London Is the Place for Me

TRANSGRESSING BOUNDARIES

Studies in Black Politics and Black Communities

Cathy Cohen and Fredrick Harris, Series Editors

London Is the Place for Me

Black Britons, Citizenship, and the Politics of Race

KENNETTA HAMMOND PERRY

OXFORD
UNIVERSITY PRESS

OXFORD
UNIVERSITY PRESS

Oxford University Press is a department of the University of
Oxford. It furthers the University's objective of excellence in research,
scholarship, and education by publishing worldwide.
Oxford is a registered trademark of Oxford University Press
in the UK and certain other countries.

Published in the United States of America by
Oxford University Press
198 Madison Avenue, New York, NY 10016, United States of America

Cataloging-in-Publication data is on file at the Library of Congress
ISBN 978–0–19–024020–2

1 3 5 7 9 8 6 4 2
Printed in the United States of America
on acid-free paper

To the memories of those women who paved the way-
Mary Tucker Hammond and Louise Elbert Patrick.

CONTENTS

LIST OF ILLUSTRATIONS

ACKNOWLEDGMENTS

Writing a book has been one of the hardest things that I have ever done. But I am grateful for nothing short of a divinely orchestrated process that has afforded me an opportunity to travel to new places, see familiar sites with new lenses, meet helpful archivists, librarians and local historians, collaborate and engage with brilliant scholars, and build relationships that remain a source of encouragement, support, and inspiration. Some of my earliest questions about Black Britain were shaped during my undergraduate years in the History Department at North Carolina Central University. There, I received my first foray into the histories of Europe and the African Diaspora as I sat in lectures and witnessed the pioneering work of Carlton Wilson and Lydia Lindsey. Alongside Sylvia M. Jacobs, Percy Murray, Oscar Williams, Freddie Parker, and Lolita Brockington, their efforts to continue the tradition of seeing NCCU's History Department serve as a training ground for future generations of Black historians has made an indelible mark on my journey as a scholar, teacher, researcher, writer, and creator of new knowledge.

This project has benefited from financial support from The Graduate School and the Department of History at Michigan State University, the Carter G. Woodson Institute for African and African American Studies at the University of Virginia, the American Historical Association, Duke University's Provost's Postdoctoral Scholars' Program, the American Council of Learned Societies, the Moore Undergraduate Research Apprenticeship Program at the University of North Carolina at Chapel Hill and from funding through the Division of Research and Graduate Studies, the Faculty Senate, and the Department of History at East Carolina University. Archivists, librarians and staff at the Schomburg Center for Research on Black Culture and Duke University as well as those in the UK at The National Archives, the British Library, the Manchester Labour History Archive and Study Center, the Imperial War Museum, the London Metropolitan Archives, the Institute of Commonwealth Studies, the Metropolitan University Trades Union Congress Library, the School of Oriental and African Studies, and the University of Warwick have been helpful throughout the research process. Moreover, the staff at the Lambeth Archives, the Institute for Race Relations, and the Black Cultural Archives deserve special thanks for not only helping me to navigate their collections, but perhaps more important, for their larger dedication to preserving and building archives to study the textured histories of Black Britain in the twentieth century and keeping sources publicly accessible even in the midst of budgetary and staffing constraints. Beyond brick and mortar archives, I am also indebted to conversations with scholars based in the UK who have paved the way for work on Black Britain including Hakim Adi, Marika Sherwood, and Harry Goulbourne, all of whom lead me to collections that I may not have discovered without their prompting. Additionally, I am grateful for the opportunity to have consulted the personal collections of novelist, journalist, educator, and activist Donald Hinds and his lovely wife, Dawn, who opened their home to me and generously shared their memories and portions of their personal family history to aid my work on this topic.

While I take the credit for all shortcomings and limitations that this book may possess, there is no doubt that the measure of its contribution can be attributed to the questions, comments, conversations, criticisms, affirmations, and words of wisdom that I have received from a community of teachers, mentors, colleagues, sistah scholars, and friends. This project began as a series of graduate seminar papers in courses taught by Darlene Clark Hine and Leslie Page Moch. I will be forever grateful for the type of "mentorship through proximity" that Darlene Clark Hine has offered me through the years by allowing me to bear witness to the work ethic, integrity, and professionalism of a Black woman academic who leads in such a way that blazes trails for others to follow. Likewise, I am deeply appreciative of Leslie Page Moch's willingness to provide guidance and much-needed affirmation that helped me to move this project from seminar paper, to dissertation, and now to book form.

I am grateful to Frederick C. Harris, Cathy J. Cohen, David McBride and readers at Oxford University Press for seeing merit in this project. I am also thankful for the critical feedback and valuable insights offered on various aspects of the project at different stages in its development from Anne-Marie Angelo, Felix Armfield, Jordanna Bailkin, Daina Ramey Berry, Antoinette Burton, J. Kameron Carter, Niambi Carter, Laurent Dubois, Christienna Fryar, Thavolia Glymph, Steve Gold, Reena Goldthree, Joshua Guild, Reginald Hildebrand, Winston James, Amy Johnson, Robin D. G. Kelley, Priscilla Layne, Ashley Lucas, Gordon Mantler, Mark Anthony Neal, Jason Parker, Susan Pennybacker, Rosa Perelmuter, Lara Putnam, Meredith L. Roman, Ula Y. Taylor, Stephen Tuck, Maurice Wallace, and Eric D. Duke, who has been my friend and writing partner at every stage of this project since grad school. As a postdoctoral fellow at Duke University, Tina Campt and Susan Thorne took me under their wing and continue to be sources of encouragement that have helped to sharpen my ideas and keep me focused on the big picture. To the members of the 2005–2007 Woodson Fellows community at UVA's Carter G. Woodson Institute, including Yarimar Bonilla, Regine Jean-Charles, Jamillah Karim, Cynthia Hoehler-Fatton, Vicki Brennen, Brian Brazeal, and Sarah Silkey, along with the fall 2012 faculty fellows at UNC–Chapel Hill's Institute for Arts and Humanities including Genna Rae McNeil, Lisa Lindsay, Neel Ahuja, and Laurie Maffly-Kipp, and to the members of a short-lived, but useful writing group of faculty in East Carolina's History Department, I offer thanks for reading some of my roughest drafts, raising engaging questions, and helping me to more clearly articulate my ideas and imagine a wider audience for this work.

During the course of my research I have been blessed to have friends, family, and colleagues who have opened their homes, cooked meals, and provided wonderful company after long days in the archives. Armena V. Richards, I cannot thank you enough for taking a chance on a stranger during my first research trips to London. You and your family have helped make Bermondsey a home away from home over the years. Thanks to Reena Goldthree for extending an invitation to crash for a couple of weeks during your time in Seven Sisters and to Jonathan Patrick, Stephen and Alecia Howard and Monica Spencer, who introduced me to wonderful guides during my most recent stay in Jamaica. I am especially grateful to Daina Ramey Berry, who gave me my first official lessons in how to be proactive, efficient, productive, and savvy as a curious Black woman in archival institutions that did not typically encounter scholars like me asking the kinds of questions that animate this study. Thank you for paying it forward and equipping me with a set of crucial skills as a historical researcher.

Besides engaging a scholarly community that has no doubt enhanced this book in ways that I could have never imagined, I have also been blessed to be a part of a growing network of Black women in academia who have helped me attend to the crucial business of nourishing my soul and keeping my spirit intact when this journey became most taxing. Talitha L. LeFlouria, Sowande M. Mustakeem, Marisa J. Fuentes, Dierdre Cooper Owens, LaShawn Harris, Sasha Turner Bryson, Marshanda Smith, Baiyina Muhammad, Natanya Duncan, Catherine Adams, and Eleanor Seaton, I am a better thinker, teacher, writer, friend, and woman for having known each of you. We have laughed, cried, shopped, prayed, mourned, wined, dined, road-tripped, and shared memorable "good times" over the years. Most importantly, we have reminded each other not to take ourselves or the ebbs and flows of this profession so seriously.

Thanks for keeping me grounded, connected, and encouraged especially in the moments when this process seemed overwhelming.

Most of all I am forever grateful to my family, who has always seen a degree of potential in me that is often greater than I see in myself. Kenneth and Evelyn Hammond have been the type of parents who let me choose my own path, but who have always provided light along the way. Your faith, wise counsel, and unconditional love and encouragement have given me the confidence and motivation to see this through. Brandon Hammond thank you for continually teaching me that new and better futures are always possible. Kathye Perry, you have supported me and helped take care of the people that I cherish most when I have had to travel for research and deal with the everyday grind of my job. Isabella Sofia Perry, you are the greatest God-given gift of light and love that I could have ever imagined. You have changed my life in all the best ways and it has been sheer joy to see the world through your eyes. And to Brandon Perry—my love, my friend, my partner for life (in Spades and in all other things!)—thank you for believing in me, accepting me (flaws and all), rooting for me, coaching me, having my back, and loving me with a force that defies logic. You have helped me to survive this journey and building a life with you has made it all more meaningful and enjoyable. To God be the glory for making this journey possible and giving me the strength to see it through.

Introduction

Windrush Politics

In June 1948, in homage of his impending arrival in Britain, Aldwyn Roberts began composing lyrics to "London Is the Place for Me," a calypso that eventually became part of the soundtrack chronicling the history of Caribbean migration to Britain following World War II.[1] Roberts did not formally record "London Is the Place for Me" until 1951. However, he publicly debuted the first two stanzas of the song before the glare of *Pathé* news cameras and a crowd of spectators who had gathered as he and over 500 people who claimed residency in the Caribbean disembarked from the SS *Empire Windrush* at Tilbury Docks in Essex on 22 June 1948. Although the ship's manifest included a total of 1,027 passengers, including British heiress, writer, and activist Nancy Cunard, who boarded in Havana along with a contingent of Polish migrants who had boarded in Mexico, it was the arrival of male travelers from the Caribbean that garnered media attention.[2] Anxious to retrieve a sound bite from the man who had been touted as "*the* king of calypso singers," an ITV News reporter approached Aldwyn Roberts with a simple query: "May I ask you your name?" To which he replied with a confident grin, offering the name that had made him famous in the world of calypso, "Lord Kitchener." Obliging the reporter's request for an impromptu serenade to mark the *Windrush* passengers' arrival in England, he cheerfully sang this song:

> London is the place for me,
> London this lovely city,
> You can go to France or America,
> India, Asia or Australia,
> But you must come back to London city.
>
> Well believe me I am speaking broadmindedly,
> I am glad to know my Mother Country,

I've been traveling to countries years ago,
But this is the place I wanted to know,
Darling, London, that's the place for me.[3]

Decades later, when asked to reflect on the creative energies that produced his lyrical homage celebrating his arrival in London, Roberts explained that with four days remaining before the completion of his steamship journey across the Atlantic, he was overcome with a "kind of wonderful feeling that I'm going to land on the mother country, the soil of the mother country."[4] According to Roberts, it was this "wonderful feeling" that inspired him to compose an ode that conveyed a sense of optimistic expectancy about life in Britain. The decision to express the "feeling" that led him to pen "London Is the Place for Me" and display his talents before the gaze of cameras at Tilbury Docks most likely came with little reservation. Aldwyn Roberts was a man who had grown accustomed to fanfare and the glare of the media, having traveled Trinidad's premiere calypso circuit during the 1940s and adopting the sobriquet Lord Kitchener, a name that spoke to the realities of an Empire at war and a history of colonial rule.[5] In addition to showcasing calypso music as part of the cultural baggage that Caribbean migrants unpacked as they made a place for themselves in Britain, undoubtedly his decision to perform reflected a desire to publicly convey his sense of attachment to Britain and articulate that not only did he want "to know" London but perhaps, more importantly, that London was a place where he belonged.[6]

Ultimately, however, what became newsworthy and iconic about Kitchener's song was not what it communicated about the beliefs, expectations, and aspirations of its composer and his *Windrush* compatriots. Instead, the song's ability to provide a sound bite for a particular story about postwar Caribbean migration to Britain—a narrative that was framed by visuals and a scripted voice-over that announced the arrival of what was thought to be 500 unemployed Jamaican men, "discouraged" about economic conditions in their homeland, "yet full of hope" about securing jobs in Britain—became the route by which the song and Kitchener's performance entered a largely White viewing public's cultural imagination.[7] As part of ITV's carefully crafted news story about the arrival of the *Windrush* passengers, there was a fleeting mention that many of those traveling from the Caribbean were entering as "citizens of the British Empire."[8] But the voice-over included this description as a preface to emphasize, and perhaps reassure viewers, that the hundreds of Black male work seekers that they were watching as they alighted in Britain were "coming with good intent." To underscore this point for viewers, the voice-over announced, "their spokesperson sings his thanks to Britain," just before the camera cut to Kitchener's interview.[9] From this vantage point, Kitchener's performance of

"London Is the Place for Me," as captured for the gaze of White British audiences, helped to forge and congeal an enduring mythology about the *Windrush* passengers that rested upon the imagery of crowds of West Indian men looking to Britain with gratitude in search of acceptance. In this scenario, although the *Windrush*'s Afro-Caribbean passengers are in the camera's eye, the story about their arrival is told from the short-sighted glimpses of the White British metropolitan society in which they ostensibly aspired to ingratiate themselves as colonial laborers. And it would be from this narrow field of vision that popular images of these colonial migrants were eventually seen as *the* source of Britain's "colour problem" in the two decades following World War II.

But what untold *Windrush* stories lie beyond the gaze of media images produced for the consumption of White audiences? What desires and perspectives did *Windrush* passengers bring that escaped notice by White observers vested in the news story that captioned the arrival of the *Windrush*? Raising these questions compels historians to ponder more than what became news about the journey of the *Windrush* passengers and move beyond the reproduction of historical narratives about postwar Afro-Caribbean migration and the formation of postcolonial Black Britain that reflect a White viewing public's fascination with the "colour problem" that the laboring bodies of Black men from the colonies posed for the imperial metropolis. Part of writing that story and, in effect, reinterpreting the Windrush moment involves considering Kitchener's performance on its own terms as a moment of claim making with political implications. Although the ITV reporter initially solicited Kitchener's performance to simply entertain, as Kitchener sang, news cameras also captured a type of cultural politics at work that spoke to how he envisioned his rightful place as a colonial subject and imperial citizen in metropolitan Britain. By refocusing the analytical lens to consider Kitchener's dockside rendition of "London Is the Place for Me" outside of the news-making media production—which, for White audiences, became synonymous with the migration of unemployed Black men attempting to obtain economic opportunities unavailable in their colonial homelands—one can unearth alternative narratives about the *Windrush* passengers and the significance of their journey to Britain.

At the very moment when Lord Kitchener confidently sang the refrain "London is the place for me" in a locally recognized standard English that suggests that he was very aware of his audience, not only did he express a sense of belonging for himself and his fellow passengers within the physical confines of the British Isles, but he also performed within the conventions of calypso, a musical genre born and bred in the crucible of Trinidad's inter-imperial histories of colonization, enslavement, occupation, and migration.[10] During the nineteenth century, calypso emerged in a variety of forms as a medium of entertainment, social commentary, political expression, resistance, and empowerment, primarily among generations of formerly enslaved people of African descent. By the late 1930s and early 1940s it had become firmly implanted in the cultural landscape of Trinidad and embraced as a national artifact integral to carnival celebrations, and even subject to state-sponsored policing and surveillance because of the subversive cultural and political critique of colonial authority that lyricists and performers infused into the music. [11] While much of this history would be lost to those interested in the "news" of Kitchener's performance, calypso's role as a medium of political expression is integral to understanding the broader context that made his performance and all that it signified possible. Paying closer attention to what Kitchener actually sang and how he communicated conceptions of belonging as he performed "London Is the Place for Me," provides an opportunity to think beyond a social history of Caribbean migration to Britain that revolves around White Britons' reactions to a growing Black presence. Moreover, turning to Lord Kitchener's assertion "London Is the Place for Me" as a type of historical claim of belonging and attachment, as opposed to an ambient soundscape for a news story, invites a more nuanced conversation about the political ideologies and vernaculars that colonial subjects of African descent articulated about the meaning of British citizenship and their status in the imperial body politic even before they set foot upon British shores. [12]

Taking a cue from Lord Kitchener's impromptu performance marking his journey to London, this study examines how Afro-Caribbean migrants made claims of belonging that fundamentally shaped the politics of race in postwar British society in ways that subsequently transformed notions of citizenship and ideas about what it meant to be British. It is precisely the claim "London is the place for me" that stands at the heart of understanding how *Windrush* passengers like Lord Kitchener and a generation of Afro-Caribbean migrants who journeyed to the so-called Mother Country in the two decades that followed shifted the political landscape in postwar Britain by asserting their sense of belonging and exposing anti-Black racism, all while challenging the state to acknowledge and guarantee their rights as British citizens. This book demonstrates that for Afro-Caribbean migrants, citizenship denoted much more than a juridical status that conferred a predetermined set of legal entitlements and or obligations. Rather, for migrants, citizenship was a pliable discourse that offered a language to make claims about rights, assert political identifications, contest the power and prerogatives of the state, and articulate expectations of belonging within the imperial body politic. [13] Focusing largely on the period between when Lord Kitchener set sail for England aboard the *Windrush* and the late 1960s when the very meaning of Blackness in Britain found new political salience against the backdrop of public policy debates about race relations, my work chronicles how the politics of race effectively impeded Caribbean migrants of African descent from fully realizing their right to belong in Britain as citizens. By revisiting some of the landmark moments in postwar Black British history with fresh eyes and the perspectives of Black Britons and those who were at times racialized as Black in full view, this book examines how race and anti-Blackness were conditioned in part by imperial ideologies of White supremacy; de facto discrimination in housing, employment, and access to public resources; state-sponsored efforts to restrict Afro-Caribbean migration and disenfranchise Commonwealth migrants; and, most virulently, by acts of violence. Perhaps most importantly, the book is concerned with unveiling a political dialogue about race and racism—a dialogue in which Black Britons were active and engaged participants and not merely objects of concern or subjects of curiosity, anxiety, scrutiny, or surveillance.[14]

By both attending to how race and anti-Black racism shaped Afro-Caribbean migrants' experiences in postwar Britain *and* their political responses to what was commonly described as the "colour bar," this study broadens the scope of current scholarship in postwar British history on race, non-White Commonwealth migration, and citizenship by venturing beyond the corridors of Parliament and the public and private commentaries of British policy makers.[15] Although the state and, more specifically, the actions, intentions, and policy prescriptions of British officials are constitutive elements of the history of postwar race politics, they do not tell the whole story. The power that state officials possessed to impose, regulate, and police boundaries of citizenship rooted in racialized visions of Britishness did not grant them a monopoly on what British citizenship could mean and who could lay claim to it.[16] What has been all too often neglected in histories detailing the relationship between migration and the racialization of citizenship in postwar Britain, a relationship that this book brings to the fore of historical analysis, is a consideration of the perspectives, organizing strategies, and political activities of Black Britons who continually insisted, much like Lord Kitchener, that London and the spaces of metropolitan Britain were places where they rightfully belonged.

Because this study considers the political voices and experiences of Afro-Caribbean migrants as they encountered anti-Black racism, confronted the state, and navigated the dynamics of being both Black and British in metropolitan Britain, it employs, by necessity, a range of conventional archival records as well as alternative historical texts to represent perspectives that may not readily appear in official records. Through an analysis of a range of sources that include migrant narratives, records of grassroots political activists, domestic and international press reports, community-specific periodicals, music, and visual culture, alongside the official records of the political establishment, this study offers a more nuanced accounting of the web of historical agents involved in politicizing race and drawing public attention to the realities of racism as experienced by Black Britons. The everyday lives of people of African descent who migrated from the Caribbean colonies and those who were racialized in the postwar era through media, popular ideology, and the racially disparate impact of public policies and social customs in ways that conflated Blackness in Britain—as it was constituted to a large extent by phenotype, and or perceived Caribbean or African colonial origins—with an "immigrant" outsider second-class citizen status are crucial to this story.[17] However, those who take center stage most often in the narrative are the individuals, activists, intellectuals, and organizations whose political activities involved a public critique of the state's role in safeguarding the rights of Black British citizens even before this more contemporary nomenclature was consistently invoked. At times this cast of historical actors includes those disenfranchised by discriminatory policies and practices, as well as victims of racial violence, including Kelso Cochrane, whose 1959 murder was described by Black activists as a "lynching".[18] In other moments, it includes those seeking to mobilize coalitions to challenge the particular cultural and political configurations of anti-Black racism in British society, including the Afro-Asian Caribbean Conference (AACC) and the Campaign Against Racial Discrimination (CARD), as well as activists and political campaigners such as Universal Negro Improvement Association (UNIA) cofounder Amy Ashwood Garvey and David Pitt, who lobbied the Labour Government for anti-discrimination policy during the mid-1960s. By examining the ways in which Black activists and organizers engaged Government officials and the power of the state to make claims about citizenship and the disenfranchising conditions associated with being Black in Britain, this book provides a broader view of the various stakeholders involved in transforming race, migration, and citizenship into overlapping wedge issues that recalibrated the political landscape of a decolonizing imperial metropolis in profound ways during the postwar era. My book argues that as Afro-Caribbean migrants made choices to exercise their imperial citizenship and rhetorically and symbolically insist that "London is the place for me" by journeying to the "Mother country" and asserting their right to belong, they made race, and more precisely, the problem of racism a subject of public dialogue and political debate. In doing so, they subsequently remapped the very boundaries of what it meant to be both Black and British at a critical juncture in the history of empire and transnational race politics in the twentieth century.

Backdrops to the *Windrush* Moment

Lord Kitchener and his fellow *Windrush* passengers represented a small frac-
tion of what became an unprecedented number of more than half a million
non-White migrants who journeyed to Britain from different parts of the
British Commonwealth between the late 1940s and the early 1960s.[19] During
this period, the largest percentages of Commonwealth migrants consisted of
people of African descent moving from the Caribbean colonies. Although
postwar migration produced one of the most significant increases in Britain's
Black population, people of African descent had long been a part of British
society. Even before Elizabeth I issued a royal directive to expel the "blackamoors" in 1596, there has been a continuous Black presence in the British
Isles.[20] During the era of the transatlantic slave trade, as Britain built the
wealth of an empire with the labor of enslaved Africans, there remained a
steady flow of people of African descent routed through major slave-trading
ports in Bristol, Liverpool, and London. In the nineteenth century, after the
abolition of slavery in the British Empire and throughout the first half of the
twentieth century, transient Black communities comprised of seafarers, students, soldiers, intellectuals, and entertainers took shape in various cities
in England.[21] By the close of World War II, the total non-White population
in Britain was estimated to be between approximately 10,000 and 30,000.
However, by 1961, when the British Government introduced the first in a
series of migration controls designed to limit a predominately Afro-Caribbean
Commonwealth migration, Britain's population of color had increased more
than tenfold.[22] And under the terms of the British Nationality Act of 1948,
Commonwealth migrants possessed full British citizenship rights, which
included the right to migrate, settle, work, and become fully incorporated
into metropolitan society.

When the *Empire Windrush* departed Kingston, Jamaica in May 1948,
Parliament was still debating the rudiments of a new nationality policy
that formally introduced the language of citizenship into the official political grammar of the British state. Passed by Parliament less than a month
after Lord Kitchener landed at Tilbury, the terms of the British Nationality
of 1948 codified a long-standing notion of imperial belonging by creating a
universal British Commonwealth citizen category that comprised all British
subjects in the metropole, colonies, and dominions.[23] Likewise, as dominion nationalism and decolonization spurred the creation of local nationality
policies among Commonwealth partners, the Act also established a citizenship classification that acknowledged the ongoing imperial relations between
Britain and the dependent territories—Citizens of the United Kingdom and

Colonies (CUKC). Whereas the particular entitlements of Commonwealth citizenship afforded to British subjects were separately acquired and delineated according to local nationality policies, one of the rights extended to all Commonwealth citizens—in part to mark their shared British subjecthood—was the right to migrate to Britain and settle with a claim to British citizenship and a political relationship to the state that was indistinguishable from that which was held by British-born subjects.[24] When considering the historical formation of citizenship as a gateway to British identifications, one is tempted to focus on the formal codification of this political nomenclature within the context of imperial governance. But thinking about how discourses of citizenship informed the contested regimes of British imperial rule requires that one adopt a more expansive perspective that accounts for the ways in which ideas about the rights of citizens and who belonged to the imperial body politic were not merely juridical matters. In fact, as Chapter 1 explores, languages about imperial citizenship and ideas about belonging were part and parcel of the post-emancipation colonial experience that made it possible for someone like Aldwyn Roberts to refashion himself as Lord Kitchener and imagine that London, the urban epicenter of the British imperial enterprise that made him a colonial subject, could indeed represent a place of belonging to which he could lay claim.[25]

Just as this book explores the imperial history that produced Lord Kitchener's claim "London is the place for me," a secondary theme of this work involves situating the claims of citizenship and belonging that Kitchener and an entire generation of Afro-Caribbean migrants made within the context of the racially charged international political landscape of the postwar world. Months before Aldwyn Roberts sang, "London Is the Place for Me," as he exited the *Empire Windrush,* protests erupted in Accra, Ghana that proved pivotal to Kwame Nkrumah's rise as leader of a burgeoning nationalist movement culminating in Ghanaian independence less than a decade later. In that same year, 1948, the National Party in South Africa gained ascendancy on a platform advocating apartheid, and US President Harry Truman issued Executive Order 9981, a directive that effectively called for the desegregation of the American military. While the reign of the National Party in South Africa more definitively codified a political system rooted in ideologies of White supremacy in an effort to sustain Black disenfranchisement and racial inequality, in many ways Truman's order foreshadowed a wave of policy reform in American society that ultimately began to dismantle many of the legal underpinnings of Jim Crow.[26]

At the same time that individual nations grappled with the relationship between racial (in)equality and Black citizenship rights, in a postwar world still deliberating the causes and devastating consequences of World War II, these issues also became part of a burgeoning international dialogue about the protection of human rights. On 10 December 1948, the General Assembly of the United Nations adopted the Universal Declaration of Human Rights, a document that provided a working blueprint for the organization to pursue a broad agenda that subsequently linked debates about human rights with a global challenge to eradicate racial discrimination in the decades that followed.[27] The global turf wars wrought by a burgeoning Cold War exacerbated these international dialogues. And for those like Trinidadian-born Claudia Jones who resided in the center of Western power while launching radical critiques of the contradictions of liberal democracy, 1948 brought increasing state surveillance. At the very outset of 1948, officers from the US Immigration and Naturalization Service, along with a special agent from the Federal Bureau of Investigations, placed Claudia Jones under arrest at her home in New York for the first time and incarcerated her at Ellis Island because of her political beliefs and ties to the Communist Party. This would be the first in a series of arrests and incarcerations for Claudia Jones that ultimately lead to her involuntary departure to Britain, where she became a central figure in grassroots political organizing among Black British communities in London during the late 1950s and early 1960s.[28]

Most students of twentieth-century Black Britain would agree that it is impossible to write about how Afro-Caribbean migrants shaped race politics in the early postwar era without paying attention to the work of Claudia Jones. Criminalized and deported from the United States during the height of McCarthyism for her unapologetically radical political ideas, Claudia Jones voyaged to Britain in 1955 as a political exile. In 1958, she established one of the earliest and most widely circulated Black newspapers in London, the *West Indian Gazette and Afro-Asian Caribbean News,* which effectively helped to forge an imagined diasporic political community that encompassed people of African and Asian descent throughout the Anglophone world. During her tenure in Britain, Jones actively campaigned for decolonization and for support of the fledging West Indian Federation. She lobbied Government officials against the passage of racially discriminatory migration policies, participated in anti-apartheid protests, organized events in London to promote solidarity between Black Britons and Black Americans against racial injustice, and was instrumental in organizing London's first Trinidadian-style carnivals featuring the calypso music that figures like Lord Kitchener had used to infuse the cultural paraphernalia of Empire in the Caribbean into postwar metropolitan life.[29] By tracing the political work of figures like Claudia Jones, this study demonstrates how the struggles of Afro-Caribbean migrants to assert and claim rights of belonging as British citizens were reflective of and refracted through a transnational and diasporic postwar dialogue among people of

African descent about civil rights, human rights, racial justice, political independence, and the contested meaning of freedom and democracy. In doing so,
this study highlights a largely unexplored dimension of the history of postwar
race politics and the legacy of the Windrush generation in Britain by demonstrating the extent to which Black Britons' quests for the recognition of their
citizenship and rights of belonging was not simply a domestic affair. Rather,
these struggles for social justice represented a critical moment in the political
history of the African Diaspora, interfacing the histories of people of African
descent in Britain, the Caribbean, Africa, and the United States.

Transnational Race Politics in Twentieth-Century Britain

In the past two decades, historical scholarship has begun to develop more
nuanced analyses of interactions between domestic race politics and international affairs during the postwar period. Scholars of American and, more
specifically, African American history have emphasized the degrees to which
anti-colonial and civil rights reform agendas advocated by Black Americans
commanded center stage in a contested international theater defined by the
racial politics of the Cold War and decolonization.[30] At the core of this his-
toriographical turn in the writing of African American, and subsequently
African Diaspora history, is a critical analysis of how Black activists, organizations, and intellectuals seized upon the wide chasm between the nation's
liberal democratic promises of freedom, equality, and full citizenship and
the realities of racially specific forms of injustice and disenfranchisement to
exact political change. In the case of twentieth-century Britain, recent work by
Susan Pennybacker, Minkah Makalani, Hakim Adi, and Marc Matera is part
of a growing body of scholarship that has expanded our understanding of the
transnational landscape informing race politics in Britain during the interwar
period.[31] Their work showcases how urban spaces like London functioned as
key sites of exchange, networking, and mobilization among activists throughout the African Diaspora. Moreover, it indicates that twentieth-century British
history is tethered to transnational histories of what Robin D.G. Kelley, Tiffany
Patterson, and Brent Edwards have described as Black globality.[32]

In the first half of the twentieth century, as a seat of imperial power and
encounter, as Marc Matera notes, the cityscapes of metropolitan Britain "functioned as both facilitator and provocateur" of a type of Black global political
culture.[33] During this time, places like London and Manchester became home
and provided temporary respite for a host of Black activists and intellectuals
like Henry Sylvester Williams, George Padmore, C. L. R James, Jomo Kenyatta,

Paul and Eslanda Goode Robeson, and Amy Ashwood Garvey, all of whom worked to institutionalize and mobilize cross-national and intra-imperial Pan-African and anti-colonial solidarities through organizations like the Pan-African Conference, the International African Service Bureau, the Negro Welfare Association, the Council of African Affairs, and the Pan-African Federation.[34] In chronicling how interwar Britain functioned as a central node of diasporic formation within the context of race-specific political organizing, recent scholarship is shedding much needed light upon how a constellation of Black intellectuals and leftist activists based in Britain anchored their agendas for radical social change in a critique of the contradictions of British liberal imperialism.[35] Viewed alongside work by Laura Tabili and Jacqueline Jenkinson, who have documented how Black maritime workers in port cities such as Cardiff and Liverpool called attention to the gulf between the promise of a notion of imperial justice that transcended race and the domestic realities of racial violence and discriminatory labor conditions, the history of race politics in twentieth-century Britain is clearly one that has been shaped by what local conditions in the imperial metropolis made possible and how people of African descent framed their anti-racist political demands in relation to the interests of a global Black world.[36]

Although scholars are making strides in reimagining political histories of early twentieth-century Britain that attend to the local and global aspects of Black activism and anti-racist organizing, there is still much more to understand about these dynamics following a mid-century world war whose victors extolled the defeat of Nazi racial doctrines and trumpeted the pursuit of national self-determination, human rights, democracy, and freedom for all. This study intends to fill in some of the gaps in the existing scholarship on transnational race politics in Britain during the twentieth century by exploring the continuities between pre- and postwar Black political activity and anti-racist organizing. Work on the interwar period illuminates how the campaigns of Black workers, activists, and intellectuals for self-government, political inclusion, labor rights, and social justice exposed the limits and inherent contradictions of liberal imperialism. However, the antipodean logics of British imperialism—which Winston James and others have observed proffered universal subjecthood, imperial citizenship, and British identifications that transcended race for colonials of African descent, just as they produced racialized hierarchies of inclusion that disavowed Blackness—did not dissipate following World War II.[37] Instead, in the wake of the decline of official imperial power, the longstanding racialized paradoxes of imperial belonging that had historically sustained Empire were in fact reconstituted as part of the very process in which metropolitan Britain reckoned with the cultural politics of decolonization.[38]

An examination of the inter-imperial movements of Afro-Caribbean migrants offers a fruitful point of departure to reconsider how Black subjects contested and reordered imperial relations by crossing the geographical borders that delineated colony and metropole and making citizenship claims that rendered Blackness coterminous with Britishness. It was precisely claims of citizenship and belonging rooted in an understanding that Blackness could be British and Britishness could be Black that provided the cultural and ideological force for colonial migrants to strike back at the Empire in such a way that disoriented ways of thinking about who or what constituted belonging in the British nation.[39] In the vein of recent work by Bill Schwarz and Jordanna Bailkin, which grapples with what the end of Empire meant for the imperial metropolis, *London Is the Place for Me* demonstrates that as Britain, the global Empire, contended with an emerging postwar crisis of liberal democracy fueled by the Cold War and more fervent calls for national self-determination by colonialized and disenfranchised people, Afro-Caribbean migrants' efforts to challenge the British nation to honor democratic promises of citizenship exposed another front of decolonization—the Empire at home.[40] This book tells a story that demonstrates how Afro-Caribbean migrants' demands for citizenship as Black Britons represents a segment of a broader postwar history of the decolonization of metropolitan Britain's ideas about race, nation, and belonging, as well as the cultural logics that reinforced their power to include and exclude. As others have persuasively argued, decolonization and the end of Empire amounted to much more than a shift in official governance in overseas territories. The process of decolonization, much like that of Empire building, involved the reconfiguration of political, cultural, and racial ideologies that simultaneously implicated the colonies and the metropole. And one aim of this book is to demonstrate how the experiences of Afro-Caribbean migrants in Britain provide an instructive opening to explore these dynamics.[41]

Revising the Narrative: Imagining Windrush Politics

Due in part to the fact that the landing of Aldwyn Roberts and his *Windrush* cohort in England was visually captured and archived in *Pathé* newsreel footage taken at Tilbury Docks in 1948, the arrival of the *Windrush* has provided an iconic optic—both in a visual and in a narrative sense—that scholars have used to chart the history of Caribbean migration to Britain following World War II and the formation of postcolonial Black Britain. Much of the historiography and scholarship pertaining to the history of postwar Caribbean migration to Britain and many of the attendant questions of race, British national identity, and citizenship that animate scholarly debate on this subject tend to privilege the arrival of the *Windrush* as a watershed moment. At the core of these scholarly conversations lies a critique of how an imperial nation-state and, more specifically, a policy-making elite conceived of what it meant to be British and legally delineated who had the most legitimate claims to the rights of British citizenship through nationality and migration policies.[42] From this trajectory, the arrival of the *Windrush* operates as an opening scene for narrating how officialdom grappled with how postwar Caribbean migration exposed the historic tensions between Britain, the multiethnic, multiracial imperial body, and prevailing notions of Britishness, as a racialized and exclusive White metropolitan identity.[43]

A corollary narrative about the landing of the *Windrush*'s role as a historical marker also pervades popular representations of postwar Caribbean migration and its relationship to a broader history of what has been described as "the irresistible rise of multi-racial Britain."[44] Unlike many of the state-centered histories of postwar Caribbean migration, public discourses of commemoration have invoked the *Windrush* moment as a preface to explain the emergence of settled Black populations in Britain and underscore how people of African descent from the Caribbean have contributed to various social, political, and cultural transformations in British society since World War II. In 1998, to commemorate the fiftieth anniversary of the arrival of *Windrush* passengers, the BBC produced a documentary series, *Windrush,* and commissioned the writing of a companion history with hopes that both might convey to a mainstream British public the "epic untold story of Britain's black population and its impact on the politics, culture, identity and self-image of British society."[45] The BBC-sponsored volume included a cursory mention of the imperial relationship that had facilitated a long history of movement and settlement by people of African descent between Africa, the Caribbean, and the British Isles. However, the underlying theme of the BBC's commemorative activities and the numerous other Windrush celebrations held in 1998, 2008, and, more recently, with the redevelopment of Windrush Square in Brixton is to cement and extol the centrality of the arrival of the *Windrush* as *the* quintessential historical portal through which one should commence a narrative about how people of African descent have shaped contemporary British society and forged Black British identifications.[46] While state-centered and commemorative Windrush discourses amplify distinct yet dialogic perspectives that have undoubtedly informed the history of Caribbean migration to Britain, both traverse common ground by situating the landing of the *Windrush* passengers as a symbolic point of origin. As a result, the *Windrush* moment has assumed an iconic stature—both in the scholarly literature and in popular memory—on the premise of its ability to provide a landmark of beginnings rather than a historically interpretative guidepost for understanding how Caribbean migrants

perceived their relationship to and within the British Empire as colonial subjects and imperial citizens.

More recently, there has been a critical interpretive shift toward dismantling and rethinking the utility of Windrush narratives made most forcefully
by scholars actively engaged in the burgeoning field of Black British cultural
studies. Paramount to these conversations resides the overarching argument
that invocations of the *Windrush* moment present a deficient and myopic
accounting of the historical genealogy, context, and implications of postwar Caribbean migration to Britain. When deployed within a state-centered
race-relations paradigm,[47] scholars such as Stuart Hall have insisted that the
Windrush moment has functioned as a signifier used to equate the emergence of the problem of race with increasing postwar Caribbean migration.
Doing so has rendered the accompanying problem of racism in metropolitan
Britain as an ahistorical phenomenon that is largely a byproduct of postwar
demographic change rather than a reflection of the longstanding imperial logics that fortified the relationship between Whiteness and colonial power.[48]
Race-relations-oriented Windrush narratives have little room for histories
chronicling the existence of forms of institutional racism including those that
prevented Black men from becoming military officers or those documenting
the type of everyday "colour bar" practices that compelled West Indian cricketer Learie Constantine to bring suit against London's Imperial Hotel when
denied a room, purportedly so as not to offend White American patrons in
1944.[49] Likewise, the histories of anti-Black violence in metropolitan Britain
that ravaged the small Black seafaring communities of Cardiff during the
interwar period, along with those which occurred in Liverpool in 1948 only
two months after the arrival of the *Windrush* also stand outside of the purview
of this narrative of race and nation.[50] Conversely, as a commemorative souve-
nir signaling the emergence of contemporary Black Britain, scholars of postcolonial Black Britain contend that the landing of the *Windrush* distorts the long
and diverse history of the Black presence in the British Isles and summarily
neglects the extent to which people of African descent both in the British Isles
and in the Empire fundamentally transformed British society well before they
appeared in the metropole in more recognizable numbers, following World
War II.[51] To be sure, what scholars in the field of Black British cultural studies have tended to find most unsettling about this form of historical amnesia
is the dislodging of Britain's racialized imperial past from its contemporary
development as a multiracial nation constituted in part by and through Black
Britons.[52]

In one of the most pointed critiques of what could be described as a type of
Windrush-as-origins discourse, Barnor Hesse raises several concerns about the
"representational difficulties" attached to the *Windrush*.[53] Hesse acknowledges

that more recent invocations of the *Windrush* moment have managed to move the story away from an emphasis on the embodied "colour problem" that Black migrants posed for British cities like London during the postwar era in an effort to position Afro-Caribbean migration as part of a public narrative about British national identity. However, he cautions that this shift "does not manage to dislodge the visual regime which established the Windrush as the intrusive object of an unreflexive white gaze." Therefore, he concludes, "the assumptions underlying this particular discursive repetition are not sufficiently different from those installed in a race-relations narrative which would have us believe that the development of racism in Britain (like the significance of Black Britain as a formation) simply arises from the impact of post-war migration."[54]

In addition to highlighting the pitfalls of representing the *Windrush* moment as a point of origin for understanding how race and those who were racialized as Black fit within narratives about the British nation in the twentieth century, Hesse also brings attention to the particular stories that are privileged and those which are subsequently elided in accounting for the formation of postcolonial Black Britain proceeding from the *Windrush*. As previously noted, what made the news regarding the arrival of the *Empire Windrush* was that it reportedly brought "500 Jamaicans to Britain."[55] Perhaps because Kingston, Jamaica was the last port of call before the ship crossed the Atlantic, or more likely because Jamaica, as the largest of the British Caribbean colonies, had historically represented a type of imperial shorthand for the West Indies in the metropolitan cultural imagination, the news of the journey of the *Windrush* passengers sealed their place in history as part of a narrative about Black Britain that foregrounds postwar movement between the Caribbean and Britain.[56] Accordingly, as Hesse explains, not only does the Windrush-as-origins narrative advance a Caribbean-centric story about Black Britain that obscures the presence of African colonial subjects and the place of Pan-Africanism in shaping Black political life in the metropole, but it also neglects regionally specific early twentieth-century Black communities in places like Merseyside and Cardiff and their relationship to the forms of Black Britishness that emerged after World War II.[57]

[This book is explicit about taking the experiences of postwar Afro-Caribbean migrants as its starting point for analyzing how Black Britons shaped race politics by making claims about citizenship in postwar Britain.] Some may argue that this choice will undoubtedly reproduce some of the limitations that Hesse attributes to the Windrush-as-origins discourse, particularly in its emphasis on the role of the Caribbean and Afro-Caribbean people in cultivating Black Britishness. However, although migration between the Caribbean and Britain is not the only imperial axis that one may engage to explore the formation of postcolonial Black Britain and postwar race politics, it is no doubt an indispensible one. *London Is the Place for Me* adopts this vantage point in part because Afro-Caribbean migrants were by far the most numerically significant Black population during this period. Beginning in the late 1940s and throughout the early 1960s, when the British Government began introducing racially motivated policies designed to curb Commonwealth migration, historians have definitively shown that officials erected these policies with the intent of regulating the movements, and infringing upon the rights of a "coloured immigrant" population that had become synonymous with the news of the *Windrush* moment and the purported influx of Afro-Caribbean male work seekers. Until 1958, when the numbers of Afro-Caribbean women newcomers began to surpass their male counterparts, this particular demographic remained the largest category of non-White migrants entering Britain through the early 1960s.[58] But to be sure, the numbers alone do not account for the historical impact of postwar Afro-Caribbean migration on race politics. More importantly, as a condition of their demographic majority, this study shows that the political activities of Afro-Caribbean migrants and the ways in which West Indians registered and represented themselves as racialized subjects fundamentally shaped the configuration of a diasporic and globally oriented Black British political culture that at times encompassed and intersected with the interests of a range of Caribbean, African, and South Asian nationalities and ethnicities. And for this reason, the Caribbean angles of postcolonial Black Britain's historical formation remain one of the most instructive—as opposed to the exclusive—conduit for understanding the racial politics of citizenship and belonging.

Since the *Windrush* moment reinforces historical lines of inquiry that have in many ways conflated the history of intra-imperial migration between the Caribbean and Britain with a strictly postwar story about race relations and the origins of contemporary Black Britain, the question remains, why return to this news-making event to rewrite a political history of Black Britain in the twentieth century? Rather than discard the *Windrush* moment, this study asks whether or not there are alternative ways of reading this historical site that might reorient and or complement debates about how we think about the ways in which postwar Caribbean migration reconfigured the metropolitan political landscape and destabilized racially exclusive notions of Britishness. What happens to the *Windrush* moment when seen from Lord Kitchener's point of view rather than from the perspective of White audiences who desired to see his performance at Tilbury Docks as one that merely expressed "his thanks to Britain," as the ITV voiceover suggested? What new and alternative interpretative possibilities emerge by locating Kitchener's declaration "London is the place for me" within a longer history of claim making and Black political activity within the British Empire? What can be learned from writing a narrative of Windrush politics where Black migrants are at the center of historical analysis?

And what can be gained by viewing the racial politics of postwar Caribbean migration through a framework that attends to the overlapping imperial, diasporic, and global valences of this history as opposed to that of a national story demarcated within the geographical borders of the British Isles and the temporal boundaries of a post–World War II script? These questions are some of the questions that inform this book.

Chapter Overviews

Chapter 1, "Race, Empire, and the Formation of Black Britain," intends to chart a new genealogy for understanding the claims to British citizenship and subsequently the Black British identifications articulated by Caribbean migrants, including Lord Kitchener and the *Windrush* passengers, in the postwar period. Even before the abolition of slavery, one can locate evidence that men and women of African descent understood that their relationship to the imperial body politic pivoted on the dynamics between their racialized status as Black workers and their membership in what was consistently defined in universalist terms as an imperial community of Crown subjects. Focusing largely on Jamaica, where the majority of postwar migrants to Britain hailed, this chapter explores the long history of how people of African descent in the Empire articulated claims to British citizenship by looking at how peasant petitioners, late-nineteenth-century Black nationalists, laboring insurgents, and military service personnel from the Caribbean appropriated discourses of imperial citizenship by invoking and acting upon their perceived rights as British subjects throughout the late nineteenth and early twentieth century. This chapter suggests that Afro-Caribbean migrants arrived in Britain with ideas about what it meant to be Black and British, and these identifications were born in the imperial world of the Caribbean as part of the process of articulating and substantiating the meaning of freedom in the post-emancipation era. Exploring this terrain situates the *Empire Windrush*'s passengers as part of an imperial history of claim making and reframes the trajectory through which the history of Black Britain is conceptualized and understood.[59]

In 1948 Lord Kitchener proudly sang, "London is the place for me," but after nearly four years of living in Britain, in 1952 he recorded "Sweet Jamaica," a song expressing nostalgia for his Caribbean homeland. In one of the verses of "Sweet Jamaica" Lord Kitchener sang,

> Many West Indians are sorry now,
> They left their country and don't know how,
> Some left their jobs and their family,

> And determined to come to London city,
> Well they are crying, they now regret,
> No kind of employment that they can get,
> The city of London they have to roam,
> They can't get their passage to go back home.[60]

Contrary to "London is the place for me," "Sweet Jamaica" conveyed a shattered sense of expectation about life in Britain, coupled with feelings of disappointment akin to a type of buyer's remorse. In "Sweet Jamaica," Lord Kitchener alluded to many of the themes that would characterize the experiences of a generation of Caribbean newcomers in Britain during the postwar period, including the difficulties of finding employment and the problems associated with securing safe, decent, and affordable living space. Perhaps the most disheartening of circumstances shaping the experiences of Caribbean migrants, including Lord Kitchener, was the absence of a widespread recognition that as members of the imperial body politic, they too, like their White metropolitan counterparts, possessed the right to belong in the imperial space of London. Although the disconnect between the racially egalitarian promises of imperial belonging and the realities of a color-coded hierarchy of access to political rights, social resources, and economic opportunities was an old and familiar imperial story for many Afro-Caribbean migrants, this history did not erase a desire for them to give substantive meaning to their status as British citizens in Britain.[61]

Chapter 2, "Migration, Citizenship, and the Boundaries of Belonging," considers the relationship between migration to Britain, citizenship, and the racialized contours of Britishness. According to the terms of the British Nationality Act of 1948, Parliament formally established a British Commonwealth citizenship status that, in theory, applied universally to all British subjects, irrespective of race, color, nationality, or regional origin. For policy makers, the Act was about maintaining the fiction of Commonwealth uniformity in an age of imperial decline. Yet its de facto effect facilitated the growth of a multiracial British citizenry in the British Isles, marked in large part by the unprecedented number of Afro-Caribbean migrants who substantiated their claims to British citizenship through the very act of migration.[62] Incorporating first-generation Caribbean migrants' narratives archived as oral histories and in family photography, this chapter offers an examination of the multiplicity of factors that facilitated increased migration from the Caribbean to Britain after World War II. An understanding of migrants' relationship to and within the British imperial body politic, economic incentives, the ease of border crossings, immigration restrictions in the United States, as well as the encouragement and sponsorship of relatives and acquaintances, all informed the choices that migrants made to journey to Britain after the war. To be sure, this study understands migration as a process of both movement and settlement.[63] Therefore, with a particular emphasis on the arenas of housing and employment, this chapter is also concerned with how race and the dilemmas of Blackness in Britain placed limitations on the degree to which Caribbean migrants could fully belong in British society and actualize all of the rights, privileges, and entitlements that accompanied British citizenship.

Chapter 3, "'Race Riots' and the Mystique of British Anti-Racism," turns to the issue of racial violence—a problem that flagrantly displayed the virulent extremes of the types of racism, disfranchisement, and denied rights of belonging experienced by Afro-Caribbean migrants in postwar Britain. While racial violence against people of African descent in Britain was not something new, when violence erupted on the streets of Nottingham and London during the summer of 1958, the international attention that news of "race riots" in Britain attracted created a nefarious image crisis for the British national brand in the global arena. What was seemingly an implosion of racial violence in 1958 created an intense questioning of what it meant to be British as images of racial conflict destabilized and contradicted widely held perceptions of the anti-racist values and ideals buttressing representations of Britain as a nation. As international audiences consumed the news of racial violence in Britain, the tone and content of their responses unearthed the workings and persistence of what is referred to as the mystique of British anti-racism. The mystique of British anti-racism is an analytic referent that denotes the collective narrative myths engendered historically that have allowed Britain as a nation to imagine, caricature, and represent itself as a paragon of racial liberalism, tolerance, and benevolence toward people of African descent. Over time, the existence of these myths has in turn replicated and simultaneously silenced conversations about and confrontations with the realities of quotidian, structural, and institutional racisms in British society and the disfranchisement of Black British citizens. In a postwar international climate acutely sensitive to issues pertaining to race, this chapter explores how White Britons' responses to the violence functioned as an attempt to preserve the mystique of an anti-racist Britain and reframe, both domestically and abroad, a tarnished image of Britain as a nation by explaining the violence as the result of a "problem" of West Indian men of African descent whose increasing presence stirred violent responses from a deviant sector of White working-class society.

While racial violence compelled White Britons to formulate new narratives about race and race relations in Britain in an effort to safeguard and preserve the mystique of British anti-racism, the murder of Kelso Cochrane, a thirty-two-year-old Antiguan carpenter, provided a pivotal moment of organization and mobilization in which one sees Afro-Caribbean migrants create and participate in grassroots campaigns to expose the problems of racism, violence, prejudice, and discrimination encountered by Black Britons.

Chapter 4, "Are We to Be Mauled Down Just Because We Are Black?" pays particular attention to the gendered "Black body politics" campaign waged by a coalition of Black British organizations, including the Committee of African Organizations, the Inter-Racial Friendship Coordinating Council, the Coloured People's Progressive Association, and the Association for the Advancement of Coloured People. Whereas the increasing presence of what were perceived as sexually aggressive, deskilled laboring bodies of Black men had become symptomatic of the "problem" of Caribbean migration, the combined efforts of these organizations in the aftermath of Kelso Cochrane's murder transformed his body into a marker of struggle and a conduit of advocacy whereby Black activists could articulate the concerns of Black British constituencies and beckon British officials to reinforce their investment in maintaining the solvency of the mystique of British anti-racism. In addition to placing the activities of Black British organizations into a transnational context that locates their activism within an ongoing international dialogue on race, citizenship, and human rights influenced by Black freedom struggles in the United States and debates over apartheid in South Africa and decolonization, this chapter also situates the agendas and activities of these organizations in relation to an earlier history of diasporic and internationalist Black political activity in Britain during the twentieth century.

Even before the arrival of the *Empire Windrush,* British officials actively participated in problematizing Caribbean migrants in an effort to rationalize the exclusion of colonial workers from postwar labor recruitment programs. As the pace of Caribbean migration to Britain accelerated during the 1950s, many of the same arguments against recruiting colonial workers of color from the Caribbean were then salvaged, repackaged, and redeployed to justify implementing migration restrictions.

Chapter 5, "Exposing the Racial Politics of Immigration Controls," begins by examining some of the formal and informal lobbying efforts that various British officials employed throughout the 1950s to forge a coalition of support within the walls of Government to favor an official policy of race-based disfranchisement with the specific intent of curbing the "influx" of Black workers from the Caribbean colonies—who were, by legal definition, British citizens. Although the clandestine maneuvering of Government officials clearly reveals the racial undertones defining the intent of the Commonwealth Immigration Act of 1962, the outward face of the bill reflected what appeared to be a race-neutral policy that vetted migrants on the basis of their employment credentials and prearranged job prospects. Moving within and beyond the corridors of Whitehall, this chapter demonstrates how a chorus of dissenting voices shaped both domestic and international perceptions of the implications of the Commonwealth Immigration Act of 1962 as an institutionalized praxis of racial discrimination. Members of Parliament, West Indian officials, Black newcomers, and activists in Britain expressed opposition to the bill and proved instrumental in framing a wide-ranging debate about the relationship between migration, citizenship, and the politics of race.

Despite the fact that the opponents of the Commonwealth Immigration Act of 1962 proved successful in formulating a public debate about institutionalized racism and the disfranchisement of Black Britons, it was not until the passage of the Race Relations Act of 1965 that Parliament erected a national policy explicitly addressing racial discrimination. Under the provisions of the Act, British officials established a national Race Relations Board structured to operate as a forum to mediate issues concerning racial discrimination in public places. Initiated in the wake of the United Nations Declaration on the Elimination of Racial Discrimination and the passage of historic civil-rights legislation in the United States, the Race Relations Act of 1965 represented a formal acknowledgement of the circulating ideologies, social relations, economic conditions, and practices facilitating racism and the potential for acts of racial discrimination to occur in Britain.

Chapter 6, "The Limits of Campaigning Against Racial Discrimination," examines the role that Black Britons played in shaping the content of the first Race Relations bill as well as the direction of the implementation of a regulatory regime that would ostensibly affirm the citizenship rights of Black Britons. To engage this issue, this chapter pays particular attention to the work of activists and organizers affiliated with the Campaign Against Racial Discrimination (CARD), an interracial anti-racist coalition formed in the aftermath of Martin Luther King, Jr.'s historic address at St. Paul's Cathedral, with the intent of becoming a political voice for the collective interests of Britain's Black and Asian communities. What the short-lived history of CARD unearths is a contentious ideological battle over the representation of Black British political interests. At the heart of these struggles remained an intra-racial and interethnic debate over the mechanics of collective advocacy and the viability of seeking to work within the confines of the state and existing political structures to achieve the type of meaningful change that would allow Black Britons to fully realize the rights, privileges, and entitlements afforded to them as citizens.

As a whole, this book intends to explore two intertwining histories that informed the views and experiences of Caribbean migrants like Lord Kitchener in postwar Britain. One is a story firmly grounded in Black British histories that seek to understand the roles that Black people as historical agents have played in the production of British culture and society. Part of that narrative in the postwar period is concerned with Caribbean people of African descent and their struggles and negotiations to give substantive meaning to their membership in an imperial community of British citizens. It was not necessarily that Caribbean migrants came to Britain with the expectation that life in Britain would not have its difficulties, stages of adjustments, and even disappointments. Rather, they came with a desire to at least belong and to maximize the opportunities available for social and economic mobility. Author Donald Hinds, who migrated to Britain from Jamaica to join his mother in 1955, explains,

> When a migrant makes up his mind that he is going to Britain, he hardly expects to find an earthly paradise. He expects to work for his living, and doubtless to do royally well . . . He believes he ought to be accepted, and his being a British subject is reason enough.[64]

Hinds's insightful comments remind us that it was not enough for migrants to simply have the opportunity to move to Britain to substantiate their status as British citizens; just as important, migrants intended that their movement and settlement would be qualified by the experience of being "accepted" as citizens, workers, neighbors, patrons, entrepreneurs, men, women, and children, perhaps at the very least by the state, on a similar basis as their White metropolitan counterparts. In recognition of this important insight, my work acknowledges the ways in which the labels "immigrant" and or "coloured immigrant," the most frequent monikers used in sources from the postwar era to describe Afro-Caribbean newcomers and other populations of color, including newly arrived Asian and African populations and those who had been settled in Britain well before World War II, served as a part of a larger racialized discourse of disenfranchisement. As such, these labels provided a public vocabulary of non-belonging that inherently denied Caribbean migrants the rights, respect, and recognition afforded them as British citizens. Although some of the scholarship on this period continues to invoke these terms, this study resists this practice and uses the terms in quotations only when referencing those who possessed citizenship and rights of belonging. As Winston James succinctly notes in his study of the Black experience in twentieth-century Britain,

> there have been relatively few black immigrants to Britain. Most of those who entered Britain in the twentieth century, including the post-war years, were simply moving from one part of the British empire to another as British citizens. . . . Unless one is prepared to call Yorkshiremen in London immigrants, then we should not call Barbadians entering London on British passports immigrants.

The immigrant label attached to such persons largely developed in the 1960s precisely to deprive black Britons of their citizenship rights.[65]

Considering this argument is essential for understanding the relationship between migration to Britain and questions of citizenship because it focuses our attention on the fact that migration during the postwar period represented an imperial right, a condition of belonging within the Empire, exercised and articulated by Caribbean newcomers by way of their journeys to places like London.

The second storyline interwoven throughout this study concerns the ways in which Black Britons, White Britons, and British policy makers articulated and contested the racial character of British citizenship and ideas about what it meant to be British, both as an ideal and a lived experience at a particular moment when issues of race and race relations mattered and remained integral to international politics. Just as policy makers debated the rights of entry for Commonwealth citizens and the social and political implications of an increasing Black presence in metropolitan Britain in a postwar world that was conscious of race, racism, and the stakes of disfranchisement, so too were Afro-Caribbean migrants cognizant that their denied claims to the rights of citizenship and belonging in Britain were entrenched within broader diasporic and transnational struggles against the vestiges of European imperialism and ideologies of White supremacy. This study hopes to provide a starting point to rethink the politics of Caribbean migration and issues of citizenship and race in postwar Britain and add to a growing literature on the metropolitan dimensions of the end of Empire and its legacies in the second half of the twentieth century. Most importantly, however, this study demonstrates that the voices, perspectives, activities, and experiences of Caribbean migrants mattered and held transformative social and political power.

Race, Empire, and the Formation
of Black Britain

In 1772, Maurice Morgann published a short pamphlet titled *A Plan for the Abolition of Slavery*. In it, Morgann offered one of the earliest blueprints for gradual emancipation throughout the British Empire. His essay described an Empire without slavery that would liberate and civilize former slaves and incorporate "black subjects of Britain" into a unified imperial body politic.[1] In the same year that Morgann published his treatise on abolition, Lord Mansfield issued his celebrated judgment in the case of an enslaved man by the name of James Somerset, who had absconded from his owner after being brought to England. When authorities recaptured Somerset, his owner, a Boston, Massachusetts customs official made arrangements for him to return to slavery in Jamaica. Represented by Granville Sharp, a well-known anti-slavery advocate in Britain, Somerset eventually won his freedom when the court ruled that English law prohibited slave owners in England to forcibly take a slave for the purposes of selling him or her abroad.[2]

Although Mansfield's decision in the Somerset case did not outlaw the practice of slavery in England, nor did it signal the emancipation of enslaved persons in England, it was widely regarded as a referendum on slavery that characterized the institution as "un-British" and essentially incompatible with the underlying principles of British law and tradition. As the anti-slavery movement unfolded in the late eighteenth and early nineteenth centuries, leading advocates, including William Wilberforce, framed abolition campaigns in the same light—as a defense of British tradition and a vindication of laws designed to protect the interests of the Crown's subjects.[3] Accentuated by a broader intellectual current shaped by European Enlightenment thinkers' preoccupation with ideas of rights and individual liberties, both the publication of Morgann's treatise on the meaning of abolition and the Somerset case represent important examples illustrating how ideas regarding emancipation and the rhetoric of anti-slavery produced new ways of defining both the imperial community and, subsequently, the rights and privileges of belonging to the imperial body politic. Whereas Morgann envisioned the demise of slavery as a foundation for the formation of a class of Black British subjects, the English court's recognition of James Somerset's right not to be reenslaved in accordance with the tenants of British law and tradition established the notion that one's race, class, and status did not necessarily prevent that person from certain legal protections enjoyed by all British subjects. To be sure, both Morgann's treatise and the Somerset case outlined a particular discursive terrain allowing for the possibility that Empire—more specifically, an Empire that denounced slavery—might indeed operate as a space where Black people, including the enslaved and the emancipated, might come to expect, assume, and assert certain liberties, rights, and identities as members of a British imperial community of subjects and, later, citizens.

To understand the historical genealogies of the claims that *Windrush* passengers, including Lord Kitchener and an entire generation of Afro-Caribbean migrants, made to British citizenship and rights of belonging during the postwar era, it is important to situate them within a broader history of race, Empire, and competing conceptions of emancipation, imperial belonging, and citizenship via subjecthood. As both Maurice Morgann's vision of the emancipatory possibilities of abolishing slavery in the Empire and the legal victory achieved in the Somerset case demonstrate, the unfolding of the series of ideological, social, and political movements that would culminate in the abolition of slavery in the British Empire produced universalizing discourses of imperial belonging. Subsequently, these discourses of imperial belonging articulated crucial links between the demise of slavery and the rise of nominally free wage-labor societies that would incorporate freed people into an imperial community of British subjects, and later one of British Commonwealth citizens.[4] Outlining some of the key ideological positions that came to define the mobilization efforts waged by the leading abolitionist organization in Britain during the late 1820s and early 1830s, the Anti-Slavery Society, Thomas Clarkson vehemently argued in 1823 that in slavery, "Africans or Creoles, *have been unjustly deprived of their rights.*" He further contended that the necessary redress was "to *compensate* to these wretched beings *for ages of injustice*" and "*to train up* these subjects of our past injustice and tyranny *for an equal participation with ourselves in the blessings of liberty and the protection of the law.*"[5] Although his appeal came laced with paternalistic overtures toward enslaved workers, Clarkson's writings no doubt challenged the legalities of slaveholding and insinuated that slavery was a form of disfranchisement. Likewise, he suggested that emancipation was the only tenable recourse that would lead to the restoration of rights and the full incorporation of enslaved laborers into the imperial body politic.

In the same year that Clarkson wrote, some 30,000 enslaved insurgents from over 50 estates rose in opposition to the plantocracy on the island of Demerara. Communicating their intentions to avoid violent confrontations, Demerara rebels informed the colonial Governor that their cause was driven by a simple desire for "Our rights." They insisted that forthcoming reforms designed to ameliorate the conditions of their enslavement "were of no comfort to them," because "God has made them of the same flesh and blood as the whites, [and] that they were tired of being Slaves to them." They contended that their "good King had sent Orders that they should be free and they would not work any more."[6] Much like Clarkson and other anti-slavery reformers, as Demerara abolitionists justified their opposition to the conditions of their enslavement, they did so in a language that invoked imperial authority to validate their claims to freedom. To be sure, the "great buckra," or King, as the consummate symbol of the Empire represented the progenitor of their right not only to challenge the terms of their enslavement, but also to assert the freedom to be recognized as members of the same imperial community of subjects as White colonials.[7]

In his work on the ideological and political currents shaping the history of British abolitionism, Christopher Leslie Brown has argued that the social processes that eventually resulted in the abolition of slavery were consequentially the defining tenets through which the British Empire began to recognize and construct Black men and women of the Empire as British subjects and members of the imperial community. Although Brown pays little attention to the role that the agency of the enslaved played in facilitating abolition, he is clear that while emancipation provided opportunities to make claims to the rights of British subjecthood, "winning the rights of the subject . . . did not free the liberated from the constraints of race, or the taint of their former status."[8] Brown's point is critical to this chapter's consideration of the ways in which the history of post-emancipation Caribbean society unveils how the very production of subjecthood for newly freed men and women of African descent involved a contest between marking relationships of imperial belonging and realities of imperial hierarchies grounded in racialized exclusivity. In essence, emancipation within the context of Empire manufactured a particular type of subjecthood for the formerly enslaved that was marginal and second-tier from its very inception. Nevertheless, it was precisely from this position that freedpeople and their progeny engendered embodied practices of citizenship and what Lara Putnam describes as "vernacular theories of rights" that allowed them to actively participate in a contentious dialogue about the meaning of British subjecthood, citizenship, and the rights and entitlements tethered to one's membership in the imperial body politic as part of their process of actualizing freedom.[9]

With particular attention to Jamaica, the island where the majority of postwar Afro-Caribbean migrants hailed, this chapter explores how people of African descent employed British subjecthood and adapted discourses of Britishness by leveraging claims to imperial belonging and citizenship, in a challenge to metropolitan elites' ideas about their place within the Empire and colonial society.[10] It is within the pendulum of what Frederick Cooper and Ann Stoler have aptly labeled as the "dialectics of inclusion and exclusion" that one can track how people of African descent in the Caribbean strategically appropriated the rhetorical paraphernalia of Empire to produce British identifications that did not negate and, in fact, oftentimes coexisted and constituted affirmations of Blackness as part of the process of giving substantive meaning to freedom.[11] This identification, of course, was not the sole axis that the formerly enslaved and those who followed engaged to make meaning of freedom, but it was no doubt one that many understood as a route to navigate the cultural politics of colonial society.

Although the codification of imperial citizenship via British subjecthood did not materialize in any juridical form until the mid-twentieth century with the creation of the category of Citizen of the United Kingdom and Colonies (CUKC), metropolitan elites' inability to embrace this idea did not eclipse and perhaps only heightened beliefs in the emancipatory promises of a type of imperial belonging that secured rights and protections irrespective of race even as the imperial state persistently failed to deliver.[12] One finds that appropriating and remaking ideas about what it meant to be British was part of a repertoire of strategies—embedded in the claims of laboring insurgents, the texts of late-nineteenth-century Caribbean writers, the petitions of working class people, and the choices of those who elected to offer their lives in defense of Empire—used to articulate the meaning and, to a greater extent, the problem of freedom.[13] Moreover, cultivating British identifications as a form of imperial belonging and a mode of practicing a type of everyday citizenship that oftentimes challenged colonial authority and summoned the power of state was fundamental to how people of African descent asserted their humanity and attempted to obtain economic security, political inclusion, and civic justice. To be sure, race was at the core of these contests. At times, as was the case under the slavery, the Empire clearly delineated rigid racial boundaries that functioned to classify people of African descent as Black and relegate them to inferior positions in the labor market, exclude them from political institutions, and systematically impede their abilities to access rights that would lead to full participation in the economic, social, and civil life of society. But the politics of Empire in the post-emancipation era also, by necessity, produced expectations—even if only rhetorically—that a sense of shared allegiance to the Crown might supplant the stigmas attached to Blackness and provide opportunities to claim and secure rights and privileges afforded to all British subjects, regardless of race. In sketching how people of African descent in the Caribbean mobilized a transracial and inclusive sense of Britishness and citizenship via subjecthood that was more often than not denied by the state, this chapter is most concerned with tracking how these identifications were deployed rather than their ability to garner specific responses from the state. Here again, much like the analysis in the Introduction of Lord Kitchener's arrival, the focus is on the history of claim-making being represented, as opposed to how an elite White colonial power structure measured the validity of those claims.

British Subjecthood and the Meaning of Freedom

As the clock struck midnight on 1 August 1838, a crowd of over 2,000 gathered at the Baptist Chapel in Falmouth, Jamaica to hear Reverend William Knibb declare the official end of the apprenticeship system marking the transition from slavery to freedom in the British Caribbean. Emotions ran high as the crowd listened to Knibb declare, "THE MONSTER IS DEAD! THE NEGRO IS FREE! THREE CHEERS FOR THE QUEEN!" Early the next morning, a large crowd convened at a local schoolhouse to commemorate the end of a painful chapter in the history of the island by literally burying chains that had become symbols of its nearly 300-year history of enslavement. As the assembly of missionaries and formerly enslaved laborers sang in unison, "Now Slavery we lay thy vile form in the dust, and buried for ever, there let it remain," they eagerly cheered as the Union Jack was raised in celebration. They were now free subjects under the banner of the British flag.[14]

A decade later in 1848, Governor Charles Edward Grey issued a widely circulated edict emphasizing the inextricable ties between freedom and the rights, privileges, and obligations of membership in a British community of subjects. Writing in large part to undermine rumors of reenslavement and quell rumblings of a planned rebellion among former slaves, Grey charged:

> The Freedom, which was given to the Negro People of Jamaica, was given without recall or reserve, and the rights of the Labourers of that Race now stands on the same foundations as those of the Planter or Proprietor, or those of the People of England, and are a part of the Constitution of the Empire. The Crown, to which the allegiance of all its Subjects is equally due, will afford to all equally the protection of the Laws, and will secure to all the enjoyment of their rights, and especially that first and greatest and most precious of all rights—their personal freedom.[15]

Not only did Grey, as the highest ranking local representative of the imperial Government, outline a binding relationship between ideas of freedom and the promises of British subjecthood but, perhaps more importantly for the Black masses of formerly enslaved communities, Grey also showcased a language of possibilities legitimated by imperial authority that might potentially collapse overlapping boundaries of race, place, and class under the banner of a shared allegiance to the British Crown. To be sure, just as Grey invoked a democratic discourse of imperially recognized rights and entitlements, he also clearly acknowledged and simultaneously attempted to subvert the radical potential of this same ideology of universal male subjecthood. He added that

> whilst this Warranty and Assurance of their Freedom, and their Rights, is willingly given to the Negro People of Jamaica. . . . That as good Subjects of Her Majesty they will abhor and prevent the employment of Violence or Threatening Language to others, and that in the enjoyment of the perpetual and Constitutional Liberty which is gladly recognized as belonging to them, they will abstain from all Riotous and Rude Behavior, which might alarm the minds of Peaceable Persons; and will endeavor, by Soberness and Steadiness of Demeanor, and by Prudence of Conduct and of Language, to shew that they are worthy to sustain the Character of freemen, and to be the Fathers of Free Families.[16]

It is important to note the overarching ideological currents shaping the presentation of Governor Grey's provocative statements. Although the legalities of emancipation in Jamaica had crystallized with the passage of legislation abolishing slavery in the Empire in 1834 and the ending of the apprenticeship system in 1838, the terms by which emancipation might gain substantive and material value from the perspective of the formerly enslaved themselves had yet to be fully negotiated. Thomas Holt has persuasively argued that the liberal ideology espoused by British elites focused largely on the ways that emancipation would provide for a nominally free wage-labor force that still operated within and sustained the interests of a White male elite plantocracy. Holt emphasized that in the minds of British supporters of abolition, emancipation authorized the masses of ex-slaves to exercise their freedom and marginal social mobility to the extent to which they would maintain preexisting social, economic, and political hierarchies.[17] Governor Grey's decree highlights this peculiar paradox of British elite liberalism and its conception of the position of Black people in the Empire. While his words clearly illustrate the enabling ideological characteristics of British elite constructions of emancipation—access to universal rights based on a shared subjecthood that transcended race, place, and class;

equality before the law; and a sense of individual liberty—at the same time, they most certainly established concrete boundaries for the exercise of Black freedom. According to the description provided by Governor Grey, Black freedom could exist only as it remained confined to a set of prescribed codes of conduct that inherently attempted to contain the possibilities of revolutionary change to the status quo. However, despite British liberals' desires to construct a model of Black freedom and Empire to enable formerly enslaved communities inasmuch as it constrained their abilities to dismantle the social structure that sanctioned their enslavement, freed men and women throughout the Caribbean colonies consistently challenged the limits of British liberalism. In doing so, oftentimes ex-slaves employed the same democratizing language of Empire implored by British liberal ideology, just as they transformed, reappropriated, and remapped its boundaries in their pursuits to actualize their own visions of emancipation.

During the early post-emancipation period, one of the major controversies involving the imperial Government, the Jamaican planter elite, and freed people involved the uses of large tracts of uncultivated, underdeveloped, and oftentimes abandoned "backlands." William A. Green has noted that between 1832 and 1847, some 465 coffee estates alone were abandoned, amounting to more than 300,000 acres of vacant land for redevelopment and new settlements.[18] Whereas the Black masses viewed access to land for provision grounds and greater economic autonomy as a means of substantiating their freedom, colonial authorities and local planters recognized the possibilities that Black claims to land might eventually undermine not only the economic basis of a planter class of White male elite authority but also, perhaps just as significant, the social and political hierarchies overdetermined by race and class structuring colonial society.

In addition to providing opportunities to generate earnings and subsistence outside of the demands of the plantation economy, land also provided a means for greater access to civic participation and political power. According to the provisions of the Franchise Act of 1840, men had to either own land valued at least £6, pay or receive rent on property valued at £30, or pay £3 in direct taxes to become eligible to vote. Qualifications for candidates were even more restrictive. Assemblymen had to demonstrate proof of a net annual income from estate property of £180, possess land valued at £1,800, or possess assets worth £3,000. Over time, these restrictions became more stringent. Coupled with increasing poll taxes, by 1863, only 1,457 males out of a total population of roughly 450,000 voted for the overwhelmingly White planter-controlled Colonial Assembly that abolished the constitution in 1865.[19]

Despite suggestions by the Colonial Governor that "Crown lands" remain solely under imperial authority, in September 1836, the Colonial Office

granted control over these estates to the Colonial Assembly. Supported by the
Colonial Secretary, local policy makers set minimum prices for the lands and
sold parcels to the highest bidder. In addition, the local Assembly instituted
a number of policies, including increased land taxes and more expensive procedures for securing legal titles for purchased lands—policies that, in combination with escalating prices for land, formed successful barriers to Black
land ownership. Behind these measures resided the underlying premise that
access to land, and in particular the rise of a significant class of Black landowners, would surely undermine the process by which a Black laboring majority
might exercise political power and become economically independent from
the demands of White-controlled plantations.[20]

Although the conciliatory posture of the imperial Government in regard
to the implementation of these measures in the colony clearly indicated that
the uses of these lands securely fell within the regulatory prerogatives of local
authorities, the idea that these lands were "Crown lands" served as a basis
for Black resistance to the post-emancipation plantocracy and shaped Black
visions of the promises of emancipation. Just as imperial and local authorities
recognized that access to land could potentially alter their prescribed course of
Black freedom by creating greater economic opportunities that might distance
former slaves from the interests of a White-controlled plantation economy,
freed men and women also view land as a means of bolstering the quality and
economic value of their freedom. According to Thomas Holt, throughout the
1850s and 1860s the Jamaican masses buttressed numerous petitions for economic justice by asserting their rights of access to land. Holt writes that oftentimes laborers made "a direct connection between popular notions of Crown
land, public land, and the people's land." He contends that "peasants grounded
their right to the land in the logically consistent belief that abandoned properties should revert to the queen, thereby returning it to the public domain,"
and in the minds of Jamaican masses, "They were the public."[21] In this sense,
"Crown lands" became a symbol of public space, and consequently claims to
these imperial lands represented vital instruments whereby the Black working classes defined and clarified, in their own terms, their relationship to and
membership within a broader imperial public. Thus the right to land represented a crucial means of asserting one's position in the Empire and a sense of
imperial belonging as subjects of the British Crown.

Although a number of legal cases involving disputed lands emerged during the 1850s and 1860s to challenge the notion that uncultivated or unused
"Crown lands" could be occupied and or claimed as public property by virtue of being a part of the imperial domain, no single event dramatized issues
related to land access by a Black-majority colonial public than the 1865 Morant
Bay Rebellion, orchestrated in large part through the efforts of Paul Bogle, a

small farmer and Baptist deacon from Stony Gut. On 10 October 1865, one day before Paul Bogle led a mass insurgency organized around a matrix of working class issues that had become symptomatic of the early post-emancipation period, including depressed wages, unemployment, high taxes, disfranchisement, unequal justice, and, most essential, access to land, Bogle and other representatives of the Jamaican laboring masses issued a petition to the imperial Government to seek redress for abuses of power sanctioned by local colonial authorities.[22] In their appeal to the Queen for protection against local authorities, Bogle and his associates argued, "we are Her Majesty's loyal subjects; which protection, if refused we will be compelled to put our shoulders to the wheels, as we have been imposed upon for a period of twenty-seven years, with due obeisance to the laws of our Queen and country, and we can no longer endure the same."[23] Finding no reprieve from colonial authorities, one day later Bogle led a parade of several hundred men and women to Morant Bay into a violent confrontation with local police, military forces, and other local authorities. Over the course of the following day, reports estimated that between 1,500 and 2,000 local men and women, including estate workers, small landowners, farmers, traders, craftsmen, domestics, mothers, fathers, churchgoers, and a variety of other segments of the Black peasantry, participated in the insurgency. The outbreak ended as a result of a violent suppression sanctioned by the colonial Governor, yielding some 439 deaths, hundreds of floggings and approximately 1,000 burned properties.[24] In launching the Morant Bay rebellion, Paul Bogle and his compatriots continued in a broad tradition of post-emancipation protest strategies that included the invocation of imperial authority to make claims upon certain rights and entitlements on the basis of their perceived membership in an imperial community of subjects.

Even before the ending of apprenticeship, newly freed people in Jamaica relied upon petitions to the imperial Government as a vehicle of protest and claim making. At a meeting organized in conjunction with the Baptist missionary society in May 1838, between 3,000 and 4,000 fieldworkers resolved in a message directed to the Queen that they would "hail the day as one of [the] brightest in human prosperity" when they would be granted "perfectly equal and just participation in the laws." Anticipating the continuation of a struggle for complete emancipation even beyond the legal demise of slavery and apprenticeship, the petitioners asserted, "We feel that we are entitled to all the immunities of free subjects without distinction, yet we are determined not to be betrayed by the schemes of our adversaries into acts of subordination."[25]

Mimi Sheller's work on what she terms as the development of "independent black publics" in the years preceding the Morant Bay rebellion offers valuable insights on working-class political culture in post-emancipation Jamaica. According to Sheller, Black public spheres developed their own political ideologies, forms of leadership, and modes of articulating their cause, oftentimes employing petitioning at mass meetings as a tool of protest and claim making.[26] In the process of engaging these forums of Black resistance and oppositional culture, Sheller not only unearths a range of concerns defining Black men and women's visions of the material value of their freedom but, just as significantly, she also reveals in her work how Black people imagined and projected self-inscribed political identities as freedpeople. Between 1858 and 1865, various sectors of the Jamaican peasant majority organized and participated in numerous mass public meetings, producing a variety of texts that illuminate their own constructions of their post-emancipation identities.

Responding to the passage of a new electoral law in 1858 that increased voter registration fees, working-class petitioners from the parish of St. David urged that the Queen recognize that with the institution of the new policy, "a serious injury is done to the class of your Majesty's subjects, who were emancipated from slavery, and invested with the rights of British Freemen." Petitioners underscored that the tenets of the legislation would impede the masses from the most basic right of civic participation and continued to concentrate political power "in the hands of an exceedingly small minority of fellow Citizens." This "small minority," the petitioners noted, mostly "belong to that class who but too recently owned our bodies and souls and who seem loth [sic] and backward to accord to us the equality of political rights secured by the British Constitution, alike to all classes."[27]

In another set of petitions addressed to the Queen in 1859, over a thousand signatories representing five rural parishes near Kingston expressed concerns over election laws, unpaid wages, harsh working conditions on estates, indentured immigration from Asia, high taxes, and a corrupt justice system. Petitioners insisted that, overall, the state of colonial policy reflected "retrograde steps to a refined state of slavery or something akin to it." In formulating their grievances to imperial authorities workers and small landholders represented by the memorials used a variety of titles to describe themselves, including "loyal and Devoted Subjects," "Mechanics and Peasantries," "sable subjects of Jamaica, of African descent," "African descendants," "British subjects," and "black."[28] Taken together, these petitions elucidate a critical dimension of the identity politics shaping the relationships engendered between Empire and the Jamaican peasantry in the post-emancipation period. By addressing their appeals to the Queen, the most potent symbol of Empire and guarantor of imperial rights and privileges, petitioners automatically positioned themselves within an imperial community of subjects. Juxtaposing their relationship to the Empire with collective identities denoting race, color, place, and class gave even more substance and elasticity to their conceptions of their own British subjecthood and the boundaries of the larger community of imperial citizens.

To be sure, not only do these labels illustrate the complexity and multipositionality of the Jamaican peasantry, but they also allude to a democratic understanding of the possibilities of an all-encompassing British imperial identity and community that could unite those under Crown authority across boundaries of race, color, region, and class.

Britishness and Nineteenth-Century Black Nationalism

Fifty years after the ending of apprenticeship in Jamaica, in 1888 C. A. Wilson, a Presbyterian minister, along with four other Black Jamaicans whom Wilson later described as "men of vision," published one of the earliest treatises expressly articulating Black nationalist thought in the Caribbean during the post-emancipation era, titled *Jamaica's Jubilee; Or What We Are and What We Hope to Be.*[29] In part, the authors sought to document the progress of former slaves in Jamaica since emancipation for metropolitan audiences. Referencing the post-emancipation struggles of Jamaican Negroes, they insisted, *"no other people could, under similar circumstances, have reached a greater height on the ladder of social advancement within the same period of time."*[30] As anti-Black colonial discourses calcified in the latter half of the nineteenth century, particularly in the wake of the Morant Bay Rebellion, the authors hoped that their work would serve to celebrate and vindicate the achievements made by a generation once removed from slavery and still living under socioeconomic conditions and colonial policies that impeded their economic and political advancement.[31] Moreover, the authors of *Jamaica's Jubilee* also intended for their work to provide a blueprint for imagining Jamaican futures for the Black laboring masses, a plan that consisted of following paths toward respectability and proprietorship through land ownership, the development of a self-reliant peasant class, and subsequently the demonstration of a type of moral fitness for self-government and entrance into the "brotherhood of nations."[32]

Casting the idealized future of a Black majority Jamaican nation in these terms involved articulating a vision of a British imperial world where the Jamaican people would be rightly acknowledged as "the subjects of a common king, the servants of a common Maker; possessing the same rights, entitled to the same privileges, claiming the same regard and affection, and having the same destiny" as their White metropolitan counterparts.[33] In this scenario, their rights as subjects and ostensibly their claims to Britishness would be both welcomed and authenticated. In her work on the political sensibilities expressed in *Jamaica's Jubilee*, Deborah Thomas has noted that the authors anchored their ability to make claims for the types of reforms in colonial governance that would propel Jamaica on a path of continued progress toward responsible self-government within the Empire in their understanding of their rights as British subjects. Claims of British subjecthood became the very discursive platform through which nineteenth-century Jamaican nationalists launched a critique of colonial racism and imperial policies that adversely affected the lives of the laboring Black masses. To be sure, the appropriation of British subjecthood and accompanying claims of imperial loyalty did not necessarily undermine diasporic or nationalist identifications. These claims were neither mutually exclusive nor fundamentally contradictory. Instead, as Thomas argues, among members of the Black intelligentsia, including the authors of *Jamaica's Jubilee*, "their simultaneous loyalty to Britain and to Jamaica coexisted with their recognition that the position of blacks in Jamaica was part of a worldwide conception of blacks, Africa and African civilization."[34]

In the same year that the authors of *Jamaica's Jubilee* issued their vision for the future progress of a Jamaican nation whose majority Black population had made tremendous strides since emancipation, English historian James Anthony Froude offered a scathing account of Black life in the Caribbean in the publication of his book *The English in the West Indies*. Based on anecdotal experiences during his brief sojourn to the Caribbean during the early 1880s, Froude's book set out to defend the virtues of Englishness and imperial rule.[35] Whereas the authors of *Jamaica's Jubilee* found every reason to celebrate the progress of Black Jamaicans fifty years after the demise of slavery as they imagined a future of self-government, Froude characterized this same population as an "inferior race" comprised of "docile, good-tempered excellent and faithful servants" with "elementary notions of right and wrong" who had shown "no capacity to rise above the condition of their ancestors except under European laws, European education and European authority." For that reason, he concluded that while freedom and prosperity was a destiny that "one would wish to see" the Black man achieve, "left to himself and without the white man to lead him, he can never reach it."[36] Trafficking in familiar tropes of Black deficiency that had been central to Thomas Carlyle's infamous essay, "Occasional Discourse on the Negro (and later "Nigger") Question," originally published in 1849, Froude's work furthered Carlyle's case against Black political power in the Caribbean for a new generation of metropolitan audiences while maintaining a stance that Black colonial subjects were inherently lacking and best suited for White rule, servility, and permanent tutelage by their more civilized English (White) metropolitan counterparts.[37]

A year later, in response to what he dubbed as the "Negro-repression campaign" demonizing Caribbean life explicit in Froude's work, John Jacob Thomas, a Trinidadian educator, civil servant, and writer, penned a book-length rebuke of Froude's polemic, simply titled *Froudacity*.[38] Describing

himself as a member of "a progressive, law-abiding, and self-respecting section of Her Majesty's liege [of] subjects," Thomas challenged the methodol-
ogy, tone, and logic informing Froude's racially incendiary rhetoric about the
necessity of preserving White power in the Black-majority colonies of the
British Caribbean.[39] Questioning Froude's "pathetically eloquent" characterization of the racial divide that advantaged Whites on the basis of "centuries
of training and discipline" rather than prejudice and power, Thomas asserted
that, ultimately, skin color and opportunity rather than aptitude and experience defined differences between Black and White.[40] While Froude found
Black West Indians inferior to their White counterparts in the colonies and
the metropole, Thomas made it clear throughout his text that the logic of
White supremacy espoused in Froude's work was untenable, as he considered
himself a member of "Her Majesty's Ethiopic West Indian subjects" who were
"black fellow-subjects" of those Britons of the "Anglo-Saxon race."[41]

In addition to rejecting the racist presumptions of Froude's arguments about
the virtues of imperial rule in the Caribbean, Thomas also issued a broader
indictment of the underlying contradictions of the liberal Victorian Empire's
mission of advancing civilization and promoting progress by exercising the
moral imperatives of justice, benevolence, and fair play. Attempting to shame
the British nation and the imperial state through an overstated comparison
between the status of Black people in the Spanish and the French Empires, in
critiquing Froude, Thomas connected the threads between the protections of
subjecthood and entitlements of citizenship that legitimated Afro-Caribbean
claims to a sense of Britishness and imperial belonging. He charged, "Are the
Negroes under the French flag not intensely French? Are the Negroes under the
Spanish flag not intensely Spanish?" In his view, although the British Empire
prided itself on molding people of African descent into free subjects, it had
proved less than accommodating of, and in many instances hostile toward, the
aspirations of its Black subjects. While embellishing the dynamics of race and
citizenship for Black people in Spanish and French territories—more likely
to dramatize his critiques of British imperial policy rather than to accurately
reflect other European imperial realities—he explained, "By Spain and France
every loyal and law-abiding subject of the Mother Country has been a citizen
deemed worthy [of] all the rights, immunities, and privileges flowing from
good and credible citizenship."[42] In striking contrast, Thomas insisted this was
typically not the case, as even the most intelligent class of Black British subjects could not find acceptance or equal opportunity within the ranks of the
British imperial regime.

J. J. Thomas's *Froudacity* is an important text for understanding the complexity of the political work that articulations of Black Britishness served in
contesting the racialized imperial regime that ultimately sought to transform

people of African descent in the Caribbean into loyal and "civilized" subjects.[43] Undoubtedly, it is clear that for Thomas and other members of an emergent nineteenth-century Afro-Caribbean intelligentsia, which included those who had accumulated educational credentials, professional standing, or other measures of bourgeoisie refinement, claims of Britishness reflected their aspirations toward and desires to fulfill elite Victorian notions of civility. But as Thomas's biographer Faith Smith notes, Victorian standards of progress, upward mobility, and respectable subjecthood were not the only metrics that Afro-Caribbean intellectuals used to define themselves and their status within the Empire.[44] Instead, as demonstrated in *Froudacity*, invocations of Black Britishness provided a viable political language for Afro-Caribbeans to contest imperial hierarchies that privileged Whiteness, Englishness, and metropolitan culture. For Thomas and others who challenged Froude's racist presumptions, their identifications as Black Britons, or "black fellow-subjects," gave them the authority to engage and talk back to Froude and a broader current of ideas about the place of people of African descent in the imperial order. Moreover, in suturing their claims of Britishness and subjecthood to their understanding of their Blackness and racialized coloniality in ways that linked their experiences and destinies to a transnational African Diaspora, Thomas and his contemporaries, including the authors of *Jamaica's Jubilee*, offered notions of Britishness that transcended the prescriptions of liberal Victorian ideologies. Britishness then became a means of advocating for Black political empowerment in the form of political representation, national self-determination, and a Pan-Africanist–oriented liberation for people of African descent in the Americas and continental Africa.

By the turn of the century, Pan-Africanism would gain greater political currency as an organizing motif of transnational Black political activity with the establishment of the Pan-African Association and the convocation of the first Pan-African Conference by Trinidadian Henry Sylvester Williams in London in 1900. Initially organized in 1897, the Pan-African Association took as its aim "to promote and protect the interests of all British subjects claiming African descent."[45] Although Williams was less than successful in establishing branches of the Association in the Caribbean, with the support of Joseph Love's newspaper the *Jamaica Advocate*, Williams did manage to organize a chapter that adopted a primary objective of securing civil and political rights "for Africans and their descendants throughout the world," which attracted nearly 500 members across the island. During the late nineteenth and early twentieth century, Love's *Advocate* emerged as the premiere organ of local Black political agitation in Jamaica. Decades later, celebrated Black nationalist Marcus Garvey would credit Love's paper with playing a formative role in developing Garvey's sense of "race consciousness" in such a manner that helped him draw crucial links between racism, colonialism, and the economic and political struggles of the Black working-class masses. [46]

In the pages of the *Advocate*, Love oftentimes featured excerpts of the writings of prominent Black intellectuals and Pan-Africanists, including Edward Blyden, J. E. Casely-Hayford, and local writers, including Theophilus Scholes. In 1905, Scholes penned *A Glimpse of the Ages,* one of three works dedicated to racism and British imperialism that highlighted the ways in which the promise of British justice had failed to materialize in the lives of "coloured British subjects" in the Empire. Pointing to what he described as a "dual standard of justice" that resulted in a regressive tax structure favoring White elites, a "defective system of education," and restricted access to land for the laboring Black masses in colonies like Jamaica, Scholes insisted that in general, in terms of political and economic power, "the coloured subject . . . is excluded and where it is impossible to exclude him, custom has so arranged that he may not upon equal terms compete with the colourless subject."[47] Scholes was careful to note that, despite the inequities of access and opportunity between Black and White British subjects, these circumstances reflected imperial conditions that required redress and as such were not indicative of Black inferiority or deficiency. From his view, the terms of emancipation had qualified people of African descent to live as free subjects within a transnational imperial community. And while it may have been a "popular fallacy" for Englishmen to refer to colonials of color as "our subjects," he maintained that it was important they recognize that "coloured members of the British Empire are not subjects of the colourless, but subjects of the king of Great Britain and Ireland, Emperor of India and fellow-subjects of Englishmen."[48]

Black Britishness from Below

Just weeks after the Governor of Jamaica proclaimed Saturday, 2 February 1901 as an official day of public mourning to commemorate the death of Queen Victoria, the *Daily Gleaner* reprinted an article that had previously been published in the *New York Tribune,* titled "Negroes and the Queen." The article contended that while the Queen had been widely loved and cherished by various people throughout the British Empire, "nowhere, perhaps, was she so adored as in the West Indies among the black population." The author explained that Black West Indians held a "belief in the all powerful magic of her name" and attributed the virtues of British law that, unlike the American South, "protects Black and white alike, and punishes them with equal severity," to Queen Victoria. The article suggested that the image of the highly esteemed Queen loomed large among Black people of all classes and conjectured that "every house and shanty has its picture of the beloved ruler" that served as an ornament of her reign and a symbol of their loyalty. The article noted that in honor of the Queen, and as an expression of their admiration, Victoria had become a common name among West Indians and on occasion "the name 'Victoria Regina' has been solemnly given to an ebony infant," a sign implying that people of African descent felt a type of familial attachment to Queen Victoria and could then confer that attachment to their progeny. For these reasons, the author surmised that as the reign of King Edward VII commenced, "none will find it harder than the West Indian negroes to say with steady voice and undimmed eyes, 'God save the King.'"[49]

The *New York Tribune* article took a somewhat sarcastic tone in articulating how the death of Queen Victoria resurrected a ubiquitous sense of reverence and obeisance toward royal authority among the Crown's Black subjects in the Caribbean. However, it did convey how some of the dynamics of what Brian Moore and Michele Anderson have described as the "cult of monarchy and empire" permeated the everyday lives of people of African descent in islands like Jamaica at the turn of the century. According to Moore and Anderson, the cult of monarchy and empire refers to the ways in which the practice of the so-called civilizing mission of the Victorian Empire depended upon actively promoting the symbols, rituals, and pageantry associated with British royalty and imperial belonging to mold a majority Black Jamaican populace into proper, respectable, and, most importantly, loyal British subjects.[50] But as Moore and Anderson caution, it is important to understand that the goal of transforming Black people into British subjects in the Caribbean was not without contestation and negotiation. Just as imperial authorities and metropolitan elites held ideas about what British subjecthood meant for people of African descent in the Caribbean, so too did the Black populations whom they sought to remake and reform. Thus the cult of monarchy and empire reflected a complex and nuanced set of contestations that people of African descent actively shaped as they engaged its manifestations. And certainly an event like the death of a longstanding royal figure like Queen Victoria provided a critical moment when a broad cross section of Jamaican society demonstrated varying degrees of affinities toward imperial culture, the monarchy, and identifications with loyal British subjecthood as they participated in an Empire-wide period of mourning.

On 2 February 1901, the day that Queen Victoria received her last rites in London, as part of an island-wide day of mourning, memorial services were held across Jamaica at local churches. In the countryside over 1,500 mourners joined a procession from the courthouse to the Parish Church in Montego Bay. That same afternoon, another crowd estimated between 3,000 and 4,000 gathered for services in Port Antonio, while others convened in the community known as "Little London" in the parish of Westmoreland. In Black River, as bells from the Anglican and Wesleyan churches rang throughout the parish, mourners who reportedly ranged from "the highest magistrate to the poorest peasants" gathered to hear a eulogy of the Queen.[51] In anticipation of the official period of public mourning in Jamaica, workers in St. Ann's Bay kept busy for most of the preceding day, draping public offices, local businesses, and houses "with black and white hangings," a practice that was repeated in other areas, including the rural community of Christiana, signifying that the town was in mourning. That evening, many in St. Ann's Bay gathered at the local Wesleyan Church for a memorial service that featured a local brass band that attempted to comfort the weeping crowds with "sacred selections," including the classic "Dead March."[52]

In summarizing the significance of the passing of Queen Victoria for the majority Black population of Jamaica, an editorialist for the *Gleaner* judged that the "universal mourning" among Jamaicans of all segments of society was not surprising, given that most inhabitants of the island from an early age viewed her as a figure worthy of their "love and fealty." Moreover, the writer noted that the Jamaican people, most of whom were slightly two generations removed from slavery, had "special cause" to lament Victoria's passing because of her perceived relationship to emancipation in the British Empire. The article explained that

> she was on the throne when absolute freedom was given, and in the West Indies her name has always been associated with the new condition of liberty. She has been regarded as the beneficent Protector of the people and the sense of her Presence and Power, dim as it has been in many cases, has been a potent factor in their lives.[53]

So as a figure embodying the Empire's extension of emancipation for those whose ancestors held memories of enslavement, Queen Victoria represented a type of cultural icon that stood not only for their freedom, but also as a guardian and trustee of that freedom—a freedom that also granted them a claim to imperial belonging and British subjecthood.[54]

Even before her death, commemorations of the life of Queen Victoria had for some time been part of the culture of post-emancipation life in Jamaica. Although the masses of metropolitan Britons did not readily participate in rituals extolling monarchal power until the latter decades of the nineteenth century, by the turn of the century in Jamaica, a post-emancipation tradition of celebrating Victoria Day on May 24 in honor of her birth had long been established.[55] In an effort to keep her legacy alive in the aftermath of her death and the installment of a new monarch, in 1904 colonial officials designated

May 24 as Empire Day, a public holiday designed primarily to instill loyalty and cultivate allegiance by celebrating the virtues of the British Empire and responsibilities of imperial belonging, particularly among school-aged children. In 1907, the Board of Education in Jamaica sanctioned the preparation of a pamphlet aimed to offer lessons on the "importance of patriotism and imperial-thinking" that adopted materials from an Empire Day catechism designed by British officials to be read as part of the island's Empire Day celebrations for the year. Touting the Empire-wide theme of "One King, One Flag, One Fleet and One Empire," the pamphlet declared the British Empire "the greatest empire the world has ever seen." In addition to highlighting the constituents of the Empire, including the "Mother Country," consisting of England, Scotland, Wales, and Ireland, along with the settler colonies and dependencies such as India "gained by conquest," the pamphlet also reminded Jamaican students that the Empire "comprises people of all races, languages and religions." And because of these things, British officials hoped to remind Empire Day observers that they should "be proud of our Empire" and "endeavor to make our Empire proud of us." Moreover, it called upon Jamaicans to demonstrate their "duty bound" allegiance to the King and explained, "in honoring him we honor ourselves and the Empire to which we belong."[56]

In that same year, 1907, children who attended schools in St. Andrew had a full day of activities that were very likely typical of Empire Day celebrations across the island. Their day included assembling around the Union Jack, listening to addresses by local officials about the meaning of Empire Day and history of Queen Victoria's role in Empire-building, and joining in the chorus of a number of patriotic songs extolling the virtues of imperial power, including "Rule, Britannia!" "Flag of Britain," and "Freedom's Land."[57] Reflecting on the "inherited allegiance" that Empire Day celebrations facilitated between generations of Jamaicans, Jervis Anderson recalled that singing "imperial anthems" was a cornerstone of Empire Day festivities during the first half of the twentieth century. At the school that he attended in Falmouth as a boy, his headmaster "drilled and rehearsed" him and his mates for nearly a week in advance of Empire Day so that they would be well prepared for "patriotic singing." Anderson remembered that Britain's national anthem, "God Save Our Gracious King," was compulsory; but he noted, "we sang none of them so fervently as we did 'There'll Always Be an England,' 'Land of Hope and Glory (Mother of the Free),' and 'Rule Britannia'—its refrain proclaiming militantly that 'Britons never, never, never will be slaves.' "[58]

In her work on the relations of Empire, Hazel Carby has suggested that Empire Day celebrations during the early twentieth century functioned as key "sites for producing multiple meanings of Britishness" both in the metropole and the colonies.[59] They reinforced a larger educational system designed to produce loyal subjects versed in metropolitan history and tradition, and they also inculcated a sense of imperial pride and civic duty among the most impressionable of subjects.[60] Likewise, Empire Day provided a moment when subjects in different part of the Empire could articulate and make their own claims to versions of Britishness. For many Black Jamaicans, this claim meant demonstrating their loyalty to the British monarch and exalting an Empire that had enslaved their ancestors and continued to exercise forms of colonial governance that created barriers to political power and rebuffed their aspirations to create economic opportunities outside of the purview of the plantation. But for Black Jamaicans, Empire Day also resurrected ideas about Britishness rooted in folkloric memories of the rule of a Queen who had overseen their emancipation from slavery and protected their newfound freedom. On the island of Jamaica, these associations with Britishness in the post-emancipation era were not incontrovertible, but they certainly held sway. And over generations, by the early twentieth century, whether Black children actually believed that the British world that they sang about on Empire Day truly existed, in many ways their loyalty was to a set of rituals handed down to them by their forebears that had become a part of the racialized colonial landscape into which they had been born. Thus, their history as the progeny of Black slaves was the very conduit through which they realized Empire Day's ultimate goal of affirming their British subjecthood.[61]

While annual Empire Day celebrations promoted ideas about imperial citizenship and belonging and ignited a sense of patriotism among a cross section of a majority Black Jamaican populace during the first half of the twentieth century, the advent of two world wars provided some of the most dramatic moments shaping how people of African descent in the Caribbean articulated Black British identifications as colonial subjects. Beginning in the late eighteenth century, the British Empire relied upon colonial soldiers from the West India Regiments to pursue and defend imperial interests in the Americas. But by the early twentieth century, these battalions had significantly diminished.[62] As fighting escalated during the first year of World War I, the organization of the British West Indies Regiment (BWIR) in 1915 provided an opportunity for a majority Black male contingent of Jamaican military recruits drawn from the socioeconomic ranks of the peasantry and the working and middle classes to serve the Empire by literally placing their lives on the line in hopes of securing victory for the Allies. Of the nearly 16,000 men recruited from the Caribbean during World War I, over 10,000, or nearly two-thirds, hailed from Jamaica.[63] Even among those who did not take up arms for the Empire during World War I, a broader patriotic atmosphere aroused their support for the British war effort and the hope for victory.

Just as the war began in October 1914, Amy Ashwood and Marcus Garvey's newly formed Universal Negro Improvement and Conservation Association and African Committees League (UNIA) submitted a resolution to King George V that expressed members' "love for, and devotion to, His Majesty and the Empire." Characterizing the British Empire as a "great protecting and civilizing influence" and agent of justice, "especially to their Negro Subjects scattered all over the world," the organization's resolution declared that in this time of "National trouble" its members would "rejoice in British Victories." Moreover, they offered prayers for soldiers on the front lines as they proudly proclaimed, "God save the King! Long live the King and Empire."[64] In later years, Marcus Garvey would describe the UNIA's Jamaican outposts as an organization of "British Negroes."[65] But the unifying goal of UNIA activity from its inception throughout the first half of the twentieth century focused upon promoting racial pride and self-help throughout the African Diaspora.[66]

With Harlem as its base as the UNIA movement took shape and gained currency in the 1920s, establishing branches throughout the Caribbean, Latin America, Africa, and Britain, Marcus Garvey emerged as a staunch critic of the British Empire's failure to deliver justice, political empowerment, equality, and economic opportunity for its "black British subjects."[67] Part of Garvey's critique of British imperial power reflected the frustrations of generations of British Caribbean migrants abroad to levy what they believed to be the entitlements of imperial belonging in an effort to secure the protections of subjecthood and practice a type of citizenship that guaranteed political rights and economic justice. Whether it was the petitions of railway workers, canal builders or banana plantation farmers in Spanish-speaking countries in Latin America, or dock workers and sailors in Britain, throughout the early twentieth century the historical record is clear that Afro-Caribbean migrants did not view Blackness and Britishness as mutually exclusive.[68] In a plea sent to King George V by Clayton Lloyd Alexander Jeffers, a native of St. Kitts who had taken up residence in the Dominican Republic in the 1930s, Jeffers decried local British consuls, whom, he argued, "were appointed to defend us and also to protect our rights," but instead proclaim that they were not sent here for the "Blacks." According to Jeffers, he and his fellow British Caribbean comrades had found themselves living "not as free-born British subjects—but actual slaves for these American sugar plantations." He therefore requested that the King relieve their suffering by affording passage to British West Africa. Grounding their status as a British subjects in a history marked by being descendants of "enslaved ancestors whom the Good and Honourable Deceased Queen Victoria herself, signed the documents of slavery 'abolition' " and members of a race who had "fought side by side with some of England's most valiant and noble sons for the defense and preservation of the throne," in pleading for aid in the form of resettlement, Jeffers insisted, "England owes every black subject of hers the debt to return him back to his ancestral home Africa when we her sons cry unto Thee."[69] Just as Clayton Jeffers invoked a history of soldiering on behalf of the Empire to bolster Afro-Caribbean emigrants' claims to economic aid and relief, in his study of Jamaican service volunteers during World War I, Richard Smith has shown that the same patriotic fervor compelling men and women on the island, including Garveyites, to support the war and enlist for military service oftentimes nurtured a heightened racial consciousness that ultimately began to inform burgeoning nationalist movements on the island. Accordingly, Smith notes, memories of wartime service and sacrifice—arguably some of the defining tenets of loyal British subjecthood and a sense of imperial belonging—became some of the central points of reference used to demand economic opportunities, citizenship rights, equality, and representative government.[70]

The public commemoration of the service of soldiers in the British West Indies Regiment and other volunteer military personnel was a prominent feature of Peace Day celebrations held throughout the island of Jamaica in July 1919 to celebrate the end of World War I and mark the official signing of peace treaties with Germany. In Montego Bay, returning soldiers were honored with a special luncheon, and in places including Port Antonio and Buff Bay, soldiers marched in local parades alongside school children as they listened to the sounds of joy bells ringing and passed buildings decorated in the national colors of Britain.[71] In the rural township of Falmouth in the rural parish of Trelawny, as part of a daylong Peace Day celebration that included a cricket match and a torchlight parade, in a message to war veterans one local official praised their service and insisted their efforts showed the world that there were "loyal British subjects" in Jamaica. And because of this demonstration of loyalty, he added, "You have made Jamaica earn a place in the Empire."[72] Interestingly, as the interwar period witnessed the growth of colonial nationalism alongside calls for imperial reform and self-rule, much like African American veterans of the First World War, those who had fought to defend the Empire would prove pivotal in redefining the terms of Black citizenship in the British Caribbean by invoking military service to reframe Jamaica's relationship to and position within the British Empire.[73]

With the imposition of Crown Colony rule following the 1865 Morant Bay Rebellion, in addition to the dissolution of the local legislative assembly, this model of colonial governance also resulted in draconian limitations on the extension of the franchise as part of a broader agenda to stifle Black political participation. Much of this form of disenfranchisement took place through restrictive property requirements that kept voting rights and local political power concentrated in the hands of a small minority of White male elites with significant landholdings. Following the war, property requirements were temporarily lifted so that veterans could vote in the 1920 Legislative Council elections. Seeing this move as an opening, Alfred Mends, a prominent local journalist and trade unionist, rallied veterans to support democratic governance and work toward extending the franchise to all Jamaicans by casting their service as part of a larger island-wide contribution to the war effort and a pillar of their civic duty. In making the case to colonial authorities, Mends insisted, "Jamaicans fought heroically" during the Great War "to uphold the glory of the British Empire." Despite this fact, he charged that for the many Jamaican men and women who sacrificed home and family and gave their lives, their bodies, and their labor to defend the Union Jack, "Where is the reward?"[74]

Jamaica did not institute universal adult suffrage until 1944. However, the push for this marker of citizenship and instrument of representative government gained traction during the interwar period, particularly alongside a rising tide of working-class unrest during the mid-1930s that swept through several British Caribbean islands, including Trinidad, Barbados, Antigua, Belize, and British Guiana. The disillusionment of demobilized soldiers who anticipated that their military service would provide a pathway to affirm their imperial citizenship both in war and peace helped to fuel agitation for working-class reforms, including higher wages, access to land, and minimum-wage laws. And against the backdrop of worldwide economic depression that exacerbated the incessant problems of poverty and unemployment throughout the British Caribbean, disenchanted veterans who held memories of being excluded from commissioned positions, receiving unequal pay, and serving as manual laborers on the front lines because of their race became part of a growing chorus of working-class protests across the island of Jamaica, a movement that reached an apex in the spring of 1938.[75]

On 2 May 1938, World War I veteran St. William Wellington Wellwood Grant lead the first in a series of protests in Kingston that erupted in response to the violent repression of workers protesting low wages at the pay office of the West Indies Sugar Company in Frome. Although several smaller-scale revolts had regularly occurred among plantation workers in various parts of the island beginning in 1935, the uprisings in Frome elicited greater attention as news that four people, including a pregnant woman, had been killed by armed policemen sent to disperse the crowds that had gathered at the company's offices.[76] In the weeks that followed, workers from a cross section of Jamaican society, including agricultural workers, dockworkers, sanitation workers, and public-transportation workers, went on strike to protest working conditions, low wages, and unequal pay. Rallying a crowd of insurgents just days after protests in Frome took a deadly turn, William Grant captured one of the central themes that laboring insurgents hoped their demonstrations would communicate to colonial officials. He charged, "We want better living conditions." More specifically, he insisted, "We want the ordinary Jamaican to get the wages of Englishmen."[77]

In framing the goals of the uprisings in this manner, not only did Grant state protesters' demands for adequate living wages, but he also offered a metric for defining precisely what those desired conditions would consist of in the form of wages that would be suitable for "Englishmen." Ironically, at the same time that his plea for change acknowledged the distinctions that the colonial order made between Jamaicans and Englishmen, he also conveyed the sense that this same Empire had the ability to and, perhaps more precisely, the duty to pursue economic parity between these two groups of imperial subjects. For Grant, having the Empire substantively acknowledge that Jamaicans should have the rights, privileges, and economic opportunities held by Englishmen was the first step in a longer trajectory of claim making that would buoy the British Caribbean's move toward self-government. Indeed, national self-determination and political independence would be one of the most powerful symbols that Jamaicans held the same rights as Englishmen.

The political uprisings that took place throughout the British Caribbean during the late 1930s did not go unnoticed by the British Government. In the summer of 1938, the Government appointed a royal commission known as the Moyne Commission with a mandate to gather evidence about social and economic conditions in the Caribbean. After nearly six months of fact finding, the Commission prepared a report that acknowledged chronic unemployment, poor economic growth, and industrial stagnation throughout the region. In response, the Commission proposed a palliative program of reform that involved establishing a social safety net in the form of an annual welfare fund that would be used toward areas including health services, education, and unemployment assistance.[78] The program of reform and economic rehabilitation outlined in the Moyne Commission would ultimately take a back seat with the onset of World War II. Likewise, as war unfolded, the Empire actively worked to revive and cultivate a sense of loyalty, patriotism and civic duty among its British subjects in the Caribbean—and British Caribbean subjects responded.

In contrast to World War I, World War II brought the day-to-day realities of war, including the threat of attack, directly to the Caribbean colonies. In doing so, it widened the warfront and expanded the various opportunities for service. Although more formal military institutions, including the Royal Air Force (RAF), recruited thousands of men from the Caribbean who would serve in places such as Britain and Canada, local units such as the Barbados Volunteer Force, the Jamaican Volunteer Training Corps, and the Women's Auxiliary Territorial Service (ATS) also recruited Caribbean workers.[79]

Reginald George Mason, who joined the RAF at age eighteen and traveled to Britain from Jamaica in 1944, recalled that every morning before he graduated from school, his teacher would offer his class daily updates on the war. Shortly after graduating, he volunteered so that he would have an opportunity to "get to know the Mother Country."[80]

Like many ex-service personnel who would later settle in Britain during the late 1940s and the 1950s, Mason framed the motivations of his wartime service by highlighting his individual desire to obtain a more intimate glimpse of what life was like in the country that he maintained a type of familial attachment. According to Odessa Gittens, a native of Barbados who joined the ATS in 1943, the decision to join the war effort came from her "love for Britain (because we were British)" and a desire to advance her education. She explained that working for the ATS gave her an opportunity "to do my duty to Britain and to myself."[81] Gittens's insights are crucial to understanding how a host of West Indians who participated in the war effort in a variety of martial and civilian roles in support and defense of their colonial lands and the broader British imperial world adopted a sense of Britishness that was both patriotic and capable of serving autonomous desires for social and economic mobility. Thus war became a context that commanded British loyalties but also fertilized the seeds that would nurture Black aspirations for better jobs, economic security, and routes to a more prosperous future than the Caribbean described in the Moyne Commission's investigative reports could offer. In terms of understanding their wartime service, Anne Spry Rush writes that during World War II, "West Indians were fighting for their own cause, but they saw that cause as including the survival of the British Empire, and themselves in it."[82] In many ways, this point is reflective of a critical theme embedded in the long history of imperial formations of Black British identifications. As people of African descent in the Caribbean made claims to Britishness and articulated their ideas about what it meant to be part of a transnational community of imperial subjects, they did so with an understanding that their cause, their experiences, their expectations, and, perhaps most importantly, their aspirations were part and parcel of the very existence and survival of the Empire. And it was this sense of belonging that would encourage Aldwyn Roberts to declare, "London is the place for me."

Migration, Citizenship, and the Boundaries of Belonging

Descended from a family of Morant Bay farmers, Isolyn Robinson departed her home on 12 September 1954 to begin the first leg of a journey that would take her from Jamaica to Southampton, where she hoped to find a "change of scenery" and begin a new life in Britain. Leaving behind her husband, as she discovered that they "couldn't really get on as a couple," and a daughter, Isolyn planned to stay with an aunt who lived in Brixton until she found a job and a place of her own. By 1954, Brixton was slowly becoming a hub of Black settlement in London, with a growing array of social activity. Isolyn quickly found employment at Lyon's Corner House in Piccadilly, a popular cafe and restaurant franchise where she washed dishes for a little over £4 per week. But this position was short lived. By the time she paid for food, taxes, and rent for the small room she occupied in a house with no indoor toilet or running water, she had little to show for her labor. After a few weeks, she quit Lyon's Corner and managed to find what she described as a "cleaner" job designing costume jewelry. Although she had come to Britain in search of work, Isolyn Robinson was more than a laborer and refused to let White employers take advantage of her. Recalling her experiences with Whites who viewed her presence in Britain strictly through the prism of her status as a migrant worker, she explained, "Sometimes white people said to me 'Do you think this country is a goldmine?'" To which she unflinchingly replied, "All my life I've been drilling up and down in front of the Union Jack and I've got a right to be here. So don't blame me, blame your King & Queen who made me a British citizen."[1]

Isolyn Robinson's response to those who questioned her motives for being in Britain and ostensibly the legitimacy of her claims to any opportunities for economic mobility and prosperity that working in the metropole might afford her opens a keyhole to understanding the importance of migration within the broader history of race, empire, and the articulation of Black British identifications. Not only did Isolyn recognize that she had a right to belong in

Britain, but she also clearly registered that the genealogy of that right resided in her legal status as a British citizen. According to the terms of the British Nationality Act of 1948, Isolyn Robinson and all British subjects resident in metropolitan Britain, the colonies, and Commonwealth countries became formally united under the banner of a universal Commonwealth citizenship that ideally transcended social divisions marked by race, ethnicity, region, class, and gender. In addition, the policy established a shared national sub-category of British citizenship specifically between metropolitan and colonial communities—"Citizen of the United Kingdom and Colonies"—and officially institutionalized the long-held tradition of intra-imperial migration to Britain as a legal provision of the broader Commonwealth citizenship. Along with the right of migration to Britain, colonials and other Commonwealth citizens assumed the full privileges, entitlements, and responsibilities of British citizenship enjoyed by their metropolitan counterparts, including the right to permanently settle and work in Britain.[2] Thus, as Isolyn Robinson reminds us, Jamaicans, Trinidadians, Barbadians, and other West Indians who journeyed to Britain in search of work and other economic opportunities were not merely part of a larger international postwar labor migration. Rather, through the very act of migrating to Britain, Afro-Caribbean travelers participated in a long history of claim making that involved reimaging the conditions of subjecthood, reordering boundaries of the imperial body politic, and reconfiguring the racial contours of British citizenship.

As noted in Chapter 1, the post-emancipation history of the British Empire has been indelibly marked by countless examples of Black men and women's relentless struggles to articulate and substantiate their claims to Britishness and imperial belonging. Focusing on the dynamics of this particular current as it informs the history of postwar migration between the Caribbean and Britain, this chapter highlights the ways in which the act of migration functioned as one of many channels through which Afro-Caribbean migrants practiced citizenship and, in the process, authenticated what it meant to be British on their own terms. Actualizing the provisions established by the British Nationality Act of 1948, as Caribbean migrants settled in Britain, not only did they make claims upon their rights as British citizens, but in doing so, they also constructed a vision of Britishness whereby the bonds that sustained Empire became the very mechanisms used to recalibrate British identifications that suited their desires to incorporate themselves into the social, political, cultural, and economic life of metropolitan society. As thousands of Caribbean migrants entered the British Isles during the 1950s and early 1960s, their acts of migration demonstrated an understanding that their position in the Empire and membership in the imperial community established and guaranteed them the rights, privileges, protections, and freedoms of

British citizens. Regardless of their race, color, ethnicity, or colonial origins, British citizenship was theirs to realize in its fullest form as they took up residency in the metropole.[3]

To situate this conversation, this chapter begins by briefly revisiting some of the claims to imperial belonging made by Black British subjects in the metropole during the interwar period, as a critical yet oftentimes neglected antecedent for understanding postwar debates about citizenship in metropolitan Britain. Just as the Empire abroad produced iterations of Black Britishness that informed ideas about imperial citizenship well before this concept received official sanction in 1948, so too did the dynamics of Empire at home. From there, the chapter moves to the juxtaposition of the coincidental, yet historically revealing timing of the Parliamentary debates surrounding the consideration of the British Nationality Act of 1948 and the arrival of the SS *Empire Windrush*. Taken together, these two events represent a critical moment when the ideological possibilities of imperial belonging collided with the practical realities of British citizenship.[4] Exploring the competing visions of a racialized imperial world as articulated by British officials and Caribbean migrants on the eve of what would become a generation of unprecedented migration from the Caribbean to Britain forms a crucial backdrop for understanding the character of postwar Caribbean migration and interrogating the various elements facilitating a migration process encompassing both actual movement and settlement.[5] In addition to detailing some of the major social, political, cultural, and economic dynamics structuring movements between the Caribbean and Britain during the 1950s, this chapter delves into the cultural demography of postwar Afro-Caribbean migration by literally taking a glimpse at who was migrating and how these individuals represented themselves as their arrivals were documented and captioned for White British audiences, and as part of their own repertoires of cultural expression. Perhaps, most importantly, a final yet critical piece of the puzzle of constructing a history reflecting some of complexities of Afro-Caribbean migrants' experiences in postwar Britain involves examining some of the material conditions shaping how migrants began to settle in Britain and confront the lived realities tethered to their efforts to make cities like London the place for them. To be sure, there is no singular narrative of West Indian migration to Britain. As Jamaican writer Donald Hinds has aptly noted, "Each migrant's story is another volume in the incredible saga of West Indian emigration."[6] However, the individual voices of migrants grant us a series of useful impressions about a rich history of movement, settlement, and social transformation that begs to be understood from the perspective of those who made the journey.

Visions of Imperial Citizenship
in Metropolitan Britain

Nearly three years before the arrival of the *Empire Windrush* became a headline-grabbing news story that would begin to shape popular perceptions among White Britons about the "colour problem" that Afro-Caribbean new-comers posed for the imperial metropolis, UNIA co-founder Amy Ashwood Garvey presided over the first day of sessions of the Fifth Pan African Congress, which convened at Chorlton Town Hall in Manchester on 15 October 1945. For over twenty years England served as the base of Amy Ashwood's political work, following her divorce from Marcus Garvey. Throughout the 1920s and 1930s she established her own brand of Pan-Africanist politics through her activities with the Nigerian Progress Union, the International African Service Bureau, and the Florence Mill Social Parlor, a restaurant that she established with calypso singer Sam Manning that became a critical hub of diasporic coalition-building and exchange between Caribbean and African activists and intellectuals such as C. L. R James, George Padmore, Albert Marryshow, T. Ras Makonnen, and Jomo Kenyatta. Thus Amy Ashwood Garvey's role as moderator of sessions concerning Britain's "colour problem" as an action item within the context of the Pan-African movement was quite appropriate, given that much of her own history of activism had been informed by living and organizing in the imperial metropolis.[7]

Organized on the heels of the end of the Second World War, the 1945 Pan-African Congress represented a watershed moment when the intellectual vanguards of Pan-Africanism, including George Padmore and W. E. B. Dubois, joined forces with mounting nationalist campaigns, civil rights advocates, and emerging labor movements, primarily in Anglophone Africa, the Caribbean, the United States, and Britain. Alongside declarations urging colonial work-ers to use the "weapons" of strikes and boycotts to combat imperialism and to make demands for self-government in the colonies, the Congress beseeched the newly formed United Nations for greater representation by political organs concerned with the "rights of African Negroes and descendants of Africans in the West Indies and the United States of America."[8] Because much of the preparation for the Congress had been conducted by Black coalitions based in Britain, and considering that Britain remained a critical diasporic space of encounter and crossroads of Black internationalism, it was perhaps quite fit-ting that the opening day of the Congress focused solely on the issue of "The Colour Problem in Britain." Moreover, the juxtaposition of domestic race politics with the explicitly diasporic agenda of the meeting underscored the ways in which its organizers understood the extent to which the conditions of anti-Black racism or the "colour problem" as viewed throughout the eyes of Black people in Britain had been produced within the architecture of the same racialized imperial structures that the meeting's attendees and supporters sought to dismantle in their pursuit of self-government, political independence, and economic empowerment in Africa and the Caribbean.[9]

During the first day's sessions, delegates from several British-based organizations, including Cardiff's United Committee of Coloured People's Association and Liverpool's Negro Welfare Centre, raised a number of concerns that had informed Britain's Black communities' view of "the colour problem" throughout the interwar period, namely, racial violence, lack of employment opportunities, orphaned children, poor housing conditions, and unjust treatment by police. As delegates sat in the hall adorned with flags from Haiti, Liberia, and Ethiopia with a map of Africa in full view, they listened as Peter Abrahams, a delegate for the International African Service Bureau (IASB), recounted a story in which police arrested "coloured and white men" on gambling charges that resulted in fines and imprisonment for the coloured men and a warning "not to associate with coloured men" for their White counterparts. Many in the room most likely agreed with those who expressed that the time had come for Black people in Britain to demand "that which is ours" and hold the Colonial Office accountable for attending to the needs and bettering the conditions of Black workers and students. As the session came to a close, F. O. B. Blaize, a Nigerian representative of the West African Student Union, reiterated many of the talking points raised throughout the day and suggested that the gathering of intellectuals, organizers, and activists had a vital role to play in seeking justice on behalf of the particular conditions of Black communities in Britain. Blaize implored, "If the British people think they have the right to live in Africa, then we have the right to stay here. We have the right to get together and see that something is done for us here."[10]

While George Padmore and the organizers affiliated with the Pan-African Federation are certainly key in understanding the broader anti-colonial agenda of the historic Manchester conference, as it relates to the specific issue of the "colour problem" or, more precisely, racism as experienced by Black people within the confines of the imperial metropolis, arguably one of the most influential figures shaping this dialogue throughout the interwar period and in the run-up to the Congress meeting was Jamaican-born doctor Harold Moody. Although Moody had been in contact with W. E. B. Dubois and Amy Jacques Garvey about the prospects of planning such a meeting in the preceding year, he did not actually attend the Manchester Congress, nor was there official representation from the organ of his political work, the League of Coloured Peoples (LCP). Founded in 1931 to promote the social, political, and economic interests of people of color, by the onset of World War II, the LCP represented itself as "the only organ in the country which is making a conscious effort to create a new climate in the racial relations between black and white" in Britain "by explaining the aims and aspirations of the black man and endeavoring to relate them with those of the white man."[11] And while the roster of delegates and their affiliate groups at the Fifth Pan-African Congress meeting demonstrates that the LCP was one of several organizations lobbying on behalf of the interests of Black people in Britain, it is certain that the LCP was one of the most active in terms of taking their claims for equity, access, opportunity, and civil rights before British officials to demand justice and compel the state to honor the purportedly quintessentially British commitment to fair play.[12]

Throughout the interwar period, as the League took their grievances about what was customarily described as the "colour bar" to British officials and the press, claims to imperial belonging and British citizenship stood at the core of their arguments for redress. Whether the League was speaking out against racist language used by the BBC, challenging discrimination in housing and employment, or protesting the treatment of prominent members, including famed Trinidadian cricketer Learie Constantine, who filed suit when a London hotel denied him accommodations, LCP activists consistently staked their positions in relation to their sense of being entitled "citizens" in an Empire that had promised rights and freedoms even if the guarantee fell short.

In October 1939, following the Colonial Secretary's announcement that the Government planned to issue emergency wartime commissions to any eligible British subject seeking military enlistment, thereby abandoning the requirement that commissioned officers be persons of European descent, the League embarked on a campaign to lift this condition permanently. In an appeal to the Colonial Secretary as "loyal subjects of the British Crown, and as representatives of colonial peoples from Africa and the West Indies and as persons believing that Britain stands for justice and equality amongst peoples," LCP members insisted that entrance into the armed services should be determined solely on the basis of "qualifications rather than skin color." Highlighting specific cases of discrimination in the military against "loyal citizens" with impeccable educational credentials, middle-class professions, and ostensibly all of the traits of respectability that would merit favorable consideration, in their petition to call upon the state to permanently embrace a policy that truly reflected the Empire's rhetoric of color-blind justice and equal opportunity, the League insisted that such a move would represent a "permanent acknowledgment of the rights of citizens of the Empire."[13] In a follow-up letter further clarifying the LCP's position, Harold Moody argued that the removal of barriers for people of color seeking to demonstrate their allegiance and loyalty to the Empire through military service was not about creating opportunities for people of color without merit. He explained,

> We are not seeking for specialist treatment in every case. We are merely seeking to establish our spiritual, cultural, and mental equality, as members of the British Empire, with every other member of the British Empire and to embody the term "British citizen" with some meaning and some reality as far as we are concerned. We claim the right to that freedom, which is the cherished possession of every Englishmen.[14]

To be sure, Harold Moody's vision of a British imperial citizenship that did not equate Britishness with Whiteness was deeply rooted in a gendered and class-conscious ethos of respectability that valued education, family background, adherence to Christian codes of morality, and social status.[15] However, what is most interesting to note about Moody and his LCP supporters' articulations of citizenship is how they positioned Black Britishness as part of the very realization of the type of inclusive sense of imperial belonging that had historically constituted imaginaries of a transnational British Empire bound by a shared and universal category of subjecthood that made no distinction in regard to race. In a speech before members of the Baptist Union in Glasgow in the formative years of the LCP, Harold Moody declared his pride in his British citizenship, but offered, "I am still more proud of my colour, and I do not want to feel that my colour is going to rob me of any of the privileges to which I am entitled to as a British citizen."[16] In doing so, Moody presciently expressed some of the ways that a generation of Afro-Caribbean migrants would seize upon and exercise claims to British citizenship, practice inclusive forms of imperial belonging that accommodated Blackness, and challenge popular metropolitan conceptions of the racial contours of Britishness when the British Nationality Act of 1948 formally codified the imperial citizenship that Afro-Caribbean subjects had long understood themselves to possess.

With the passage of the British Nationality Act of 1948, the term citizenship entered the official political lexicon of British public policy. Under the terms of the Act, imperial belonging via subjecthood in the metropole, colonies, and dominions received a new nomenclature, Commonwealth citizenship. Likewise, the imperial nationality of British subjects resident in Britain and the colonies alike gained official recognition through the creation of the category Citizen of the United Kingdom and Colonies (CUKC). It is important to note that while ideas about imperial citizenship had long been debated in policy-making circles, the contours of the British Nationality Act of 1948 emerged as a Parliamentary response to developments in the Commonwealth, specifically, the passage of the Canadian Nationality Act of 1946. Under the terms of the Canadian policy, British subjecthood became a derivative of, rather than a precursor to, Canadian citizenship. As such, the policy represented a decisive departure from the nationality principles maintained under the provisions of the British Nationality and Status Aliens Act of 1914. This act implemented uniformed naturalization procedures and provided for a shared universal British subjecthood status throughout metropolitan Britain, the dominions, and the colonies. The common status was to serve as the primary nationality of British subjects throughout the Empire and Commonwealth. However, recognizing the nationalistic impulse that undergirded the very idea of having a dominion status, dominion states had the option of establishing local citizenships as subcategories of British subjecthood.[17]

Throughout the 1920s and 1930s, the dominions persistently engaged in various means of distinguishing their individual national communities, including restrictive immigration policies and selective enfranchisement, as part of a broader move to distinguish their own sovereignty and constitutional authority aside from the realm of metropolitan interests. In spite of these measures, however, what remained intact was the primacy of British subjecthood. The institution of the Canadian Nationality Act of 1946 altered the principles buttressing the common status because it inverted the relationship between local citizenship and the historic imperial nationality. Canadian citizenship then became the gateway to British subjecthood, which meant that the imperial status became secondary to an individual's locally defined national status.[18] As a result, this move to supplant the traditions that had fortified the common status forced the British Parliament to not only look for avenues to preserve the historic sense of imperial nationality but, more importantly, to also reexamine the metropolitan community's own ideas about British citizenship and the parameters of Britishness.[19]

Parliamentary debates over the British Nationality Act of 1948 raised a number of issues, including the prerogatives of Commonwealth dominions to establish their own local citizenships, the ambiguities of British subjecthood for residents of Northern Ireland who maintained political ties to the United Kingdom, and the denaturalization of British women married to non-British subjects. But the most critical point of contention involved questions concerning the creation of an applicable local citizenship status for both the metropolitan and colonial communities. If Parliament was to acknowledge the right of the Canadian government to enact a unilateral citizenship status that trumped British subjecthood, it would also have to anticipate that the Canadian legislation might indeed represent a new paradigm of Commonwealth relations that would be adopted by other Commonwealth nations. In February 1947, the British Government hosted a meeting of nationality experts from throughout the

Commonwealth to outline a proposal for legislating British nationality in light of the new Canadian policy. As a result, the contours of the British Nationality Policy of 1948 took shape. Taking a cue from Canada, the plan at the heart of the proposal was to create a new category of local citizenship—"Citizenship of the United Kingdom and Colonies"—which would then serve as the portal through which individuals in the British Isles and the colonies would be considered British subjects.[20] Explaining the need for such a policy, Home Secretary Chuter Ede argued that the bill was "a natural sequel" to the provisions established in the 1931 Statute of Westminster.[21] Under the terms of this agreement, Parliament formally acknowledged the limits of its power in the dominions and officially recognized the dominions of Australia, Canada, New Zealand, South Africa, and Eire as equal partners along with Britain in a Commonwealth of Nations bound by an allegiance to the Crown for the principal purposes of security, trade, and economic development.[22] Ede, who had been instrumental in lobbying the Cabinet to explore amendments to the British nationality policy after the Canadian government expressed intentions to depart from the common code system, was one of the leading proponents of the bill. He insisted that in accordance with the Statute of Westminster, creating a local citizenship for the metropole and colonies would serve as a necessary endeavor "so that our fellows in the Dominions can understand and can realise that we are in fact recognising the equality of status with this country of each of the Dominions."[23]

In addition to noting the demise of the common system and the need to align the United Kingdom with the shifting politics of the Commonwealth, Ede urged his Parliamentary colleagues to consider the ways that a shared local citizenship between the metropole and colonies could serve as "an essential part of the development of the relationship between this Mother Country and the Colonies who are administered in varying degrees of self government and tutelage by the Colonial Office." Anticipating many of his critics, Ede recognized that many of his colleagues felt "that it would be a bad thing to give the coloured races of the Empire the idea that, in some way or other, they are the equals of the people in this country." However, adopting the type of patronizing racial lenses that framed the civilizing mantras of Victorian imperialism, he conceded, "It is true that we cannot admit all these backward peoples immediately into the full rights that British subjects in this country enjoy," but urged, "we must give these people a feeling that on that homespun dignity of man we recognise them as fellow citizens."[24] Even though Ede supported the bill because it reflected a move toward Britain's acceptance of the egalitarian principles of the Commonwealth ideal, his logic for establishing a shared citizenship between residents of the United Kingdom and those of the colonies was clearly tempered by racialized notions of both the colonial populations and the meaning of the most authentic sense of Britishness.

As others have noted, although the British Nationality Act of 1948's proposal to codify Commonwealth citizenship and establish Citizenship of the United Kingdom and Colonies espoused notions of egalitarianism and universalism, in constructing their arguments about the boundaries of Britishness and citizenship in consideration of the bill, Parliamentarians on both ends of the political spectrum relied upon a set of assumptions about the people of the colonial territories and the dominions rooted in racial hierarchies that had historically justified imperialism.[25] But in spite of stringent opposition in both Houses of Parliament against the creation of a shared local British citizenship between Britain and the colonies, the Act prevailed. To understand why it did requires looking beyond the racially exclusive visions of the British world represented in the Parliamentary debates on the question of citizenship and contextualizing the bill's passage in relation to the larger imperial and transnational political dynamics in play in the aftermath of World War II. Not only did the Canadian government's move to institute a new nationality policy represent a break from the historic relations of Empire but, perhaps more importantly, the British Government's willingness to reexamine questions of nationality and citizenship in the wake of the new Canadian legislation illuminates a broader postwar trend defining Britain's changing relationship to its imperial past.

Following World War II, one of the central paradoxes shaping British politics involved reconciling desires to maintain the legacies of world dominance shaped by the history of imperial relations, and adjusting to new realities presented by the declining significance of the British Empire as a geopolitical construct. In the period between World War I and World War II, because of its extensive imperial resources, Britain could have easily been regarded as the world's sole superpower.[26] However, even before the end of the war a new phase in international politics emerged that was marked by the rise of American economic hegemony, the emergence of the Cold War, heightened expressions of colonial nationalism and the streamlining of imperial military and political commitments in part to facilitate the recovery and reconstruction of Britain's own domestic economy. Coupled with the shifting demographic landscape in the imperial metropolis, these elements collectively contributed to what Chris Waters has described as a postwar "crisis of national self-representation" that reflected a series of cultural dislocations and anxieties during the late 1950s and 1960s and in turn produced an "intense questioning about what it now meant to be British."[27] Moreover, as Clement Atlee's Labour Government prepared itself to face the practicalities of decolonization, including the extant realities surrounding the partitioning of India, not only did British officials cleave to the language of New Commonwealth partnership and its connotations of consanguinity and mutuality as a means of preserving the global power status that

Empire had historically bestowed to the nation, but they also cultivated more inclusive discourses of British/Commonwealth citizenship to capture a sense of what the Empire was becoming. Whereas subjecthood emphasized shared loyalty to the British Crown and reified the superiority of the metropole as the centrifuge of British power to which subjects owed their allegiance, the idea of citizenship, even imperial citizenship, reflected republican values emphasizing universal rights of belonging that extended equally to all members regardless of race or national origin.[28] Therefore, not only did the discourses of citizenship reflected in the new nationality policy complement the Commonwealth's egalitarian and democratic ideals, but they also articulated a multiracial and transnational vision of Britishness that did not distinguish between colonizers and the colonized.

It is then in this context that one can consider how the racially egalitarian premises buttressing the British Nationality Act of 1948's categories of citizenship could be adapted as official policy in light of policy makers' hierarchical vision of the racial communities encompassing Empire/Commonwealth and the exclusive parameters of Britishness. Essentially, the British Nationality Act of 1948 represented a means to redress the fading image of Britain's imperial legacy through the institutionalization of a transracial, trans-regional citizenship category that bolstered the perception of imperial and Commonwealth uniformity. It was then British policy makers' preoccupations with maintaining what one MP regarded as "the appearance of concord and unity throughout the Commonwealth," rather than a pressing commitment to principles of racial democracy embedded in the egalitarian rhetoric of the British Nationality Act of 1948 that led to its adoption as official policy.[29] Thus it is important to see the debates over nationality policy as more of a testament to the ways that imperial logics persisted in shaping how a decolonizing British state aimed to remake itself in the world rather than a measure of the Labour Government's liberal credentials.

Although the Labour Government's considerations of the British Nationality Act of 1948 focused primarily on its intended role in redefining British citizenship, upon its passage, the bill provided the legal structures of both a citizenship and, somewhat indirectly in the eyes of Parliamentarians, a domestic migration policy. British subjecthood had historically granted access to British passports, and passports undoubtedly conferred mobility rights both within the Empire and beyond. Therefore, by simply engaging the question of British citizenship, not only did the act concern defining the parameters for determining who would be included in the imperial community of British/Commonwealth citizens, but as a derivative of that, the act also pertained to mobility rights and reinforced a long-held tradition of entry for all of subjects of the British Empire and citizens of Commonwealth countries.[30] While the goal of preserving the appearance of Commonwealth unity might have provided the ideological premises for the adoption of the British Nationality Act of 1948, it would be the issue of migration—and, more specifically, a largely Afro-Caribbean colonial migration and the emergence of more visible Black populations in Britain—that would test the substantive value of the new policy and force the metropolitan community to again confront the competing imperial visions of what it meant to be British.

Migration and the Meaning of British Citizenship

On 16 June 1948 in a telegram to the Acting Governor of Jamaica, Colonial Secretary Creech Jones urged that it was "essential" that he "should know whether [the] decision of Jamaicans to travel by *Empire Windrush* to England was of their own motion."[31] On that same day, Jones answered questions in the House of Commons about the Colonial Office's preparedness concerning the housing, employment, and general welfare of the *Empire Windrush*'s passengers. In his statements to Parliament members, Jones noted that "the West Indians in question booked their passages privately." He explained that even though most had not made prior work arrangements and had been warned of uncertain employment prospects in Britain before departing, it appeared "that the men concerned are prepared to take their chances of finding employment." When asked if the Colonial Office might institute measures to screen potential migrants to judge "if they are likely to be suitable for employment" in Britain, Jones responded, "We recognise the need for some vetting, but obviously we cannot interfere with the movement of British subjects," adding, "It is very unlikely that a similar event to this will occur again in the West Indies."[32]

Jones's telegram to the Governor of Jamaica and his comments to Parliament members unearth an important yet underprivileged perspective shaping the significance of the *Empire Windrush*'s passengers. The passengers of the *Windrush*, along with the thousands of other Caribbean migrants who journeyed to Britain during the 1950s and early 1960s, did so on their own accord—meaning outside of the confines of Government regulations, wartime service, or attachments to particular institutions, including specific employers.[33] Therefore, if one is to speak of a "Windrush generation," what most clearly defines this referent of postwar movement from the Caribbean to Britain is that it was an unprecedented movement of choice by self-selected individuals. While certainly the terms and conditions of individual migrations were shaped by a broad spectrum of social forces, mediating structures, and informal networks and affiliations, the fundamental yet all too often overlooked element of the significance of the sailing of the *Windrush* is that migrants made a choice. Migrants chose to leave behind the familiarities of their homelands. Migrants made conscious decisions to part ways with spouses, children, and other relatives—even if only temporarily. Most importantly, migrants elected to face the uncertainties of life in Britain—a place where most Caribbean colonials had knowledge of, but relatively few had journeyed. As one examines the choices that Black migrants made to travel to Britain, one must consider the aggregate social, political, economic, and ideological elements that prompted Caribbean migrants to choose Britain as a destination during the 1950s and 1960s. In doing so, this investigation must begin by exploring Caribbean migrants' conceptions of Britain, their expectations of life in Britain, and, perhaps most importantly, their own ideas about their relationship to and within British society.

In their companion volume to the BBC television series commemorating the fiftieth anniversary of the arrival of the *Empire Windrush*, journalists Mike and Trevor Phillips poignantly remarked, "the people on the Windrush . . . regarded their 'Britishness' as non-negotiable."[34] Connie Goodridge-Mark, who migrated to Britain in 1954 with her daughter to join her husband after serving as a secretary at a military hospital in Jamaica, recalled longing to return to Jamaica before she eventually decided to make a home for herself and her family in West London. For her, the question of her sense of being British and having a claim to belong in Britain had been settled long before she arrived in England. Reflecting on her middle-class upbringing in Jamaica, Connie recalled being inculcated with a sense of her own Britishness and a connectedness to a British world that encompassed both Jamaica and England, as she explained, "We were British! England was our mother country. We were brought up to respect the royal family. We didn't grow up with any Jamaican thing. We grew up as British."[35]

Arthur Curling, a passenger on the *Empire Windrush* who had served in the Royal Air Force during World War II, shared similar memories of life in Jamaica during the 1940s. According to Curling, Jamaican society was infused with an imperial culture that encouraged reverence toward England and the monarchy and actively cultivated affinities toward British identifications among colonial subjects. Reflecting on the colonial world that he left behind as he journeyed to England in 1948, he insisted,

> We were always British. In Jamaica I can remember, when it was the Queen's birthday or the King's birthday or the Coronation, everything was done the way Britain wanted us to. We hadn't our own identity. . . . England was "the mother country," as they used to say, and anything the English did or the British did was always right, you know.[36]

Not only do the sentiments expressed by Connie Goodridge-Mark and Arthur Curling underscore imperial hierarchies that ascribed England to be the maternal standard-bearer for British subjects in colonized spaces such as Jamaica, but they also illuminate how the relations of Empire and the "structure of feeling" that it produced shaped how colonial subjects imagined themselves and their position within the imperial community.[37] Scholars and writers alike have noted that the trope or "myth" of Britain as the "Mother Country" was a powerful appellation that commanded cultural and political authority. Much like the royal celebrations, imperial pageantry, and annual Empire Day festivities that promoted patriotism through the singing of songs such as "Rule, Britannia!" and "There'll Always Be an England," the idea of Britain as Mother Country was part of a tool of colonization that served as a means of molding Caribbean men, women, and children into loyal British subjects.[38] But the authority of the cultural narratives about the Mother Country and all its attendant glorification of Britishness, Victorian notions of respectability, and all things English were not necessarily absolute. Instead, as Brian Moore and Michele Anderson have persuasively argued in their work on British cultural imperialism in Jamaica during the late nineteenth and early twentieth centuries, the Black masses' identification with and acceptance of this particular narrative and mechanism of social engineering did not overshadow Jamaican colonials' ability to exercise cultural autonomy. Rather, as noted in Chapter 1, just as this narrative was *selective* in framing an untainted view of Britain that would be used to justify and define the virtues of imperial rule, the narrative of Britain as Mother Country was also strategically *selected* and appropriated by colonial subjects to make claims to political rights, economic aid, and access to routes of social mobility. [39]

In accepting the narrative of Britain as Mother Country, potential migrants also reaffirmed a relationship to the Empire that permitted inclusion into a transnational body of British citizens whose shared rights, privileges, and freedoms were made universal in the imperial space of the metropole. And it was this imagined relationship to and within the imperial body of British citizens that is critical to understanding the broader cultural and ideological context shaping the decisions that Caribbean migrants made to journey across the Atlantic to Britain. The decision to migrate inherently involved migrants interpreting that their relationship to Britain allowed for the possibilities that without any form of Government intervention, they would be able to successfully negotiate geographical borders, settle in Britain, search for opportunities to secure employment, and potentially access new avenues of social mobility unavailable in their home society. In essence, as migrants made choices about their movement to Britain, they also made claims upon the Mother Country, used those claims to their advantage, and affirmed their membership in the

imperial body politic. As Walter Lothen, a Jamaican carpenter who made the
trek to Britain in 1954 explained,

> People did think England was the mother country. When I came here
> [London] I didn't have a status as a Jamaican. I was British and going
> to the mother country was like going from one parish to another. You
> had no conception of it being different.[40]

While it is clear that Lothen identified with imperial hierarchies that privileged metropole (England) over colony (Jamaica), his statements also suggest that his own sense of Britishness—which was available to him in both
spaces—allowed him to evaluate the possibilities of migration as one of the
privileges or, perhaps more appropriately, an entitlement of his membership in
the imperial community of British citizens. Lothen's comments illuminate a
keen awareness of the limits of his Jamaican colonial identity in Britain and jux-
tapose this reality with the possibilities garnered via his claims to Britishness.
In this sense, Walter Lothen draws attention to the ways that one cannot easily classify Caribbean migrants' claims to Britishness or British citizenship as
simply a conditioned hegemonic response to the pervasiveness of the culture
of British imperialism in the Caribbean colonies. His claim to Britishness or a
British citizenship did not obscure his own sense of his Jamaicaness and perhaps quite possibly a host of other identities, including his Blackness, his masculinity, and his working-class status. Rather, his Britishness served as a type
of metalanguage that, when appropriated, allowed him to actualize the privileges and entitlements of British citizenship in spite of the prescribed social
limitations of race, gender, class, or colonial status.[41]

   Examining the ways that migrants perceived their relationships to Britain
and membership in the imperial body politic represents a crucial starting
point for understanding the myriad social forces at work that influenced the
decision to migrate. And as Chapter 1 illustrates, ideas about Black people's
claims to Britishness and membership in the imperial body politic, as well as
their attempts to substantiate those claims, has been a defining point of the
post-emancipation history of race and Empire. In locating the various elements contributing to the choices that migrants made and the motivations
behind those decisions, one must consider a host of structural and subjective
factors. It is clear that socioeconomic conditions in both the Caribbean and
Britain coalesced with the international politics of migration at a particular
moment, creating a ripe climate for nearly a quarter of a million Caribbeans
to choose Britain as a migration destination in the early postwar period. In
addition to these structural determinants, quite often, less quantifiable factors such as emotional attachments to family and friends or a migrant's own

personal perceptions of potential opportunities in Britain in comparison to that in the home country played the most significant roles in influencing an individual's decision to migrate at a particular moment.

Factors Influencing Postwar Caribbean Migration to Britain

Pointing to the importance of migration as an integral theme in understanding the history of Caribbean societies in the twentieth century, author Mike Phillips, whose family migrated to Britain from Guyana in 1956, recalled, "By tradition, men from our region looked for work and advancement abroad." Phillips recalled,

> My uncles had worked, on and off, in the Trinidad oilfields, in Panama, in Costa Rica and in Florida. My father had traveled the eastern Caribbean looking for a foothold, before trying to England. On leaving school my older sister, my brother and their classmates had scattered some to the University of the West Indies in Jamaica, some to Brazil and Venezuela, others to colleges in the USA or Britain. For anyone with almost any ambition, spending a period of time in another country was inevitable."[42]

Since the early post-emancipation period, migration has been a recurring motif endemic to Caribbean societies. As noted by Thomas Holt, physical movement served as an important tool allowing newly freed men and women in Jamaica and other former slave societies to test the meaning of their freedom, exercise greater autonomy over their labor and families, and broaden their access to certain economic opportunities outside of the purview of the plantation.[43] Faced with a declining local sugar industry, decreased employment opportunities, the consolidation of Crown lands, declining wages, and natural disasters in the late nineteenth and early twentieth century, thousands of Jamaicans and workers from other British Caribbean islands moved throughout the Caribbean and Latin America to such places as Panama, Costa Rica, Honduras, and Cuba to work on railroad construction projects, banana and sugar plantations, and multinational investment ventures, including the construction of the Panama Canal. [44] In the 1850s, some 5,000 Jamaicans worked on the construction of the Panama Railroad. Thirty years later, when the French initiated work on the Panama Canal, an estimated 78,000 Jamaicans migrated to Panama during the 1880s. By the turn of the century, after the French had abandoned the project (later completed under the auspices of the American-controlled Isthmian

Canal Commission in 1914), approximately 91,000 migrants had departed for Panama.[45] In the meantime, the expansion of American interests in the fruit trade and the growth of the Cuban sugar industry lured large numbers of Jamaican migrants to Cuba and Costa Rica. As early as 1887, Jamaica experienced an estimated net outward movement to Costa Rica of 1,736, while labor movement to Cuba peaked at the close of World War I with annual migration figures of some 21,573 in 1919. By the 1930s there were some 60,000 Jamaicans who had settled in Cuba.[46]

Although substantial numbers of British Caribbean migrants settled throughout Latin America during the early twentieth century, until the passage of more stringent immigration restrictions in 1952, the United States was often a prime migratory destination. During the decade between 1911 and 1921, no fewer than 30,000 Jamaicans entered the United States. Overall, this pattern somewhat shifted during the 1920s in part because of the introduction of new immigration restrictions in 1924, peppered with nativist undertones designed specifically to curtail migration from southern and eastern Europe and regions with majority populations of color. This policy instituted quotas for countries in relation to the proportion of American citizens who traced their origins to a particular country and reduced the total number of immigrants admitted per year to 150,000.[47] Because the populations of the British Caribbean were included in the generous annual quota of 65,000 reserved for citizens of Great Britain and Northern Ireland, the prospects associated with actual border crossings between the Caribbean and United States did not change dramatically until the passage of the McCarran-Walter Act of 1952. What did fluctuate, in terms of migrant settlement opportunities, were the economic climates and labor conditions greeting migrants upon their arrival in the United States. With the onset of the Great Depression in the late 1920s and early 1930s, job competition at all levels of the working classes reached dire proportions. As a result, foreign-born workers along with Black Americans and other people of color were oftentimes marginalized, or in some instances, completely shut out from accessing positions in certain spheres in the US labor market. This situation changed somewhat with the onset of World War II. Between 1943 and 1946, the United States actively recruited some 100,000 industrial and agricultural workers from the Caribbean for temporary assignments to supplement the loss of domestic manpower during the war and to meet labor demands in wartime industries.[48]

Despite a veto by President Harry Truman, the passage of the McCarran-Walter Act on 27 June 1952 represented a decisive political turning point influencing the direction of migrations from the Caribbean after World War II. Essentially, the new policy expanded many of the provisions outlined under the national-origins quota system implemented under the

1924 Immigration Act. In regard to the British Caribbean, the most significant policy shift involved the extraction of the colonial territories from the generous quota allotted to immigrants from Great Britain and Northern Ireland. Proposed at the height of McCarthyism and the resurgence of nativist rhetoric, the McCarran-Walter Act granted each Caribbean territory an annual allotment of 100 border crossings and effectively redrew the boundaries of British citizenship by making distinctions between metropolitan and colonial subjects. At the time that the legislation received approval, it was estimated that an average of 2,600 immigrants moved from the Caribbean to the United States annually.[49] But as American borders closed, those in Britain remained opened, easily navigable and ripe with economic opportunities unavailable in the Caribbean.

Recalling the reasons behind his decision to move to Britain in 1956, Claude Ramsey, an active member of the Barbados Labour Party and Trade Union movement during the 1930s who also served in the British army during World War II noted, "As the War ended I found myself back in Barbados with its poverty and lack of opportunities.... My reasons for leaving were simple—the Barbadian economic depression, and the greater employment prospects in Britain."[50] As was the case throughout the late nineteenth century, during the first half of the twentieth century socioeconomic conditions in the Caribbean territories spurred a steady stream of international emigration. Worldwide economic depression during the 1930s, which contributed to a series of labor uprising throughout the archipelago only heightened pre-existing economic problems, including declining wages and unemployment. In the wake of increasing unemployment during World War II, the colonial government in Jamaica, the largest of the Caribbean colonies and the region where most Caribbean migrants entering Britain hailed during the late 1940s through the early 1960s, established a social welfare system that provided benefits and employment opportunities for workers in the most destitute areas of the island. By 1943, estimates indicated that the Jamaican government provided over 11,000 workers with some form of relief per month. In that same year, according to census reports, the overall rate of unemployment was likely as high as 29 percent. In the construction industry, rates in some areas rose as high as 40 percent. After the war and throughout the 1950s, overall unemployment rates slowly declined, although the economy still failed to generate an adequate supply of labor opportunities for significant portions of the Jamaican populace. A 1957 survey estimated that unemployment had fallen to 18.5 percent, while the 1960 census reported a figure of 12.7 percent[51] Coupled with the economic strains induced by widespread unemployment and underemployment, overpopulation also contributed to greater job competition, escalating poverty rates, and an increasing surplus population that postwar economic conditions could not adequately sustain. During the first half of the twentieth century the total population in Jamaica had doubled, with no visible indicators of declining birth rates.[52]

In striking contrast to postwar employment conditions in Caribbean territories such as Jamaica, after the war ended, a number of industrialized western European countries, including France, Germany, and Britain, experienced labor shortages and actively sought foreign workers to meet postwar labor demands and to facilitate economic reconstruction. In 1946, the newly elected Labour Government issued an economic survey that projected labor shortages between 600,000 and 1.3 million and an overall decline in the working-age population. A later survey taken in January 1947 identified widespread labor shortages and a maldistribution of available labor as critical issues facing the British postwar economy. Many of the industries hit hardest by the shortage of workers were essential to postwar economic recovery and reconstruction, including coal mining, textiles, agriculture, steel, and construction.[53] In response, a committee of seven Cabinet members, including the Home Secretary and the Minister of Labor, formed the Foreign Labor Committee in February 1946 with an initial mandate to explore temporary initiatives to address labor shortages in British industries.[54] In May 1946, the committee announced the establishment of the Polish Resettlement Corps, a program designed to recruit Polish veterans for civilian employment through the Ministry of Labour. With the passage of the Polish Resettlement Act in February 1947, the Government outlined a system of pensions and welfare benefits for immigrating veterans and their dependents. By 1950, no less than 120,000 Polish veterans and their families had migrated to Britain with plans for permanent settlement.[55]

Although the recruitment of Polish veterans represented one of the largest Government-sponsored migration programs instituted in the early postwar years, the Labor Government initiated a number of smaller-scale recruitment schemes designed to attract foreign workers from continental Europe. Under the "Westward Ho" initiative, the Ministry of Labour facilitated the recruitment of over 78,000 displaced persons lodged in camps throughout Austria and Germany for temporary employment between 1946 and 1951. Eventually, the Ministry of Labour negotiated permanent settlement for these workers, who became known as European Volunteer Workers (EVWs). Although many of the recruitment programs targeted male workers to meet labor deficiencies in industries such as construction and coal mining, shortages in domestic service, health care, and textiles opened more gender-specific opportunities for women workers. In March 1946, the Foreign Labour Committee agreed to recruit 1,000 women from eastern European countries, including Latvia, Lithuania, and Estonia, to work in hospitals, sanitariums, and other health care facilities. During the summer of 1948, three programs, the "Blue Danube," the "North Sea," and the "Official Italian Scheme" facilitated the immigration of roughly 13,600 women from Austria, Germany, and Italy to work in the textiles industry, domestic services, and nursing.[56]

At the same time that the British Government actively supported and sponsored the immigration of foreign labor from continental Europe, officials expressed serious reservations about the prospects of recruiting colonial workers—who were legally bona fide British citizens—to address deficiencies in the postwar domestic labor market. In September 1948, just months after the arrival of the *Empire Windrush*, the Colonial Office distributed a memo throughout the Cabinet, detailing "the difficulties that arose from the presence of coloured workers in Great Britain." As a result, by February 1949, the Colonial Office spearheaded the formation of a Working Party on the "Employment in the U.K. of Surplus Colonial Labour" to explore the potential consequences of recruiting colonial labor to address employment deficiencies in Britain. In one of the first reports issued by the Working Party, the committee noted that although there were some 367,000 employment vacancies that had been reported to the Employment Exchanges in major industries, including coal mining and textiles, "there are several obstacles to the use of Colonial labour for the purpose of relieving labour shortages over here." In addition to noting that colonial workers, as British citizens, could not be subjected to labor regulations imposed on foreign workers such as those which confined foreign workers to certain industries for specific periods of time, the report also maintained that "it has to be realised—that while there is no formal 'colour bar' in this country . . . neither the employers nor the workers, in industry would look with favour on the introduction of coloured workers in factories and workshops where up to now they have not previously been employed." The report added, "many employers—even the most broadminded among their number—tend to look with disfavour on the idea of using coloured labour to relieve even the most obstinate and persistent labour shortages."[57]

Although the report concluded that large-scale recruitment of colonial workers would not be a viable source for addressing postwar labor market demands, the Working Party did note that more gender-specific arrangements might be more conducive to filling vacancies in certain areas. The report also suggested that while "no case could be made out in present circumstances for the importation of *male* colonials for any industry. . . . In the case of industries employing women . . . we are impressed with the fact that both in the textile industries [and] in the field of hospital domestic employment there are large unsatisfied demands for female labour."[58] An earlier memo from an official in the Ministry of Labour poignantly captures at least some of the gendered opposition to the influx of Caribbean male migrants. The memo explained that there is relatively little objection to the importation of women, for example, for domestic employment where their living conditions would be controlled, since the worst troubles concern men who settle in unsatisfactory districts and get into street fights owing to quarrels about coloured men associating with white women, etc.[59]

These statements help to illuminate the ways that gender played an active role in shaping White Britons' perceptions of and officials' reactions to Caribbean migration. In the process of crafting political responses to the issue of Caribbean migration, policy makers constructed images of and racialized Caribbean migrants through a gendered prism of ideas about Black men. In turn, these ideas were then appropriated as the consummate symbols of the consequences of Caribbean migration and then used as a means to rationalize and institutionalize race-based social policies that sought to exclude both Caribbean men and women from exercising their right of migration and entitlement to full citizenship in British society.[60]

In addition to the macro economic and political elements that facilitated Caribbean migration to Britain, including high rates of unemployment in the colonies, the tightening of borders in the United States, the open-door migration policy in Britain, and the promise of economic opportunities in the post-war British labor market, it is clear that throughout the 1950s and early 1960s, Caribbean migrants tapped into a wide range of formal and informal networks, including Government-sponsored initiatives, local travel agencies, advertisements, and exchanges between friends and family that mediated migration and shaped migrants' expectations of life in Britain.[61] The British Caribbean Welfare Service, which eventually became known as the Migrant Services Division of the West Indies Commission after the formation of the West Indies Federation in 1958, was one of the most important Government-sponsored agencies facilitating Caribbean migration during the late 1950s and early 1960s. Established in June 1956, the organization began as a joint venture backed by the Colonial Office and funded by local colonial governments as a mechanism designed to offer support to Caribbean migrants upon their arrival in Britain. Before this agency took shape, only the governments of Jamaica and Barbados had attempted to make arrangements for settlement assistance for migrants. During its lifespan, which coincided with the collapse of the West Indies Federation in 1962, Migrant Services maintained two primary departments—Welfare and Reception, and Community Development. The responsibilities of the Welfare and Reception department included receiving migrants at various ports upon arrival, locating family and friends, informing migrants of prospective employment opportunities, negotiating housing contracts, arranging travel to areas outside of the landing port, and providing information on health care and legal services. The Community Development department offered vocational training and education for workers; served as a liaison and advocate on behalf of migrants with Labour Exchanges, employers, and trade unions through an Industrial Relations component; and arranged social clubs and other activities for migrants to incorporate themselves into the fabric of British society.[62]

While the chief focus of the Migrant Services Division centered on aiding migrant communities in Britain, the agency also prepared a pamphlet for distribution in the Caribbean territories to orient prospective migrants to conditions in Britain. The pamphlet, *Before You Go to Britain,* instructed migrants to take into account a range of issues relating to the rudiments of settlement before migrating. In addition to urging migrants to bring ample funds to cover incidentals and expenses associated with securing housing, the pamphlet also suggested that they make an effort to secure accommodations and employment in advance of arrival and take into account the difficulties "of living and working in a cold and wet climate which is different as it could possibly be from the one to which you are accustomed." Offering a more somber portrait of the realities facing prospective migrants, the pamphlet advised migrants to recognize that migration would entail "separation from family with little hope of raising enough money to either send for them or return." Officials for the Division hoped to remind migrants that contrary to popular opinion, there were indeed "great risks of making a success of the venture." [63]

Along with pointing out some of the factors that informed adjustment and settlement in Britain, Migrant Services also provided prospective travelers with details of some of the financial particulars associated with migration to Britain. The brochure gave estimates of prices for train tickets to London, a range of average wages for manual laborers, reasonable prices for accommodations, and a sample budget of typical living expenses. Likewise, migrants were encouraged to bring employment credentials, including "satisfactory evidence" of labor skills such as records of previous employment, trade union membership, character references, and tool kits, and to anticipate delays in finding suitable employment. The pamphlet warned, "DO NOT BELIEVE that high wages are being paid in Britain from laboring work" and further cautioned migrants that there was significant job competition between them and "long standing residents of Britain" for vacancies in skilled labor positions.[64] It is clear from the tone of the pamphlet that although the Government agency had a mandate to assist migrants in their settlement to life in Britain, Migrant Services was not necessarily an official proponent of migration. In many ways, in collusion with broader interdepartmental initiatives involving the Colonial Office, the Home Office, and various Cabinet officials, the Migrant Services Division attempted to suppress increasing migration to Britain just as it functioned as a critical intermediary of adjustment for migrants arriving in Britain during the 1950s and 1960s.

Despite the circulation of publications, including those prepared by Migrant Services presenting a somewhat dismal picture of settlement in Britain, prospective migrants tapped into an array of information that portrayed the prospects of finding amenable economic opportunities in Britain in a more favorable light.[65] In the early 1950s, the local government in Barbados entered into partnerships with the Ministry of Health, the Ministry of Labor, and the Colonial Office to advertise and recruit laborers in Barbados to work for some of the key sectors of expansion in the postwar welfare state, including hospitals, domestic service industries, the London Transport Executive, and the British Transport Commission. Overall, migration functioned during this period as an important avenue of economic relief in Barbados in the midst of growing unemployment and declining GDP per capita. As a result, workers overwhelmingly looked to Britain as a destination with alternative economic opportunities.[66] Under these programs, the Barbadian government provided loans to cover the cost of passage and incidentals, conducted background checks and medical screenings, and offered training courses to equip prospective migrants with the necessary skills to adjust to employment in various British industries.[67] In the case of Barbadian women recruited as domestics and nurses, often the local government established a temporary migration program with a three-year contract, during which time workers made weekly contributions to the government to cover the costs associated with repatriation.[68] Though the British Government did not pursue labor recruitment in Barbados or any of the Caribbean territories on the same scale as it did in continental Europe after World War II, programs such as those facilitated through the Barbados government most certainly created a greater awareness of labor shortages and employment opportunities available in Britain during a period of economic turmoil throughout the Caribbean.

In addition to government-sponsored initiatives, an array of private and more informal agencies and networks played pivotal roles in motivating Caribbean migrants to seek out different opportunities in Britain. By the mid-1950s, several new travel agencies in Jamaica had been established in both rural and urban areas to address the growing demand for passage to Britain. These agencies often courted prospective migrants with advertising campaigns that promised competitive rates for mass bookings, advisory services related to arrival and settlement in Britain, and credit programs for those unable to make full cash payments at the time of purchase. One woman recalled, "There were adverts everywhere: 'Come to the Mother Country!' The mother country needs you!"[69] Bolstered by growing interest in migration to Britain, travel agencies flourished and offered flexible packages and services in large part because of a corresponding growth in the transportation sector. Throughout the early 1950s, there were more ships available to provide passenger accommodations for travel from the Caribbean to Britain, coupled with an increase in the number of aircrafts departing the island.[70]

While developments in the travel industry would create greater opportunities for migration to Britain during the 1950s, for many migrants ties to and exchanges with family members and/or acquaintances who were planning, or had already journeyed to Britain were some of the most important factors influencing their decision to migrate. Whitfield Jones, who departed for England in 1956 from Barbados, recalled "coming to England in those days was kind of a fashion." It was the au courant thing to do. He explained, "John Brown gone, your friend gone and you found out, well, you haven't got many friends home now, so then you come too."[71] A government-sponsored study of Jamaican migration to Britain during the 1950s concluded that one of most critical factors shaping migratory flows between the Caribbean and Britain involved what could be described as a "multiplier process." The report explained that typically, when one person traveled to Britain, he or she would oftentimes encourage friends or relatives to make the journey. And in many cases, wages earned in Britain would be used to supplement or finance the cost of journeys of others through remittances sent back home or by securing a friend or loved one's travel arrangements in England.[72] To be sure, this form of encouragement and incentive to migrate held its own narrative about the promise of life in England for prospective migrants. In a tangible and material way, it gave them a glimpse of the possible prosperity, economic benefits, upward mobility, and wages available to them in England—incentives that would allow them to support themselves and have income to spare to support their loved ones at home. But who were some of these individuals who made the choice to migrate? What skills did they bring to the British labor market? And how did they make impressions of themselves to those in metropolitan society?

The Character of Postwar Caribbean Migration to Britain

One of the most iconic visual archives documenting postwar Afro-Caribbean migration to Britain includes images of hundreds of newly arrived West Indians passing through British customs ports in 1956, published in the pages of London's *Picture Post* under the heading "Thirty Thousand Colour Problems" (See Figure 2.1). Estimating that some 30,000 West Indians would arrive in Britain that year alone, the article, which included several snapshots of men and women flanked by luggage as they waited in customs lines, sought

Figure 2.1 West Indian arrivals in *Picture Post*, 1956. Getty Images.

assistance from local welfare agents, and anticipated reconnecting with friends and relatives, suggested that the outlook for these individuals' desire to secure work and homes in Britain looked bleak. The paper declared that with their presence, "Trouble and distress are brewing."[73]

It is important to recognize that the documentary intent of *Picture Post* journalists centered upon showcasing the embodied "problem" of an increasing West Indian migrant population for White metropolitan audiences just as these individuals set foot upon British shores. However, the interpretative value of these images lies not only in understanding the perspective of those who sat behind the camera's gaze, but also in considering the vantage point of the bodies and individual aspirations reflected under that gaze. It is clear that the camera angles of *Picture Post* photographers were vested in capturing and, more importantly, captioning a narrative about West Indians in such a way that problematized the very sight of their presence in British cities like London. In the pages of the *Picture Post*, West Indian migrants' "problem" status is one that is defined and captioned not by their living in British homes, working in British industries, occupying seats on the tube, sitting alongside White children in British classrooms, participating in British consumer life, or displaying familial attachments. Rather, it is engendered by their mere arrival, their embodied presence, and the act of simply being in sight in London. Yet the gaze of White audiences is only half of the story of these images. For these images also offer us glimpses of what West Indians migrants aimed to reflect and project about themselves as they arrived in metropolitan society.

In his work on the photographic representations of West Indian migrants appearing in the *Picture Post,* Stuart Hall contends that aside from documenting arrivals, the images juxtaposed with headlines declaring, "Thirty Thousand Colour Problems" also represented some of the earliest moments when migrants would consciously be aware of being seen by metropolitan spectators who included the family and friends whom they might have come to join, as well as a predominately White British society. As such, these images can also be read as moments when migrants were also hoping to make a first impression, (re)present themselves, and intentionally communicate their aspirations by the ways in which they literally fashioned and styled themselves.[74] When Michelle Charlerly arrived in Britain from St. Lucia in 1959, she vividly remembered that she was "wearing a suit my mum did make for me. It was very stylish and fashionable and I had a scarf or hat she'd given me to wear with it."[75] According to Stuart Hall, who also journeyed to Britain during the 1950s, migrants from his homeland of Jamaica traveled "in their 'Sunday best.'" The clothes they wore when they arrived and the manner in which they wore them conveyed their intent to survive and thrive in Britain.[76] Charlerly and Hall's reflections suggest that West Indian migrants came in attire occasioned to command respectability and dignity under the glare of those who would be watching and waiting as the newcomers alighted in Britain. Women arrived in dresses accessorized with hats, gloves, earrings, necklaces, and neatly coiffed, pressed, and curled hair. Men typically wore suits with collared shirts, neckties, and brim hats. People carried mementos and monikers displaying their particular island attachments, but they were also steadfastly determined to (re)present themselves as bona fide British citizens who had not only arrived with British passports in tow, but who also planned to belong.

Aside from documenting how Afro-Caribbean migrants attended to the act of being seen in such a manner that conveyed a desire to belong and prosper in the public realm at the very point of their arrival in Britain, image making as a cultural practice also became an important mechanism used to express how they imagined themselves and their aspirations within the interiors of their own families and communities, both in Britain and in a larger Caribbean diaspora. Much like generations of formerly enslaved people and their progeny hoping to qualify the meaning of emancipation, migrants employed photography and the technologies of portraiture as a tool to both chronicle their hopes and create a vision of the promise of full citizenship and incorporation within the nation, oftentimes through depictions of familial attachments and domestic life.[77] Photos functioned like messages on a postcard to relatives at home who were concerned about a migrant's well-being in Britain. Smiling faces

Figure 2.2 Black family arrival at Waterloo, 1964. George Rodger, Magnum Photos.

conveyed happiness and a sense of contentment. Trendy clothing and chic styling suggested that one had money to buy new clothes, attend to grooming, purchase more than the bare necessities, and actively participate in consumer culture in Britain. An upright posture or poised demeanor communicated an air of confidence, coolness, and ultimately a sense of self-assuredness about one's status.[78] As one woman who migrated to Birmingham in the 1950s recalled, for newcomers, having portraits made and being seen in photographs "was about communicating in a way that words couldn't."[79]

Although it was not until the early 1960s that larger numbers of West Indian women and children began to form the demographic majority of Afro-Caribbean newcomers, even before the issue of migration as a source of family reunification became a matter of public policy concern, depictions of a migrating Black family life as seen in photographs (see Figure 2.2) showcase some the glaring ironies about the visual archives documenting Afro-Caribbean migration and postwar Black British history.

Just as photographs served to aid White audiences in seeing a media-driven narrative about Black newcomers as a "colour problem," they also became instruments that subverted those stories. More specifically, whereas the news of West Indian migration and its social implications often invoked tropes of transient, Black male bachelors and absentee fathers who stoked fears of miscegenation and prompted the *Picture Post* to ask its readers in the mid-1950s

Figure 2.3 Donald and Dawn Hinds wedding photo, 1961. By permission of Donald Hinds, courtesy of the Lambeth Archives, Landmark Ref# 20259.

"Would you let your daughter marry a Negro?", family photographs and scenes of Black formations in the domestic sphere offered glimpses into an alternative narrative about who and what constituted the conditions of Black life in Britain.[80] Pictures from family photo albums such those shown here (Figures 2.3–2.7) from Jamaican writer, Donald Hinds, who moved to Britain in 1955, where he married Dawn Bruce in 1961 before a host of family and friends at Raleigh Park Baptist Church in Brixton, contain images that document what news stories about the "colour problem" presented by popular typecasts of male West Indian migrant workers could not. In contrast, these photographs register Black men in intimate relationships with Black women and present in the everyday lives of their children. They place Black men in a position to contribute to or help marshal the financial resources necessary to migrate, provide a home, purchase indulgences, dress children in their "Sunday best," and perhaps commission the services of a photographer. Moreover, while the "colour problem" and, consequently, the racialized discourse about "immigrants" that emerged in full view during the 1950s turned on gendered stereotypes about Black masculinities in ways that rendered Black women and ideas about Black femininity invisible, by visually capturing Black men as husbands, fathers, sons, and brothers, photographs also provide sites for seeing

Figure 2.4 Donald and Dawn Hinds wedding cake photo, 1961. By permission of Donald Hinds, courtesy of the Lambeth Archives, Landmark Ref# 20260.

Figure 2.5 Hinds family wedding photo, 1961. By permission of Donald Hinds, courtesy of the Lambeth Archives, Landmark Ref# 20257.

Figure 2.6 Donald, Dawn, and Jacqueline Hinds. By permission of Donald Hinds, courtesy of the Lambeth Archives, Landmark Ref# 20265.

Figure 2.7 Baby Jacqueline Hinds. By permission of Donald Hinds, courtesy of the Lambeth Archives, Landmark Ref# 20267.

Black women as they constituted family, domestic life, consumer culture, and the formation of Black communities.[81]

Given, as Wendy Webster has noted, that postwar visions of Englishness and White respectability celebrated domesticity, homemaking, familial life, and the virtues of motherhood, the absence of representations of Black femininities as wives, mothers, and caretakers of domestic space served to cement Black newcomers as an "immigrant" other that stood outside of the bounds of the nation. Therefore, family photographs and, more precisely, the framing of images of Black family life can be viewed as a mechanism through which newly arrived men and women claimed spaces in and relationships to the domestic sphere in a manner that paralleled and appropriated a type of ideal citizenship through marriage, parenting, and recreating a sense of "home" during the 1950s and early 1960s.[82]

A combination of experienced and amateur photographers operated the technology that was used to frame, capture, document, and preserve images of Black family formations in postwar Britain. However, as shutterbugs like Harry Jacobs, a Jewish studio photographer who became a self-described local institution among Brixton's Black communities beginning in the late 1950s and early 1960s would himself attest, sitters brought their own ideas and cultural logics about what they wanted to project and reflect before the camera.[83] In the visual archives of Black Britons, one can see that men, women, and children exercised great care to create, model, and document images of thriving two-parent households, milestone events, family celebrations, and the growth of children who would carry their legacy forward.[84] Moreover, photographs give us a glimpse of how migrants aimed to create demographic profiles of themselves that moved beyond their status as colonial migrant laborers to embrace their social, cultural, and economic realities and aspirations. While these images cannot present a full accounting of the character of postwar Afro-Caribbean migration to Britain, they do offer an alternate way of viewing some of the everyday practices of settlement in inclusion. They are important fragments that take us outside of White Britons' projections of Black newcomers as a newsworthy "colour problem" and usher historians into the interiors of Black Britons' lives to generate a wider frame for understanding how they imagined their best selves and the things that made them proud, attractive, sentimental, and worthy of remembrance. These are the stories of Black Britain that are oftentimes most elusive in the archive and obscured by a focus solely on the numbers used to quantify their existence.[85]

Although photographs provide a viable means of expanding the scope of how one constructs demographic profiles of Afro-Caribbean migrants, official data oftentimes designed to track and quantify the economic dynamics of the flow of labor also provide insights into understanding who was coming to Britain. In the early postwar years, men dominated the migratory flows between the Caribbean and Britain, and this trend of majority male migration continued until 1958, the first year when female migration surpassed male migration.[86] Throughout the 1950s and into the early 1960s, the greatest numbers of Caribbean migrants hailed from Jamaica. According to Jamaican Government statistics in the early 1950s, nearly 65 percent of male migrants were classified at the time of their departure as "skilled" or "semi-skilled" workers, occupying such positions as carpenters, mechanics, painters, and shoemakers. Whereas the majority of male migrants identified themselves as workers, many of their female counterparts did not claim a position in the public labor market at the time of their departures. Of the female migrants who did declare occupations in Jamaica between 1953 and 1955, nearly half fell into the category of seamstress, while roughly 16 percent were classified as domestic workers.[87]

In 1955, the Caribbean Welfare/Migrant Services Division of the West Indies Commission in London began compiling demographic information on West Indian migrants to Britain. Although their statistics accounted only for those migrants who had some form of contact with this agency upon their arrival in Britain, they do offer general composite information about large segments of this population.[88] According to data maintained by the Division, during the 1950s the majority of Caribbean migrants settled in major urban areas, with the highest concentrations in London. Of these numbers, most tended to reside in West London in such areas as Paddington, North Kensington, Notting Hill, Shepherd's Bush, and Hammersmith, and in South London in places that included Brixton, Stockwell, and Lambeth.[89] In one of the earliest studies analyzing this data, sociologist Ruth Glass estimated that most male and female migrants were between the ages of 20 and 30 when they arrived in Britain and fewer than 15 percent were over 44 years of age. In terms of occupational status, nearly half of all male migrants and over a quarter of female migrants were classified as "skilled" laborers in their respective home labor markets, occupying both manual, professional, and paraprofessional positions.[90] Thus Afro-Caribbean migrants tended to be in the prime of their laboring years when they arrived in Britain and had a vast repertoire of work experiences, skills, educational credentials, laboring knowledge, and personal ambition to bring to a vibrant postwar British labor market.

Although Ruth Glass found that only approximately 5 percent of the majority male migrant population of workers from the Caribbean who came to Britain in the latter half of 1950s in search of better employment opportunities obtained jobs in a higher occupational category, and instead would have been classified at a lower rank on the occupational scale in Britain than that of their previous employment in their homeland, most migrants did not necessarily envision themselves as downwardly mobile due to their migration. Through the eyes of migrants, higher wages and the availability of jobs, even in lower-ranking positions in the British labor market, oftentimes allowed migrants to view their migration as economically beneficial. For women in particular, as Nancy Foner's work on Jamaican migrants suggests, migration to Britain afforded wage-earning opportunities that allowed them to increase their financial independence and gain more influence over the economic resources of their families.[91] Therefore, even though Black migrants' initial employment prospects may have consigned them to menial jobs in service industries that did not correspond with their credentials, skill sets, or previous employment background, these jobs did represent avenues unavailable in their homelands to secure a place in a labor market where working opportunities were readily available and subsequently where steady and relatively higher wages could be obtained. But as many Caribbean migrants discovered, there was indeed a social cost of living in Britain that oftentimes obstructed their attempts to fully realize their aspirations of upward mobility. And this cost was most conspicuously attached to the racial politics of Blackness.

Encountering the Social Dilemmas of Race and Blackness

In a calypso titled, "If You're Not White, You're Black," written during his tenure in Britain during the 1950s, Lord Kitchener poignantly addressed the presence of a Black/White dichotomy of race in British society during the postwar era, differing from the color/class racial hierarchies found in Caribbean societies. Mocking those individuals who could not lay full claim to a European lineage because of their mixed-race heritage, yet attempted to distance themselves from darker-complexioned people of African descent and define themselves as racially superior, Lord Kitchener explained,

> Your father is an African
> Your mother may be Norwegian
> Your pass me, you wouldn't say goodnight
> Feeling you were really white
> Your skin may be a little pink
> And that's the reason why you think
> That the complexion of your face
> Can hide you from the Negro race
> No you can never get away from the fact
> If you're not white, you're considered black.[92]

Kitchener's lyrics draw attention to the ways in which the experience of Blackness in Britain was less negotiable, particularly in terms of one's skin shade or perceived phenotype when compared with those existing in the Caribbean. In Jamaica, for instance, the island from which the majority of West Indian migrants to Britain hailed during the 1950s, the overlapping legacies of slavery and colonialism produced an intricate hierarchy of race, or what Winston James has referred to as a "pigmentocracy" that intimately connected skin color, class, and social status. Evolving from the social relations that buttressed Jamaican slave society, fair-skinned White people of European descent were at the top of the social pyramid and generally had the greatest access to land, wealth, education, and political power. Beneath this group were "coloureds" or "browns," who were typically people of mixed racial heritage who often did acquire middle-class respectability through formal education, skilled or professional occupations, wealth, and limited political power. At the bottom of the social hierarchy were the Black working-class masses who typically were darker-complexioned people of African descent that generally had less education and the least amount of political power.[93] To be sure, none of these racialized categories of social belonging were absolute. Although gradations of skin pigmentation contributed to the stigmatization of people of African descent, the blemish of Blackness assumed by one's skin color could be negotiated, and in some cases, even transcended by social markers such as education, occupation, wealth, and one's affinity toward the adaptation of European physical attributes, cultural norms, and sensibilities. As a result, although skin color functioned as a salient characteristic of Blackness, it was in no way a definitive marker of social inferiority and therefore did not preclude people of African descent from accessing privileges or positions associated with Whiteness.[94]

Whereas stratifications associated with skin color and rooted in material and ideological constructs of class and social status may have been more fluid and diverse as they applied to defining the parameters of Blackness in Caribbean societies, alternatively in Britain, the markers of Blackness were less fungible and oftentimes more rigid and impermeable.[95] According to one fair-skinned Jamaican woman who arrived in Britain during the 1950s,

> providing you are black at all ... they [White Britons] feel there is nothing good in black people. No black people are clean and decent. We is not human being, we is something else. It gives me at times to know that because of the color of your skin they class you in that condition, beneath them in every way."[96]

This Jamaican woman's observations capture some of the ways that skin shades of all hues not considered as White or of European stock qualified one as Black in Britain. And as such, this homogeneous racial classification erased important social distinctions that helped defined one's cultural capital in the Caribbean, including lighter skin, wealth, education, or a respectable profession or family background, and instead attached all of the attendant negative imagery associated with Blackness and coloniality, including deficiency and inferiority.

Ironically, just as the markers of Blackness became more concrete and intractable for Afro-Caribbean migrants, particularly as they related to skin color and national origin in Britain, for many Caribbean migrants, their encounters with the social hierarchies of class in Britain destabilized and complicated their ideas about the conditions of Whiteness. A Jamaican migrant who moved to Britain in 1955 recalled,

> I would look from my window and see a white man sweeping the streets, and fear that, in the shop nearest where I should live, a white girl would sell me cigarettes. Now I was seeing my colonial society in a terrible light. I had never hoped to challenge the whites in Jamaica for a job. I realized in the confusion of the crowded station that I was starting on a desperate phase of life. If the white man was sweeping the streets, then any job I asked for would mean a challenge to him. I was not one of the "mother country's" children. I was one of her black children. That was to be my first lesson on arriving in Britain."[97]

This migrant's narrative of encountering working-class Whites in British society illuminates the contrasts between the image of Whiteness and the experience of Blackness in the Caribbean as compared with Britain. While mutually constitutive hierarchies of color and class in Jamaica privileged Whiteness in such a way that qualified it as a social category representing a protean sector of elites, in Britain the saliency of class created stark social divisions that fragmented representations of Whiteness for Caribbean migrants, just as they calcified the experience of Blackness. Winston James has argued that at the same time that British society provided a context structured by racial ideologies and practices that (re)produced collective Black identities that collapsed distinctions such as skin color, class, occupation, and education among Caribbean migrants of African descent, the presence of a White working class debunked "the mystique of whiteness" cultivated in the colonial setting, as Caribbean migrants encountered White people occupying positions at even the lowest rungs of the social ladder, performing menial labor, living in squalid accommodations, and experiencing poverty. To be sure, there were working-class and poor Whites in Caribbean societies. However, James's point suggests the ways in which the migration experience transformed commonly held ideas of the social meaning attached to Whiteness as Caribbean migrants witnessed greater proportions of White people in more diverse, non-elite positions within the socioeconomic hierarchy.[98]

For Afro-Caribbean migrants in postwar Britain, their Blackness was most distinctly marked by their skin color and their national/colonial origin; however, as a racial identity, Blackness was also structured by material conditions.[99] Two of the areas most critical to settlement where one's Blackness presented particular obstacles for Caribbean migrants included housing and employment. Noting the widespread appearance of housing advertisements barring Black tenants, May Cambridge, who migrated during the 1950s to attend a training course for nursing, noted, "The 'no Irish, Blacks or Dogs' signs are no myth—sometimes you would knock on the door with a vacant sign on the window, some would say the room had just gone, others would slam the door in your face while the less forthright wouldn't bother opening the door but you could see the curtains twitching."[100]

In her study of the conditions that West Indian newcomers encountered as they attempted to settle in Britain during the 1950s, Ruth Glass found that in a three-month span, between November 1958 and January 1959, the *Kensington Post*, a weekly newspaper serving West London, contained over 300 housing ads that barred persons from tenancy on the basis of race and or national origin. Some of the ads specifically excluded persons of color, while others read "Europeans only" or "English only," which implied a reference to both color and national origin.[101] Prior to Glass's study, a *Manchester Guardian* editorial acknowledged that "anyone who has searched for accommodation in London will testify to the large number of advertisements which specify 'No Coloured Applicants' or 'White Tenants Only'; any coloured person in London will confirm that an impossibly high percentage of the remaining accommodation has 'already been let' when the landlord sees the colour of the applicant."[102] The article's conclusions echoed the experience of Baron Baker, who had initially come to Britain as part of the Royal Air Force during World War II. Baker noted that for him, the practice of racism became most apparent during his search for housing. He insisted that "usually, once you told people you were coloured, they would say their place has been let."[103] For Black women, who more often than men migrated with children, or for anyone seeking to secure housing for an entire family, the effects of these practices could be more acutely felt, as some adverts stated, "So Sorry, No Coloured, No Children."[104] According to Mildred Deacon, who arrived from Jamaica in 1963 to join the father of her children, only to discover that he had begun seeing another woman, it was particularly hard for single women hoping to find housing in a tight market for Black people that had traditionally accommodated single men. Deacon recalled that if a potential landlord or landlady discovered "you were a single person—and especially being pregnant—you is nothing . . . you is nothing."[105] Taken together, these discriminatory housing practices had a twofold outcome. By placing restrictions on the areas where Caribbean migrants could reside, they also facilitated the concentration of Black people in areas such as Notting Hill and Brixton in major cities like London.

Although racial prejudices certainly kept White property owners from opening their doors to Black newcomers during the 1950s and early 1960s, following World War II, massive housing shortages plaguing a number of British cities also contributed to a strained housing market for migrants. Throughout Britain, residential property loss and destruction was a major wartime casualty that became a central concern of postwar reconstruction and recovery efforts. In a White Paper issued in September 1944, Parliament estimated that roughly 202,000 homes had been completely destroyed during the war and approximately 255,000 more were no longer inhabitable. Likewise, Parliament records indicated that while they remained in livable condition, over 4 million homes had suffered wartime damage and needed repairs.[106] Compounding this issue, in areas such as London, with higher birthrates and greater numbers of returning demobilized military personnel and evacuees, the demand for housing proved staggering in relation to the figures for lost property. According to a report issued by the Commission on Housing in Greater London in 1951, the city had an excess of 500,000 more households than available homes. Thus, as the British Government confronted the realities of postwar social conditions, the deficiencies in residential property, overcrowding, and rising prices for accommodations transformed housing into a major postwar political issue. [107]

The scarcity of housing, particularly in urban areas with larger population densities such as London, served as a major point of social competition and, in some cases, conflict in many communities.[108] In addition to an overall lack of suitable accommodations, overcrowding, and the ability of private landlords to impose higher rents, because of the deregulation of rent controls under the 1957 Rent Act, and issue unfair lease agreements due to increased demand, further aggravated social tensions related to living space.[109] While the issue of housing was a source of contention among indigenous residents—particularly in many working-class communities—for Caribbean migrants, the competition over living space was punctuated by their position as social outsiders because of their migrant status and the stigmas attached to their racial identities. Before local authorities would even consider a resident for public housing in the London borough of Lambeth, which included the Brixton community, an area with some of the largest proportions of Caribbean settlement, a person had to document local residency for a period of at least three years. As a result, many new migrants were virtually shut out of wait lists for local council-housing programs during the 1950s because of residency requirements receiving little or no assistance from local authorities.[110] And as Susan J. Smith has noted, these practices of de facto discrimination interfaced with a larger process of disenfranchisement that effectively kept migrants from reaping some of the public benefits made available through the postwar welfare state.[111]

Not only did Caribbean migrants face discrimination in their pursuit of housing, but oftentimes even when they did secure housing, they were subject to indecent living conditions, the constant gaze of suspicious landlords, and exorbitant rental fees.[112] Jamaican migrant Walter Lothen recalled that in the mid-1950s, when he arrived in Britain, "Accommodation was appalling. A lot of landlords didn't want to know you. Half the houses had no bath. You had one toilet for five or six houses and had to go to the public baths."[113] Although May Cambridge, who also hailed from Jamaica, secured housing in Britain through her nursing program, she vividly remembered the frustrations of friends and relatives who were forced to rent rooms "at the princely sum of £2.04sh with six or seven people sharing the facilities." Cambridge also explained the rigidity of life under strict landlords. She noted, "Tenants were subjected to rules and regulations for army recruits," adding that "one of [her] landladies charged 1d for toilet tissue, and if the lights were left on you'd get a knock on the door. You also had to be in at a certain time and all clothing was washed and dried in bedroom."[114] When Claude Ramsey arrived in 1956 from Barbados, he remembered having to rent a room that he shared with some thirty people "with only one bath and toilet." Ramsey insisted, "The conditions were appalling, and it cost me £3 a week in rent," a sizable sum when the average manual laborer netted little more than £5 per week during the 1950s.[115]

One of the most infamous landlords notorious for capitalizing on the racial politics of housing was a Polish immigrant named Peter Rachman. At the peak of Rachman's real estate career during the 1950s, he maintained interests in over 23 separate companies controlling over 144 properties in North Kensington and Paddington, where large proportions of Black migrants in London had settled. Although many of the properties owned by Rachman were dilapidated and oftentimes in unsanitary conditions, for Caribbean newcomers, they provided some of the few places where they could easily secure lease agreements. Feeding off the overall housing shortage and a looming reluctance by many Whites to rent to Black tenants, Rachman and other local landlords easily exploited Caribbean migrants' demand for the most basic of socioeconomic necessities through the imposition of what was commonly described as a "colour tax" that entailed paying higher than average rental rates for less than adequate accommodations.[116]

Not only did discriminatory leasing practices and exclusionary housing policies reflect how racism operated to deny Afro-Caribbean migrants the right to equitable living conditions, but the labor market also proved to be an arena where the racialization of Black workers limited their access to opportunities. When Cecelia Wade arrived in England from Montserrat at the age of thirty-four in 1956 to join her siblings, she figured that her education and experience as a schoolteacher would serve her well as she negotiated the British labor market. On the first Monday after her arrival, she confidently entered a local labor exchange and, after presenting references documenting her teaching career in Montserrat, she recalled that the woman behind the counter sarcastically queried, "Oh, you were a teacher back home were you?" before promptly telling her, "Well you won't get a job teaching here!"[117] In one of the earliest sociological studies of White employers' impressions of West Indian workers conducted in Brixton during the late 1950s, including a survey of a number of public and private establishments in industries with some of the highest concentrations of labor shortages, Sheila Patterson tracked a general degree of hostility toward "foreign" labor. But for Black workers, their perceived alien status as non-indigenous workers was compounded by derogatory racial stereotypes about their aptitude as workers. British employers often characterized Black workers as lazy, slow, and irresponsible as compared to their White counterparts. Moreover, Patterson noted that the archetypical male Caribbean worker was oftentimes perceived "at best semi-skilled," more suited to "rough labouring jobs" that involved more repetition than intellect. Patterson suggested that these stereotypes were often used to justify unofficial quotas in hiring Black workers and/or overlook them for supervisory positions.[118]

Although local government-sponsored employment agencies like the one that Cecelia Wade encountered as she ventured for a job in London did not officially institute quotas or employment exemptions for Black workers, as her experience suggests, the stereotypes that Patterson found among individual employers also shaped informal practices and procedures at these agencies, which ultimately placed Black workers at a disadvantage as local employment officials typecast them as "unskilled" or uncredentialed and therefore less suited to certain types of higher-paying industrial and/or professional positions.[119] To be sure, Patterson's study found that the racialization, stigmatization, and marginalization of West Indian workers in the British labor market were not gender neutral. Officials at labor exchanges often viewed Black women as particularly unable to adapt labor skills acquired in the colonies to meet the demands of the British labor market. Local labor officials noted that Black women were oftentimes perceived as ill suited to industrial labor and generally unwilling to accept domestic-labor positions, which they regarded as demeaning, making them difficult to employ. Regarding the employment of Black women as the greater "labour problem" as compared to men for a number of reasons, one local labor official explained,

Employers find them [black women] slow, touchy, unadaptable, choosy, hypochondriac, and lacking in stamina. . . . They [employers] say they need more supervision than white workers. Many employers prefer the lighter-coloured ones and ask for them in preference to "black-mammy types" and "dark ones." Some employers find them not worth training because of their habit of "making a baby" every year or so. Employers also claim that their white women employees object to working side by side with them for personal hygienic reasons.[120]

This particular labor-exchange official's views speak to the gendered terms of racialization that Black migrant workers encountered. But more importantly, what it underscores is that the gendered stereotypes used by White employing sectors of the economy to evaluate Black men and women's aptitude for jobs functioned in similar ways to relegate them into less desirable jobs and, in some instances, exclude them from certain industries and employment opportunities.

The process whereby Black men and women found themselves in lower-paying menial positions as newcomers to the British labor market was not one completely born of White racial prejudices and racially exclusionary employment practices. Whereas British economists projected labor shortfalls during the late 1940s and early 1950s, it is important to note that these shortages were generally limited to certain segments of the economy. Typically throughout this period, overall projected labor shortages were most acute in manual, low-waged, entry-level positions in industries such as construction, coal mining, and textile production. These were the industries with greater demand for laboring bodies and oftentimes more willing to hire Black workers with fewer degrees of scrutiny. Moreover, even when the economy did produce higher-ranking positions with better wages, the labor shortfall was still more keenly felt at the lower rungs of the labor market, as this dynamic most immediately facilitated the upward mobility of indigenous White laborers into higher-paying industries.[121] In her study of West Indian workers in Birmingham, Lydia Lindsey characterized this particular process of marginalization experienced by West Indian and other migrants of color in the postwar era as part of a "split-labor phenomenon" that stratified workers within the same market on the basis of race. According to Lindsey, "Although they were full citizens, the West Indian immigrants could not become racially integrated. Their skin color and backgrounds in addition to discriminatory policies prevented their movement in higher-paying jobs. Color determined social class and work status. White skin ranked higher than black skin in the social hierarchy."[122]

For many Black Britons, experiences of housing segregation and labor market segmentation represented a clear contradiction to the ideology of racial egalitarianism inherent in the Commonwealth ideal as legally prescribed by the provisions of a transracial British citizenship, guaranteed by the British Nationality Act of 1948. While the promises of British citizenship allowed Caribbean migrants to fashion themselves as members of the imperial body politic and substantiate the meaning of that sense of belonging through the act of migration, the experience of racism and discrimination in Britain created a penetrating schism between the possibilities of British citizenship and the realities of exclusion and non-belonging. Moments of racial violence dramatized the fractures between the ideal and the reality and caused both Black and White Britons to closely examine their own definitions of what it meant to be British and to fully belong as members of British society.

"Race Riots" and the Mystique of British Anti-Racism

On the evening of 1 September 1958, a crowd of approximately three hundred men and women remained barricaded in two adjacent buildings at Blenheim Crescent, prepared to defend themselves to the death against what was described in the local press as a "mob of marauding white rowdies."[1] Armed with Molotov cocktails and makeshift weapons such as bricks, iron bars, bicycle chains, and milk bottles, the group, largely consisting of West Indians, joined forces in response to a rumored planned attack on Black people in the area during what had become the third consecutive night of mass racial violence in the streets of West London. Frightened yet resolute in their desire to defend and protect their lives, their property, and their rights as citizens, the members of the group undoubtedly found their courage to stand and fight growing as they overheard an angry White mob that had gathered in the street, surrounding them shouting, "Let's burn the niggers out!"[2]

The fear that enveloped the men and women who had gathered to confront the White mob at Blenheim Crescent was quite justifiable. Earlier that day, as Seymour Manning exited the Latimer Road Tube Station, he met the taunts and jeers of a vitriolic White crowd incited by the death cheer "lynch him!"[3] Described in press reports as a "young West African student," Manning had journeyed to Notting Hill for the day from Derby to visit friends but quickly found that the color of his skin was attracting contempt and violence.[4] Manning narrowly escaped a brutal beating by a "gang" of young White men. However, it was only after a local shopkeeper's wife opened her doors and called police after watching him run for his life and gasping, "Help me. For God's sake, help me. They are going to kill me," that Manning found refuge from the racial terror that he had encountered while doing nothing more than being a lone Black man walking the streets of Notting Hill.[5] When questioned by a reporter about the reasons for the attack on Manning, one of his attackers boasted, "We'd have tore 'im apart if it hadn't been for the police," while another explained,

"We've got a bad enough housing shortage around here without them moving in. Keep Britain white."[6]

Perhaps some of the men and women assembled in the tenements at Blenheim Crescent had learned of Seymour Manning's attack and decided that enough was enough. For over a week, reports of anti-Black violence in the streets of Nottingham and West London captured national headlines as news of "Negro-baiting" White mobs and "Teddy boys" brandishing knives, razors, and other weapons of expediency, including bicycle chains and broken bottles, prowling for victims and fueling "race war" circulated in the British press.[7] While patrolling in Notting Hill on the evening before Seymour Manning's attack, local constables made several arrests as they encountered hundreds of "hostile" Whites, who hurled bottles and iron railings while referring to them as "nigger lovers" as they taunted police for permission to "get at" the "dirty coloured bastards."[8]

In the hours before a group of West Indians convened at 9 Blenheim Crescent above Totobag's Café to launch their counterattack on the anti-Black street violence, Jeffrey Hamm, secretary of Oswald Mosley's Union Movement, a fascist organization that avidly protested the "coloured invasion," gave a fiery speech condemning Commonwealth "immigrants" and inciting hundreds of Whites who had gathered outside of the Latimer Road Tube Station to "get rid of them."[9] After a speech that tapped into the fury that had been on display in the streets by a speaker obviously hoping to cultivate and exploit White anxieties about the consequences of Commonwealth migration, one can imagine that seeing supporters cheer in agreement with Jeffrey Hamm's incendiary rhetoric only strengthened Black Britons' resolve to fight back. Whereas on previous evenings Black Britons had oftentimes found themselves largely on the receiving end of mob violence, as darkness fell on the streets of West London on the evening of 1 September 1958, the tide was shifting. Groups of West Indian men entered the streets while challenging Whites to "come and fight!"[10] As homemade petrol bombs cascaded from the rooftop of Totobag's Café into the streets at Blenheim Crescent, White crowds would, if only temporarily, scatter. In West London, police would amplify their efforts to tame the mobs to restore order in the streets, and the press would declare that in the face of another night of vigilante efforts to "Keep Britain White," on the evening of 1 September 1958, "this time colored people fought back."[11]

Within forty-eight hours of what was described as the "siege of Blenheim-Crescent," the violence between Black and White Londoners began to subside.[12] Evening rains coupled with an intensified police presence helped to calm the atmosphere as ongoing racial strife transitioned from a blistering boil back to a more passive simmer. By the time that the major fighting reached an armistice, police had made 108 arrests, the overwhelming majority

being young White working-class men.[13] As defendants answered to local
magistrates on a host of charges, including assault, using insulting behavior,
obstructing police, possessing offensive weapons, and "fighting to the terror
of Her Majesty's subjects," even before the violence tapered, an assortment
of commentators both in Britain and beyond began to render opinions about
what the news of "race riots" in Nottingham and London meant.[14] Was the violence simply a local story about a sudden, geographically specific "outburst"
of racial conflict? Could it be explained as a product of "hooliganism," the
depravities associated with working-class urban life or growing right-wing fascist agitation? Was the so-called colour problem precipitated by a largely Black
male Commonwealth "immigrant" population, or did its origins lie elsewhere?
More importantly, what did news of "Britain's race war" say to the world about
the nation as a whole?[15]

   This chapter focuses on the competing logics offered by both domestic and
international audiences to explain and make sense of the causes and consequences of news of "race riots" in Britain. While incidents of anti-Black violence
during the summer of 1958 have been customarily viewed as landmark events
in charting a social history of White Britons' hostilities to Commonwealth
migration and the growing presence of non-White communities in Britain,
this domestically oriented reading obfuscates the transnational political
impact that news of "race riots" had on perceptions of race and race relations
in Britain.[16] News traveled. And sensational headlines describing the exploits
of "lynch mobs" in Nottingham and the "Nazis of Notting Hill" made copy in
papers throughout the world and garnered an international audience of observers.[17] As a decolonizing imperial power and proprietor of Western democracy in a political moment driven by racially charged Cold War imperatives,
Third World movements, and debates over the protection of human rights, for
Britain—much like the United States—inflammatory images of race and race
relations encapsulated in news stories, including those chronicling events such
as the desegregation crisis in Little Rock, Arkansas, held the power to potentially compromise the nation's moral leadership on a world stage.[18] Moreover,
news of "race riots" struck at the very heart of postwar discourses about race
in Britain, manufactured to recalibrate ideas about the nation's evolving relationship to a post-imperial Commonwealth community of former colonial
states. It is only by incorporating a transnational framework that attends to
the interplay between the local and the global through the prism of Empire
that the racial conflict that erupted in the streets of Nottingham and Notting
Hill during the summer of 1958 can be properly located within a broader history of shifting ideas about the character of Britain as an imperial nation-state
and the meaning of Britishness in an age of imperial atrophy.[19] What then
emerges from this discussion is a deeper awareness of how the experiences of

Caribbean migrants provide a critical point of entry for examining how race shaped perceptions of what it meant to be British both at home and abroad during the postwar era.

Tracking the range of domestic and international commentary generated in response to the news of "race riots" in Britain captured in press reports, the public statements of Government officials, editorials, cartoons, and diplomatic correspondences brings into sharp focus the gulf between the purported ideals of the nation and the quotidian realities of Black British citizens. Whereas the nation touted values of tolerance, multiracial inclusiveness, and racial progressivism, news of "race riots" told a different story that stood diametrically opposed to this narrative of the nation. To be sure, inasmuch as international responses to the news of "race riots" helped to distill this terrain, they also provide a useful window to gauge the workings of what I term the mystique of British anti-racism. The mystique of British anti-racism is a concept used to describe the collective myths engendered historically that have over time sustained and reinforced anti-racist perceptions of British liberalism, tolerance, and ostensible benevolence toward racialized colonial subjects. Rooted in the reconstituted "moral capital" accrued by Britain's investments in shaping a humanitarian legacy of abolitionism, the mystique of British anti-racism in the postwar era functioned as a potent element of representations of Britain and Britishness both at home and abroad.[20] News of "race riots" certainly challenged this depiction of race and nation, compromising the legitimacy of the mystique and threatening its survival. Therefore, this chapter is also concerned with the ways in which domestic reaction to the violence was tempered by an attempt to manage the contradictions between the racialized ideals that were tethered to how the British imperial nation-state fashioned itself in an increasingly post-imperial world and the extant racial realities of metropolitan society embodied in the experiences of Afro-Caribbean migrants.

"Race Riots" in Britain as International News

As the intensity of the interracial clashes in Nottingham and London grew during late August and early September 1958, London's *Daily Herald* reported "world uproar" as news of "Britain's race war" circulated internationally.[21] Reporting on three consecutive nights of violence in Notting Hill on 3 September 1958, Ghana's *Daily Graphic* featured the comments of C. J. M. Alport, a Commonwealth Relations Office official, as part of a headline declaring, "Race Riots are unBritish." Condemning both the incidents of racial violence that had erupted in Nottingham and London in the preceding weeks, as well as the sensational media coverage of the conflicts, Alport insisted that the very idea of "race riots" in England was "wholly unBritish" and could not be explained as a product or indicator of the existence of "colour prejudice" in Britain.[22] Explicit in Alport's characterization of the violence was the idea that the very rudiments of what constituted what it meant to be British were antithetical to the realities of violent racial conflict.

The theme of the "unBritish" nature of news of race riots in England resonated in media coverage throughout the world. Whereas an editorialist for *The Star* in Johannesburg assessed that Britain was a nation where racial discrimination was "essentially alien to the whole spirit of the people and the laws," other international news outlets, including Australia's *Sydney Morning Herald*, ran headlines announcing, "Race Riots Give Britain a Shock" to capture the unexpected and seemingly foreign concept of violent racial conflict in Britain.[23] This point of view also permeated the filters of British diplomats charged with measuring the pulse of international opinion about the violence and keeping government officials in London abreast of the shifting views of race and race relations in Britain from abroad. From the outset, several British overseas observers reported that much of the commentary surrounding the news of "race riots" centered on the seemingly uncharacteristic nature of images of racial violence in Britain, given the nation's international reputation as a beacon of liberalism, tolerance, and egalitarianism.

Summarizing the extensive coverage of the violence in the French press, a British diplomat asserted that "the British are renowned in France for their tolerance and liberal outlook and it has come as a shock to many that racialism can rear its ugly head in the country of Wilberforce."[24] Invoking William Wilberforce, an iconic figure in the history of British abolitionism, as a synecdoche representing the moral and political investments of the nation in the racially charged history of anti-slavery accentuated the racially progressive values associated with British liberalism and ideas of tolerance, which the diplomat concluded had been compromised in his survey of French media. A report on coverage of the violence filed by a British diplomat stationed in New Zealand expressed similar sentiments and included an excerpt from the *Wellington Dominion* that noted that racial violence in Britain was particularly shocking "because such disorder [was] so out of character with [the] British whole reputation for tolerance," which the paper added was now "impaired."[25]

The idea that news of "race riots" loosened the threads of the moral fibers of a British nation that had imagined itself and was regarded as a land governed by its seemingly impartial principles about the significance of race also circulated in US coverage of the violence. *Washington Post* editorials and reports on the violence referenced "the strong British tradition of civil liberties," which ran counter to the news of racial conflict, a dynamic that the paper described as producing a "sociological shock" to the conscience of a "nation which likes to regard itself as wholly free of color bias."[26] Collating media reports throughout the United States, British diplomats in Washington reported comment in the *Tulsa Tribune* that described how the violence was "searing the conscience of a nation so traditionally dedicated to fair play," while an editor for the *New York Times* remarked that it would "be interesting to see how the British reassert their normal tolerance and good sense," given that "no people in the world had achieved a more urbane sense of tolerance than the British."[27] It was not simply that news of "race riots" challenged the legitimacy of the virtues of tolerance and racially blind liberal justice in Britain, but in doing so, the news also struck at the heart of perceptions of the nation's role as a political leader internationally.

Commenting on the violence upon arriving in England just days after the dust began to settle in London, Norman Manley, Premier of Jamaica, echoed many of the sentiments expressed in the *New York Times*. Manley declared news of race riots a "tragedy" for a nation that he insisted had "always led the world in tolerance and decency."[28] Carefully maneuvering the tensions between his diplomatic role as advocate for a largely Jamaican West Indian community in Britain, and broker for the official political interests of the Jamaican nation in the British Commonwealth, in his comments Manley underscored how the racial politics of Britain as a nation was configured in a global political imaginary. Britain was not simply a nation with its moral compass facing forward when it came to (anti)racism, but its imagined national virtues of being tolerant, just, liberal, and decent also translated into a global brand that allowed it to be perceived as racially inclusive, democratic, egalitarian and, most importantly, politically respectable as a type of standard bearer for these desired traits in the eyes of a world community attuned to the politics of race and representations of race relations.

During his visit to England in the days immediately following the height of the London violence, Manley joined a special envoy of West Indian leaders, which included Carl La Corbiniere. Deputy Prime Minister of the newly formed West Indies Federation, and Hugh Cummins, Prime Minister of Barbados, assembled to investigate the causes and consequences of the violence. In addition to visiting areas most severely affected by racial conflict, including London's Notting Hill district and the St. Ann's Road section of Nottingham, the envoy had as the goal of what became a two-week tour to convey a message of official support for West Indian nationals in Britain. Moreover, the presence of West Indian officials in England served as a public gesture of concern and solidarity that allowed them to harness a type of bully pulpit to lobby British officials on behalf of the interests of their mutual constituencies in Britain and their respective national political interests as members of the Commonwealth. In the course of holding several public meetings attended by hundreds of West Indians during his tours of neighborhoods in

London and Nottingham, Manley reminded West Indians to remain vigilant and undeterred by the violence. Emphasizing their status as citizens, he urged a crowd convened in London to "exercise every single right you possess," and reminded a crowd in Nottingham, "you have a right to be and here and you will stay here as long as you want."[29] In framing his public critique of the violence as both an affront to the citizenship status of West Indian nationals residing in Britain and a product of anti-Black or, at the very least, anti-non-White racism, Manley's narrative about the violence articulated the ways in which West Indians were indeed disenfranchised casualties of racism rather than colonial denizens whose mere presence engendered a racialized "immigrant" problem in British society.

West Indian officials were not alone among predominately non-White Commonwealth governments in their expressions of concern for their nationals residing in Britain in the wake of the violence. African and Asian nations, including Ghana, Nigeria, Kenya, and Pakistan, all made direct appeals to British officials to seek clarification on the nature of the violence and the steps being taken to ensure the protection and safety of their nationals.[30] While anxieties about the plight of their respective national constituencies figured most prominently in public and private dialogues between Commonwealth and British officials, these exchanges also highlight a preoccupation with the ways in which the violence marked a particular construction of anti-Black racism that crystallized in specific ways upon the non-White, colonized, working-class bodies of West Indian men of African descent. Acknowledging that "the negroes" appeared to be the "main targets" of the violence, Pakistani diplomats warned the Commonwealth Relations Office that "there is no knowing when the teddy boys will direct their wrath at the large population of Pakistanis" resident in the United Kingdom.[31] In their appeals to British officials, representatives of the High Commissioner of Ghana cited confusion in press reports that did not clearly distinguish between the "different kinds of 'coloured' people" involved in the violence, noting that "there was all the difference in the world between Indians and Pakistanis on the one hand, West Africans on another and West Indians in the third place."[32] As British officials considered these appeals, they too agreed that a finer point should be given to distinguishing between "one type of coloured person and another," particularly as it related to the sexual politics of race, concluding that "no Teddy Boy is likely to feel that some undersized little Pakistani or Indian will steal his girl friend from him; but West Africans are almost certainly to be classed with West Indians as the major menace where women are concerned."[33]

Although Commonwealth nations formed differing opinions about the stakes of the violence rooted in racial classifications of "coloured people"—views that were shaped by ideas about the phenotype, gender, sexuality, nationality, and socioeconomic status tethered to the Black bodies involved—they did seem to agree that the violence posed a grave threat to the sense of solidarity that governed the principles of a multiracial British Commonwealth. According to Australia's *Sydney Morning Herald*, the rioting in Britain had aroused "dark subjects['] anxiety" throughout a Commonwealth community with an overwhelming majority of non-White British subjects.[34] Reporting on media coverage of the violence in Pakistan, a British diplomat included excerpts from an article appearing in the *Times of Karachi* that suggested those involved in the violence, namely, "teddy boys," deserved to be "flogged to within an inch of their lives," given that "the good work done in our multi-racial association may be now in jeopardy simply because of some teenage wise guys and hoodlums."[35] Jamaican Premier Norman Manley concurred with this assessment and determined that "the whole future of the British Commonwealth of Nations—much of which is peopled by non-white races—depended on Britain's conduct in the face of racial incidents."[36] Just as the British Nationality Act of 1948 institutionalized the notion of a British Commonwealth community of citizens whose ties transcended the boundaries of race, region, and nation, the Commonwealth itself, at least in theory, represented a multiracial political entity comprised of equal nationalities, where markers of race purportedly had no pertinent social value in determining Commonwealth citizenship rights in Britain.

Addressing a largely West Indian audience in London during his two-week tour in the aftermath of the violence, Manley noted that Britain's open-door migration policy was "a principle which has helped to build the very foundations on which the Commonwealth rests."[37] Also stressing the importance of migration as an essential element defining Commonwealth relations, a Nigerian official expressed concerns similar to Manley's, warning that if Britain decided to restrict migration from Commonwealth nationals, it would "do irreparable damage to Commonwealth unity and mutual understanding."[38] Future Nigerian President Nnamdi Azikiwe agreed. During a state visit as he anticipated his country's march toward independence, Azikiwe noted that while the British Commonwealth had taken a liberal stance on race relations, a shift in migration policy would fundamentally alter Commonwealth relations. Accordingly, he warned, "We would not like to be in the Commonwealth where we could be second-class citizens."[39] Since people of color and, more specifically, Afro-Caribbeans, represented the overwhelming majority of migrants from the Commonwealth in Britain during the 1950s, inherently, the issue of migration, particularly the question of migration restrictions, came embedded with racial undertones. How could British officials consider migration restrictions amid racial conflict involving Black Commonwealth migrants without signaling that controls were indeed a de facto race policy designed to limit the entry of Black British citizens?

South Africa's *The Star* in Johannesburg addressed this controversial question in an editorial suggesting,

> No doubt Britain would be reluctant to depart from the principle of the open door or to give any appearance of racial bias. But when she is faced with an immediate practical problem, the obvious thing is to check the inflow of people whose coming at this moment could only aggravate the troubles of the authorities as well as the non-whites already in the country."[40]

In an editorial appearing in the leading nationalist pro-Government paper, Cape Town's *Die Burger,* one South African observer attributed the "racial explosion" directly to Britain's reluctance to implement migration controls that would appear to discriminate against the entry of people of color "in the interest of good relations with the multi-racial empire and Commonwealth." The editorial suggested that, "such intolerance towards people who are coloured is completely in opposition to the picture of a liberal, colour-blind Britain which is shown to the world."[41] To be sure, British diplomats observed that in general, articles related to incidents of racial violence in Britain reported in the South African press tended to highlight what was regarded as "the very real conflict between the principle of the open door in a multi-racial Commonwealth and the practical problem of controlling the influx of those who are difficult to assimilate."[42] South African opinion clearly articulated how the news of "race riots" in Britain—the premier Commonwealth state—clearly exposed the ways that the principles governing the Commonwealth ideal formed inextricable ties between race and migration.

As racial conflict and its international implications prompted British officials to more carefully reevaluate the relationship between race and migration within the context of notions of "Commonwealth," two scenarios emerged. Either migration could continue to function as one of the chief mechanisms through which the ideals of a multiracial egalitarian British Commonwealth community acquired substantive value or, in striking contrast, it could serve as a medium of remapping the racial hierarchies that had defined Empire onto the citizenship rights afforded to Commonwealth nationalities. By even contemplating the latter, particularly in response to racial violence, Britain could not avoid international conjecture that when it came to freely opening its borders to the Commonwealth community, race did indeed matter.

Not only did South African public opinion emphasize how the violence unearthed tensions between a British migration policy reflecting the ideals of a multiracial Commonwealth and the practicalities associated with forging a multiracial society but, more importantly, news of "race riots" in Britain offered South African observers an opportunity to attempt to vindicate their own abhorred racial practices and appeal for greater understanding from British critics. J. O. Wright, a representative for the South African High Commission monitoring public opinion in South Africa, noted that after the violence spread from Nottingham to Notting Hill, South African commentators had "a real field day" reporting on the riots.[43] As accounts of violence in Nottingham emerged, *The Times* reported that South African papers referenced the events as "a case of the biter bit." Under the heading "No more the cry 'Holier than thou,'" the Johannesburg's *Star* reprinted a cartoon appearing in Britain's *Daily Express*, portraying British Prime Minister Harold Macmillan dodging a scuffle between a "Nottingham 'teddy boy' and a coloured man" as the Governor of Arkansas, Orval Faubus, who had become legendary for obstructing federal mandates to desegregate public schools in Little Rock, Arkansas, and a figure "vaguely resembling" Nationalist Party leader Charles Swart labeled "South Africa" watched (Figure 3.1).[44]

A British correspondent reporting from Johannesburg explained.

The incidents at Nottingham have roused considerable interest here. . . . Many South Africans feel that as their own racial troubles

Figure 3.1 Daily Express Cummings cartoon, 1958. (Permission *Daily Express*/Solo Syndication.)

-develop the British, like the United States, are likely to be more sympathetic to the Union's [South Africa's] difficulties, and this gives
them a feeling of relief.[45]

Editorial commentary appearing in Die Burger, the organ of Afrikaner
Nationalists, evoked a similar tone. One writer contended that Britain was
"ill-equipped to deal with the problems of a multi-racial community." The
editorialist insisted that because British perspectives of "colour problems"
derived chiefly from its role as a colonial power, Britain's answers to issues
of race had been resolved through what the commentator labeled as "total
apartheid" rather than through any serious consideration of "multiracial exist-
ences." Clearly, the commentator was attuned to the ways that historically,
notwithstanding small and oftentimes transient enclaves of seafaring, student,
and military communities, Britain's experience with forging multiracial non-
White communities had largely been shaped within the context of an imperial structure in which majority White metropolitan communities were more
accustomed to governing from abroad rather than accommodating a sizable
population of color on its own shores. The article maintained that, for this reason, British perspectives "on the problems of colour are often stupid and intol-
erable" and suggested that Britain was unqualified to critique South Africa's
use of apartheid policies to regulate race relations within its borders. Rather,
the editorialist concluded, Britons should offer Africa "less advice, but not
without greater understanding."[46]

Just as South African opinion conveyed a hope that the racial violence displayed in Nottingham and Notting Hill might cause British critics of apartheid to reexamine their self-righteous posture on issues pertaining to race,
observers in Germany, France, and the US South also expressed a degree of
vindication for racial practices and policies scrutinized by the British public.
In their surveys of German reaction to news of "race riots" in Britain, British
officials reporting from Bonn described what was detected as "an undertone of
German satisfaction" that Britain had proven itself "not immune to anti-racial
feeling" despite pompous denouncements of Nazi anti-Semitic sentiment in
Germany.[47] Similarly, British officials in Paris noticed that a certain degree
of schadenfreude characterized French reactions to the violence, particularly among "right-wing Frenchmen" who recognized Britain's self-righteous
"tendency to preach to others" on the subject of race and colonialism, as
exemplified in British criticisms of French policies in Algeria.[48]

Among US critics, one of the most stinging indictments of what news of
race riots in Britain articulated about the nation's international position as a
moral authority on the subject of race came directly from Arkansas Governor
Orval Faubus. In the wake of the 1957 Little Rock desegregation debacle,

which seared images of Black students encountering a military-style perimeter as they sought to exercise their right to access the same institutions of public education afforded to their White counterparts into the consciousness of international audiences, Governor Faubus had become for many British observers the embodiment of America's continuing failure to secure racial equality in a purportedly democratic society. In response to a report in an Arkansas newspaper indicating that Governor Faubus had admonished, "The British had better not point the finger at us anymore," as news of intensifying racial conflict in Notting Hill had surfaced, a reporter for the *Daily Mail* issued a reply that aimed to make clear distinctions between Jim Crow America and the streets of Nottingham and London. Presumably addressed to Faubus and any others feeling absolved of British moral indignation about their racist policies and practices, in an article titled "Dear Governor Faubus . . .," the reporter noted, "There is no law for the white and another for the black in this country." And while America's race troubles were compounded in part because local authorities, including Faubus, had "defied the law of the land," in the case of the recent fighting in Nottingham and London, those who had violated law in Britain by committing acts of violence were not those endowed with the responsibilities of enforcing the laws that governed the nation, but rather were "a bunch of rowdies and no-goods" whose actions would be punished to the full extent of the law.[49] By challenging Faubus's suggestion that news of "race riots" placed Britain on a similar plane with the United States in respect to the question of racial politics, the reporter hoped to remind Faubus and other international detractors that the violence did not reflect the values of the nation. In doing so, the reporter's response points to the ways in which news of "race riots" placed the British nation in the precarious position of having to defend the seemingly anti-racist mystique of tolerance, liberality, and multiracial inclusiveness that it touted as the defining features of what it meant to be British in the postwar world.

Historicizing the Mystique

If one examines international conjecture in the aftermath of the violence in Nottingham and London, three dominant narratives about race and race relations in metropolitan Britain emerge. The first of these narratives focused upon Britain's image as a racially liberal nation that touted ostensibly progressive values, including tolerance, decency, and equal justice. A second narrative revealed how Britain was envisioned as the "Mother Country" or progenitor of a multiracial Commonwealth defined by a sense of Britishness that was inclusive and universalist, while a third narrative addressed Britain's image in the arena of race relations as a foil to the extremes of White supremacy practiced in the Jim Crow South in the United States and under South Africa's postwar apartheid regime. To be sure, these narratives about race and race relations in Britain did not exist in isolation from one another, nor were they absolute or uncontested. Rather, they functioned as converging discursive frameworks that informed a broader portrait of race and race relations in Britain—a composite portrait that I refer to as the mystique of British antiracism.

As a means to account for the ways in which a litany of foreign observers shared overlapping visions of a racially enlightened British nation, the mystique of British anti-racism describes a powerful constellation of narratives that worked in concert to secure and indeed normalize the credos that sustained the ostensibly racially progressive virtues of British liberalism. Moreover, it is a concept that captures the ever-elusive, unstable, and fungible character of the credos that constituted ideas about what the nation is or what it is perceived to represent both at home and abroad. As conventional definitions suggest, a mystique carries with it a certain ineffable quality that commands power and, to some extent, reverence even through its very character of being nondescript and normalized oftentimes to the point of a type of common-sense hegemonic invisibility.[50] Thus the mystique of British anti-racism functions as a conceptual device to open up an analytical space to explore the contours of the chasms and contradictions between the purported values and ideas that informed imaginaries of the British nation and what was actually happening within the social and political life of the nation, particularly in respect to questions of race. Whereas the mystique of British anti-racism provided a powerful frame to interpret the politics of race in Britain, under the weight of news of "race riots" the mystique fractured. And on the basis of the responses noted above, it is clear that during the summer of 1958, for many international observers throughout the Commonwealth, Europe and the United States, ideas of a tolerant, just, and liberal Britain simply did not comport with images of mob violence perpetuated in the name of keeping Britain White.

In unearthing what *appeared* to be a dislodging of racial ideals and racialized realities one has to consider how international audiences came to adapt such views of race and nation in postwar Britain—albeit to varying degrees and with different political motivations. It is important to note that the internationally legible discourses that collectively articulated the mystique of British anti-racism did not emerge as a type of spontaneous initial reaction to the violence in London and Nottingham. Rather, when viewed in concert, they were part of a preconditioned schema for thinking about race and nation that was then used by international audiences to read and make sense of the news about "race riots" in Britain. Considering the existence of the mystique of British anti-racism requires paying attention to both the narratives that constitute its articulation and some of the historical currents that breathed life into these visions of nation, giving them political efficacy and staying power over time. To engage this issue within the context of 1950s Britain, it is first necessary to distill the relationship between the three dominant narratives about race and race relations that framed how international audiences began to respond to news of "race riots" during the summer of 1958. It can be argued that the narratives informing ideas about Britain as the standard-bearer of a multiracial Commonwealth that promoted universalism, egalitarianism, and transracial camaraderie, along with those which emphasized metropolitan Britain's position as a counterpoint to the racial orders that sanctioned Jim Crow in America and apartheid rule under the National Party in South Africa, were indeed postwar iterations of post-abolitionist narratives about Empire and British racial liberalism shaped by the exigencies of imperial crisis that arose during World War II.

Fortified with the "moral capital" accrued by the politicization of a partic-ular narrative of abolitionism that emphasized humanitarianism, the idea of the Empire as a liberal "anti-slavery state" and benevolent protector supplied the logic and cultivated the rhetorical levers that British imperialists used to qualify their claims to exploit, govern, civilize, and create colonial subjects in Africa, the Caribbean, and Asia throughout the late nineteenth and early twentieth centuries.[51] To be sure, versions of a liberal, abolitionist, and human-itarian British nation also circulated in the metropole during the Victorian era and figured into the political campaigns of anti-lynching crusader Ida B. Wells as a means of highlighting "American atrocities"—as opposed to domestic and imperial racial realities—to gain the sympathies of British audiences in her opposition to racial violence and disenfranchisement as experienced by Black Americans.[52] Although military conflicts such as the Anglo-Boer War and World War I exposed the waning strength of British imperial power and raised questions about its virtues both at home and abroad during the early twentieth century, it was not until World War II that the representations of a benevolent British Empire underwent the most intensive scrutiny.[53] During World War II, the convergence of several factors, including the loss of imperial fronts in the East to the Japanese during the early years of the war, Nazi propa-ganda, American anti-imperialist rhetoric, and the critique of anti-colonialists in India, the Caribbean, Africa, and within the imperial metropolis, chal-lenged the integrity of this image of Empire.[54] Juxtaposed with the task of defining the Allied cause as one steeped in a defense of wartime credos such as national self-determination, human rights, freedom, and democracy against an enemy that threatened those prospects on a global scale by advocating a racially extreme, violent, and imperialistic brand of fascism, the very idea of Empire found itself imperiled. In response, part of creating an official wartime propaganda front involved adopting strategies to refurbish the view of Empire by promoting liberality and tolerance as national virtues as a means of branding Britain as a just nation tethered to a "temperate empire that was neither racist nor oppressive."[55] Tantamount to the project of both reviving and vindicating the virtues of Empire was a move toward the discursive deracialization of imperial relations that involved engendering a new lexicon to describe Britain's relationship with its Empire.[56]

The first layer of this initiative entailed the adaptation of the universalist language of Commonwealth as shorthand for Empire. During the postwar era, the British Nationality Act of 1948 became the signature policy that institutionalized a narrative about Commonwealth that emphasized the multiracial and inclusive character of Britishness. Driven in part by an attempt to blunt the emergence of racially exclusive British nationalities in the majority White dominions, the British Nationality Act of 1948 fully encapsulated a vision of a "New Commonwealth" that recognized an inclusive and transnational definition of Britishness transcending race and space. And while the passage of the British Nationality Act of 1948 is typically regarded as an attempt to redress the fading image of Britain's imperial legacy rather than a display of a pressing commitment to the principles of racial democracy, it is important to acknowledge how the embrace of a multiracial Commonwealth ideal managed to resuscitate post-abolitionist discourses of imperial benevolence and goodwill that explicitly disavowed the violent and oppressive racial ideologies of Empire.

Just as wartime critiques of the practice of Empire prompted a move toward the universalist and egalitarian ethos of Commonwealth, as Sonya Rose notes, fighting a war against the racial prescriptions of Nazi rule "made British tolerance a particularly salient aspect of national identity during the war."[57] According to Rose, "The British understood themselves to be tolerant of racial difference, identifying racialist practices with the United States, Germany and South Africa."[58] During the war, nothing underscored this claim more pointedly than British reactions to a Jim Crow US military presence in England. Eager to distance themselves from US segregationist policies and the racism of White Americans, the Ministry of Information produced a pamphlet that attempted to make clear distinctions between British dispositions toward African Americans and those found in America. The pamphlet boldly declared, "Any American Negro who comes to Britain must be treated by us on a basis of absolute equality." Reminding British audiences of proper racial etiquette in Britain, the pamphlet added, "And remember *never* call a negro a 'nigger.' "[59] Ultimately, by accommodating Jim Crow during the War, but not overtly condoning it, British officials hoped to articulate an ahistorical narrative about the imposition of racism as a burden of war imported by the United States, an imposition that the British bore as a type of necessary evil associated with allying with American forces in the greater cause of giving a final death blow to Nazi rule. In doing so, this narrative accomplished at least two complementary political agendas. First, it clearly established a barometer for measuring the substance of British notions of tolerance as a Western liberal power. The perception of tolerance is relative. The cultural and political cachet of those who are deemed tolerant is always tethered to the ways in which the tolerant can measure themselves against an intolerant or less tolerant entity of perceivably similar status.[60] For Britain both during and after the war, as its position as a world power dramatically strengthened, Jim Crow America provided the requisite contrast necessary to claim the moral high ground associated with being regarded as a tolerant nation. Although US President Harry Truman would issue an executive order in the years immediately following World War II to desegregate the military and the Supreme Court would render a series of decisions, including the celebrated 1954 Brown v. Board of Education decision, that would slowly begin to dismantle the legal underpinnings of Jim Crow segregation, over a decade following the war, British audiences could still lay claim to being a more racially "tolerant" nation as stories of Emmett Till's lynching, images of federal troops escorting Black children to school in Little Rock, Arkansas, and international outrage about the death sentence passed down to Jimmy Wilson for the crime of stealing $1.95 from a White woman reminded the world that American democracy continued to betray some of its most vulnerable of citizens.[61] Indeed, as news of "race riots" in Britain began to dominate headlines during the summer of 1958, British audiences would declare that they did not want to see the seeds of "Little Rock" germinate in Britain, to remind themselves and international audiences that racism and racial violence were particularly American social concerns that had no place in British society.[62] And it was the preservation of this narrative of a tolerant, liberal-minded, and comparatively racially progressive Britain—all pillars upholding the mystique of British anti-racism—that British audiences sought to defend as they responded to and account for the news of "race riots."

Preserving the Mystique

In the days following the violence in Notting Hill, British Foreign Office officials dispatched a confidential telegram to all Government representatives in Commonwealth territories and those serving in such places as Italy, Japan, the United States, and Russia, with an expressed goal to "dampen down public interest" in the violence that it noted had been "given exaggerated importance in the United Kingdom press." To further this effort, the telegram included

[handwritten margin note: ≠ not like US at all]

a list of talking points that London officials felt would allow overseas representatives to place the news about the violence in its "proper perspective" as they
communicated with local officials and media outlets in their respective outposts. First and foremost, British officials hoped to alter international opinion
by changing the parlance surrounding how what was happening in the streets
of Nottingham and London was being reported. Whereas "race riots" had been
one of the most commonly deployed descriptors of the violence, the telegram
explained that it was important to emphasize that given the scale of the events,
"by foreign standards" the violence occurring in Nottingham and London
would not be considered a "riot." To further underscore the aberrant quality of
the incidents, the memo's talking points were careful to remind international
audiences that the violence had been widely denounced and that, unlike places
such as the United States and South Africa, "organized racial discrimination
has never been part of the pattern of British life, nor of the laws of the country."
While British officials conceded that the "disturbances" had an unspecified
"racial aspect," they noted that race was merely a "pretext" for understanding
the violence rather than a determining factor that could account for it. The
memo concluded by encouraging foreign representatives to impress upon
their local audiences that "all British subjects, white or coloured enjoy absolute
equality before the law." [63]

In addition to offering overseas diplomats succinct talking points on the
British Government's perspective on the violence, Foreign Office officials
issued a separate addendum to the same recipients that provided a more
detailed statement seeking to clarify media reports related to what they
termed the "so-called 'race riots.'" [64] Whereas the talking points memo had
emphasized that the label of "race riot" was inaccurate to describe the conflicts in Nottingham and London, on the basis of how foreign audiences might
have understood the use of this appellation in their own domestic contexts, the
addendum aimed to provide specific references to buttress their characterization of the violence as being something other than a "riot," and certainly not a
"race riot" by any standard. Riots conjured mobs of people; however, officials
noted that while there had been over a hundred arrests, there were relatively
few people injured. Moreover, "race riots" happened in societies brimming
with racist bigots and racism. Insisting that Britain was no such place, officials
noted, "There is very little racial prejudice" in Britain and suggested that when
incidents of racial conflict surfaced between "coloured immigrants" and local
White residents, "they have almost invariably arisen from under-currents of
jealousy over extraneous things," such as "accommodation, employment or
women," rather than any entrenched form of racism or racial prejudice. [65]

For further context, the telegram explained that it had been only since the
close of World War II that British cities had witnessed a "considerable influx of

coloured immigrants"—the majority of whom were "unskilled" West Indian workers—and only recently had this pattern of "immigration" begun to reach "disconcerting proportions" as postwar labor shortages began to level. Foreign Office officials reasoned that because migrants of color were "easily recognizable 'foreigners'"—and in the particular case of West Indians—were "sometimes more flamboyant in their behavior," they were "easy targets for hooliganism." The memo concluded that although "the presence of the city's coloured population had been used as an excuse to create a violent disturbance" by the dregs of society, the news from Nottingham and London did not reflect widespread racial dispositions among the British public or the character of the nation. Instead, British officials wanted an international public to understand that news of "race riots" cast an unwelcomed "blot on the conscience of Britain."[66]

The telegrams issued by the Foreign Office in the wake of the violence elucidate at least three key points concerning how one might consider domestic responses to the violence. First, British spectators, particularly those in Government, were acutely sensitive to the impressions that news of "race riots" made among international observers. Although identifying and addressing the sources of racial tensions, as well as reprimanding the perpetrators of violence and devising preventive approaches to subdue future outbreaks all fell within the purview of the domestic community, one cannot ignore the broader international context of British responses and interpretations of the meaning of racial violence. In the postwar world in particular, issues of race could never quite simply be confined to a nation's domestic sphere. Rather, they represented contested transnational terrain that defined an individual nation's image in world politics and tested its legitimacy on a host of racially charged international concerns. Intensifying civil rights campaigns in the United States, the inherent racial undertones of the disengagement of European colonial powers in Africa, Asia, and the Caribbean, as well as United Nations' debates concerning South Africa's apartheid regime, all kept the issue of race firmly ensconced in an international political landscape defined by shifting and competing Cold War diplomatic alliances. In this climate, questions of race mattered, and Britons certainly knew that when news of "race riots" captured headlines, the world would be watching.

Secondly, British officials were concerned about influencing international perceptions of race and race relations in the wake of the violence. In much the same way that incidents such as the Little Rock debacle served as powerful symbols of race in America providing fodder for international critics to besmirch what Mary Dudziak has referenced as the "image of American democracy," news of "race riots" potentially threatened to dismantle widely held perceptions of British anti-racism.[67] Just as the real and imagined impact of racial narratives emerging from Jim Crow America induced US officials to repackage tarnished national myths pertaining to visions of American democracy, it is important to understand that British officials' reactions to news of "race riots" were also mediated by a desire to preserve certain contested notions of the mystique of British anti-racism. The images of interracial violence projected throughout the world showcased realities of racial conflict that severely crippled the liberal myths of racial tolerance, inclusiveness, egalitarianism, and moral authority fortifying the mystique of British anti-racism. Not only did images of "race riots" run counter to the underlying claim that racial differences had no social value in British society but, more importantly, they also provided alternative narratives of race and race relations that unveiled the existence of anti-Black racial hostilities, prejudice, and discrimination. How could the mystique of British anti-racism survive as a viable optic for imagining the virtues of the nation amid reports of "nigger-hunting," "race war," and vigilante campaigns taking place on the streets of Nottingham and London and celebrating the mantra "Keep Britain White!"?[68]

A third theme highlighted in the Foreign Office telegrams is that the narratives about race in British society that were exposed for international consumption during the summer of 1958 represented a critical moment compelling various sectors of a majority White metropolitan British society to take an introspective gaze at the nation and the dilemmas associated with what was more commonly described as the "colour problem." Whereas London's *Evening Standard* cast news of "race riots" as "London's Shame," a *Daily Express* report noted that while Britons had long "observed the colour problems of the United States and South Africa with an aloof and somewhat superior detachment," the violence in London and Nottingham had "brought the problem right up to their doorsteps."[69] As news of the violence spread, White British audiences began to cultivate a media-driven narrative that aimed to reconfigure shattered perceptions of race and race relations and rationalize the violence to circumvent a broad indictment of espoused national values and ideals regarding race. Alongside news of fresh outbreaks of violence in the days and weeks immediately following the initial flare-up of street brawls in the St. Ann's Well Road area of Nottingham, newspapers consistently carried headlines including "What Fans the Hate?" "Reasons for Racial Tension," "Our Colour Problem," "Who is To Blame?" "Why Racial Clash Occurred," and "London Racial Outburst Due to Many Factors," all of which undertook the task of explaining and, to varying degrees, reframing the nature of racial violence in Britain and its broader social and political implications domestically and, perhaps more importantly, for the consumption of international audiences.[70] For many British observers, one of the very tenets of British national identity was at stake in the aftermath of the Nottingham and Notting Hill incidents.

Thus reconciling the violence became a means of safeguarding the mystique of British anti-racism and essentially reifying and retooling the very myths about the nation that silenced a broader imperial history of anti-Black violence and racial hierarchies of power and belonging that also worked in the service of keeping Britain White.[71]

In the weeks immediately following the disturbances in Nottingham and Notting Hill, British observers began to construct an intricate web of social commentary to analyze what was described as the "colour problem" and explain the factors contributing to racial conflict. In the process, two overlapping and somewhat complementary explanations emerged as British officials, media outlets, organizations, and private citizens debated and attempted to account for the sources of racial tensions that led to the outbreak of violence. The first aspect of these explanations emphasized the ways in which the violence could be explained as a series of localized incidents confined to a wayward sector of White society. To frame this argument, observers oftentimes conceded that the violence was, on the whole, the result of racially motivated attacks on Black residents; however, these racist overtures were largely attributed to the reckless actions of "irresponsible youths" commonly described as Teddy boys, who were in no way representative of the larger White society's values or dispositions toward Black people. Not only did this explanation rely upon caricatures of Teddy boys—who were typically believed to be young White men—who were figured as the primary agents of violent racist behavior, but it also located the emergence of Teddy boy violence as part of a broader context of degenerate conditions characteristic of working-class urban life in particular neighborhoods in Nottingham and West London.

A second and indeed corollary theme emerging from White Britons' considerations of the causes of racial conflict focused on the ways in which racial conflict could be directly linked to the recent "immigration" of large numbers of people of color from Commonwealth communities—the overwhelming majority being Caribbean men of African descent. Issues of interracial sex, living space, and work dominated this line of discussion. British observers highlighted how sexual relations (real and imagined) between Black men and White women, housing shortages, and employment competition created hostile social relations between Black newcomers and indigenous White residents. In the process of articulating these two explanations—one of which confined racist behavior to an aberrant sector of White society and another of which attributed racial tensions to the problems of adapting to a new "immigrant" population—British audiences provided a means of accounting for what appeared to be an eruption of racial conflict in Britain and translating its implications for both domestic and international audiences in such a manner that disavowed the racism that news of "race riots" implied had taken root in

British society. To be sure, the glue that ultimately held these interlocking narratives together contained a critical subtext about gender, race, and nation that associated the sources of racial violence with male culprits who could be imagined as deviant and categorically un-British in order to preserve and defend the mystique of British anti-racism.

In an article appearing in the *Manchester Guardian Weekly* just days after reports of interracial violence in Nottingham surfaced, a special correspondent for the newspaper posed the question, "What produced the tension in this community?" At first glance, the reporter argued that the "real causes" of the violence involved "the whole complex of prejudice, envy, and mutual irritation inadequately known as the 'colour problem.'" In an attempt to further explain the essential features of the "colour problem" the reporter explained that

> many people put the verdict credibly into one word—"women." You might add as one equal factor general anxiety about the presence of coloured men, or "prejudice"—including white residents' dislike of mixed marriages. Some distance behind these causes comes a complex of irritations: coloured people's manners and mannerisms; rivalry for employment in a time of slight recession in the area; and envy of coloured men who have been able to buy houses and 'flash' cars.[72]

The report added,

> The 'women problem' seems to mean no more than that some West Indians and other coloured men have acquired white girl friends. This is resented by some white male residents—vaguely known as 'teddy boys' though their age range seems to run from over 20 to at least over 30—who do their best to humiliate coloured men in general.[73]

In an editorial appearing in the following week's edition of the paper, Myrtle Shaw, a resident of Nottingham, responded to the special correspondent's arguments concerning the nature of the "colour problem" and suggested that while the article could be commended for its objectivity, "the question 'What went wrong in Nottingham?' is not easily answered." From Shaw's perspective, "to lay the blame on 'teddy boys' or 'irresponsible' coloured men, or to conclude that it is due to jealousy over women," was an inadequate response. Instead, Shaw insisted that any interrogation of the societal problems that the violence exposed should extend beyond a focus on what she described as "surface causes" and attend to larger socioeconomic problems, including rising unemployment and housing shortages, rather than "hastily concluding that the affair was the handiwork of youth."[74] Although Myrtle Shaw hoped to

elicit a public dialogue about the violence and highlight some of the structural
factors that contributed to the violence, as news of racial conflict spread from
Nottingham to London, much of the initial commentary seeking to explain
the sources of the violence fixated on personalities rather than conditions. As
news of "race riots" in Nottingham and London unfolded, public discourse
about the violence captured in press reports framed the story as one of competing deviant masculine personas—young White Teddy boys and West Indian
"immigrant" men who competed over urban working-class resources, including White female sexual partners, means of economic mobility in a recessive
labor market, living space in era of housing shortages, and the right to articulate their own brand of British masculinity. Even when public chatter raised
socioeconomic issues, it typically did so merely to underscore antagonisms
between these two deviant masculine personalities—images that ultimately
became the central caricatures employed in an intricate set of narratives that
worked to absolve the nation of the blemish that news of "race riots" projected
to the world.

In a special report on the causes of the violence in Nottingham, a correspondent for *The Times* began by insisting that "Nottingham has had no
apparent colour bar." [75] Instead, the reporter maintained that the reasons for
the "racial clash" boiled down to more interpersonal issues of "envy, resent-
ment, and sometimes fear of eventual domination of white by black." Sampling
opinion among White residents in the St. Ann's Well Road area, where most
of the fighting took place, the reporter found that Whites complained of being
"elbowed off the pavement by groups of young coloured men, and that [white]
girls are accosted and molested." Moreover, the reporter found that "white
people, particularly those of low intelligence" were jealous of the "sight of coloured men walking along with white women," and especially irritated by Black
people who appeared to make "good wages," purchase homes, drive "flashy"
cars, and display a "happy-go-lucky temperament." Although the reporter
noted that West Indians in the area expressed resentments about being mis-
understood, humiliated, and attacked by "white toughs," the crux of the article
outlined a rationale about the causes of the violence that envisioned the streets
surrounding St. Ann's Well Road as working-class spaces of masculine aggres-
sion. In this narrative, fighting became recourse for weak-minded White men
to defend vulnerable White women, their neighborhoods, and their liveli-
hoods against Black male predators who flaunted their access to the spoils of
settlement in Britain. [76]

As reports of racial violence spread from Nottingham to London, reporting
on the violence fixated on variations of a similar narrative that sought to further explain the "wave of lawlessness" that was sweeping through British cities
at the hands of young White male "rowdies" and "irresponsible ruffians" who

comprised a "lunatic fringe" aiming to 'Keep Britain White."[77] These behaviors became most associated with Teddy boys, an idiom used to describe the seemingly errant qualities of postwar British youth culture, which, according to Dick Hebdige, reflected broader social anxieties about working-class respectability, imperial decline, and Black "immigration."[78] In response to a headline raising the question "Who is to blame?" in the days after the violence in London seemed to calm, an editorial in *The Observer* cited Teddy boys as a primary concern. Describing the evolving stereotypes circulating in popular discourse about Teddy boys, the article insisted that the nomenclature had become a "generic term for the Whites who seemed to be leading the riots," adding that for Americans, the equivalent referent would be "poor white trash."[79] Referencing research that had been conducted by the Home Office, *The Times* featured an article discussing the Teddy boy phenomenon as part of a broader "Hooligan Age" characterized by increasing rates of crime and delinquency among British youth whose "impressionable years" had been shaped by the dislocations of World War II. The article suggested that it would be short sighted to place blame for the rioting solely at the feet of these "immature and excitable" sectors of society; nevertheless, it concluded that it was important to understand that the source of the outbreaks of racial violence was in fact confined to this "tiny submerged hooligan element" whose antics would continue to reflect the views of an inconsequential minority whose actions deserved the "contempt of the civilized majority" and severe consequences from legal authorities.[80]

Ensuring that international audiences, particularly those in places accustomed to attracting headlines tarnishing their own reputations in the arena of race relations, understood that the violence in Britain could be traced to the likes of a deviant Teddy boy youth subculture was of paramount importance to B. R. Wilson, an affiliate of the University of Leeds who wrote a letter to the editor of the *The Times*, insisting that the "citizens of Bulawayo, Pretoria and Little Rock," including the infamous Governor Faubus, needed to be clear that "no widespread hostility towards coloured people in Britain" existed. Rather, the problem that the violence exposed was a problem of "ill-disciplined, overpaid, frustrated youth" who had not been properly socialized to "either preserve our traditional values or to effectively forge them for a new way of life." According to Wilson, the deviant nature of Teddy boys, which had most recently directed its frustrations toward West Indians, was driven in large measure by a shifting postwar socioeconomic climate that offered high wages and economic security through the welfare state to "unskilled, untrained, socially illiterate youth" influenced by an American youth culture that scoffed at authority and a mass-media industry that celebrated violence. [81] Therefore, audiences must not misconstrue the violence as a political statement about race relations in

British society. Instead, as a *Daily Express* cartoon depicting two young men aimlessly smoking on a street corner with the caption "Heads we go to Notting Hill, tails we go to the pictures," suggested, Wilson and ostensibly the editors of *The Times* hoped that the "sadly misnamed 'race riots'" would be viewed as a series of inchoate, reckless choices made by bored young White men flipping coins over whether they should waste an evening at the movies or journey for entertainment by causing trouble in neighborhoods like Notting Hill.[82] In this configuration, young Teds did not possess the political consciousness to contemplate the implications of participating in "race riots" even if racist ideas informed the thrill-seeking violence that they directed toward Black people.

Yet the rebellious nature of violent-prone Teddy boys was only part of the problem. In addition to a fixation on the reckless behavior of Teddy boys, inflamed by the presence of Black newcomers who threatened young White working-class men's socioeconomic positions and took sexual liberties with White women, the local communities themselves became spaces of degeneracy that served as breeding grounds for socially deviant behavior. Describing the St. Ann's community, where most of the violence occurred in Nottingham, one paper suggested that episodes of interracial violence erupted in a "squalid district" of the city "where the popular idea of a good time . . . is "beer, fish-and-chips, and a good fight on Saturday night."[83] No doubt seizing upon historical narratives about Notting Hill dating from Charles Dickens's mid-nineteenth-century depictions and resurrected in contemporary novels of the mid-1950s, including Colin MacInnes's *City of Spades,* press commentary about the Notting Hill community was even more condescending. Describing Notting Hill Gate as a neighborhood with decrepit flats, plagued with a history of street violence, and heavily populated by West Indian and Irish men and "others whose roots are not in London," a reporter for the *Manchester Guardian* concluded that the "very nature of the Notting Hill area must in part be responsible" for the violence.[84] Expressing similar sentiments about the demographics of Notting Hill, a report in *The Times* described Notting Hill as an impoverished area that had "always been tough." In characterizing the residents of the community, the article explained,

> Many of the long-established residents are of gypsy stock settled in the Dale before London filled it. They are, as they say themselves, tough, clannish people. Many of them are self-employed in the used-car trade, which has its lawless fringe. They have no love for the police; several of them have boasted to your Correspondent that "I've been in trouble with the bogies all my life." Many of the newer arrivals are Irish labourers—who work for good money on the building sites, and then many take a week off to drink their earnings.[85]

Judging from this view, one can understand that the demographics of Notting Hill made it ripe for all sorts of violence—not just racial violence—but the types of violence and social degeneracy that that could be found only amongst foreigners, criminals, shiftless workers, Teddy boys, and other outsiders on the peripheries of respectable British society. In the press, Notting Hill became more than the geographical location for racial conflict; it became a metonymy marking the undesirable spaces of urbanity within the nation—spaces that did not properly conform to the cultural norms and values of popular conceptions of a "little England."[86] In the wake of the violence, Notting Hill became the outsider within London to such an extent that one journalist found that even gauging the pulse of the community required the acquisition of a type of cultural knowledge of "the Notting Hill argot," which included supposedly locally specific lingo like "shackie," which was used to describe White girls who lived with Black men; "yobbo," a reference to a Black man known as a pimp or hustler; and "slag," a more generic term that described White women who were friendly with Black men or women.[87] Inhabiting its own world filled with foreign and rogue personalities who devised parochial dialects that needed to be decoded by reporters, clearly, the Notting Hill that emerged in the British press in the aftermath of news of "race riots" may have been in London, the metropolis of the nation, but it certainly was not London.

In defense of Notting Hill, one resident who had been born in the area suggested that in the wake of the violence, the entire public conversation in the press about the area had shifted from one about the problem of colour prejudice to a narrative "actuated by class prejudice" about the problems of the neighborhood. Describing herself as a "Government clerk, unmarried, supporting a widowed mother," the resident contended in a letter to the editor of the *Manchester Guardian* that she hardly recognized the images of Notting Hill that had come to dominate headlines. She insisted that one would glean on the basis of press reports that "we in Notting Hill are a brothel-bred rabble inhabiting leprous tenements who have no right to complain of anything." Challenging this view, she contended that the majority of Notting Hill's residents were "honest working people" whose sense of security was being threatened by the encroachment of "Jamaicans" acquiring property in the area and attempting to settle in "with their juke boxes and ragged curtains." [88] From her view, Black newcomers represented the problem that needed attention, not necessarily the White communities whose welcome had been less than inviting.

From the very outset, news of "race riots" in Nottingham and London was framed by a narrative that captured White angst about how Black newcomers would erode a sense of security within the domestic space of the neighborhood and perhaps even the home, as expressed by the unmarried White clerk from

Figure 3.2 Daily Express "Race Riot" headline, 1958. (Permission of *Daily Express*/Solo Syndication.)

Notting Hill. As news of racial fighting in Nottingham broke, the *Daily Express* ran a front-page headline, "Race Riots Terrorise a City" and accompanied the story with a photo (Figure 3.2) of "Mrs. [Mary] Lowndes" and her daughter Josephine, along with the caption "a woman is punched, then violence flares out...."[89]

Although there would be numerous stories that would eventually circulate about the origins of the street fighting, stories of married White women's proximity to violence involving Black men, including those relayed by Mrs. Mary Lowndes, who described being attacked by a "black man" without provocation as she and her husband returned home to their children, abounded in early reporting.[90] The juxtaposition of married White women, who could be imagined to embody the vulnerabilities of the sacred domestic space of the family, femininity, sexual virtue, and respectability, with the "terror" of street violence, which implicated Black men, buoyed widely held myths about the cultural threat that a largely Black male Caribbean migrant population posed to British society. Journalists covering the violence in Notting Hill and aiming to foreground local perspectives about the causes of racial tensions peppered their reporting with anecdotes describing West Indian men as pimps, sexual predators, and indolent workers who depended on the largesse of the British welfare state and exploited White women's bodies for their own immoral economic and sexual benefit.[91]

While most reporters tended to include only local White residents' opinions about the reasons behind racial tensions in the area, a reporter for the *Manchester Guardian* sought out the perspective of a "young Jamaican" who had opened a garage in Notting Hill, whose opinion projected a host of White anxieties about West Indian men in what had become known as "Brown Town." The reporter's informant explained,

> "Let's face it man. Not all West Indians are prepared to work for a living when they get here. Some of them are lazy bums who didn't fit in at home . . . I don't blame those English people for getting mad. [Pointing to a house with smashed windows] Everyone here in Brown Town knows there's three West Indian men living up there, and each one has a white girl living with him as his wife. And every one of those girls has to go out at night and work as a prostitute . . . as long as this goes on people here are going on breaking windows and I don't blame them. Why can't those no-good Jamaicans get a decent job?"[92]

No doubt providing an additional layer of credence to popular stereotypes about Black men by speaking both racially and geographically as a type of cultural insider, the Jamaican mechanic's comments reinforced popular mythologies about Black masculinity cultivated in the colonial Caribbean context that figured West Indian men as the antithesis of White bourgeois British manhood by being trifling workers, dysfunctional family men, and a dangerous and illicit sexual presence, particularly in proximity to White women. According to Marcus Collins, it was these colonial discourses of Black masculinity that were remapped onto the public imagination of West Indian men and therefore shaped the terms of their experience as newcomers in postwar Britain.[93]

The distinctions between fact and fiction about Black newcomers became the central theme of a *Daily Mirror* series, titled "Black and White," that sought to address the reasons behind the violence in Nottingham and London. Hoping to contribute to a broader public dialogue about reasons for racial conflict, Keith Waterhouse, the author of the column, designed the series to educate a White public about Black newcomers in an effort to combat the ignorance that the paper asserted "enables thugs—Fascist or otherwise[—]to foment the violence that has disgraced the name of this country throughout the world."[94] The first article in the series, which adopted the logo of a male figure with his face divided into two halves, each with images of a White and a Black man on opposite sides, featured a headline introducing the "Boys from Jamaica."

Noting that the overwhelming majority of West Indians in Britain hailed from Jamaica, Waterhouse used the island as a proxy for understanding the economic conditions that shaped Caribbean migration to Britain, including

Figure 3.3 Daily Mirror "Black and White" series image, 1958. (Mirrorpix.)

high unemployment and depressed wages in a largely agricultural labor market. Waterhouse explained that the search for jobs fueled Caribbean migration and, with little economic incentive for migrants to return to islands like Jamaica, jobs would keep West Indians in Britain.[95]

In contrast to the "Boys from Jamaica," who would most likely become a permanent fixture in British society, in introducing his audiences to "The Men Who Come Here from West Africa to Learn," Waterhouse emphasized that in West Africa, unlike in the Caribbean, there was "unlimited opportunity for a coloured man" in such nations as Nigeria and newly independent Ghana. Therefore, it should be expected that Britain was a temporary attraction for West African "men" seeking to earn professional credentials and technical skills while gaining a first-person education in British models of civil service, democratic governance, and freedom.[96] Waterhouse's overt gesture toward distinguishing between the masculinities embodied by "boys from Jamaica" and the "men from West Africa" illuminates the different ways in which nationality shaped popular mythologies about Black men. While the purveyors of anti-Black violence may have made little distinction between the bodies of Black men from Africa and those from the Caribbean, Waterhouse's column articulated the ways in which West African men could be regarded as migrants arriving in Britain for the noble purpose of seeking education and knowledge that would ultimately be used to complete British Africa's march toward responsible self-government and inclusion as an equal partner in the Commonwealth.[97] Their status as students made them British men in training and, in comparison with West Indian masculinity, which Waterhouse depicted through a narrative about labor migration and adolescence, West African men emerged <u>as a more matured example along</u> the spectrum of Black masculinities. To be sure, race precluded either category of Black men from being fully regarded as British men, particularly when their very existence was the subject of public inquiry and explanation.

As Waterhouse attempted to refute popular myths about West Indian men's criminality, their cultural difference, and their perceived sexual and socioeconomic threat to British society <u>by highlighting that increasing numbers of West Indian women were migrating to join their husbands; most Jamaicans were Christian; those with a criminal past could not migrate; and many West Indians were oftentimes acquiring accommodations that "white people would not take"</u> and jobs that employers could <u>not find White workers to fill,</u> he also showcased the variety of stigmas attached to West Indian masculinity that defined its exclusion from popular ideas about what constituted the most legitimate forms of British masculinity.[98] <u>Likewise, as he reassured White audiences that the British men in training from West Africa were merely a temporary presence,</u> in his column Waterhouse also reaffirmed a notion that African men <u>had no intention to make permanent claims of belonging in Britain</u> as British men, a theory that made their existence more palatable, even if it was not necessarily desirable.

As alluded to earlier, <u>narratives about the deviant British masculinities embodied by Black "immigrant" men and young white Teds were more than media fictions created to rationalize racial violence.</u> Perhaps more germane to understanding how the nation spoke to the world about what news of "race riots" meant and its broader political implications for measuring the nation's moral compass on issues pertaining to race and perceptions of race relations, <u>it is critical to track how officialdom appropriated discourses of deviant masculinities to extricate the nation from the violence of racism and to preserve its anti-racist veneer.</u> Hoping to influence "overseas opinion, particularly in the Commonwealth," Vincent Tewson, General Secretary of the <u>Trades Union Congress (TUC),</u> one of the most powerful lobbies of British labor interests both domestically and abroad, issued a statement on behalf of the General Council, <u>condemning what he labeled as "isolated outbreaks of vicious hooliganism [in] Nottingham and one area of London."[99] Hinting of the possibility that the violence might be attributed to Fascist agitation,</u> the official statement issued by the Congress noted, "Evidence is accumulating that elements which propagated racial hatred in Britain and Europe in pre-war days are once more fanning the flames of violence." As TUC delegates launched their annual Congress meeting during the same week that reports of violence in West London began to surface, <u>the connections that TUC delegates made between the hooliganism that had been associated with Teddy boys and Fascist organizers underscored some of the circulating conjecture illustrated</u>

in a provocative cartoon that appeared on the front page of the *Daily Mirror* during the same week of the Congress meeting that linked the London violence in particular to Fascist groups. The most visible was Oswald Mosley's Union Movement, which actively promoted a "Keep Britain White" campaign opposing Black "immigration." The cartoon reminded British audiences that nearly twenty years before, "Adolph Hitler started the Second World War," and portrayed an image of a White male figure labeled "our own racialist thugs" being enjoined by a figure dressed in Nazi military garb resembling Adolph Hitler to take the fight for ideas of "racial persecution, intolerance and prejudice" to the streets as he whispered, "Go on, boy! I may have lost that war, but my ideas seem to be winning …"[100]

Not only did TUC delegates appropriate this explanation for the violence—which essentially involved imagining racism to be a foreign social trait that had previously infiltrated British society but was nonetheless

Figure 3.4 Daily Mirror Hitler cartoon, 1958. (Mirrorpix.)

fundamentally un-British—but also the organization was careful to remind its imagined domestic and Commonwealth audiences that the Trades Union Movement in Britain had traditionally practiced British ideals of tolerance, as it "freely accepted" migrants from other countries into its ranks and remained outspoken in condemning "every manifestation of racial prejudice and discrimination in any part of the world." And just as the TUC had remained a bulwark of British values, it suggested that in the wake of the violence, local communities pursue efforts to "further tolerance" and greater understanding of the "difficult problems" facing "immigrants" adjusting to life in Britain.[101]

Just as the TUC understood that its response to the news of "race riots" would be scrutinized by global audiences, the international ramifications of the news of "race riots" also concerned high-ranking Government officials as they too attempted to weigh in on the possible causes of racial conflict and formulate working narratives to publicly account for the violence. Concerned that the violence might be "exaggerated at home or overseas," the Tory Government, issued its first public response to the violence in a statement issued by Prime Minister Harold Macmillan three days after headlines of violence in London began to circulate. The statement stressed that the most pressing issue involved "the maintenance of law and order." [102] Avoiding any specific references to the racial undertones of the Nottingham and Notting Hill violence, Macmillan statement characterized the situation as unbridled acts of lawlessness and further implied that the violence was a breach of some sort of established code of social conduct for which the Government and local authorities could and would exercise the "utmost strictness" in restoring through existing legal channels.[103] Hugh Gaitskill, leader of the opposition Labour Party, noted, "Nothing can justify the rioting and hooliganism." Gaitskell insisted, "Such behavior can only damage the reputation of our country in the world, weaken the unity of the Commonwealth, and increase racial tension without . . . solving the underlying social and economic problems."[104] Both Gaitskill and Macmillan tapped into discourses of hooliganism and vigilantism. These discourses appropriated tropes associated with the social deviance ascribed to Teddy boys to mark an imagined boundary of Britishness that encompassed an orderly society with laws intolerant of racial violence, a boundary that the White hooligans responsible for the violence had flagrantly violated.

A report on the violence in Nottingham and London compiled by Home Office officials which informed the Prime Minister's initial public response underscored this view as it outlined four key factors contributing to racial conflict in Nottingham and London. First, the report that was circulated in the national press listed White men's jealousy "because white girls are attracted to coloured men." Second, the report noted that increasing unemployment and job competition among largely "unskilled" workers "has undoubtedly increased the antagonism between white and coloured." Third, the report made reference to Teddy boys, who had been induced by "local public opinion to stir up still more trouble" for Black residents in the area already experiencing White apprehensions about their presence. Finally, the report added that in the arena of housing, "where there is overcrowding, whites sometimes become embittered because they feel that the immigrants are increasing their difficulties."[105] Ultimately, the report aimed to provide a rationale and a context for understanding the behaviors of the instigators involved in the violence who were imagined as gullible White males whose sense of sexual and economic security had been challenged by the presence of Black newcomers. However, as the Prime Minister's response suggested, the Government wanted the world to be clear that the nation's rule of law and practice of legal justice would demonstrate that the nation did not sanction the actions of these individuals and that their behaviors and attitudes offended the sensibilities of all that defined what it meant to be British. Indeed, from the perspective of these high-ranking officials, one of the most effective means of demonstrating the deviance of the White masculinities that ostensibly generated news of "race riots" was to convey that the full weight of state power had mobilized against them.

The opportunity to project this message, however, did not emanate from the national level. Instead, it came in the form of decisions by local magistrates in Nottingham and London. Although local magistrates in both cities imposed fines and prison sentences ranging from a couple of weeks to several months for Black and White defendants arrested in the street fighting, Justice Cyril Salmon's decision at the Old Bailey to sentence nine young men ranging in age from seventeen to twenty to four-year prison terms for their guilty pleas to the crimes of assault and wounding with the purpose of inflicting "grievous bodily harm" attracted the most media attention.[106] As courtroom spectators reportedly gasped in shock and mothers of the defendants shed tears of disbelief, Salmon spoke on behalf of the interest of the nation to a broader audience vested in how Britons would confront the violence. Recalling the crimes for which the defendants had pled guilty, Salmon reminded them that "[you stand] convicted on your own confessions of a series of extremely grave and brutal crimes" that included attacking "five peaceful, law-abiding citizens without any shadow of an excuse" other than that "their skin happened to be of a colour of which you apparently did not approve." In a striking admonishment, which would be quoted extensively by British and international news outlets, Salmon charged,

It was you men who started the whole of this violence in Notting Hill. You are a minute and insignificant section of the population who have brought shame upon the district in which you live, and have filled the whole nation with horror, indignation, and disgust.... Everyone, irrespective of the colour of their skin, is entitled to walk through the streets in peace, with their heads erect, and free from fear. That is a right which these courts will always unfailingly uphold.... As far as the law is concerned you are entitled to think what you like, however foul your thoughts; to feel what you like, however brutal and debased your emotions; to say what you like providing you do not infringe on the rights of others or imperil the Queen's peace, but once you translate your dark thoughts and brutal feelings into savage acts such as these the law will be swift to punish you, the guilty and to protect your victims."[107]

Salmon's remarks were clearly crafted to capture the umbrage of the nation toward the White culprits who had been found guilty of exacting racial terror on the streets of London. But Salmon was careful not to implicate the nation as a context for fomenting the ideologies that informed the "dark thoughts and brutal feelings" that incited violence against Black people. While the actions of the individual defendants had torn at the moral fibers of the nation, Salmon's firm sentence offered a type of reminder that the justice of the nation was intolerant of this behavior and would rise to protect the eroded rights of those who fell victim to the violence of racist bigots. In this scenario, racists stood trial for a type of anti-Black racism that was seared into the hearts and minds of a small White few and not embedded in the structure of a nation whose racialized imperial history had wedded Whiteness to the most privileged forms of British national identity.

On the same day that British news outlets printed the magistrate's remarks, a reprint also appeared in the *Trinidad Guardian*, along with the following editorial commentary:

The Judge's action should go far in helping not only to nip in the bud the burgeonings of further racial troubles . . . but [also] in restoring to coloured people in Britain a sense of being under the shelter of the great rock of British justice, which has stood the test of time."[108]

Two days later, the *Trinidad Guardian* carried an editorial by James Nestor noting that the four-year prison terms issued to the "English hooligans" responsible for attacking Black men in Notting Hill had restored Trinidadians' "faith in the British Government and "in one breath shown to the world that British justice still remains the highest achievement of man." Nestor maintained that the triumph of "British Justice" should offer an example to Britain's "American cousins."

Citing the looming injustices of American racial politics most recently high-lighted in the international coverage of Jimmy Wilson's death sentence for steal-ing less than two dollars from a White women, a conviction that was upheld by the Alabama Supreme Court just days before Justice Salmon rendered his deci-sion at the Old Bailey, Nestor reinstated Britain's position as a morally superior foil to Jim Crow America as he queried, "Could the Americans rise above their sordiness [sic] of Jimmy Wilson and Little Rock? Can they really redeem them-selves and enforce justice as impartially as the English?"[109]

According to British diplomats, Justice Salmon's decision also played well to both German and French audiences as part of a redemptive story about what the violence said about the nation. British diplomats in Germany noted that overall in the German press, "the sharp sentences passed at Old Bailey on white youths who beat up coloured people have received wide approval," adding that this "attitude contrasts with German criticism of [the] latest devel-opment at Little Rock."[110] Similar to the view in Germany, British officials in France suggested, "The bad impression made by these 'riots' has since been to some extent corrected by the severity of the sentence passed on four of the ringleaders."[111] These sorts of remarks suggested that international observers bought into British interpretations that the violence was the result of a breach of law and order instigated by reckless youth rather than any pervasive exist-ence of racism or widespread hostility toward Black people. Moreover, these comments highlight that the punishments meted out by the British legal sys-tem to the perpetrators and the restoration of public order in the aftermath of the violence served as means of redeeming the tarnished image of race and nation in Britain.

While both liberal and conservative wings of officialdom appropriated nar-ratives problematizing acts of "hooliganism" committed by Teddy boys bred in urban working-class communities—acts that could best be resolved through the punishments meted out through a legal system that was seemingly intol-erant of the injustice of racial violence—for those who chose to concentrate blame largely on Black male West Indian "immigrants" whose presence incited the ire of the likes of Teddy boys and other White locals who perceived them as a social threat, the solution to this problem centered upon controlling and curbing West Indians' right to migrate to Britain. In a telegram dispatched to all Commonwealth governments, including colonial territories, sent just one day after news reports began to circulate pertaining to racial violence in Nottingham, an official of the Commonwealth Relations Office noted,

> While police reports make it clear that coloured persons involved in last Saturday's rioting in Nottingham were almost exclusively West Indian, press comment here tends to see this incident in round terms

of coloured versus white. Publicity, is moreover, bound to lead to further pressure for some form of immigration control.[112]

As the violence spread to London, debate over migration restrictions became firmly implanted in public discussions concerning the incidents of racial discrimination. Just two days after the fighting began in Nottingham, J. K. Cordeaux, a Conservative MP for Nottingham Central, linked the conflict to Britain's open-door Commonwealth migration policy that had in recent years facilitated the growth of an unprecedented Black population in Britain.[113] Cordeaux's Parliamentary colleague and fellow party member, Norman Panell of Liverpool, agreed with Cordeaux's logic and maintained, "The Nottingham fighting is a manifestation of the evil results of the present [migration] policy." Panell reasoned that "unless some restriction is imposed we shall create the colour bar we all want to avoid."[114] Cyril Osborne, Conservative MP for Louth, proposed a one-year moratorium on all Commonwealth migration except in the case of *"bona fide* students," imploring that the Nottingham violence should serve as "a red light to all of us." According to Osborne, the alternative would be devastating to race relations in Britain. Referencing US racial tensions, he insisted, "It will be black against white. We are sowing the seeds of another 'Little Rock' and it is tragic."[115]

When British Prime Minister Harold Macmillan issued his first public statement on the incidents of violence in Nottingham and Notting Hill, although he emphasized that the events represented a breach of law and order requiring "the utmost strictness" by law-enforcing agents, he also noted that the Government had "for some little time" been examining the impact of "the country's time-honoured practice to allow free entry" to those migrating from Commonwealth territories. Macmillan pointed out that the Government would not make any hasty decision regarding a major policy change on the subject of Commonwealth migration without "careful consideration of the problem as a whole." But the timing of his comments drew clear connections between racial tensions and the effects of Commonwealth migration.[116] In fact, the subject of Commonwealth migration controls had been actively pursued in various Government departments as early as 1952, when the Ministry of Labour established a commission on the Employment of Coloured People in the United Kingdom to study and collect data pertaining to "coloured immigration," a study that was later used in Cabinet discussions resulting in a draft immigration restrictions bill in 1955.[117] Racial violence breathed new life into this long-discussed agenda and, perhaps more importantly, it provided a more volatile and receptive public climate to test the case for restricting Commonwealth migration—in this instance, as a means of addressing racial tensions and quelling the spread of interracial conflict.

What dominated public debate on the question of migration controls in the wake of the Nottingham and Notting Hill violence was the unavoidable racial undertones that any form of restriction might convey and the larger implications concerning the concept of British citizenship. In an editorial appearing in *The Times*, T. E. M McKitterick summarized this issue in an appeal against the introduction of migration controls. McKitterick concluded that any form of Commonwealth migration restriction "would be a breach in the basic principles behind the phrase 'citizen' of the United Kingdom and Colonies.'" He further added that "it would inevitably lead to colour discrimination and the creation of two classes of citizenship."[118] McKitterick's remarks captured one of the major subjects framing current historical debate over race, citizenship, and migration in postwar Britain. As McKitterick rightly surmised, migration, under the terms of the British Nationality Act of 1948, became an institutionalized right of British citizenship that extended to all nationals of Commonwealth territories. Therefore, the introduction of Commonwealth migration restrictions inherently dismantled the egalitarian principles buttressing the ideal of a transracial, transnational British citizenship by excluding certain categories of Commonwealth nationals from enjoying the migration privileges attached to their British citizenship.

Suggesting that curbing a largely Afro-Caribbean Commonwealth migration might remedy racial conflict represented yet another discursive medium to preserve the mystique of British anti-racism. Reducing the social dilemmas of race and race relations in British society to a problem of migration and the presence of racialized "immigrant" bodies presented an ahistorical narrative implying that racism and racial conflict had no place historically or structurally in British society until the advent of large-scale Caribbean migration and the growth of more visible Black communities in the postwar period. This narrative ignored the long history of negative racial stereotypes about Black colonials circulating in metropolitan culture historically and the history of racial conflict in cities such as Cardiff, Liverpool, and Birmingham during the early twentieth century and in the years immediately following World War II.[119] Moreover, this assumption relied on the notion that Caribbean migrants by virtue of their very presence alone prompted and exacerbated racial conflict and virtually exonerated the nation as a whole from addressing its own history of racial prejudices, stereotypes, stigmas, exclusionary practices, and anti-Black violence.

In the days after the dust began to settle in the wake of mass violence in London, West Indian officials continued to make rounds in the various West Indian enclaves in London. Before launching his tour of Brixton, Jamaican

Premier Norman Manley commented, "I am satisfied the great majority of the English people are not against West Indians, only a narrow section of the community. No doubt this is agitated by the 'Keep Britain White' Fascist movement." Manley's remarks suggested that he agreed with White British assessments that the violence was indeed the result of an aberrant section of society influenced by extremist propaganda rather than an endemic social problem.[120] Hugh Cummins, the Premier of Barbados, echoed Manley's position on the causes of the violence. Cummins noted, "We feel that the trouble is the result of gangster-type Teddy boys and probably Fascism. . . . We feel that the average Englishman doesn't explode into intense racial feeling."[121] Manley and Cummins's comments suggest that the rationales for the violence offered by mainstream media outlets and British officials about the causes of the violence held sway among influential international observers. But in many ways these narratives about the virtues of metropolitan culture were not new. They were familiar in that they made it possible to separate socially deviant violent White racists from respectable Englishmen who were thought to embody the highest ideals of Britishness, including the mystique of British antiracism. But news of "race riots" did leave an unsavory residue. And it is clear that the images of race and race relations in Britain that emerged in the aftermath of violent racial conflict between Black and White residents on the streets of Nottingham and Notting Hill in London did much to challenge widely held perceptions of British racial liberalism and tolerance. News of "race riots" put White Britons on the defensive. These news stories contradicted the mystique of British anti-racism that informed the ways that White Britons viewed themselves, their relationship to the Commonwealth, and Britain's image in international politics. Less than one year after news of "race riots" occasioned White Britons to take an introspective examination to account for images of race relations that countered the mystique of British anti-racism, another instance of racial violence, the murder of Kelso Cochrane, would create a moment when visions of Britishness, race, and nation were fractured, contested, and reconfigured—this time through the grassroots political activism of Black Britons.

4

Are We to Be Mauled Down Just Because We are Black?

On 6 June 1959, over a thousand mourners gathered in Ladbroke Grove in London to pay their final respects to thirty-two year old Antiguan-born Kelso Benjamin Cochrane. One local newspaper remarked that although the Prime Minister of the West Indies Federation, the High Commissioner of Ghana, and the Mayor of Kensington took part in the interment, which displayed a casket adorned with a wreath "From the Martyrs and Victims of Oppression" in Nyasaland, sympathy messages from the People's National Party in Trinidad, and condolences from the Liberian Government, Cochrane's "only claim to national fame was that he became the murder victim of a gang of white boys."[1] Three weeks earlier around 10:30 p.m. on the evening of 16 May 1959, Kelso Cochrane informed his fiancée, Olivia Ellington, a nurse trainee from Jamaica, that he planned to go to Paddington General Hospital to seek treatment for a severe pain in his thumb caused by a minor work injury. While Olivia Ellington assumed that the man that she was set to wed would surely not be gone for long, hours later she received a call from local police informing her that her groom-to-be was dead.[2]

Before his death, many of the details of Kelso Cochrane's life would have seemed quite unexceptional to many working-class Caribbean migrants in Britain. Born in Johnson's Point, Antigua on 26 September 1926 to Johanna Valentine and Stanley Cochrane, from whom he learned his trade as a carpenter, Kelso Cochrane arrived in England in 1954 with plans to eventually pursue a career in law. Like many Caribbean migrants of his generation, Cochrane viewed emigration as a means to obtain economic opportunity and routes to social mobility unavailable in his homeland during the early twentieth century. In 1945 Cochrane moved to Dominica, where he remained for three years before deciding to return to Antigua and setting his sights on making the journey to America, the destination that proved to be most attractive to Afro-Caribbean migrants before stringent immigration controls instituting restrictive quotas were introduced under the McCarran-Walter Act in 1952. Less than a year after his return to Antigua in 1949, Cochrane moved to the United States, where he began working in Florida on an agricultural labor contract. Shortly thereafter, he married Kansas Green, with whom he had a daughter, Josephine, before moving to New York. Establishing himself in New York proved difficult for Kelso Cochrane. In 1954, as he witnessed the dissolution of his marriage, he faced deportation orders because of his expired visa. Cochrane spent less than six months back in Antigua before deciding to cast his fortunes in England, where he arrived by ship in September 1954. Although he had intended that his stay in England would be temporary—even petitioning to return to the United States in 1956—after meeting Olivia Ellington, a nursing student from Jamaica, Kelso Cochrane most likely desired to make England a more permanent home.[3]

Kelso Cochrane's transatlantic journey to London by way of the Caribbean and America would have been quite unremarkable to many of his West Indian compatriots in the city and throughout the British Isles during the postwar era, who came in search of jobs with dreams of building a better life for themselves and their families. In death, however, he embodied an existence that stirred the hearts and minds of London's Black communities in such a way that prompted an international outpouring of sympathy and a national dialogue about race, rights, and citizenship in postwar Britain. According to Joy Okine, a twenty-one year old White woman who was one of the few witnesses Cochrane's the murder, shortly before 1 a.m. on 17 May 1959 she heard loud banging followed by the voice of someone in a group of what appeared to be five or six young White men shouting words that resembled the phrase, "Hey Jim Crow." Minutes later, Okine watched in horror as the group of men attacked a lone Kelso Cochrane from behind in a brief scuffle that ended only after he fell to the ground with a single stab wound to the chest. With the aid of two bystanders, Cochrane made it alive to St. Charles's Hospital, where he reportedly uttered to the two Samaritans who came to his assistance, "They asked me for money. I told them I had none," shortly before he was pronounced dead.[4]

While Scotland Yard officials offered Cochrane's purported dying declaration and an empty wallet found tucked away in one of his jacket pockets as proof that the circumstances surrounding his death had "absolutely nothing to do with racial conflict," but rather were more likely motivated by robbery, many Black Britons had a starkly different view.[5] For many Black Britons, in the early-morning hours of his death, Kelso Cochrane became a more intimate nomenclature for a cycle of violence against Black bodies, a cycle that had only become publicly perceptible with the breaking news of "race riots" less than one year earlier. In the weeks and months following the news-making violence in Nottingham and London, political organizing in defense of the interests of Black communities became more pronounced as activists, including Amy Ashwood Garvey, who had long been entrenched in struggles to address Britain's anti-Black "colour problem," joined forces with more recent newcomers like Claudia Jones, editor of the *West Indian Gazette and Afro-Asian Caribbean News*, a fledgling grassroots periodical founded in March 1958 that ultimately became the voice of an emergent Black British political consciousness during the late 1950s and early 1960s. [6]

On the day following Cochrane's murder, Alao Bashorn of the London-based Committee of African Organizations (CAO) and representatives of various African and West Indian organizations, including staff at Jones's *West Indian Gazette*, met and drafted an open letter to British Prime Minster Harold Macmillan addressing what they believed to be the inherent racial overtones of the murder. Drawing a clear connection between the violence that was associated with the summer of 1958 and the murder of Kelso Cochrane that extended well beyond their geographical proximities, the letter to the Prime Minister admonished, "Hardly the ink has dried on the screaming headlines in the national press about the racist disgrace of Nottingham and Notting Hill Gate of last August, [and yet] another heinous crime has been committed." While the police saw Cochrane's murder as a robbery gone awry, the organizations insisted that there was compelling "evidence" indicating that "Kelso Cochrane was murdered because he was coloured."[7] Invoking the extant iconography of Jim Crow America as an analog rather than a counterpoint to pinpoint the fallacies of the mystique of British anti-racism, the organizations declared in an adjunct statement issued to the press that the Cochrane murder "rivals what we have seen or heard in Little Rock or the recent lynching of Mr. M.C. Parker of Poplarville, Mississippi."[8] In their petition to the Prime Minister, the organizations urged that Government officials publicly "condemn" the murder as "a sign that at topmost levels, the rights of Commonwealth citizens, irrespective of colour are held sacred." Moreover, they revealed that an official response was especially warranted because "Africans and West Indians are bitter over the murder of one who, but for the Grace of God, might have been any one of us," leaving many wondering, "Are we to be mauled down just because we are black?"[9]

This chapter examines the politicization of Kelso Cochrane's murder and traces the processes through which his Black body in death became a site of advocacy that Black Britons employed to articulate the perils and promise of their citizenship status and the dilemmas of Blackness in postwar Britain. Mobilizing powerful symbols of the ways in which state authority was complicit in the disenfranchisement of African American students in Little Rock, Arkansas and the death of Mack Charles Parker, who was kidnapped and murdered while awaiting trial in a Mississippi jail just weeks before Cochrane's death, the CAO's letter to the Prime Minister set in motion a narrative about how Black Britons imagined what the death of a "quiet and pleasant" carpenter revealed about relationship between state power, violence against Black bodies, and the entitlements of citizenship.[10] In the weeks following Cochrane's murder, grassroots activists waged a political campaign that included exchanges with public officials, organized protests, community petitioning, and the orchestration of a high-profile funeral, all of which aimed to reframe the public consciousness about what was commonly described as "the colour problem," associated with postwar Caribbean migration.

Whereas newsworthy narratives of the "race riots" of 1958 prominently featured the trope of imperiled Black male bodies being injured and threatened by White "hooligans" to explain the various manifestations of the "colour problem," as noted previously, they did so in part within the context of producing a narrative about race relations and Britishness that tethered this perceived "problem" to a series of myths about Black masculinities rooted in racialized colonial discourses of hypersexuality, degeneracy, (dis)respectability, and criminality. Kelso Cochrane's death provided Black Britons with an opportunity to retool the injured Black body as a grievable subject and citizen in such a way that recalibrated the parameters of public debate over the dimensions of *Britons'* "colour problem." When Black Britons posed the question, "Are we to be mauled down just because we are black?" they transformed the terms of engagement over the "colour problem" most importantly by articulating the existence of Black British subjects, who could speak on their own terms about the politics of race and Blackness in postwar Britain as a lived experience and as a broader social dilemma of citizenship and belonging that all Britons had a particular stake in interrogating and remedying. To be sure, by deploying Kelso Cochrane's murder as the embodiment of the problem of racism and the condition of race and, more specifically, Blackness in Britain, Black activists and supporters of a burgeoning postwar Black British grassroots anti-racist movement transmogrified the public trope of the injured Black body from one of abject "immigrant" denizen into that of disenfranchised citizen.

Mobilizing at the Grassroots Roots

Part of understanding the process in which Kelso Cochrane's death registered as a political event requires considering how the highly publicized episodes of violence in Nottingham and London during the summer of 1958 began to resurrect and reorient grassroots activism among Black Londoners. In the wake of the violence, leftist organizations concerned with race relations and interest groups run by Black Britons channeled their focus towards race work as a social welfare issue with political implications. In the days and weeks immediately following the climax of violence in West London, members of the Kensington Communist League rallied Black and White residents in Notting Hill for an "anti-colour bar demonstration," at which protestors walked the streets with signs displaying messages such as "No Little Rock Here" and "There's Only One Race, The Human Race" that promoted interracial harmony.[11] Two weeks later, Labour MP Fenner Brockway, Chairman of the Movement for Colonial Freedom, one of the leading anti-colonial lobbies in Britain, helped to organize a "Mass Demonstration of Inter-Racial Friendship" in Trafalgar Square to protest attacks on people of color in Nottingham and London.[12] During visits to West London by representatives from the West Indies Federal Government, Brockway joined Jamaican Premier Norman Manley and David Pitt, a local West Indian doctor vying for a seat in Parliament, in headlining a rally at St. Pancras Town Hall, organized by the London branch of the Trinidadian-based People's National Movement, Claudia Jones's *West Indian Gazette*, the West Indian Students' Union, and an organization founded by Amy Ashwood Garvey that was known as the Association for the Advancement of Coloured People (AACP) which took its namesake from one of the most prominent US civil rights organizations.[13]

Given that the Mayor of Kensington selected Amy Ashwood Garvey as a representative for Black residents on a new committee tasked to address race relations in the borough following the eruption of violence in West London during the summer of 1958, it is clear that she maintained a significant degree of local political capital accrued through a long history of activism in Britain.[14] However, one of the first major undertakings of Garvey's Association in the aftermath of the violence entailed creating a legal defense fund to assist Black defendants sentenced with fines from charges stemming from the clashes in Nottingham and London. The establishment of the defense fund brought together a host of key organizations and activists that would shape the course of Black politics in Britain throughout the late 1950s and 1960s.[15] Alongside Amy Ashwood Garvey, David Pitt also served on the AACP's executive as first Vice-Chairman, along with Fenner Brockway, who served as second Vice-Chairman. Beyond lobbying on behalf of the fund among members of the Movement for Colonial Freedom, Brockway also solicited support from the Parliamentary caucus of the British Caribbean Association, a newly formed group hoping to foster interracial cooperation and promote public policy beneficial to Caribbean peoples.[16]

Pitt and Brockway brought a type of official political legitimacy to the work of the AACP. However, Claudia Jones, who served as General Secretary of the Association, was one of Garvey's most important co-collaborators. Their ties ran deep. Not only did they both embrace an internationalist and diasporic perspective on Black liberation and the vestiges of White supremacy, but they also envisioned Black women workers, organizers, and intellectuals including themselves as central to the quest for radical social transformation. Although many of her contemporaries, including George Padmore, foregrounded the inextricable ties between White supremacy, imperialism, fascism, and the exploitation of the working classes, Jones embodied an intellectual trajectory that positioned Black women and their (re)productive labor at the center of liberatory possibilities that could radically reconfigure the citizenship status of Black and Brown people, women, colonial subjects, and unpropertied workers across racial lines, beholden to a global system of capitalist economic relations. Pushing the boundaries of dominant leftist, Black nationalist, and White and Black bourgeoise feminist thought during the first half of the twentieth century, in an essay titled, "An End to the Neglect of the Problems of Negro Women" published in the CPUSA's *Political Affairs,* Jones insisted that the experiences of Black women workers provided a particularly rich intellectual space to imagine and mobilize a broad and radically democratic politics of liberation as she explained,

> The Negro woman, who combines in her status the worker, the Negro and the woman, is the vital link to this heightened political consciousness. To the extent, further that the cause of the Negro woman worker is promoted, she will be enabled to take her rightful place in the Negro-proletarian leadership of the national liberation movement, and by her active participation contribute to the entire American working class, whose historic mission is the achievement of a Socialist America—the final and full guarantee of women's emancipation. [17]

Just as this vision of Black women's place in social-movement building had guided her work in anti-racist, leftist, and internationalist politics during her time in the United States, when she arrived in Britain as an American deportee on a British passport acquired through her status as a Trinidadian national with rights as a citizen of the United Kingdom and Colonies in December of 1955, the same vision continued to shape her activism in Britain's Black communities.

During her time in the United States, the Communist Party functioned as the central outlet of Jones's activist work. In Britain, however, the focal point of her political work remained the *West Indian Gazette,* which she established in March 1958 and to which she invited Amy Ashwood Garvey to contribute articles and serve on the editorial board. Jones launched the *West Indian Gazette,* one of the earliest Black newspapers with a mass appeal, during the postwar era in the tradition of earlier London-based Black internationalist periodicals, including Duse Mohamed Ali's *African Times and Orient Review*, George Padmore's *International African Opinion*, and *The Keys*, the organ of Harold Moody's League of Coloured People, all of which to varying degrees championed anti-colonialist and anti-racist causes in Britain and around the world. Carrying forth this legacy of diasporic activism through print media, in its early years the paper addressed transnational causes such as support for the burgeoning West Indies Federation and the civil rights campaigns of Black Americans. Moreover, as Jones envisioned the paper as a conduit for the formation of distinctly Black British identifications and communities that would be born through and between groups of people of African and later Asian descent with varying racial, ethnic, and national loyalties and affinities, the *West Indian Gazette* featured articles, editorials, literary supplements, and advertisements appealing to the cultural and social interests of a largely Afro-Caribbean Black community in Britain. At the same time, it provided a political space of transnational dialogue between West Indians, Africans, and primarily South Asians about the specific conditions of race and racism in Britain.[18] In the wake of the 1958 violence in Notting Hill, Jones and her editorial team spearheaded the planning of the first Caribbean carnival in January 1959 held at St. Pancras Town Hall, where Jones designated part of the proceeds to the AACP's efforts to build a legal fund for Black defendants in London.[19]

Figure 4.1 Limbo Dancers at Notting Hill Carnival, 1960. By permission of Donald Hinds, courtesy of the Lambeth Archives, Landmark Ref# 20304.

Bringing to Britain the Trinidadian tradition of carnival, a cultural institution that had historically challenged the machinations of colonial authority in the Caribbean, was an explicitly political act for Jones, who famously wrote "a people's art is the genesis of their freedom."[20] The costumes, dancing, singing, artistry, steel bands, and contests celebrating Black women's beauty provided an opportunity for West Indians to share in a common assertion of pride in their Caribbean heritage and express their intent to belong as Black Britons on their own terms by creating a social and cultural medium to, in Jones's words, "transplant our folk origins to Britain."[21]

Beyond the members of the AACP's executive council, the legal fund also drew supporters from student organizations such as the West Indian Students' Union and those which had recently formed the Committee of African Organisations (CAO), a politically oriented alliance of predominately African student groups. In the weeks following the Notting Hill violence, CAO Chairman Alao Bashorun solicited support from the Labour Party and the Trades Union Congress to sponsor a campaign to educate the public on racial prejudice. Likewise, the Committee urged that Government address routine racial discrimination occurring in employment and housing and prohibit extremist groups such as the Union Movement and a homegrown British front of the Ku Klux Klan, which had recently grabbed headlines after sending a threatening message to Claudia Jones at the *West Indian Gazette* offices on letterhead containing the slogan "Keep Britain pure and white" signed by "A. Whiteman" just days before news of violence in Nottingham.[22]

Given that the CAO had already begun to flex its activist muscles by advocating against anti-Black violence and petitioning the state for redress following the summer of 1958, from the very outset of learning about the circumstances of Kelso Cochrane's death, members of the Committee were well aware of the political implications of his murder. Not only did his death speak to a particular reality of anti-Black violence, but it also conveyed an alarming message about the positions of marginality that Black Commonwealth citizens occupied in British society. This was a message that Black activists and their supporters were determined to force British officials to reckon with as they formulated a response to the violence. For many, much like the news of "race riots" less than one year earlier, the political subtext surrounding what they deemed to be a racially motivated murder challenged the liberal ideals that the nation stood for in the world, and their calls for justice sought to mobilize the mystique of British anti-racism as an unrealized promise rather than a collection of elusive myths used to maintain the status quo.

In their letter to the Prime Minister on the day after Kelso Cochrane's murder, several of the organizations that had banded with the CAO to support the defense fund for Black defendants, namely, the AACP, the West Indian

Student Union, and the *West Indian Gazette*, joined groups that included the Afro-Asian West Indian Student Union and the Uganda Association to draw clear links between Cochrane's death, the growth of unregulated anti-Black organizing, deficient and discriminatory policing practices, and the absence of legal recourse to address racial discrimination and incitement. By framing the stakes of the murder in these terms, these organizations aimed to demonstrate that attaining justice for Cochrane would involve more than an official display of righteous indignation or a search for the "gang of white youths" who had committed the crime.[23] Rather, Black British activists understood that Cochrane's murder was indicative of a systematic failure of the state, and ostensibly the nation, to protect and defend the rights of its Black citizens. As their letter to the Prime Minister carefully explained, Black Britons believed that if the British Government was indeed "serious about its professions of a multiracial Commonwealth of equal peoples," ensuring that the state would mobilize its power to prohibit racial discrimination, limit the public display of racially incendiary rhetoric, and encourage adequate and unbiased policing practices to protect the lives of all citizens from the threat of violence as they walked the streets of their neighborhoods and communities was just as important as bringing justice to Kelso Cochrane's killers.[24]

Two days after the CAO met to draft an open letter of protest following Cochrane's murder, the group convened to discuss further steps that should be taken to organize and advocate around the platform of racial justice that had been outlined in their letter to the Prime Minister. Part of a legacy of activism among West African students in Britain begun with the founding of the Nigerian Progress Union in 1925, the CAO operated as an umbrella organization for several social and political interests groups in the wake of the murder, including anti-apartheid coalitions.[25] One of the first orders of business involved discussions of how to streamline the work of the organization on behalf of the politics surrounding Cochrane's murder and navigate the tenuous line between public and private. While the organizers viewed the circumstances of Cochrane's death as a political marker symbolic of the racial conditions that threatened the lives of all Black Britons, Cochrane was also a man who would be mourned and missed by an intimate community of family and friends. However, Cochrane was no political figure. As Black activists considered the political stakes of his death, they were undoubtedly reminded that his public appeal rested on his ability to remain a figure embodying the respectable yet ordinary working man, who could be any person's son, brother, groom, or co-worker even across the racial divide.

As a means of resolving this issue representatives from the various organizations affiliated with the CAO, including Claudia Jones, Amy Ashwood Garvey, and Frances Ezzrecco, who had also recently launched a West London–based social welfare organization known as the Coloured People's Progressive Association (CPPA) in the aftermath of the Notting Hill violence of 1958, agreed to form a burial committee, which took on the responsibility of assisting Kelso Cochrane's family with funeral arrangements. Even though David Pitt, the Grenadian physician who was standing as a Labor Party candidate for Hampstead, raised objections about turning the family's private memorial into a political event—insisting that "the whole object of obtaining public sympathy would be destroyed" if the funeral became politicized—the newly formed burial committee, which became known as the Inter-Racial Friendship Coordinating Council (IRFCC), proceeded to help plan and raise funds to defray the cost of funeral services for Cochrane's family.[26] While the extent to which IRFCC personalities determined the actual staging of this affair is unknown, it is clear that Cochrane's funeral, held some three weeks after his death, represented a climactic moment encapsulating the ways in which a ceremony marking the personal loss of a single family became a commemoration of a public tragedy that encompassed the collective struggles, fears, hopes and regrets of entire communities. Thus it is important to consider how the IRFCC capitalized on the critical period between Cochrane's murder and his entombment to create and mobilize a public narrative about his life, the circumstances of his death and the meaning of his injured Black body that endeared him to a local community, to a nation and to Black people in Britain and beyond. To be sure, this public narrative rested upon the IRFCC's ability to reframe popular discourses of Black masculinity and implicate the state as a progenitor of racial violence.

The State of Racial Violence in Postwar Britain

Following a flurry of leads from the few eyewitnesses to Kelso Cochrane's murder, including Joy Okine, a young White woman who witnessed the attack as she looked out the window of her flat, and George Isaacs, the taxi driver who took Cochrane to St. Charles Hospital where he died following the stabbing, the early police investigations of Cochrane's murder centered upon two young White men, John Breagan and Patrick Digby, both of whom lived in the neighborhood where the stabbing took place. Within forty-eight hours of the murder, for nearly two days police held the two men for questioning after witnesses reported seeing them at a party near the scene of the murder. According to John Breagan, both men saw Cochrane's dying in the street on the evening of the attack, but neither admitted to knowing anything about the murder. Ultimately, as a conspiracy of silence enveloped the Notting Hill community and in the absence of a successful search for the murder weapon, without a confession, the police were unable to charge Breagan or Digby and did not publicly focus their attention on any other suspects.[27] Although police continued to publicly stick to their theory that Cochrane's race did not contribute to his death and that it was his "bespectacled" appearance and plastered left hand that made his attackers view him as "easy prey" as they trolled for money after a night of partying, in the days immediately following the murder a West London paper noted the growing local sentiment that even if robbery had been motive for murder, Cochrane's death underscored the reality that "the law has failed in its duty to protect the coloured man."[28] For Black British activists and organizers, this was cause for political action.

Less than one week after the Committee of African Organization's open letter of grievance reached the office of the Prime Minister, members of the IRFCC arranged for a deputation to meet with Home Office officials on 27 May 1959. In a memorandum issued to Home Secretary R. A. Butler in his absence, IRFCC representatives explained that their purpose in meeting with Home Office officials was to discuss steps that the Government might take to address, the "serious situation of insecurity facing the coloured minorities in London, particularly in the Notting Hill area, as well as the obvious weaknesses in the law-enforcing authorities to curb racist propaganda which," according to the IRFCC, "resulted in the murder . . . of Kelso Benjamin Cochrane." The memo highlighted the increasing influence of organized racist campaigns in the area, including the White Defence League, the Union Movement, and the Ku Klux Klan, and suggested that police apathy toward the potential of these groups to prompt violent encounters along racial lines has generated a "loss of confidence" in local authorities' ability to adequately provide protection for Black citizens "in the face of organised attempts to stir up race hatred." According to the IRFCC, all these factors had culminated in "a situation in which ordinary citizens of all races cannot walk the streets without fear of being involved in disturbances."[29]

It is important to note that throughout the memo, the IRFCC consistently invoked the language of citizenship as a means to frame the problem of racial violence and, more importantly, as a vehicle to demand Government action. In particular, the organization drew attention to the ways in which escalating racial conflict coupled with inadequate police protection had effectively eroded Black Britons' citizenship right to a sense of security. While official explanations of the eruption of racial conflict in British cities less than a year earlier had attributed the violence to the reckless activities of young White men, in their protests to Home Office officials, Black activists cited insufficient police patrols in areas with significant Black populations and "police bias" as contributing factors in the creation of a "situation of lawlessness," which had resulted in "a growing lack of confidence by all citizens in the law enforcing agencies." As a possible remedy for this increasingly disconcerting state of affairs, IRFCC officials suggested that the Government urge local authorities to increase the number of constables assigned to patrol "troubled areas" like Notting Hill and support the introduction of "special constables" comprising "responsible citizens *of all races*" to assist the regular patrols. For these activists, taking a proactive role in policing their communities was not meant to be a call for vigilante action; rather, the council affirmed their belief that it was their "right and our duty as citizens to demand that such duty [adequate policing] should be fulfilled, and to offer assistance if we feel that the safety of citizens demands it."[30]

To demonstrate the growing cadre of local support for the IRFCC's antiracist political campaign, along with the memorandum, the IRFCC submitted a petition to the Home Secretary that had been circulated by members of the CAO. Echoing many of the sentiments expressed in the IRFCC memo, the petitioners noted that what they considered to be the "race-murder" done "in cold blood of young Kelso Cochrane" had occasioned the need for the British Government to take immediate action to protect "our persons, property and rights . . . from violence." Moreover, they requested that "if the authorities are unable to do so with existing resources, that citizens such as ourselves be given authority as special constables to protect ourselves and our community."[31] By translating the problem of racial violence as an infringement on the basic rights of protection and security due to all British citizens, the IRFCC challenged the notion that issues of race were simply matters of interpersonal relations beyond the purview of official regulation. Whereas explanations of the "colour problem" in the wake of the previous year's "race riots" described racial tensions as a product of competition between deviant British masculinities battling over sexual and economic resources, including White women, housing, and jobs, the IRFCC sought to change the terms of the debate over the nature of the "colour problem" in such a way that moved past the personalities directly involved in street violence to engender a broader public dialogue about the politics of race and governmentality. From their view, racial violence was the manifestation of a "colour problem" that could not be rationalized through indictments of Teddy boys, urban decay, or the physical presence of "immigrant" Black men. Instead, IRFCC activists took a structural view of both the "colour problem" and ways of remedying its effects, all predicated on an understanding that Black Britons had the right to fully belong and participate in British society as citizens, and Government had a responsibility, and indeed an obligation, to address any potential impediment that race might pose as they sought to secure and exercise those rights.

The deputation recommended that in addition to expanding patrol units in certain areas with consistent patterns of racial violence, Government officials appoint a Select Committee to collect evidence "from residents of all races" in areas with "an immediate problem of racial tension," including Notting Hill, to make more informative assessments of local issues shaping racial conflict. Moreover, the Committee urged that officials support a bill criminalizing racial discrimination and propaganda and other activities that might incite racial conflict.[32] In appealing to the sentiments of Government officials, the IRFCC understood that racial violence undermined narratives about the nation that buttressed the mystique of British anti-racism at a particularly critical historical juncture when British officials would be invested in defending and preserving the mystique to maintain a sense of national legitimacy both in the Commonwealth and beyond. As their memo reminded Home Office officials that "the eyes of the world are on Notting Hill and the good name of Britain as a democratic nation," Black activists also issued a veiled warning that Government inaction would not only exacerbate racial tensions but, perhaps more important to officials, also weaken the nation's tenuous position as a global power.[33]

A survey of media coverage of the meeting between IRFCC members and Home Office officials does not reveal all of the names of the deputation; however, it is important to underscore the participation of those whose attendance did make news and speculate on the input of others who may have been a part of the group and or key figures in shaping the IRFCC's platform and agenda at the time. Published reports on the IRFCC's meeting with Home Office officials reveal that Labour Party candidate David Pitt served as spokesperson among a deputation that included Amy Ashwood Garvey; Claudia Jones; Frances Ezzrecco; her husband, Donald Ezzrecco; Alao Bashorn; and actress and agent Pearl Connor, who along with her husband, Edric Connor, had recently established an agency to promote African, Asian, and Caribbean artists in Britain.[34] Although Pitt was the publicly acknowledged spokesperson for the IRFCC, as the IRFCC evolved, Black women overwhelmingly dominated the leadership of the organization and undoubtedly played important roles in shaping the direction and content of the organization's early activities. According to Scotland Yard surveillance reports tracking the organization's early activities, particularly in light of the leftist affiliations of its leadership, the first elected executive committee of the IRFCC included Amy Ashwood Garvey as Chairman, who was described as a "known communist" but had no formal affiliation with the Communist Party; Claudia Jones, whom the report described as a "self-confessed communist," as Vice-Chairman; Eleanor Ettlinger as second Vice-Chairman; and Alao Bashorn and Trinidadian artist and organizer Pearl Connor, who served as Secretary and Treasurer, respectively. Other members who served as part of the executive committee included Abhimanyu Manchanda, a close friend and political associate of Claudia Jones and Frances Ezzrecco, who along with her husband Don Ezzrecco ran the Coloured People's Progressive Association.[35]

On the day following the meeting with Home Office officials, the IRFCC sponsored a memorial service for Kelso Cochrane billed as a community-wide event simply titled "We Mourn Cochrane" and held at St. Pancras Town Hall, the same location where Claudia Jones had convened the first Caribbean carnival celebrations just months earlier.[36] The list of speakers at the service included a range of prominent local and international political voices, including Deputy Prime Minister of the West Indies Federation Carl La Corbiniere, Labour MP Stephen Swingler, Conservative MP Richard Hornsby, David Pitt, and distinguished Pan-Africanist Eslanda Goode Robeson. In particular, the presence of Carl La Corbiniere and Eslanda Robeson is especially illustrative of both the growing influence of the IRFCC and the larger network of political affiliations mobilized by key organizers shaping the direction of the council's agenda in the aftermath of the Cochrane murder.

The decision to invite Eslanda Robeson was most likely connected to the persuasive powers of Claudia Jones. Both Eslanda and her husband, world-renowned artist and activist Paul Robeson, were close and personal friends of Claudia Jones, whom Eslanda met during her tenure in the United States. Having served as an official delegate to the historic All African People's Conference, held in Accra, Ghana in December 1958, the first continental-based meeting espousing Pan-African unity, Robeson had developed an international reputation as a staunch defender of civil rights for Black Americans and African nationalism and had become a leading member of the US-based anti-colonial organ, the Council of African Affairs.[37] Speaking to an audience of nearly 500 in front of a "larger-than-life portrait" of Kelso Cochrane purchased by the IRFCC, Eslanda Robeson underscored the racial character of his murder, stating, "I believe that Kelso Cochrane was killed because he was coloured. He died because of racial prejudice and hatred."[38] Eslanda Robeson's involvement in the IRFCC grassroots political campaign underscores the extent to which Black activists, including Claudia Jones, were keen on tethering local race politics to both a national agenda advocating for full citizenship rights for Black Britons and, simultaneously, a transnational struggle for a type of Black freedom that contested all forms of racial oppression, including colonialism, segregation, inequality, and disenfranchisement. Robeson's presence at the IRFCC public memorial firmly implanted the organization's anti-racist platform of Black British citizenship rights within a diasporic context that transformed the political implications of the Cochrane murder into a transnational "colour problem" rooted in White supremacy, and not a byproduct of Black bodies taking residence and seeking routes of belonging in what was imagined as the White British world of the metropole. As such, the "colour problem" that ultimately resulted in Kelso Cochrane's death was one that linked the struggles of Black constituencies in Britain, the United States, the Caribbean, and Africa.

Upon his arrival in Britain one week after news of Kelso Cochrane's murder broke, Carl La Corbiniere, Deputy Prime Minister of the West Indies Federation, most likely fueled growing tensions between London's Caribbean communities and the Metropolitan Police by acknowledging that West Indians in Britain and the Caribbean had largely rejected police theories that Cochrane's murder had resulted from a botched robbery attempt. Describing his visit to London as part of a "mandate" issued by the West Indies Federal Government to assess the racial situation facing West Indian migrants in Britain, La Corbiniere explained that his compatriots in Britain and the Caribbean were "deeply disturbed" by the circumstances surrounding Cochrane's death. Moreover, he noted, "I think you will find it almost impossible to convince any West Indian that this was not a racial murder."[39] Making a somewhat untenable comparison between the Mau Mau insurgents in Kenya who had been violently suppressed by the British military and those responsible for Kelso Cochrane's murder, La Corbiniere echoed sentiments expressed in Black Britons' petitions to the Prime Minister and Home Office officials by insisting that the British Government bear responsibility for taking forceful action to alleviate the racial hostilities that had spurred anti-Black violence in London.[40]

La Corbiniere's description of his tour of England as an official "mandate" to inquire about racial conditions in Britain and the specific problems confronting Caribbean migrants reflected Caribbean audiences' growing interest in the case of Kelso Cochrane's murder. Although Cochrane had roots in Antigua, where most of his family, including his mother, Johanna Valentine, resided, the mainstream press in Jamaica, where the majority of Afro-Caribbean migrants in Britain hailed from, and Trinidad, the seat of the Federal Government, offered extensive coverage of the case. In the *Trinidad Guardian*'s initial report on the death of the "West Indian Groom-to-Be," the paper made immediate connections between the attack on Cochrane and the violence that had spurred "White vs. Black street battles" during the previous summer in Notting Hill.[41] Noting that local MPs had recently advised the Home Secretary of the need for a greater police presence in West London because of increasing racial tension in the area, the *Guardian* reminded Trinidadian audiences that the previous year's violence in the streets of London had in fact resulted from "the colour of a man's skin." The *Guardian* declared, "Now there is murder. Race tension is growing again."[42]

Aside from citing Scotland Yard theories of attempted robbery as the precipitating factor in Cochrane's killing, the national press in the Caribbean focused on race as the central underlying motive for the crime committed against Kelso Cochrane. This focus ultimately made the case ripe for political posturing among West Indian officials. As news of Cochrane's murder spread throughout the British Caribbean, several members of the West Indies Federal Parliament, including A. U. Belinfanti of Jamaica, contended that Federation officials had a duty to send the British Government a clear message regarding their dissatisfaction with the conditions faced by West Indian migrants in Britain. Belinfanti argued that "the time had almost passed when they [West Indians] look on Britons as their imperial masters and oppressors" and insisted that West Indians now viewed themselves as a part of a Commonwealth brotherhood "and expected to be treated as equals."[43]

The idea of Commonwealth as a partnership among equals rather than a final attempt to resuscitate the dying hierarchies of power and White [English] privilege that held Empire intact also informed how labor leaders in Kelso Cochrane's country of birth, Antigua, responded to the violence. Hoping to eventually air their grievances before the Colonial Office, in a petition to local administrators, members of the Antigua Trades and Labour Union expressed their dissatisfaction "with the treatment handed out to West Indians in England," given their status in the Commonwealth community.[44] Just days after Cochrane's murder, the *Worker's Voice*, the organ of the Antiguan Labour Party, issued a scathing indictment of domestic race relations in Britain in the context of British colonial policy in the Caribbean. Mocking British moral claims of civility—claims that had long justified imperial rule—in light of the violence that had taken Kelso Cochrane's life, an editorialist for the paper challenged, "What could be worst [sic] than walking the streets in fear, fear of being brutally murdered in cold blood because of one's colour? This is the virtue of being among the great and cultured English—to be jeered at as 'jim crow' and foully stabbed and left to die like a stuck pig."[45]

As reports describing the protests of the CAO and their insistence that West Indians and other Black Britons had "lost confidence in the ability of law-enforcing agencies to protect them" found their way to West Indian audiences in Jamaica and Trinidad, the growing publicity fueled debate in the West Indies Federal Parliament and prompted Federal Prime Minister Grantley Adams to announce plans of flying to London to monitor the investigation of the murder.[46] It is quite possible that Adams, who had personally promised Stanley Cochrane, Kelso's father, who resided in Trinidad, that he would keep him apprised of any developments in the case, had no intentions of lending the full weight of his public office to move the investigation forward. And perhaps it is more likely that the combination of widespread publicity and challenges from West Indian Parliament members, including Opposition party leader Robert Lightfoot, pressured Adams to take a strong public interest in the case despite the fact that Colonial Office officials had discouraged his interventions and expressed that his presence in London would only "exacerbate" matters and send a message that he had prejudged the murder as a "racial happening" when this fact had "not yet been proven."[47] Upon his arrival in London nearly one week after the murder, however, Deputy Prime Minister Carl La Corbiniere placed himself and subsequently the official voice of a transnational West Indian community squarely in the middle of the fomenting racial politics engendered by the death of Kelso Cochrane.

Appearing at the IRFCC memorial as a representative of a transnational West Indian community, Carl La Corbiniere reiterated his contention that West Indians in Britain and beyond were convinced that Cochrane's death was indeed a "race murder."[48] La Corbiniere's presence at the IRFCC memorial service only reaffirmed this position. The IRFCC was a political product of the Cochrane murder, and at the center of the organization's initial mandate was to facilitate a public commemoration of the body of Kelso Cochrane that inherently involved connecting the racial character of the murder with broader political issues related to race and the experiences of Black migrants in Britain. La Corbiniere's remarks emphasized that the murder was "a tragic incident in the history of the world."[49] The fact that La Corbiniere spoke at the IRFCC's memorial service suggests that he might have viewed the organization as an important conduit of Black political interests. His appearance granted him an opportunity to publicly communicate a message of solidarity between West Indians in the Caribbean and Britain and simultaneously gave official legitimacy to the political agenda of the IRFCC and its leadership.

The central purpose of the IRFCC's "We Mourn Cochrane" memorial was to engage local London communities and the broader British public in a collective and participatory expression of anguish, outrage, sympathy, and sorrow about the loss of Kelso Cochrane's life and a culture of racial violence directed toward vulnerable Black bodies. Rather than laying blame for Cochrane's murder solely at the feet of the unapprehended "anti-law white teenagers" who had driven the stiletto through Cochrane's chest, those involved in anti-racist organizing around the case sought to cast a wider spotlight and critique the larger social conditions that rendered Cochrane's body vulnerable to attackers who deemed the color of his skin as a motive for violence and a marker that he did not belong on the streets of West London.[50] In doing so, activists raised fundamental questions about Black Britons' right to a sense of security and to freedom from the threat of bodily harm—rights that were ultimately an implicit guarantee of one's citizenship and belonging within the metropolitan body politic. Framing the circumstances of Cochrane's death as a problem of ineffective policing practices, selective law enforcement, and a lack of legal redress for confronting racial discrimination and racially incendiary rhetoric, the IRFCC and their supporters brought attention to the British Government's role in safeguarding the rights of its citizens. Although a "gang of white youth" might have wielded the knife that physically killed Kelso Cochrane, Black British activists intended to highlight the shortcomings of the state in protecting its Black citizens from becoming vulnerable to racial violence. This argument directly censured the state in cultivating a climate of racial hostilities and, perhaps more importantly, it looked to the British Government as a political resource for exacting a type of justice that would extend far beyond the search for Cochrane's killers.

To further their petitions for redress from the state on behalf of Kelso Cochrane's dead body and all the other Black bodies that race rendered vulnerable to violence as they walked the streets of British cities like London, on 1 June 1959, the Coloured People's Progressive Association (CPPA) sponsored a twelve-hour vigil outside Whitehall near 10 Downing Street. Frances Ezzrecco, who had accompanied Amy Ashwood Garvey and Claudia Jones on their visit to lobby the Home Secretary as part of the IRFCC deputation less than a week earlier, was a leading personality in both the CPPA and the IRFCC. In the aftermath of the racial violence of 1958 in Notting Hill, Frances and her husband, Donald Ezzrecco, founded the CPPA for the purposes of promoting democracy, interracial unity, social incorporation for Black migrants, equal employment opportunities regardless of race, and unrestricted Commonwealth migration.[51] In a report on community relations in North Kensington released just days before the vigil, officials of the organization echoed many of the sentiments expressed in the CAO's open letter to the Prime Minister and the IRFCC's memo to the Home Secretary. The report addressed the need for more adequate police protection for Black people in North Kensington and noted that the Cochrane murder was only the "latest outrage against the coloured people" since the "riots" of the previous year. In announcing plans for the vigil, an unnamed spokesperson for the organization insisted that the purpose for the event was "to make clear the concern felt by our organization regarding the explosive situation, and also to espress [sic] lack of confidence in the arrangements for security of coloured people and all members of the community."[52]

Beginning at six in the morning, at times in pouring rain, demonstrators at the CPPA's vigil carried placards displaying slogans such as "Racial Discrimination is Illegal," "Black and White Can Live Together in Harmony," and "Speak Out against the Colour Bar," while one person communicated a poignant message without words by carrying a placard bearing a sketch of the face of Kelso Cochrane (See cover photo).[53] The sketch of Cochrane featured at the CPPA vigil bore a likeness to the most popularly circulated visual image of Cochrane accompanying media reports about the case. It is likely that

Figure 4.2 Kelso Cochrane, undated. Getty Images.

the image, a form of vernacular photography depicting Cochrane poised and posed before a photographer's glare while seated and dressed in a dark suit, collared shirt, and tie with a trifold kerchief neatly tucked in his jacket pocket and a boutonniere attached to his left lapel, was given to the press at the behest of his fiancée, Olivia Ellington.

While the image of Cochrane circulated in the press typically only included a headshot, a less cropped version of the photo suggests that another person whose shoulder can be seen in the wider shot was seated in the original photo in intimate proximity to Cochrane, and it is reasonable to consider that Olivia Ellington, the person with whom he shared a home and planned a future that included marriage, may have been at his side as the camera captured his bespectacled face projecting an air of unpretentious aplomb befitting his attire. Even though it is unclear whether or not Olivia Ellington was actually in the original photo given to the press to aid the world in visualizing the life of Kelso Cochrane in the aftermath of his untimely death, it is apparent that Cochrane's family, the media, and subsequently activists concerned with the racial politics of the crime that resulted in his murder hoped to do as Ida B. Wells had done a generation earlier in her anti-lynching campaigns, and as Mamie Till had done just a few years earlier after the brutal lynching of her son, Emmett Till, in Mississippi and "let the world see" the life that had been lost.[54] Whereas Mamie Till's decision to hold an open-casket funeral and have images of her son's mangled and disfigured corpse published in *Jet* magazine dramatically underscored the physical pain, mental anguish, and spectacular terror that her son endured as he met his demise, the visual politics surrounding Kelso Cochrane's murder narrated a story that focused on a lived existence rooted in the mundane, and in many ways universally aspirational imagery associated with what it meant to belong as a citizen and upstanding member of society.

As the image of a well-coiffed Kelso Cochrane peering through the frames of corrective lenses found its way to the covers of national newspapers, as it stood in prominent display as a type of visual aid to the remarks made by statesmen on the dais at community-wide events, and as it was carried as a type of political banner by one of the participants in the CPPA's demonstration at the seat of British political power, this particular image disrupted popular conceptions of Black men in British society during the late 1950s. Whereas the previous year's news of "race riots" produced narratives about Black men, and West Indian masculinities in particular, that qualified their "immigrant" outsider status through recycled colonial tropes emphasizing their licentious sexual proclivities toward White women, their flamboyant nature, and their aversion toward responsible work and family lives, the image of Kelso Cochrane presented an alternative narrative of West Indian manhood. As British audiences learned about Kelso Cochrane's death, in some instances they were presented with a visual representation of a man captioned by stories describing his work as a carpenter who was "saving up for his June wedding" to a "nurse trainee," Olivia Ellington, who in some instances was pictured in a separate photo alongside Cochrane in news stories about the case.[55] The previous year's stories of "race war" and "nigger-hunting" had implicated oftentimes largely anonymous Black men in scenes of violence as unwitting provocateurs prompting violence in many cases by way of their embodied presence alone. However, in the aftermath of Kelso Cochrane's murder, Black activists, including those who took part in the CPPA vigil, provided the British public with a name, a face, and indeed a life story to attach to the experience of West Indian manhood in Britain. As stories of "race riots" equated the Black male "immigrant" with Britain's increasing "colour problem," images of Kelso Cochrane, a groom, a working man, a family man in an intimate relationship with a Black woman whose progeny would not upset conventional racial boundaries, made a compelling case for the inclusion of Black men into the body politic.

As noted previously, the production and circulation of family photos like the one that the world came to know of Kelso Cochrane's life and death were important technologies and cultural practices through which West Indian migrants imaged and imagined themselves as Black Britons. As Tina Campt has argued, these types of photos indexed "forms of industry, responsibility, intellect and erudition, dignity and elegance that were not exclusively identified with Englishness, but signified status and accomplishments for the West Indian subjects and recipients in their own right." Moreover, she notes that these images registered "forms of British subjecthood through which these individuals signify a sense of belonging" in the national landscape as Britons.[56] As CPPA activists paraded Kelso Cochrane's image alongside 10 Downing Street in hopes of engaging the British Government and the wider public about the meaning of his death, they imbued his photograph with a type of "political velocity" that helped make a powerful case about where the Black men who had become the symbols of the "immigrant" problem stood in British society.[57] Not only did they have a right to protection from the threat of racial violence and bodily harm, but they also understood themselves and wanted to literally be seen as people who belonged and were a part of the nation as British citizens, regardless of their countries of birth or the color of their skin.

Black Bodies and the Politics of Mourning

The visual politics of Black death were not the only elements surrounding Kelso Cochrane's murder that connected his history with the brutal lynching of Emmett Till in Money, Mississippi in 1955. Written most likely during her incarceration in the United States and before her deportation to Britain in December of 1955, the opening stanza of an elegy penned by Claudia Jones titled, "Lament for Emmett Till" vehemently exclaimed,

> Lynch-
> Cry murder!
> Sear the land
> Raise fists—in more than anger bands![58]

Reminiscent in tone to that of Claude McKay's "If We Must Die," the poem became an emotive medium for Claudia Jones to convey her sympathies for Mamie Till, the aggrieved mother robbed of a child by Mississippi's version of what she labeled as "white washed justice." Jones's mourning song for young Emmett Till conveyed a sense of admiration for Mose Wright, Till's uncle, "who stood firm" while "facing lynchers eye for eye." Jones concluded her poetic requiem by proclaiming, "Vengeance for this brutal hour," urging her unidentified audience to "soar above strife, to swiftly avenge young Emmett Till's life."[59] More than a mourning song about the barbaric and deplorable circumstances that culminated in Emmett Till's tragic death, Jones's "Lament for Emmett Till" signaled a call to action steeped in a critical reinterpretation of the iconographic resonance of Till's slain body. In doing so, Claudia Jones simultaneously acknowledged the ways in which his body conveyed a disturbing message about American racism and conversely represented a yet-to-be determined space ripe for new and alternative meanings and memories that could be produced by seeking a type of post mortem justice that would arise from a concerted and collective mourning of "young Emmett Till's life."

It is likely that as Claudia Jones made preparations for Kelso Cochrane's funeral that the emotions and memories that fueled her "lament for Emmett Till" resurfaced. Here was yet another Black male whose body had been fatally injured and whose life had been prematurely snuffed out in an act of violence that could only be explained by the color of his skin and the perceived prerogatives of Whiteness shared by his murderers. Unlike in the case of Emmett Till, there was no trial of Kelso Cochrane's murderers in a Jim Crowed judicial system that would result in their acquittal by an all-White jury. Yet Black Britons, including Claudia Jones, certainly felt that the lack of an arrest by Scotland Yard detectives and their denial of the racial motives precipitating the murder, coupled with a broader reluctance by law-enforcing and policy-making officials to adequately protect and ensure their everyday right to be present on British streets and belong in British society without fear of racial violence or discrimination, were eerily akin to the Jim Crow conditions that sanctioned Emmett Till's lynching and that of Mack Parker's just weeks before Cochrane's death. And for Claudia Jones and the supporters of the IRFCC's campaign to seek justice for Cochrane, this was cause for action and, more specifically, a cause that required harnessing a type of "black body politics" through the power of collective mourning to elicit political mobilization and a greater public consciousness about what it meant to be Black and British.[60]

Described by a local newspaper as "organised with a thoroughness usually associated with a demonstration," the funeral of Kelso Cochrane held on 6 June 1959 represented a definitive moment in the IRFCC's campaign to highlight racial violence and the precarious status of Black bodies in British society.[61] Because the IRFCC coordinated most of the arrangements and fulfilled all of the financial obligations for the burial of Cochrane's body, the funeral provides an instructive historical moment for understanding the process in which Cochrane's body and subsequently the memory of his body were reconstituted into political narratives about Black life in postwar Britain. According to IRFCC records, in addition to assuming the cost of the funeral services, transportation for family members, wreaths, and handbills "in respect of [the] funeral," the organization also provided support for Cochrane's brother to supplement lost wages and covered the expense of advertising the memorial service and funeral in the *New Statesman*, and sending cablegrams to officials in Jamaica, Trinidad, Antigua, Ghana, Cairo, Paris, India, and Liberia. Aided with donations from leftist, anti-colonial, and anti-racist organizations, including the London branch of the Communist Party, the Nyasaland African Congress, the Movement for Colonial Freedom, the South African Freedom Association, and the West Indian Federal Labour Party, by assuming the costs, the IRFCC made a public claim on the final interpretations of Kelso Cochrane's life and death. [62] In making these claims on Cochrane's body in death, the organization actively shaped the terms by which Kelso Cochrane's life, and particularly the circumstances in which it was ended, would be remembered.

Even though Kelso Cochrane's brother and fiancée attended the services and were recognized as the chief mourners, the predominance of the IRFCC's role in publicizing and, more importantly, politicizing the body of Kelso Cochrane through their interchanges with Government officials and memorial activities in the days leading up to the funeral, transformed the final remembrance of Cochrane's life into a public ceremony that commemorated both the personal loss of a loved one and a public tragedy that encompassed the collective interests of an entire community. As hundreds of mourners crowded into the St. Michael and All Angels Church, they were directed by well-dressed IRFCC stewards, including Trinidadian singer Pearl Connor, who wore brightly colored dresses with "red silk flashes in their lapels" and an "emblem of mourning" such as a black armband or a patch stitched into their sleeve to symbolize their affiliation with the organization. [63] Upon viewing Cochrane's casket draped in purple and gold fabric, those involved in the procession most likely took notice of one of many wreaths sent by those who had heeded the IRFCC's call to show support "for friendship between the peoples" by sending messages of condolence in memory of Kelso Cochrane, including one from "West Indian sympathisers at Paddington Post Office" and another, from Harold Sharp, bearing this inscription: "Ever-loving memory. Your death was by the hand of a blind man. His terrible deed has drawn innumerable warm hearts to love towards you and yours." [64]

Although the facts of Kelso Cochrane life provided him with a rather ordinary existence that most likely would have rendered him anonymous in the eyes of history, he died a most remarkable death that warranted a funeral akin to that of statesman. The crowd of mourners included Grantley Adams, the highest ranking official in the West Indies Federal Government; A. N. E. MacHaffie, the Mayor of Kensington; the exiled South African labor leader and anti-apartheid activist Emil Solomon "Solly" Sachs; and leaders of several London-based associations, including the Movement for Colonial Freedom and the London Communist Party. As the Bishop of Kensington, Reverend J. H. Goodman stood before the mourners, he read a lesson that struck a somber tone of hopefulness in the transformative power of death as he exhorted, "Death is swallowed up in victory. O death, where is thy sting? O grave, where is thy victory?"[65] Echoing the sentiments embedded in the political work of grassroots organizations, including the IRFCC, in the aftermath of Kelso Cochrane's murder, Goodman's words suggested that Cochrane's death would engender an opportunity to achieve or attain something desirable, to begin a conversation, to clarify and or redeem a wrong even through the act of mourning a lost life. While a grave might hold the corporeal remains of Kelso Cochrane's existence, Black activists were clearly determined that it would not bury the memory of his life and the circumstances in which he encountered death—conditions reflecting the vulnerabilities that Black bodies continued to face as disenfranchised citizens in British society.

Hundreds of spectators lined the streets of Ladbroke Grove to watch the cortège from St. Michael and All Angels Church to Kensal Green Cemetery after funeral services for Kelso Cochrane. In doing so, the individual unnamed men, women, and children, some of whom watched from windows as the procession moved slowly along its quarter-mile trek, helped the IRFCC stage a final scene of a collective public mourning in honor of the loss of Cochrane's life. Following a graveside committal by Reverend Ronald Campbell in his role as official chaplain to West Indian migrants in Britain, a voice in the crowd began to lead mourners in a rendition of the Anglican hymn "Abide with Me," which summoned a spiritual presence among the living even as they paused to acknowledge and confront the realities of death.[66] The choice of this popular Christian funeral hymn, whose final stanza enjoined, "In life, in death, O Lord, abide with me," might seem unremarkable as Kelso Cochrane's remains were laid to rest. But, in fact, given the political work that surrounded the production and performance of his funeral services through the organizing of IRFCC leaders, including Claudia Jones and Amy Ashwood Garvey, the singing of this particular hymn powerfully articulated one of the central aspects of the IRFCC's effort to cultivate a politics of mourning that transformed Cochrane's body from a site of injury and trauma into a palimpsest of collective melancholia that would contain a host of meanings and identifications for Black Britons and remind the nation of its responsibility to safeguard the lives and rights of its citizens.

In their work on the political stakes of mourning practices, David Eng and David Kazanjian note that the condition of melancholia represents a degree of mourning that involves an enduring attachment to that which is lost or an "inability to resolve the grief and ambivalence precipitated by the loss of the loved object, place or ideal." According to Eng and Kazanjian, it is precisely the inability to reconcile the loss of a particular "melancholic object" that produces a perpetual engagement with the lost object oftentimes through forms of memory that then keeps the past—even one marked by the embodied loss of death—"steadfastly alive in the present."[67] It is precisely the inability to reconcile loss that then animates a type of politics of mourning that renders a subject valuable, meaningful, indispensible, and vital to the collective or the nation. June 6 1959 marked the date when the world bid the material remains of Kelso Cochrane's life goodbye. However, because his family and the Black activists and organizations who cultivated a public and collective politics of mourning that centered upon how his life was lost in the midst of conditions of anti-Black street violence, ineffective policing practices, and the failure of the state to enact forms of redress against racial discrimination to secure the citizenship rights of Black Britons, Kelso Cochrane's existence remained palpable, alive, and effectual as a movement-making moment that encouraged a greater consciousness about the politics of race and citizenship in postwar Britain. In this sense, as activists made Kelso Cochrane publicly grievable, they also imbued his injured and violated Black body, as well as those bodies which continued to exist under the same threat of violence and disregard for Black life that caused his death, with a sense of human dignity, recognition, and consequence that mattered to those who personally knew him and loved him. Moreover, as they crafted a campaign that signaled "We Mourn Cochrane," they made this statement legible to the broader society that tolerated the conditions that marked his Blackness as expendable and unworthy of the protections and guarantees of full citizenship.[68]

Most recent histories detailing the postwar historical formation of postcolonial Black Britain reference the murder of Kelso Cochrane as a key moment of Black political mobilization that drew greater public attention to the impact of racial discrimination and violence as experienced by Black Britons.[69] In the commemorative volume *Windrush* documenting the postwar emergence of multiracial communities in Britain in the wake of unprecedented arrivals of non-White migrants from the Commonwealth, journalists Mike Phillips and Trevor Phillips explained,

> The death of Kelso Cochrane—an obscure carpenter from Antigua—and the mourning which followed it was a revelation which helped create popular revulsion against the street violence and harassment the migrants had experienced during the fifties. It also helped to move the argument about their presence on to a new plane. Political interest in the conditions which characterised Notting Dale had increased and become the subject of fierce debate.[70]

This was no accident. Rather, it was by historical design through the political organizing and claim making of Black British activists on behalf of the citizenship rights of all Black Britons living under the social and cultural stigmas attached to their racialized status as "immigrant" outsiders in postwar Britain.

On the day after Kelso Cochrane's funeral, members of organizations known as the African-Asian Congress and the United Kingdom Coloured Citizens' Association convened a meeting at Trafalgar Square, where they collected £128 to put toward the cost of fulfilling Cochrane's mother's request, pending approval from the Home Office, to have the body of her slain son returned to Antigua, where a statue was to be erected in his honor near his home.[71] It is unclear if a shortage of funds, an abandoned resolve, or a willingness to leave his body undisturbed on the part of Cochrane's family was the reason that his remains stayed buried in Kensal Green Cemetery in West London. But Home Office officials and high-ranking officials in the West Indies Federal Government, including Prime Minister Grantley Adams, were keen on keeping his body interred in London. In response to Deputy Prime Minister Carl La Corbiniere's proposal to return the body to Antigua to avoid the "danger" of the gravesite becoming a site of "annual pilgrimage" where "mischief-makers" in London could cause trouble, Home Office officials estimated that "more unfortunate repercussions" would occur if the body were removed. From their view the very arrival of the body in Antigua could become "an occasion for demonstrations on a considerable scale," which they judged would most likely "arouse fears and inflame animosities" that might "damage race relations" both in the Caribbean and in Britain.[72] In any case, British officials hoped that with time, the memories of Kelso Cochrane's life and, more specifically, the collective politics of mourning prompted by the circumstances in which his life ended would recede from the public consciousness and ultimately be buried with his corporeal remains. But Black Britons would remember. They would continue to mourn his loss and Black activists would continue to invoke his name for decades to come as a reminder of the violence and injustice that had defined their experiences as British citizens.

On the first anniversary of Kelso Cochrane's death in June 1960, the *West Indian Gazette* ran an article reminding its readers of the solidarity displayed among West Indians, Africans, Asians, and "progressive white Britons" who had joined the funeral cortège to Kensal Green Cemetery to lay Cochrane's body to rest. In addition to soliciting contributions to support an effort by the IRFCC and the Hammersmith and Kensington Trades Union Council to purchase a gravestone for Cochrane's burial site, the *Gazette* informed its readers that Cochrane's funeral represented a "climax of thousands of protests against racialism and the incidents of racial violence."[73] By framing the memory of Cochrane's death in this manner, the *Gazette* captured the intended political work that IRFCC organizers and other activists hoped that a public mourning might perform. Because of their efforts, the remembrance of Kelso Cochrane's death and the collective mourning that marked the loss of his life functioned as a site of protest against racism and violence against Black bodies occurring in Britain, and a requiem to other violated, disenfranchised, objectified, and oppressed Black populations across the African Diaspora. Moreover, for a generation of postwar Afro-Caribbean migrants, the death of Kelso Cochrane would help to solidify their desires to challenge a metropolitan culture and, more specifically, a state apparatus that regarded them as "immigrant" outsiders and denied them the rights of belonging that secured their status as British citizens.

5

Exposing the Racial Politics
of Immigration Controls

In a 1956 interview published in *Caribbean News*, the short-lived organ of the London branch of the Caribbean Labour Congress, reporter George Bowrin asked Claudia Jones, "Is there any special significance to the fact that you are a West Indian, and as such were deported from the United States?" Jones, who had only been in Britain for about six months following her deportation from the United States, answered, "Yes, I definitely think so." She explained,

> The very law under which I was deported, the reactionary Walter-McCarran law [is] widely known for its special racist bins towards West Indians and peoples of Asiatic descent. This law, which came into being as a result of the whole reactionary drive against progressive ideas in the United States, encourages immigration of fascist scum from Europe but restricts West Indian immigration, once in their thousands annually to the United States, to 100 persons per year, from *all* the Caribbean islands. This works special hardships among West Indians who have family ties and who are permanent residents and citizens of the U.S.A.[1]

Passed by Congress at the height of a resurgence of anti-Communist hysteria brought on by escalating Cold War tensions, the McCarran-Walter Act of 1952, which Claudia Jones cited as providing the legal grounds for her deportation, reflected over a half a century of US immigration policy that codified what Mae Ngai has referred to as an "index of racial desirability" that determined which bodies could aspire to notions of Americanness and legally access paths toward citizenship.[2] Aside from extending the restrictive national-origins quota system instituted in 1924, as previously discussed, the McCarran-Walter Bill established a per annum quota of one hundred immigrants from the British colonies in the Caribbean and further imposed preferences based on a potential immigrant's educational training, specialized labor skills, and/or familial ties to American citizens or permanent residents. For Claudia Jones in particular, the deleterious effects of the bill did not necessarily stem from its provisions that stripped rights of mobility for future arrivants from the Caribbean largely on the basis of racially coded quotas that privileged immigration from majority White nations of Western Europe. Rather, the most repugnant aspects of the bill involved the impact that it would have on the rights of those migrants, permanent residents, and naturalized citizens who hoped to stay and continue to create spaces of belonging and inclusion for themselves and their posterity in the United States.

Nearly ten years after the McCarran-Walter Bill became law despite a veto by US President Harry Truman, who castigated the bill as one that perpetrated "invidious discrimination," Claudia Jones and organizers of the newly formed Afro-Asian-Caribbean Conference (AACC) in London issued a call to the working-class masses of "Afro-Asian-Caribbean citizens" of Britain. Urging "nurses and medical staff from hospitals in their uniforms, bus train and transport personnel, factory, canteen and municipal workers in overalls or uniforms" to join in solidarity for a mass protest at the House of Commons on 13 February 1962, the AACC intended to rally Black Britons to demand the withdrawal of what would become the Commonwealth Immigration Act of 1962.[3] Members of the AACC hoped to expose the racially discriminatory intent of proposed Commonwealth migration restrictions that placed strictures on the citizenship rights of a largely non-White stream of West Indian and, increasingly in the early 1960s, South Asian migrant population in ways that were similar to the McCarran-Walter Bill. On the surface, the proposed bill, which had initially been introduced by Conservative Home Secretary R. A. Butler, functioned as a race-neutral policy regulating the entrance of Commonwealth citizens on the basis of their employment prospects in such a manner that applied universally to all Commonwealth migrants, regardless of race or national origin. But for many Black Britons, the devil was in the details. Not only did the provisions of the bill effectively deprive British citizens of Commonwealth nations of their right to freely migrate to Britain, but through the very process of regulating the terms of their movement to Britain on the basis of their national origins, the act also institutionalized their precarious disenfranchised status as an "immigrant" class of alien citizens subject to public scrutiny, surveillance, and expulsion as they sought to cross Britain's borders and, perhaps more importantly, as they exercised their right to stay and incorporate themselves into the fabric of British society.

Characterizing the Commonwealth Immigration Act as the introduction of "legalized apartheid," as the AACC attempted to build a coalition of support, its members insisted that the act was riddled with racially discriminatory features such that it "flouts the U.N. Charter of Human Rights, is an insult to human dignity and is a slur to the fair name" of Britain, which they regarded as "the citadel of democracy."[4] In advertising its mass-protest lobby, the AACC made a timely and politically apropos comparison between what the organization deemed as the racist intent of Commonwealth migration controls and the White supremacist logic that underwrote South Africa's apartheid regime. Just months before the Home Secretary announced plans to pursue Commonwealth migration reform, South Africa withdrew from the British Commonwealth under mounting pressure from within the largely non-White Commonwealth community of nations to reform South Africa's official policies of White minority rule. Moreover, on a global scale, the very language of "apartheid" had become a racially charged international synecdoche articulating some of the most virulent forms of White supremacy, which stood in violation of the principles of equality, national self-determination, and respect of human rights enshrined in the governing documents of the United Nations and the broader postwar international order. By invoking the extant specter of apartheid in a protest against the provisions of the Commonwealth Immigration Act of 1962, the AACC made a concerted effort to use its dissenting voice to reframe a national conversation about race, citizenship, and the social, political, and legal construction of the "immigrant." In doing so, Black British activists and their supporters exposed for public consumption a central institutional mechanism of racialized governmentality designed to transform a largely Afro-Caribbean population of Commonwealth citizens into a disenfranchised underclass of Britons.

While it is clear that news of the Nottingham and Notting Hill "race riots" of 1958 certainly fueled a greater public consciousness of the relationship between race and "immigration," it was precisely this connection that policy makers' advocating legislation to control Commonwealth migration hoped to downplay as the first Commonwealth Immigration Act moved through Parliamentary channels and circulated in the public sphere in the process of becoming adopted into law. Voices of dissent, including coalitions of communities of people of African and Asian descent represented by the AACC, made this impossible by articulating their opposition to the bill on the basis of the manner in which the policy would preclude non-White Commonwealth migrants from accessing and exercising their rights of migration as British citizens, guaranteed under the British Nationality Act of 1948. To understand how the Commonwealth Immigration Act of 1962 provoked a public dialogue about the relationship between im/migration, citizenship, and institutional racism in postwar Britain, there are at least four significant groups of dissenters that merit attention: Black newcomers, British Parliamentary critics, West

Indian officials, and grassroots Black political organizers in Britain. All of these groups from varying trajectories and in different ways challenged the underlying premise of a migration policy that inherently disenfranchised a category of citizens and codified what Kathleen Paul describes as "separate spheres of belonging" premised upon hierarchies of race and nation.[5]

Whereas the focal point of much of the scholarly debate on race politics and the Commonwealth Immigration Act of 1962 centers on the extent to which Conservative policy makers actively participated in shaping and institutionalizing a marginal citizenship status for what was, at the time of the bill's proposal, a largely Afro-Caribbean population of Commonwealth migrants, this chapter explores what was accomplished by those who dissented.[6] Those who challenged the intent, as well as the social and political ramifications of the Commonwealth Immigration Act of 1962—including the Black British communities for whom the issue of im/migration was arguably most relevant—transformed racialized discourses about the problem of "coloured immigration." As the circulation of discourses about the "coloured immigration" problem surged in the aftermath of the violence of 1958, dissenters transformed public discussion on im/migration law into grounds for debating the politics of race and citizenship and, more importantly, forging a dialogue about the processes that rendered Black Britons as second-class citizens. These discussions struck at the very heart of what Britain stood for in the world, as a bellwether of liberal democracy in an age when Freedom Rides throughout the Jim Crow South and the militarization of the African National Congress's anti-apartheid movement in response to events such as the Sharpeville massacre kept global audiences attuned to the machinations of White supremacy and the perpetuation of Black disenfranchisement, oppression, and exclusion. As Black British constituencies formed transnational and multiethnic coalitions to confront the racial politics of "immigration," they made it clear that their citizenship status was just as much about rights of mobility as it was about the freedom to establish roots and claim Britain as a permanent home.

The Open Road to Closed Borders

Despite a long tradition of intra-imperial migration between the metropole and colonies, controlling the entrance and regulating the terms of settlement for colonial and non-White migrant workers was a concern of British policy makers throughout the early twentieth century. Coming on the heels of episodes of racial violence occurring between indigenous White residents and seafaring workers of color in port cities, including Cardiff and Liverpool in 1919, the Aliens Order of 1920 empowered immigration officers to refuse entry to any arriving "Arab seamen" who could not provide proof of British nationality. In January 1921, this policy was extended to apply to all incoming "coloured" seamen, regardless of ethnicity or port of origin. Four years later, under the provisions of Special Restriction (Coloured Alien Seamen) Order of 1925, the Home Office again codified a policy that was rooted in racial difference, that privileged Whiteness, and effectively presumed the alien status of non-White migrating maritime workers. The terms of the 1925 order required that all non-White seamen resident in British ports present local authorities with documentary evidence of their British nationality or register as aliens with the police. Not only did this measure continue to make it difficult for non-White seamen, including those who were bona fide British subjects to enter Britain, but because, as many Government officials were well aware, few sailors customarily carried passports. Instead, most journeyed only with discharge books documenting their voyages that served as their sole travel documents. Therefore, the new policy forced many non-White British subjects who were automatically regarded as foreign outsiders until proven otherwise to relinquish their migration rights as Crown subjects and face possible deportation or formally register as aliens because they could not provide acceptable proof of their British nationality. [7]

The economic ramifications of this policy for seamen of color came to a head in 1935 with the passage of the British Shipping (Assistance) Act. This act made it illegal for shipping companies to claim Government subsidies if they employed alien seamen. As a result, the policy virtually shut out many non-White maritime workers from employment on state-subsidized vessels, many of whom were merely improperly documented British subjects. [8] Laura Tabili has suggested that the structure, implementation, and consequences of the Coloured Alien Seamen Order of 1925 makes the act an important precursor to understanding many of the issues that would come to define postwar considerations of race, migration, citizenship, and belonging within the national body politic. While the policy did not completely prevent non-White British seamen from migrating and working in Britain, it most certainly relied upon racial categories to differentiate between the ways in which White British seamen experienced their British nationality and the manner in which colonial seamen of color could lay claim to and access the opportunities associated with their status as British subjects. [9]

In theory, imperial relations allowed colonial and dominion residents "free" movement to Britain well before the codification of migration as a citizenship right under the British Nationality Act of 1948. Throughout the interwar period, however, as the Coloured Aliens Order of 1925 demonstrates, intra-imperial politics did not preclude the existence of de facto policies of obstruction designed to curb migration to Britain from parts of the Empire with majority non-White populations. During the 1930s the British

Government made arrangements with colonial governments, including those of India and Pakistan, that required potential migrants to obtain specific endorsements by colonial authorities before journeying to Britain. In the case of Cypriots, in addition to certain passport endorsements, colonial authorities required potential migrants to post a security bond and in some instances provide documentation from a resident in Britain stating an offer of sponsorship until he or she found employment in Britain.[10]

With the onset of World War II, as the British Government mobilized the labor reserves of Empire, the metropole witnessed an increase in the movement of colonial workers, soldiers, and auxiliary military personnel recruited to fulfill vital roles in supporting and sustaining the British military effort and wartime economy. However, while colonial workers proved invaluable to the Allied cause, the end of the war ushered in a return to a concerted interest in controlling the terms by which imperial citizens, particularly those from nations with non-White majorities, accessed their imperial right to move, work, and settle in Britain. In 1950, the Colonial Office urged all colonial governments to enforce procedures that would limit the issuance of passports to those "whose financial position was not sound" and or those who could not demonstrate steady employment.[11] By that time, High Commissions in the newly independent nations of India and Pakistan began to selectively issue British passports to primarily White applicants or those who could demonstrate that they were a descendant of someone born or naturalized in Britain. While West African governments, including the government of Nigeria, generally complied with the requests of the Colonial Office, West Indian governments on the whole were generally less cooperative in introducing formal administrative procedures to limit emigration. In heavily populated islands, including Jamaica, in a period marked by high unemployment, depressed wages, and fiscal recession, emigration served as a critical form of economic relief. Defining their economic interests apart from those of the imperial government and exercising policies reflecting rising nationalist currents, rather than implement official measures to prevent certain groups from migrating to Britain, Jamaican authorities alternatively agreed to assist in efforts to publicize the potential obstacles facing migrants, including the potential inability to secure employment or suitable housing.[12] Throughout the 1950s, Jamaica and other West Indian nations made it clear that emigration was an economic resource that they were unwilling to easily concede through backdoor channels. Therefore, as the numbers of Caribbean migrants in Britain steadily increased throughout the 1950s, British policy makers understood that controlling and restricting this migration would involve a formal policy that would ultimately restructure one of the fundamental rights defining the ties that had historically bound the disparate communities of Britons across the geographical spaces and national borders of the Empire.

West Indian officials' reluctance to enact policies and procedures to restrict emigration to Britain was not necessarily a welcomed sentiment on the part of British officials. In 1961, when the Home Secretary introduced the first Cabinet-approved legislation intended to regulate Commonwealth migration, "coloured immigration" largely from the Caribbean colonies had been the subject of previous Cabinet discussions no fewer than thirty-seven times since the end of World War II. The peak of these discussions occurred between 1954 and 1955, when the Cabinet in the Conservative Government debated a proposal for migration controls drafted in consultation with ministers overseeing the Home Office, the Colonial Office, and the Commonwealth Relations Office.[13] According to migration statistics maintained by the House of Commons between 1953 and 1954, the number of Caribbean migrants entering Britain increased more than fivefold, from an estimated 2,000 to 11,000. By 1955, the number of Caribbean arrivals had more than doubled from the previous year, totaling approximately 27,500 and accounting for nearly two-thirds of all migrants entering Britain from the Commonwealth.[14] For some Cabinet members of the Conservative Government of the early 1950s who had reclaimed power under the leadership of wartime Prime Minister Winston Churchill, these figures were alarming and justified cause for action.

By June 1955 a majority of Cabinet ministers favored investigating the means by which an overwhelmingly Black colonial migration might be regulated and moved to appoint an Interdepartmental Working Party to draft a definitive statement on the social and economic problems arising from "the growing influx" of "coloured workers" from the Commonwealth.[15] Just a few months later, however, when the Cabinet convened in November 1955 to consider a "draft bill to restrict colonial immigration," in light of what was described as "the rapid increase in immigration from the West Indies," instead of moving forward, officials elected to table the issue.[16] Citing the lack of an empirical smoking gun that could link particular social and/or economic problems with Commonwealth migration, including strains on the resources of the postwar welfare state or high unemployment among migrants, and in the absence of a clear consensus on the form that migration controls could take without appearing to be racially bias or preferential, Cabinet members ultimately decided to wait. Timing was everything. Just months earlier, the historic Bandung Conference had sent a powerful message to the international community about the political possibilities of Afro-Asian alliances and served as a reminder to Britain and its Western allies of the importance of images of anti-racism in building spheres of influence for liberal democracy and deflecting Communist encroachment.[17] Because there seemed to be no rationale for

implementing migration controls that would circumvent a widespread public
backlash both within the Commonwealth and internationally on the grounds
of racial discrimination, Cabinet members elected to follow the course that
then Commonwealth Relations Secretary Lord Swinton had advised a year
earlier. Considering how even the perception of racially discriminatory policy
might impact Britain's international credibility in the politically charged arena
of postwar race relations, Swinton cautioned,

> If we legislate on immigration, though we can draft it in
> non-discriminatory terms, we cannot conceal the obvious fact that
> the object is to keep out coloured people. Unless there is really a
> strong case for this, it would surely be an unwise moment to raise the
> issue when we are preaching, and trying to practise, partnership, and
> the abolition of the colour bar.[18]

Although Swinton retired along with Churchill after the 1955 elections, the
sentiments expressed in his prescient remarks prevailed throughout the 1950s.
But by 1961, when Prime Minister Harold Macmillan announced intentions
to proceed with legislation to control Commonwealth "immigration," the geo-
political landscape had changed. During the late 1950s and into the early 1960s, the rapidly accelerating pace
of decolonization reconstituted Britain's place in the international order. The
end of Empire steadily approached as African nations such as Ghana, Nigeria,
and Sierra Leone attained independence, while the British Caribbean colonies embraced the establishment of a West Indies Federation to negotiate the
transition toward full independence for a single West Indian nation-state.[19]
To be sure, the dissolution of Empire motivated British officials to fortify
international ties and economic relationships beyond the Commonwealth as
they began to explore integration with the European Economic Community
(Common Market). Established in accordance with the provisions of the
Treaty of Rome in 1957, the European Economic Community sought greater
economic cooperation between Western European states and supported the
free movement of European workers among its member states. In August
1961, Britain submitted a formal application for membership in the European
Economic Community, a prospect that would no doubt entail the consideration of immigration policies that would allow for greater mobility of European
workers seeking employment in British industries.[20]

Aside from the shifting dynamics of Britain's international relationships
with Commonwealth partners and European nations, one of the most significant events altering the terrain in which British officials considered regulating Commonwealth migration involved domestic race relations. Because

of the widely reported incidents of racial violence during the final weeks of summer in 1958 occurring between Black and White residents in Nottingham and London, the issue of migration and a popularly configured West Indian "immigrant" problem had clearly made the transition from being the subjects of private discussions among Government officials to being firmly entrenched topics that distinctly resonated in the public consciousness. Although news of "race riots" in 1958 might have proved an opportune time to revisit and actively pursue migration controls, the opposite occurred. As noted previously, in the aftermath of the violence, "immigration" became a racially coded political discourse that implicated single Black men as the source of White working-class anxieties about urban resources, including jobs, decent and affordable housing, and sexual partners. A Gallup poll conducted in the early weeks after the violence subsided in Notting Hill reported that while 92 percent of people had knowledge of the violence, only 9 percent attributed the violence to Black residents; yet nearly 80 percent favored some form of "immigration" controls.[21]

In 1955, when Cabinet members pursued measures to curb West Indian migration, there had been no climactic event or cohesive narrative available for policy makers to draw upon to measure or shape the broader society's disposition toward restrictions. But news of "race riots" changed this field. To be sure, at the same time that news of "race riots" gave public credence to the idea that racial conflict and social unrest was a likely consequence of "immigration," as several scholars have observed, Government discussions concerning controls after the violence demonstrated a sense of wariness on the part of many officials to introduce legislation that might easily be construed by domestic and overseas audiences as a reaction to anti-Black racism.[22] Because West Indian men of African descent were numerically the largest community of "coloured immigrants" and generally cited as either perpetrators and or victims in areas where episodes of racial violence erupted in 1958, as discussed earlier, in the midst of the violence they became the archetypical embodiment of the problem of "immigration" and therefore would most likely be viewed as the potential targets for any form of migration control that might be considered in the aftermath of the violence. Paradoxically, just as the racial character of Commonwealth "immigration"—and in particular West Indian migration—provided an impetus for officials to consider controlling the entrance of Black British citizens, in 1958, the public appropriation of this same rationale became a deterrent for moving forward with legislation, as the Government did not want to be viewed as capitulating to demands to "Keep Britain White!"

On 11 October 1961, Home Secretary R. A. Butler presented a motion to introduce legislation "to control, but not to stop" Commonwealth "immigration" to Britain at the Conservative conference of Parliament members. Addressing rank and file members of the Conservative caucus, Butler estimated that total migration from the Caribbean, India, and Pakistan would top 100,000.[23] A few weeks before Butler's speech, the Cabinet's Interdepartmental Working Party, convened to assist in developing the empirical case for regulating Commonwealth migration, submitted its latest report for Cabinet review. In it, the Working Party noted that during August 1961, there was "a net inward movement of coloured people from the Commonwealth" of 15,700, which was the "highest monthly figure ever recorded." Of that total, approximately 7,700 migrated from the Caribbean, 2,400 from India, and 3,000 from Pakistan. The report mentioned that despite an increasing influx of non-White Commonwealth migration, there had been "no serious racial disorders since 1958" and "remarkably little unemployment."[24]

Despite the Working Party's inability to pinpoint any concrete social or economic conditions necessitating immediate controls of Commonwealth migration beyond the fact that it had brought an unparalleled number of non-White British citizens to Britain in steadily increasing proportions since the late 1940s, the Party recommended the adoption of "flexible employment" controls, which Butler emphasized in introducing plans to seek legislation on Commonwealth migration. In his remarks to the Conservative Parliamentary conference, Butler suggested that, in light of current trends, the slightest economic downturn might create difficult and possibly dangerous social conditions that the Government had to attempt to circumvent. Appealing for support of the motion, Butler maintained that the employment sector presented "the only effective way" to control "immigration" and encouraged his colleagues "to think like a jury" when deciding if they would lend their support to the resolution. Alluding to the notion that the rising numbers of unprecedented migration from the Commonwealth posed an alarming threat to the social and economic life of the nation, he unequivocally made the case for restrictions exigent and compelling. Butler insisted that while the Government would be "departing from a great tradition . . . we might be able to work out a system which is humane, unprejudiced, and sensible which might help to meet economic problems that might be too much for our country." And with that said, the motion passed.[25]

Under the proposal submitted by the Working Party and later adapted as the framework for legislation by the Cabinet, a potential migrants' relationship to the British labor market determined whether or not he or she would be subject to restrictions. The proposal outlined three categories of Commonwealth migrants. Category A comprised those migrants who had a job awaiting them in Britain upon their arrival. Category B encompassed "those who have undergone apprenticeship or training or have professional or educational qualifications or experience accepted as likely to be useful" in Britain, while Category C constituted all other migrants and presumably "unskilled" laborers seeking to enter Britain. According to the Working Party's proposal, those who fell into Categories A and B would not be subject to controls and would be freely admitted to Britain under the same provisions codified under the British Nationality Act of 1948. However, those in Category C would be allowed entry on a first-come/first-served basis within the parameters of a predetermined quota established by the Ministry of Labour. In addition to creating an instrument to regulate inward movement from the Commonwealth, the Working Party's proposal also contained a component that empowered the Home Secretary to deport Commonwealth "immigrants" convicted of offences punishable by any term of imprisonment.[26]

The period between the Home Secretary's public announcement of the Government's intent to pursue legislation to regulate Commonwealth migration in October 1961 and the final Parliamentary vote making the Commonwealth Immigration Act of 1962 the law of the land produced a critical moment that laid the foundation for the political and ideological debates that would shape public discourse about "immigration," citizenship, and the politics of race in British society for decades to come. Whereas much of the scholarly debate about the racial politics surrounding the Commonwealth Immigration Act of 1962 tends to focus on the racist intent of Conservative policy makers, in order for one to fully comprehend the process in which the act came to represent an official statement on race and race relations in Britain, it is important to highlight the ways in which voices of dissent—regardless of their inability to thwart the bill's passage—mattered in terms of the ways in which the bill was viewed and interpreted both domestically and abroad. Voices of dissent exposed for public consumption the obscured objectives and hidden transcripts shielded by a migration policy structured to favor those with prearranged employment or skills deemed beneficial to the British economy, but inherently designed to establish an implicit racially inspired barrier to limit what was in 1961 a predominately Afro-Caribbean Commonwealth migration. In doing so, voices of dissent provide an important yet all too often overlooked trajectory to analyze the process in which "immigration" restrictions became a publicly recognized discourse of institutionalized racism, criminality, and disenfranchisement for Black British citizens, despite policy makers' desire to frame the public presentation of controls as a color-blind initiative.

Voices of Dissent and the Construction of Official Racial Discourse

In introducing the provisions of the Commonwealth Immigrants Bill for a second reading in the House of Commons, Home Secretary R. A. Butler emphasized the escalating rates of Commonwealth migration and reminded his Parliamentary colleagues that while the British economy was currently experiencing full employment, in the event of recession, increased employment competition coupled with an already strained housing market would lead to dire social conditions. Using this logic, Butler maintained that the possible outcomes of increasing migration warranted immediate attention as a preventive measure in reducing the possibilities of an unmanageable socioeconomic situation exacerbated by newcomers. Conceding the fact that Commonwealth migrant workers were valued contributors to the British economy, particularly in the arenas of health care and public transportation, Butler argued conversely that the increasing proportion of incoming migrants "[has] presented the country with an intensified social problem . . . by the sheer weight of the numbers," that undermined efforts to improve social conditions related to such areas as housing and urban renewal.[27]

As noted earlier, although public receptiveness to migration control peaked in the aftermath of the Nottingham and Notting Hill violence of 1958, the annual totals for Commonwealth migration sharply declined between 1956 and 1959. But by the end of 1960, this trend had reversed. In the final report issued by the Cabinet's Working Party on Commonwealth migrants, officials framed the urgency for legislation largely in terms of the dramatic increases in the rates of migration since 1959 and the rising monthly totals for non-White Commonwealth migration during the first eight months of 1961. Although Commonwealth migration slowed in the late 1950s, at the end of 1960 Government records indicated that no fewer than 49,650 West Indians of a total of 57,700 Commonwealth migrants entered Britain. One year later, the total figures for Commonwealth migration had more than doubled, at 136,400. While Caribbean migrants still dominated with 66,300 net arrivals, there were significant increases in migration from India and Pakistan.[28]

With a majority Afro-Caribbean migration stream at the forefront of the Conservative Government's efforts to enact Commonwealth immigration controls, it is important to highlight that as of 1958, Afro-Caribbean women began to match and, in many instances, outnumber the monthly and annual migration totals from the Caribbean colonies. This increase is significant in at least two regards as it relates to how Commonwealth migration was being imagined as a public policy problem. Although popular postwar discourses about "coloured immigrants" coalesced around the trope of single, Black male workers and the sexual and economic threat of Black masculinities, throughout the 1950s there existed a virtual silence about the particular anxieties attached to Black femininities and what the presence of Black women signaled in a majority White public's imagination.[29] As Wendy Webster has observed, by the 1960s, against the demographic backdrop of an increasing number of

West Indian womens' migrations, as popular discourses about Black women began to emerge in more coherent forms, their reproductive capacities and, more specifically, their purported over-fecundity became key elements of their status as "immigrants" and their racialization as second-class Britons. In the context of a postwar welfare state that offered its citizens health care, child care, and resources to pregnant and nursing mothers, even as Black women newcomers became subjects of public debate as mothers, it was in the process of configuring their sexuality and domestic life as a burden on the state.[30]

In addition to being marked as a potential economic drain on the welfare state, there is evidence to suggest that West Indian women were also regarded as a type of defense against the sexual threat that Black masculinity posed to White womanhood. As part of a series of editorials intended to "give people the facts about coloured people" in the wake of the 1958 violence, a column introducing the "Boys from Jamaica" attempted to refute arguments that West Indian men were "stealing our women" by highlighting that half of West Indian migrants were "wives and children—coming to rejoin their husbands."[31] In offering the migration of "wives" to dismantle the imagined threat that single Black men posed to White women, the author merely reaffirmed stereotypes about Black masculinity and sexuality. Ostensibly, Black men in intimate partnership with Black women offered possibilities to redeem and domesticate a pathologically wayward and unsavory Black masculinity.[32] But following this same line of thinking, as Black men partnered with migrating Black women one can also image how these dynamics produced modes of family formation and homemaking that would engender a type of re-rooting among migrants and serve as a conduit of settlement, claim making, and belonging. When imagined as unattached single men seeking work in Britain, "coloured immigrants" could retain a degree of transience. But as partners, husbands, fathers, heads of household—roles that the physical and discursive presence of Black women made possible—the problem that "coloured immigrants" embodied in the minds of those who sought to control and contain it became more entrenched and permanent.

For proponents of migration controls, the numbers of arrivals told the story. But as the Commonwealth Immigration Bill made its way through Parliament, some of its most vocal opponents included members of the Labour Party. During the second reading of the bill, the most extensive debate took place in the House of Commons. In the course of the debate, dissenters honed in on the racial character of the bill and the potentially devastating effects of the bill on Caribbean economies, Commonwealth relations, and international race politics. Leading the charge against the bill for the Opposition Party, Labour MP and former Commonwealth Relations Secretary Patrick Gordon Walker outlined a number of points of contention with the introduction of migration restrictions and the proposed formula for exercising controls. First, Walker noted that Cabinet members had introduced the bill "without adequate inquiry" or consultation with Commonwealth governments. He insisted that because the bill revoked "the long standing right of free entry to Britain" held by Commonwealth citizens, it essentially would "undermine the strength and unity of the Commonwealth." Walker also pointed out to his Parliamentary colleagues that the bill in its present form granted the executive Government "excessive discretionary powers" and introduced "a colour bar into our legislation," while at the same time failing to address the real origins of "the deplorable social and housing conditions under which recent Commonwealth immigrants and other subjects of Her Majesty are living." For Walker, all of these considerations provided grounds for Parliament to reject the bill during its second reading. [33]

In response to the Home Secretary's statistical rationale for legislation, Walker agreed that the "net figure of migration" was "absolutely critical" to any decision to regulate Commonwealth migration, but suggested that the Home Secretary's appraisals were inflated and presented a "wholly exaggerated" portrait of the potential impact of the current state of Commonwealth migration.[34] Citing a study conducted by the Economist Intelligence Unit, Walker insisted that Government figures for migration did not account for return migration among West Indians, estimated at no less that 20 percent between 1955 and 1960. Moreover, Walker asserted a laissez-faire economic argument that market relations alone would regulate acceptable levels of migration. He insisted, "There is a direct relation between labour demand and immigration."[35] While Butler had carefully noted that "one-quarter of the population of the globe" currently had the right to enter Britain,[36] Walker contended that "a limit is set on the numbers coming here by the economy itself, by the need of the economy for labour." He charged, "The truth is that there is a fairly quick adaptation of the numbers to the movement of the economy to and fro."[37]

Walker's strongest criticisms of the Commonwealth Immigration bill centered on the racial undertones implicit in its structure. Reiterating the rationale used by the Commonwealth Migrants Committee during Cabinet discussions to recommend employment-based restrictions that would appear race-neutral, yet most likely affect migration patterns along racial lines, Walker also surmised that under the bill, "Australians, Canadians and New Zealanders will overwhelmingly fall into the acceptable categories," and certainly "some coloured immigrants will come in because they have jobs and voucher." However, he insisted, "the overwhelming majority of those trying to get in on the open quota will be coloured people." With this possibility in mind, he publicly articulated what closed-door Cabinet discussions had already resolved—that "the net effect of the Bill is that a negligible number of white people will be kept out and almost all those kept out by the Bill will be coloured."[38]

Aside from the actual design of the controls, what most clearly exposed the racialized intention of bill for Walker was the exclusion of Irish migrants from any of the regulations included in the legislation. Initially, Cabinet ministers had suggested that Irish migrants—who, the Home Secretary estimated, entered Britain at a rate of between 60,000 and 70,000 annually—would be subject to controls in the same manner as all other Commonwealth citizens. However, given the tremendous strain that regulating such a heavy and, to be sure, more welcomed flow of migrants across traditionally porous borders would place on the Ministry of Labour, Government officials decided to exempt movement from the Irish Republic from controls.[39] In response to this exclusion, Walker maintained, "Before the Irish were taken out, the Bill was very careful to cover up this racial discrimination,"[40] but in its new form by exempting the Irish, Walker accused the Home Secretary of advocating "a Bill which contains bare-faced, open racial discrimination . . . written—not only into its spirit and its practice, but into its very letter."[41]

Walker was not alone in his condemnation of the racial dimensions of the bill. Fellow Labour Party member Charles Royle suggested that the bill amounted to official capitulation to the type of racial extremism promoted by "Fascist thugs" and seconded Walker's contention that with the exclusion of the Irish, the bill would disproportionately affect non-White migrants and therefore operate as "a colour bar bill."[42] Conservative MP Nigel Fisher, who along with Royle maintained membership in the British Caribbean Association, a Parliament lobby sympathetic to West Indian interests, suggested that the very idea of legislation ending unrestricted entry for Commonwealth citizens was "quite inimical to our whole concept of a multi-racial Commonwealth." For Fisher, the Commonwealth ideal of multiracialism served as a powerful internationally recognized example of anti-racism and provided a means of validating British moral legitimacy in the arena of race relations. In his opinion, Commonwealth migration restrictions—and particularly those structured to excluded non-White migrants—struck at the heart of the Commonwealth model and thus undermined Britain's position as a moral arbiter on issues of race in world politics. Alluding to what he viewed as the blatant hypocrisy of the nation captured in the Commonwealth Immigrants bill, Fisher explained,

> It seems strange to me that in Africa we attack apartheid and preach partnership, but in the United Kingdom we are today taking powers to exclude coloured British citizens, which is really a form of apartheid, and are evading our opportunity, that splendid opportunity, to practise partnership and so make our contribution to the improvement of

race relations throughout the world. Our words to Africa are incon-
sistent with our action today in the House of Commons.[43]

Elaborating on a point that had been raised during Patrick Gordon Walker's
diatribe against the bill, Fisher also agreed that that the structure of the bill did
not favor Caribbean migration in particular. Fisher insisted that because West
Indians did not generally arrive in Britain with prearranged jobs and were less
likely to meet British standards of "skilled" labor, it was most probable that
Caribbean migrants would gain entry only though undefined quotas.[44] While
Fisher qualified this assertion with a simple reference to the differing interpretations of "skilled" labor as defined by Caribbean economies, industries,
and labor markets, as compared to those in Britain, his comments highlight an
even more complicated relationship between ideas of "skilled" labor, race, and
the systematic processes of disenfranchisement affecting Caribbean migrants
which the Commonwealth Immigrants bill purposed to exploit.

The logic of the bill rested upon the notion that Black workers were inherently "unskilled," based in large part by their position within the British
labor market. In much the same way that racialized assumptions about Black
migrant laborers provided the basis for their systematic exclusion from accessing certain occupational opportunities in a British labor market in which they
had a right to expect full incorporation, the architects of the Commonwealth
Immigrants bill used a similar reasoning in crafting legislation that, in practice, largely excluded a presumably "unskilled" Black migrant working class.
To be sure, this same rationale formed the basis of Parliament members',
including Patrick Gordon Walker and Nigel Fisher, opposition to the inherent
racial character of the legislation.

Hugh Gaitskill, leader of the Labour Party, also weighed in and focused his
opposition to the bill on questions of race. Gaitskill insisted that the social
"harmony" of any multiracial society depended on the principle of "non-dis-
crimination." Gaitskill contended that "the test of a civilised country is how
it behaves to all its citizens of different race, religion and colour," and concluded, "by this test the Bill fails, and that is why we deplore it." Alluding to
similar comparisons raised by other members between the bill's intent and
the racially discriminatory policies and practices of South Africa's apartheid
regime, Gaitskill predicted that upon the Bill's passage, "the Nationalists in
South Africa will be rubbing their hands and saying, 'You see, even the British
are beginning to learn at last.'"[45] In addition to reiterating many of the racially
discriminatory features of the Bill highlighted by his Labour Party colleague
Patrick Gordon Walker, Gaitskill also paid careful attention to the potentially
devastating economic impact of migration restrictions in the West Indies.
Referencing the high unemployment rates in the more heavily populated

islands, including Jamaica, Trinidad, and Barbados, Gaitskill rehashed similar arguments asserted by West Indian officials who had consistently maintained throughout the late 1950s that migration to Britain provided a vital source of economic relief. For these reasons, Gaitskill beseeched the Government to "drop this miserable, shameful, shabby Bill," as it would surely "deal another deadly blow at the Commonwealth."[46]

In many ways, Opposition members, including Gaitskill, articulated talking points that explicitly addressed the concerns regarding the impact of the bill as viewed through the eyes of West Indian officials and other public interlocutors for West Indian communities in Britain and the Caribbean. In a telegram to the national secretary of the Labour Party dated just weeks after the Home Secretary had received approval from the Conservative Parliamentary conference to move forward with introducing legislation to control Commonwealth migration, Jamaican Premier Norman Manley expressed his apprehension about the implications of such legislation in regard to the overlapping issues of race and Commonwealth relations. Manley noted,

> This proposal we are certain will be a damaging blow to the Commonwealth. Moreover [the] proposal will vitally injure Jamaica and other parts of the West Indies at this critical moment in our history. We cannot see any economic reason for curbing migration now and recruitment in the West Indies for the British [labor] Army underlines [the] employment situation in England.[47]

In soliciting Parliamentary support against the bill, Manley reminded Labour Party leaders that from the perspective of many West Indians, the "decision [to legislate] will be interpreted widely as based on colour."[48]

When news of the Conservative conference's acceptance of the Home Secretary's recommendation to pursue migration controls reached Jamaica's Leader of the Opposition, Alexander Bustamante, he immediately issued a telegram to the Prime Minister that condemned restrictions on Commonwealth migration. Bustamante noted Commonwealth migration to Britain had been a common practice for decades, yet it appeared that it was only the recent increases in West Indian arrivals that occasioned the Government's interest in altering this tradition. Bustamante maintained that it was obvious that any restrictions on Commonwealth migration would in fact "be only a camouflage for colour discrimination," which he "vigorously" protested.[49] Bustamante's political rival, Jamaican Premier Norman Manley, concurred with his assessment and insisted that "the decision to limit migration to Britain would not have been made if the migrants had been people of European origin."[50] By November 1961, Manley had announced the commission of a Working Party established to examine the implications of the Commonwealth Immigrants bill and the potential impact on the Jamaican economy. From Manley's perspective, migration to Britain was unequivocally an "economic necessity" that provided relief for overloaded Caribbean markets and a supply of workers to fulfill labor shortages in British industries.[51]

Although Jamaican migrants represented the overwhelming majority of Caribbean migrants who journeyed to Britain during the early postwar period, the range of protests against the racial character of migration controls and their potential economic impact on Caribbean economies demonstrates the ways in which the issue represented a centripetal force uniting West Indian leaders and communities across island differences at a particular moment when it appeared that the future of a united West Indies seemed imperiled. Initially, Colonial Secretary Ian Macleod expressed reservations about the timing of the Government's announcement to legislate on Commonwealth migration in the fall of 1961 as he engaged in sensitive negotiations with West Indian officials about the transition toward independence in the form of a West Indies Federation. When the West Indies Constitutional convention met in London in June 1961, Grantley Adams, Federal Prime Minister, drew clear links between the economic solvency of a future independent West Indian nation-state and the ability for West Indian migrants to continue to exercise their historic right to migrate to Britain. Appealing to British officials for the continuation of an open-door policy, Adams contended,

> At the moment of independence we need a period of time in which to deal with the grave responsibilities of nationhood without having to suffer the indignity of having a door that has traditionally and generously been kept open now slammed in our faces. Our history has been too closely intertwined to make us think that Britain would wish to mar the moment of rejoicing with the ill tidings that a curtain is to be drawn between the peoples of our countries. We do not think migration is the solution of our economic difficulties, but we want at least time to show that the other remedies which we are preparing can make our people want to stay at home because home is able to give them opportunities which they now seek here [Britain].[52]

Adams's comments highlighted the extent to which migration to Britain provided much-needed economic relief for Caribbean colonies, including Jamaica, by serving as an additional employment market for West Indian workers and a source of indirect monetary subsidies for struggling Caribbean economies in the form of remittances, which in 1960 had totaled nearly £5.5 million in 1961.[53] But when Jamaica withdrew its support in September 1961, following a popular vote against a referendum to remain a part of the Federation, Cabinet members decided that there was no longer a pressing imperial agenda preventing an announcement of their intentions to pursue controls in the upcoming session of Parliament. As one traces dissent among West Indian officials, it is interesting to note that precisely when Jamaica's withdrawal from the West Indies Federation effectively served to diminish the concept of an independent West Indian nation, the subject of Commonwealth migration to Britain paradoxically provided a medium through which West Indian officials articulated the overlapping interests of a West Indian national community whose borders extended to Britain and trumped inter-island politics.

On the day following the first extensive Parliamentary considerations of the Commonwealth Immigration Bill, Grantley Adams registered an official protest to the consideration of controls in his capacity as Prime Minister of the West Indies Federation. In a scathing dispatch to his counterpart, Harold Macmillan Adams characterized the bill as a "flagrant disregard of every liberal principle on which Britain has based its customs and traditions since Lord Mansfield's famous judgment of 1772." Raising the specter of the nation's legacy of abolitionism, which shored up its racially liberal international image, Adams went on to invoke the benevolent paternalism enshrined in this national mystique as he noted that the actions of policy makers sought to diminish the freedom of those to whom the British "have a historic responsibility" as a result of the "rich [slave] trade in bodies and goods on which much of Britain's prosperity has been founded." Adams insisted that the transnational West Indian communities for whom he spoke were "firmly convinced" that the move toward immigration control would be "no different in kind to the basis on which the system of apartheid in South Africa is based." He concluded with a stern warning, "It will in [the] future be difficult for any person from the Commonwealth to accept unreflectingly the oft-repeated assertion of a multi-racial partnership."[54]

Barbadian Premier Hugh Cummins shared Adams's concerns about the ways in which migration controls would "do irreparable harm to Commonwealth unity," as they would devalue the meaning of British citizenship for people of African and Asian descent from the Caribbean.[55] Speaking on behalf of the government of British Guiana, Brindley Binn suggested that migration control represented a form of economic divestment in the Caribbean. Binn's remarks drew attention to the ways in which Britain's tradition of open-door migration policies for British Commonwealth citizens had long offered West Indian workers employment opportunities and routes toward social mobility outside of the limits of struggling Caribbean economies, policies that had in turn benefited not only individual workers and their families, but also the broader economic infrastructure of Caribbean societies. To be sure, Binn also noted that the manner in which the bill would curtail the freedom of movement of "British subjects and citizens" between the Caribbean and Britain also introduced an "undesirable colour-bar" into British policy that contradicted the basic foundations of Commonwealth solidarity.[56]

For Garnet Gordon, High Commissioner for the West Indies Federal Government, the timing of the bill was especially germane to West Indian opposition to the bill. Gordon drew attention to the fact that just as the British Government planned to pursue a program of migration controls largely on the premise that migration would become a detriment to the British economy and exacerbate already disconcerting social conditions in areas such as housing, the Tory Government had also begun the process of cementing their integration within the European Economic Community (EEC). Less than a month before Butler's announcement to reform migration policy, the EEC began a review of Britain's application for membership in a continental partnership premised in part upon facilitating greater freedom of movement of Western European labor across national boundaries.[57] Garnet Gordon found this coincidence especially troubling. Gordon suggested that even the "possibility of non-British Europeans, exercising rights permitted to citizens of the Commonwealth restrictively, calls for much explanation." Clearly aware of a broader racial undercurrent guiding the British government's seemingly contradictory actions, Gordon sarcastically chided, "But then, of course, the immigration from Europe would not be coloured."[58]

In making their case against the Commonwealth Immigrants bill, West Indian officials spoke directly to British policymakers, but they were well aware that they spoke on behalf of local Black British constituencies and a larger transnational West Indian community. One of the central modes by which West Indian officials communicated their opposition to the bill to their West Indian constituents residing in Britain was by having their talking points captured in the headlines of the *West Indian Gazette* (*WIG*) newspaper, edited by the venerable activist and organizer Claudia Jones. Since its founding in 1958, the *WIG* had arguably become the most powerful centrifuge of Black British culture, community, and political life in postwar Britain. Coming out of a tradition of Black internationalism, Jones initially conceived the paper as a tool for galvanizing the political consciousness of a largely West Indian migrant population around what had been a long-standing struggle among diasporic intellectuals—many of whom were based in London during the twentieth century—against the interlocking global forces of colonialism, racism, and working-class oppression.[59] During the late 1950s, the *WIG* found the base of its local audience and developed a popular appeal in the wake of urban racial violence in Britain, including the highly publicized "race riots" of 1958 and the murder of Kelso Cochrane in 1959. Along with organizing the first annual series of West Indian carnivals, beginning in January 1959, to showcase Caribbean culture and celebrate the music, fashion, food, artistry, and beauty of Caribbean people, throughout the late 1950s and early 1960s Jones and the WIG sponsored a host of community-wide events, including concerts and talent shows, that featured such artists such as internationally renowned activist and entertainer Paul Robeson, BBC personality Cy Grant, renowned Jamaican ska virtuoso Laurel Aitken, and actress and singer Nadia Cattouse.[60] In 1961, weeks after the Home Secretary announced plans to pursue Commonwealth immigration reform, in her role as WIG editor, Claudia Jones and local Caribbean, African, and South Asian political leaders hosted a reception for Martin Luther King, Jr. at a moment when he was becoming an international symbol for the long history of Black freedom struggles aimed at dismantling Jim Crow in American society.[61] By taking part in such organizing, not only did Jones continue to establish the WIG as a local Black political voice but, more importantly, she also showcased its mission to foster wide-ranging collaborations, solidarities, and cross-fertilizations of movements advocating on behalf of disenfranchised populations in different parts of the world.

The assemblage of a broad coalition of anti-racist supporters that transcended national, racial, and ethnic identifications that convened for Martin Luther King, Jr.'s 1961 visit to London placed Claudia Jones in conversation with local representatives of the African National Congress, the West African Students Union, and the India League, along with ambassadors from Haiti, Ethiopia, and Nigeria. Moreover, it reflected the vision of "Black globality" and a type of what Nico Slate has labeled "colored cosmopolitanism" captured in the headlines of the WIG, which added the phrase "and Afro-Asian-Caribbean News" to its masthead title by its second year in circulation as a show of solidarity with other anti-colonial, anti-racist, leftist, and burgeoning Third World liberation movements around the world.[62] Imagining the structures enabling White supremacy through the intersecting prisms of capitalism, colonialism, and racism, as Bill Schwarz has noted, the pages of the WIG intimately linked the concerns of West Indian migrants in neighborhoods like Brixton to stories about the Cuban Revolution, opposition to apartheid and Jim Crow, the assassination of Congolese leader Patrice Lumumba, and Socialist achievements in China.[63] And it was the imaginings of the global worlds of a "Black community" that was transnational, multiethnic, and bound in familiar yet historically distinct ways by the disenfranchising power of White supremacy that Black Britons such as Claudia Jones and other anti-racist activists joined forces to protest against the passage of the Commonwealth Immigration Act of 1962.

As the Tory Government made preparations to formally introduce a bill to regulate Commonwealth migration, Labour MP Fenner Brockway convened a series of public meetings in early November 1961 in anticipation of

Parliamentary debate headlined "No Colour Bar on Immigration."[64] Working under the auspices of his anti-colonial advocacy organization, the Movement for Colonial Freedom (MCF), Brockway shared a platform with Claudia Jones and newly elected London County Councillor David Pitt, who, along with Jones, had been on the front lines of civil rights activism in the wake of the race riots and the death of Kelso Cochrane. During the interwar period, Brockway had established a national political career based on his passionate opposition to colonial rule. As decolonization and the end of Empire became more of a political reality, he remained on the front lines of the domestic anti-colonial front that he regarded as inclusive of a struggle against fascism and racism. And to that end, throughout the 1950s he proposed legislation to address racial discrimination in public spaces, a legislative agenda that did not take shape until the Labour Party regained power in 1964.[65] From Brockway's view, racial prejudice was the sole impetus behind the Commonwealth Immigrants bill and the exemptions for Irish migrants made this prejudice readily apparent. In promoting their opposition to the bill, circulars for the MCF charged that the proposed policy "legalises colour prejudice," and contained echoes of "the jack-boots of fascism," a combination that questioned Britain's commitment to the ideals that so many had fought and died for in World War II.[66]

It is likely that Claudia Jones and David Pitt, in framing their opposition to the bill at the MCF conference, resurrected talking points that they had previously outlined in the pages of the *WIG*. Whereas Pitt, who held political office, used the columns of the *WIG* to emphasize the vital contributions that West Indian laborers and economic resources made to the British society, Jones's editorials typically took a sharper tone in laying bare the "hypocrisy and pretense" that underwrote the bill's central intent to limit the entry of non-White Commonwealth citizens.[67] As the Caribbean colonies moved closer towards self-government and independence, Pitt, a native of Grenada who helped establish the West Indian National Party in Trinidad in support of West Indian nationhood during the late 1940s, viewed migration as a tool for economic development for fledging Caribbean nations, particularly given that remittances nearly totaled colonial welfare aid in the postwar years. Moreover, Pitt saw migration as part of a larger Commonwealth economic partnership that had historically been mutually beneficial to both Britain and the Caribbean. Along with the migration of workers fueling Britain's transport and health services industries, he highlighted the goods and raw materials such as sugar, citrus fruit, bauxite, and aluminum that Caribbean colonies supplied to Britain and other Commonwealth markets.[68]

Most importantly, however, in making the case against migration reform, Pitt challenged the alarmist empirical arguments that proponents of Commonwealth migration restrictions had offered about the exigency of migration reform. In response, Pitt noted that the unemployment rate was less than 2 percent, employment vacancies surpassed the numbers of the unemployed, and net emigration from Britain in the last decade had exceeded the overall figures for immigration. When coupled with Britain's interest in joining the Common Market, a move that would surely promote the inward movement of European workers and enhanced trading partnerships with western European nations, Pitt concluded that the Conservative push for controls did not comport with any particular "economic necessity" but rather "is the entire result of racial prejudice." Thus for Pitt, halting the move toward a type of policy that would disproportionately affect what was a largely West Indian Commonwealth migration, meant bypassing an opportunity to show the world that racial integration was "not only possible but desirable." No doubt influenced by the integrationist rhetoric that Martin Luther King, Jr.'s model of civil rights advocacy espoused, Pitt asserted that the stakes of altering the time-honored universal right of Commonwealth citizens to freely move across Britain's borders would compromise the nation's moral leadership in the world at a crucial moment in the international history of race relations, as he charged,

> When we have mixed crews of white and black on our buses and trains, mixed teams of white and black in our hospital wards and operation theatres; in our canteens and our factories; when white children are taught by black teachers and black children by white teachers, there is bound to be a better understanding and there is bound to be progress towards the realisation of the brotherhood of man. Britain should not allow South Africa and the Southern States of America to tell her how to behave. We should show them how it is done and then invite them to do likewise.[69]

In Pitt's view, upholding the right of Commonwealth citizens to migrate to Britain meant denouncing the institutions of law and order that empowered ideologies of White supremacy to exclude, differentiate, selectively police, and disenfranchise Black British citizens, a sentiment that Claudia Jones shared.

As editor of the *West Indian Gazette*, Claudia Jones had consistently been on the front lines of articulating Black Britons' opposition to any form of legislation that would strip Commonwealth citizens of their right to migrate to Britain. Even before Home Secretary R. A. Butler announced the Government's intentions to move forward with the Commonwealth Immigrants bill in October of 1961, the *WIG* ran several articles making the case against migration controls as a detriment to Commonwealth relations and the fight for West Indian independence.[70] While British and West Indian officials who opposed the bill focused their dissent largely in terms of how the legislation would infringe upon the rights of those seeking to enter Britain, Jones used the pages of the *WIG* to construct an anti-immigration-control argument that threaded the ties between the international and domestic consequences of new legislation for Black Britons seeking to enter and for those seeking to stay in Britain. In explaining the components of the proposed legislation, Jones highlighted the fact that the bill had two defining features that collectively worked to create a second-class citizenship status for Black Britons and the poor. Obviously, the first of these elements related to the new powers granted to the Home Office to regulate the entry of Commonwealth citizens. Although proponents of the bill touted its ostensibly race-neutral system for regulating migration based on one's relationship to the labor market, Jones pointed out to her *WIG* readers that in addition to exempting controls for citizens of the majority White Irish Republic, for those "rich enough . . . to have a job to come to, a house to sustain you—its provisions need not apply."[71] Jones intended for readers to understand that the racial politics of citizenship had an implicit class dimension that functioned in very strategic ways to disadvantage non-White laborers migrating from struggling colonial labor markets who largely relied upon migration as a necessary means to acquire economic resources, including jobs and wages, unavailable in their homelands due to what she described as "300 years of imperialist colonial rule" in the Caribbean.[72]

While the most controversial feature of the bill involved the regulation of entry, Jones's condemnation of the proposed legislation also focused upon provisions granting the Home Office unprecedented powers of deportation that were based on the recommendations of local magistrates.[73] Arguably, nothing articulated one's imperiled citizenship status more so than being subject to deportation. Deportability essentially abrogates the process of incorporating oneself as a citizen and ultimately marks one's presence in a society as alien or criminal. Having been personally affected by the disenfranchising powers of surveillance, detainment, incarceration, and expulsion embedded in having a deportable status, Claudia Jones knew all too well that for those Black Britons who intended to stay in Britain, their potential deportability would significantly alter their juridical relationship to the state and potentially render them defenseless against everyday policing practices exercised by law enforcement officials and the society writ large.[74] Moreover, deportability coupled with official rules of entry designed to systematically exclude Black Britons meant that the rhetoric of "Keep Britain White," a mantra that underwrote the supposedly rogue activities of a so-called lunatic fringe of right-winged neo-fascists and young reckless "Teds," was now becoming a matter of policy. From Jones's vantage point, the provisions of the Commonwealth Immigrants Act essentially sanctioned quotidian practices of discrimination in housing and employment—practices that effectively barred Black Britons from certain

sectors of the labor market and opportunities to obtain decent and affordable accommodation in certain areas. Most importantly, it gave credence and
legitimacy to fomenting anti-Black sentiment on the streets of places like
West London where West Indians, Africans, and South Asians encountered
derogatory epithets on pavements, verbal assaults, and physical violence—all
of which reminded them that their presence in British society was neither tol-
erable nor welcomed.

The conference on the immigration bill organized by the Movement for
Colonial Freedom (MCF) in November 1961, at which Claudia Jones and
other local leaders made a case against the proposed legislation, was followed up with a public march held on 14 January 1962 and attended by nearly
2,000 demonstrators carrying signs from Hyde Park to Trafalgar Square,
including "No Colour-Bar for Britain." [75] In organizing both the conference and
the rally, MCF chairman Fenner Brockway hoped to build a broad grassroots
campaign that would challenge the bill's features by exposing the links between
racial discrimination and the MCF's larger anti-colonial platform. The vision
of forming a coalition of support against the bill took shape most concretely
with the establishment of the Afro-Asian-Caribbean Conference (AACC) at
a meeting of nearly 100 delegates and supporters held at Mahatma Gandhi
Hall following the MCF march. There, activists, representatives, and supporters affiliated with organizations such as the London branch of the People's
National Movement, the *WIG*, the West Indian Students Union, the Indian
Workers Association, the Committee of African Organisations, the Standing
Conference of West Indian Organisations, and the British Guiana Freedom
Association unanimously passed two resolutions. The first resolution offered
support of West Indian independence and called for the reorganization of the
West Indies Federation in the wake of Jamaica's unexpected secession, while
another protested what delegates deemed as a "reactionary and retrograde"
Commonwealth Immigration bill. Incorporating many of the points of dissen-
tion previously addressed by Labour Party members in Parliament, West Indian
officials and, in the pages of the *WIG*, the AACC's resolution determined that
the bill was "nothing but a legalizing of race prejudice and Colour discrimination" that essentially gave "a green light to racialist forces" that were the products of a history of British imperialism. [76]

The coupling of protest against immigration control and support for the
collapsing West Indian Federation underscores the particular ways in which
racial politics in postwar Britain and advocacy on behalf of Black British citizens was routed through the intersecting imperial histories of White supremacy, the racialization of laboring bodies, and colonial governance. And it was
precisely this conceptualization of anti-racist organizing that proved decisive in shaping a burgeoning Black British political culture that advocated

on behalf of all communities of color even as it remained securely oriented toward the interests of diasporic communities of African descent. Just as Claudia Jones had anticipated a *WIG* audience that had West Indians and people of African descent as its base, in changing the masthead title of the paper to the *West Indian Gazette and Afro-Asian-Caribbean News*, she also presciently imagined a local Black political culture that would be able to adapt to and accommodate the realities and political futures of postcolonial Britain. Whereas Empire had, by design, sought to partition the worlds of the colonized, the postwar migrations of West Indians, Africans, and South Asians to Britain effectively collapsed the tenuous intra-imperial boundaries that distinguished not only between colony and metropole, but also between the various colonial geographies of the Caribbean, Africa, and the Indian subcontinent. These migrations articulated claims to a type of British citizenship that could be inclusive, transracial, multiethnic, and universal. And in doing so, they allowed migrants from Jamaica, Trinidad, India, Pakistan, Nigeria, Ghana, and Barbados to employ their journeys to Britain as a type of anti-colonial project that challenged the racial hierarchies of race, space, and White privilege that had previously marked their colonial status.

To publicize and solicit support for their campaign against the passage of the Commonwealth Immigration bill, the AACC, in collaboration with organizations such as the West Indian Students' Union, the London branch of the People's National Party, the Indian Workers' Association, and the Committee of African Organisations announced plans to hold a Commonwealth Lobby on 13 February 1962, timed to coincide with final debate on the bill at the committee level. Targeting the support of the laboring masses of West Indian, African, and Asian "citizens," in order to lobby Parliament members in the House of Commons to reject the legislation, and in anticipation of the event, the AACC, made contact with officials from the High Commissions of Ghana, Canada, India, the West Indies, Nigeria, and Malaya and requested that representatives issue public statements in support of their cause. While the Indian Government expressed their objection to controls that would discriminate on account of race or color, Nigerian and West Indian officials made a more pointed attack on the deplorable "racial overtones" of bill. Nigerian officials were convinced that the bill would embolden "racialist and fascists elements" in Britain, a development that Garnet Gordon, High Commissioner to the West Indies Federal Government, felt would encourage "harmful incidents" toward West Indians."[77]

It is important to note that the leadership base of the AACC was comprised of many of the same grassroots organizers who had been key in advocating on behalf of the rights of Black British citizens in the aftermath of the 1958 race riots and the death of Kelso Cochrane. David Pitt chaired the conference,

Pearl Connor worked as its Public Relations Officer, and Claudia Jones and Frances Ezzrecco, who had founded the CPPA, served as central points of contact as the AACC built a coalition of support for its cause that included labor leaders, political office holders, Commonwealth officials, and local communities.[78] Plans for the AACC's Commonwealth lobby included a two-day vigil outside of Admiralty House and the Home Office, followed by a public protest meeting. Although it is quite likely that AACC organizers well understood that their efforts would not necessarily reverse the course of the Tory Government's legislative agenda toward regulating Commonwealth migration as the window for Parliamentary debate drew to a close, at best, arguably their goal was to create a greater public consciousness about the stakes of immigration reform and leverage that awareness to challenge House of Commons members to object to some of the more egregious aspects of the bill that would directly infringe upon the citizenship rights of Black Britons who hoped to enter and those who aimed to stay. In particular, the AACC focused attention on a subsection of the bill that made it a criminal offense for any person to "knowingly harbour" an undocumented immigrant or someone believed to have entered the United Kingdom without a proper employment voucher or in violation of any other established provisions of the bill. In selecting this particular provision of the bill as a touchstone of their Commonwealth lobby, AACC members strategically triangulated between points of dissent that centered upon the racially discriminatory intent of the bill and its impact on Commonwealth citizens seeking to migrate and those already resident in Britain.[79]

In a memo outlining its objections, the AACC explained that this particular provision of the bill provided landlords and landladies, some of whom "already practice colour discrimination," with an excuse to turn away people of color under the guise of insulating themselves from prosecution for unlawfully harboring an improperly documented migrant. Even for those proprietors more amenable to renting to Commonwealth migrants, under the law, this transaction would involve opening proprietors to a new potential legal liability and undesirable surveillance and policing of their private property and business ventures. For newcomers, entering a depressed housing market, the AACC regarded this avenue of discrimination as detrimental to their ability to secure a basic element of settlement, survival, and belonging even when they entered with the promise of employment. Perhaps more important to those West Indians, Africans, and Asian communities already in Britain, the AACC's memo noted that the bill would inherently require all Commonwealth migrants, regardless of the timing or conditions of their entry, to bear the burden of proving not only their citizenship status, but also their right to literally belong in British society by demonstrating to landlords that they were not "prohibited immigrants."[80]

In highlighting this particular feature of the bill, the AACC powerfully articulated the everyday realities of racism and disenfranchisement tethered to the underlying structure of the Commonwealth Immigration bill. The activists, organizers, and supporters involved in the AACC lobby clearly understood that the policy was not merely about regulating the inflow of Commonwealth migrants. Rather, the proposed legislation pinpointed the right of migration as an apparatus for redefining and, to be more precise, abrogating the citizenship rights of any individual who fit the profile of an "immigrant," whether they lived in Kingston or Kensington. Although West Indians, Africans, South Asians, and other non-White Britons had been surreptitiously imagined as "immigrants," and foreign outsiders in relation to the national body politic in public discourse throughout the late 1940s and 1950s, the 1958 race riots cemented the equation of the "immigrant" problem with people of color and, more specifically, caricatures of single West Indian men. Discourses surrounding Britain's "immigrant problem" provided a lexicon to speak about and oftentimes conflate the "colour problem" and what was perceived as the public nuisance of the invasion of Black outsiders. But in their protest against immigration reform, AACC activists and their supporters skillfully subverted this discourse. In their critique of the Commonwealth Immigrants bill, AACC lobbyists underscored that the idea of "immigration" controls, an institutionalized policy that would juridically disenfranchise particular groups of citizens and produce categories of "immigrants" in a manner intended to disproportionately affect Black working-class Britons, was the problem. In doing so, the AACC aimed to shift the public dialogue from an ahistorical conversation about the presence of Black "immigrants" to one that focused upon the institutional structures of anti-Black racism in British society.

Because the Commonwealth Immigrants bill ultimately received Royal assent in April 1962, most historical accounts of the racial politics surrounding its passage tend to overlook the important work that those who publicly dissented did in transforming the issue of immigration into a political wedge for debating race and race relations in British society. In the aftermath of the passage of the Commonwealth Immigration Act of 1962 and for decades to come, immigration remained a racially charged political issue that represented contested visions of citizenship, belonging, and ideas about British national identity both at home and abroad. Tracking the voices of those who opposed the bill and in particular the Black Britons who were the subject of policy makers' regulatory vision for the legislation focuses much-needed critical attention on what the passage of the Commonwealth Immigration bill meant for those who had already journeyed to Britain. In the aftermath of its passing, as activists such as Claudia Jones and her AACC compatriots had warned, the parameters of the bill significantly altered not only the terms of entry for Afro-Caribbean migrants, but also the terms of their ability to stay and belong as citizens.

Internal Immigration Control

On 1 June 1962, Part II of the Commonwealth Immigration Bill of 1962 granting the Home Secretary powers to deport any Commonwealth citizen who had been convicted of a "serious criminal offense" and who had been residing in Britain for fewer than five years took effect. On the following day Carmen Bryan, a twenty-two year old Jamaican woman who had arrived in Britain in 1960 stood before a Paddington magistrate, charged with petty larceny for stealing goods, including nylons, tomatoes, milk, and a clothesline, at a local shop, amounting to a total of approximately £2.[81] A first-time offender at the time of her arrest, Carmen Bryan was unemployed and living on national assistance since losing her position at a welding factory after experiencing a bout of extended illness.[82] Two days after her arrest, on 4 June 1962, Carmen Bryan entered a guilty plea for her crime. Because she had not lived in Britain for more than five years, she was served with a notice indicating that her conviction made her eligible for a recommendation of deportation and was immediately remanded into custody at Holloway Prison. One week later, after issuing a conditional discharge of her case, a local magistrate at Marylebone became the first in the nation to exercise new prerogatives authorized under Part II of the Commonwealth Immigrants Act of 1962 when he formally recommended that the Home Secretary deport Carmen Bryan back to Jamaica, since she "seemed not to have settled down successfully" in Britain.[83]

Carmen Bryan sat in Holloway Prison for nearly six weeks as she awaited the Home Secretary's decision regarding her recommendation for deporta- tion, which was finally approved by outgoing Home Secretary R. A. Butler on 13 July 1962. In the intervening weeks, however, most likely because it was the first of its kind, Carmen Bryan's case ignited a political firestorm that challenged the authority of the Home Secretary and exposed the underlying paradoxes of an immigration policy that applied to certain categories of British citizens. [84] Upon learning of Bryan's case nearly a month after her incarceration, Labour MP Eric Fletcher questioned the new Home Secretary, Henry Brooke, during debate in the House of Commons about the length of her detention and his intentions to fulfill the deportation orders signed by his predecessor, given that "assurances" had been made by the bill's Tory supporters that deportation would be reserved for "serious offenses."[85] On the job for less than a week, Brooks maintained that he saw no reason to reverse his predecessor's orders. To the consternation of the Opposition, he argued that to do so might encourage crimes of this sort by suggesting that he considered shoplifting a "trivial offense." Moreover, Brooks cited the fact that Bryan had not appealed the court's decision and had apparently petitioned the Home Secretary to have her return to Jamaica expedited because she had no desire to remain in Britain as further justification for his decision to move forward with her deportation. Seemingly unflappable in his decision to let the order stand despite audible shouts of dissent from many of his Parliamentary colleagues, Brooks self-righteously exhorted, "I think it would be a great act of injustice if I were to stand in the way of her returning to Jamaica."[86]

In his appeal for clemency on behalf of Carmen Bryan, Eric Fletcher challenged the Home Secretary's arguments on a number of grounds that would form the basis of a media outcry in defense of Carmen Bryan's right to stay in Britain. First and foremost, Fletcher viewed the deportation of Commonwealth citizens as a power reserved for serious criminal infractions and for habitual offenders, neither of which applied to Bryan's case. Secondly, Fletcher took issue with Brooks's contention that Bryan had been afforded full rights of due process, given that she was denied legal aid and had no access to officials at the Jamaican High Commission during a period of incarceration that did not necessarily comport with her crime. Given these circumstances, Fletcher surmised that Bryan's petition expressed the desires of a woman seeking to depart from Britain rather than continue to face the uncertainties of her incarceration. Perhaps most importantly, Fletcher wondered whether the legal and administrative procedures characterizing Carmen Bryan's case meant that the new powers of deportation authorized by the Commonwealth Immigration Act of 1962 would effectively "treat Commonwealth immigrants as regards [to] deportation worse than aliens" in the eyes of British law, a suggestion that elicited cries of "Shame" from the Opposition.[87]

Although Fletcher and his supporters were able to convince the Home Secretary to delay Carmen Bryan's deportation, pending further debate, ultimately Henry Brooks announced a decision in the House of Commons days later that he planned to cancel Bryan's deportation orders.[88] No doubt aware of the ways in which the administrative bungling of Bryan's case had begun to cast a cloud on his early days as Home Secretary, as press reports described him as "inept" and "stubborn," Brooks explained that since she had already been regrettably imprisoned for weeks and given that it now appeared that Bryan wished to remain in Britain, he felt deportation was not warranted.[89] Although Eric Fletcher had been one of the most vocal supporters of Carmen Bryan, his response to Brooks' announcement of her canceled deportation orders indicates that he too had a short-sighted view of the overall implications of the Commonwealth Immigrants Act for Commonwealth citizens. Remaining critical of the procedures for implementing deportation, given the somewhat arbitrary fashion in which they were applied in Bryan's case, Fletcher challenged that the case should serve as a reminder that in Britain "there can be no second-class citizenship for British subjects whether they are members of the United Kingdom and colonies or elsewhere."[90] But Carmen Bryan's case and those of what would become a largely Irish population of Commonwealth deportees during the 1960s would prove otherwise. Their deportability in fact qualified their "immigrant" status and effectively nullified their rights as British citizens before the law. And it was in opposition to the disenfranchising premise and practice of Commonwealth immigration policies that Black Britons voiced their dissent.[91]

Eventually, Carmen Bryan and her fiancé voluntarily decided to leave Britain and return to Jamaica. But little more than a year after her case was settled, in August 1963, as the eyes of the world fixated upon the quarter of a million marchers who convened on the national mall in Washington, DC for the historic March on Washington for Jobs and Freedom, Black Britons organized one of several solidarity marches held across the world to demonstrate to Black Americans that they shared their experience of second-class citizenship and supported their cause for a collective Black freedom as Black Britons declared on the streets of London, "Your fight is our fight!"[92]

On 31 August 1963, members of the Committee of Afro-Asian Caribbean Organisations (CAACO), a grassroots coalition of African, Caribbean, and largely South Asian organizations that grew out of the anti-immigration organizing, including the AACC, formed in response to the Commonwealth Immigrants Act, sponsored London's March on Washington in support of the highly publicized US march (Figure 5.1). In announcing plans for the march, CAACO activists, including Claudia Jones, who spearheaded the

Figure 5.1 "London Solidarity March," *West Indian Gazette*, 1963. (Courtesy of the Institute of Race Relations.)

formation of the Committee, noted that their goal in organizing was to express their solidarity with "Afro-American Freedom Fighters" and "demand justice for England's African Asian and West Indian population" who, they insisted, "also suffer from the cruel effects of racial exploitation."[93] Echoing many of the themes of the US march, Black British activists hoped that their demonstration would further their demands for "equal rights, jobs, housing and education for all," as well as the repeal of what they deemed as "racist" immigration policies in Britain.[94]

Leading a convoy of over 750 supporters, CAACO activists, including Trinidadian singer Pearl Connor, who offered a rendition of "We Shall Overcome" as marchers journeyed from Ladbroke Grove Tube Station to the American Embassy, carried placards that contained messages that included "NO IMPERIALISM, NO RACISM" and "RACIALISM DEFEATS WORKERS UNITY," along with a banner declaring "NO COLOUR BAR ON IMMIGRATION!"[95]

The March on Washington solidarity campaign served a number of strategic political purposes for Black activists seeking to continue the fight to expose the racially discriminatory character of the Commonwealth Immigration Act of 1962. By linking the citizenship struggles of African Americans with those of Black Britons and other populations of color, including South Asian migrants, the campaign clearly established that in their eyes, the bill codified the types of anti-Black racism and ideologies of White supremacy that had long prevented African Americans from experiencing full citizenship. CAACO activists and their supporters felt that, much like the disenfranchising color bars of Jim Crow, Britain's Commonwealth immigration policies made Black Britons second-class citizens subject to suspicion, deportation, and, as the case of Carmen Bryan revealed, unfair and discriminatory treatment in the criminal justice system. Moreover, aligning their fight to repeal the Commonwealth Immigration Act of 1962 with the internationally recognized Black freedom movement being waged by African Americans gave Black British activists a platform to raise the profile of their campaign and garner the attention of global audiences to the racial conditions facing Black Britons. And much like the news of "race riots" in 1958, activists told the world that Britain as a nation was not as different from Jim Crow America as the mystique of British anti-racism might have suggested.

As organizations including CAACO hoped to continue the critique of the racial politics of the Commonwealth Immigration bill that those who had voiced their dissents to its introduction in Parliament had begun before it became law, they did so with an understanding of the bill's effect on the everyday lives of Black Britons who had made the journey across the Atlantic. Immigration policy was just as much about those prospective "immigrants" seeking to enter as it was about those who had exercised their right to migrate and incorporate themselves into British society as citizens, but who were still socially and culturally regarded as "immigrant" minorities. Their lives continued to bear evidence that the law had fundamentally altered the meaning of their citizenship and their status in British society.

In July 1965, while Barbara Tomlin was traveling on a British passport issued in Jamaica on a trip to the Federal Republic of Germany with her schoolmates from Twyford School in Acton, authorities at the German Frontier at Strasbourg detained her and required her to produce a visa and pay a fee equivalent to £1 to cross the border. Although her British passport indicated that Tomlin was a "British Subject Citizen of the United Kingdom and Colonies" and therefore described her official nationality in a manner that was indistinguishable from her other mates, aside from the passport's place of issuance, in the eyes of German authorities it was deemed a "colonial" passport.[96] Disturbed by the incident, the headmistress at Tomlin's school wrote to Bernard Floud, her local MP, to express her objection to "the singling out of a British subject" in this manner.[97] While the headmistress did not directly raise the issue of race in her complaint to Floud, when he followed up with the Foreign Office to inquire about the incident, he expressly noted that the case was "bound to give the impression of racial discrimination."[98]

In light of the provisions of the Commonwealth Immigration Act of 1962, one year after it took effect, German authorities began requiring visas for all British passport holders, including Barbara Tomlin, whose nationality documents had been issued in British colonies. Based on German authorities' interpretation of the new immigration policy, because the United Kingdom could not guarantee that all "colonial" passport holders could be returned to Britain without restriction, an additional visa requirement would be necessary for these travelers.[99] Although British authorities had sought to abolish all formal visa requirements for any British subject seeking to enter the Federal Republic—particularly since all British subjects with passports issued in colonial territories, including those citizens who had been in Britain for more than five years were not subject to the provisions of the Commonwealth Immigration Act of 1962—German authorities did not budge. They rightly understood that in July 1962, the rights of British subjects, Commonwealth citizens, and Citizens of the United Kingdom and Colonies like Barbara Tomlin had fundamentally changed. And just as their rights of access and inclusion were restricted legally and in the social imagination of a British society that labeled them as "coloured immigrants," German authorities quite justifiably felt that they too should distinguish this category of British citizens from others in such a manner that would reflect the ways in which British policy had begun to institutionalize their second-class citizenship status. Just as British policy had now altered the conditions of entry for Afro-Caribbean migrants, so too would German authorities.

Shortly after Barbara Tomlin resumed her studies at Twford School in Acton, following her school trip to the Federal Republic, the newly elected Labour Government issued its first White Paper on Commonwealth Immigration in August 1965. Although Labour Party leaders had stridently opposed the Tory Government's introduction of the Commonwealth Immigration Act of 1962, their new legislative agenda outlined policies that would impose even further restrictions upon the rights of Commonwealth citizens to migrate to Britain. With this move it was clear that the regulation of Commonwealth migration was a subject in which both leading political parties had reached a degree of consensus even if their support was grounded in slightly different rationales. However, while those British subjects seeking to enter the British Isles from the Caribbean may have found their options for passage dwindling, for those who had arrived there remained the struggle to fully actualize the citizenship rights that they had claimed by migrating to Britain. This struggle would involve working toward dismantling the social, political, and economic barriers of discrimination that stood in the way of full citizenship.

6

The Limits of Campaigning Against Racial Discrimination

When three West Indian businessmen, Geoffrey Browne, Loampit Hill, and Roy McFarlane, accompanied by Sydney Hollands, a "Hong Kong-born journalist," entered the Dartmouth Arms pub in Lewisham on a late summer evening in 1964, there was no "Whites only" sign on the entrance to warn them that they would not be served. However, the men certainly anticipated this response as they took their seats at the lounge bar. Rather than place their own drink orders, they allowed Ken Vass, a White reporter for the *Daily Herald*, to order on their behalf. As expected, the bartender refused to fill the order and immediately called the owner, H. C. Hawes, to rectify the situation. Not only did Hawes defend the actions of the bartender in denying service to the men, but he also explained as the operator of a private establishment, "I can refuse to serve anyone I like." He charged, "If you want a drink, you will all have to go to the public bar," before asking the men to leave. The men refused and remained unmoved as Hawes announced that he had called to notify police that the men were causing a disturbance, presumably by their mere presence. The fact that the four men stayed suggests that they were prepared for further confrontation. But after waiting for over half an hour for police to arrive, they decided to leave on their own accord.[1]

The news of what was reported as a staged "sit-in" at the Dartmouth Arms pub to protest the "colour bar" in London made headlines just weeks before the general election of 1964.[2] Although neither of the major political parties intended to introduce race as a wedge issue in their respective campaigns, in the days following the incident at the pub, the *Times* noted that the election season had fueled "intense passions over colour" in Britain as polls indicated widespread support for controlling Commonwealth migration.[3] But even beyond the issue of rights of entry for non-White Commonwealth migrants, what reportedly occurred at the Dartmouth Arms pub spoke to those everyday realities of a "colour bar" which did not always appear in plain view, yet nevertheless insidiously banned, excluded, and denied Black Britons by way of unspoken social customs, habits, and de facto codes of exclusion.[4] This "colour bar" was unofficial, yet just as authoritative as public policies like the Commonwealth Immigration Act of 1962 in its power to discriminate and disenfranchise. And as the general election approached in the fall of 1964, not only did this "colour bar" prevent West Indians and Asians from receiving service at the Dartmouth Arms, but it also continued to make headlines as it empowered Barbara Grainger, the owner of a nursing home in Bristol, to advertise a position for a night nurse "who was not coloured" to keep her elderly patients happy, and prevented non-White students in Oxford from obtaining decent, affordable housing.[5] Thus for Black Britons, the "intense passions over colour" that *The Times* spoke of were mired in both the racialized politics of entry and that of belonging in British society.

Yet despite Black Britons' experiences with the pervasiveness of anti-Black racism and racial discrimination, it was the highly contested battle for Smethwick's Parliamentary seat that ultimately catapulted the issue of race into the national spotlight as an election issue in the fall of 1964. Stoking White working-class anxieties reflected in public discourses about the problem of "coloured immigrants"—anxieties that crystallized in the wake of news of "race riots" in Notting Hill in 1958 and reconditioned a few years later by Conservative policy makers to leverage support for the Commonwealth Immigration Act of 1962—the circulation of leaflets bearing the now infamous slogan "If You Want a Nigger for a Neighbor, Vote For Labour" transformed Smethwick into a symbolic bastion of anti-Black sentiment in Britain.[6] Although the Labour Party stood poised to regain control of Government after over a decade of Tory rule, in Smethwick, Peter Griffiths, a politically unknown local headmaster, built his public profile in a race to unseat Patrick Gordon Walker, the Labour incumbent who had been tapped to become Foreign Secretary in a new Labour Government, by shoring up his hometown credibility through a racially coded anti-immigration platform. Just three years before, Walker had led the charge against the passage of the Commonwealth Immigration Act on behalf of the Labour Party. Griffiths used Walker's opposition to the bill to cast his opponent as a pro-immigrant, anti-White working-class candidate who had lost touch with the interests of his constituents. Likewise, while Griffiths publicly disassociated himself from the tagline suggesting that a vote for Labour meant choosing a "nigger for a neighbor" to distinguish himself from Walker and to appeal to White working-class voters in the Midlands, Griffiths nonetheless embraced the inflammatory rhetoric as a legitimate expression of the sentiments of the people he hoped to represent.[7]

Griffiths went on to win Smethwick's Parliamentary seat in a stunning defeat that reminded the Labour Party that the overlapping issues of race and "immigration" had become unavoidable and contentious political concerns that could prove detrimental to their vision of erecting a "New Britain."[8] Griffiths was quickly ostracized and labeled a "Parliamentary leper" by newly elected Prime Minister Harold Wilson. But rather than confront the interlocking social, ideological, cultural, and economic structures collectively fomenting the anti-Black racism that allowed the owner of the Dartmouth Arms pub to believe he could solicit police to protect his right to discriminate on the basis of race, the Labour Party tried to straddle the fence as Party officials understood that these same sentiments drove White voters in Smethwick to cast their ballot for a candidate who promised to protect their neighborhoods from the "coloured invasion."[9] In an attempt to avoid alienating White working-class voters by being seen as a pro "coloured immigration" faction, Labour Party leaders expressed intentions to maintain controls despite their initial opposition to the Commonwealth Immigrants Act of 1962 on the grounds that the law was racially discriminatory. To distinguish the Party from the racist anti-(coloured) immigrant motives that drove Conservative policy, Labour leaders reaffirmed their commitment to pursuing legislation outlawing racial discrimination and incitement, ostensibly with an eye toward fully incorporating Commonwealth migrants into British society. But for Black activists and intellectuals surveying the political landscape in the run-up to the 1964 general election, the Labour Party's gestures toward the pursuit of anti-discrimination policy in the context of their willingness to leave a signature policy designed to systematically disenfranchise Black British citizens in fact only proved the hypocrisy of race politics within the Labour Party. From Black Britons' view, Labour was no more committed than their Conservative foes to dismantling racial inequality and guaranteeing the rights of Black British citizens.

In a column titled "Race: The Unmentionable Issue," appearing in the pacifist news magazine *Peace News* one month prior to the election, West Indian, African, and South Asian activists and intellectuals expressed alarm about what they deemed to be a concerted effort by "the three leading parties to leave the colour bar out of the elections" and to actively "conceal it as an object of controversy that might lose votes."[10] The list of featured discussants included noted figures active in Black British and leftist circles, including historian and anti-colonial theorist C. L. R. James, sociologist and peace activist Stuart Hall, and prominent Jamaican writers Barry Reckford and Andrew Salkey. Other discussants included lesser well-known figures, including Kenyan law student Ngumbu Njururi, Indian scholar, and activist Ranjana Ash, and Marion Glean, a thirty-two year old Trinidadian woman enrolled at the London School of

Economics who had arrived in England four years prior and worked as a secretary for the Quaker International Affairs Centre in London.[11]

In her response to the roundtable's query concerning the absence of substantive engagement with the politics of race by the British political establishment in the run-up to the 1964 general election, Marion Glean opined, "Race isn't an issue in the forthcoming general elections because all major parties agree on a colour-bar in Britain." From Glean's view, Tory conservatism sought to confine West Indians, Africans, and South Asians to "ghettos" and "overcrowded slum conditions," while the Labour Party's commitment to the prosperity of the White working classes effectively worked to relegate people of color to "the worst paid jobs that no one else will do." Because the mainstream political establishment virtually ignored the concerns of its non-White citizens, Glean called for a more militant political posture among Black and Asian communities to demand their rights of belonging and inclusion. Glean charged,

> The truth is that race never is an issue until those discriminated against racially make it one. Charity is never a forerunner of equality. It is time that we coloured people of Britain stop this nauseating begging for crumbs and behave like men. We have a right to share in the prosperity the three centuries of our labour has helped to build. We have a right to be ordinary citizens of Britain.[12]

When Martin Luther King, Jr. added London to his European itinerary on his way to Norway to claim the Nobel Peace Prize in 1964, Marion Glean seized the opportunity to try to bring the ideas that she had articulated in *Peace News* to life in the form of a multi-ethnic anti-racist political movement powered by "immigrant groups" with a social justice mission of advocating against all forms of racial discrimination. Working in conjunction with Bayard Rustin, who had been instrumental in organizing the 1963 March on Washington for Jobs and Freedom, Glean hoped to capitalize on the media attention that King's visit would generate to mobilize migrants of color for political action. To that end, Glean along with members of Multi-Racial Britain, a small interracial association of leftist activists, arranged for King to meet with over thirty members of local West Indian, South Asian, and African organizations, including the Standing Conference of West Indian Organizations, the Council of African Organizations, the Indian Workers Association, and the National Federation of Pakistani Associations on the evening following King's historic address at St. Paul's Cathedral. According to Ranjana Ash, the goal of the meeting was to put King before "black faces" who could by way of experience best articulate racial conditions in Britain.[13] In an interview that became the subject of

Claudia Jones's last editorial in the *West Indian Gazette* before her death in December 1964, King explained that his meeting with representatives from Black and Asian organizations was meant to encourage "the coloured population in Great Britain to organize and to work through meaningful non-violent direct action approaches" to bring the issue of racial discrimination "to the forefront of the conscience of the nation."[14] Inspired in part by the energy of King's visit, his work as an internationally recognized advocate for racial justice, and his example of coalition building and nonviolent direct-action protest in the movement to dismantle Jim Crow, Marion Glean used the meeting with King to initiate the formation of a new umbrella association that sought to build a grassroots anti-racist movement rooted in a coalition between leading Black and Asian organizations. Less than a month after King's visit, the movement that Glean imagined as an alternative political space for incorporating the overlooked voices, concerns, and issues confronting Britain's Black and Asian communities took shape as it adopted a formal name—the Campaign Against Racial Discrimination (CARD).

According to early promotional material, CARD emerged from the efforts of "a group of immigrants who were fed up with being talked about but never listened to." Part of the goal in establishing the organization was to create a type of national clearinghouse to centralize "work against prejudice and discrimination at the grassroots level" throughout Britain.[15] The short-lived history of CARD provides an illuminating trajectory to examine the role that Black Britons, in coalition with South Asian and liberal and progressive White organizers, played in shaping the development of a national race-relations policy agenda during the mid-1960s. It is clear that anti-racist grassroots political organizing among Black British constituencies had a long history that coalesced around domestic questions of citizenship in the wake of postwar Commonwealth migration. However, the history of CARD and the struggle to build a movement from the bottom up to effect policy specifically addressing the problem of racial discrimination in Britain sheds light on how Black Britons forced Government officials at both ends of the political spectrum to reckon with their status as citizens and devise juridical means of protecting their right to belong and participate in the social, political, and economic life of the nation.

In 1962, when the Tory Government implemented the Commonwealth Immigration Act, proponents of the bill publicly denied that race was a factor in the institution of public policy. Three years later, when the Labour Government proposed more stringent immigration restrictions, Home Secretary Frank Soskice found it imperative that this initiative be set forth as part of a legislative "package deal" that also included what was described in a White Paper as "*positive* measures designed to secure for the immigrants and their children their rightful place in *our* society."[16] This aspect of the legislative proposal offered by the newly elected Labour Government resulted in the passage of the Race Relations Act of 1965. Under the terms of the Act, Parliament civilly outlawed discrimination in "places of public resort" on the grounds of race, color, ethnicity, or national origin. Additionally, the Labour Government created a National Race Relations Board tasked with investigating and mediating complaints of racial discrimination brought before local conciliation committees.[17] In doing so, this piece of legislation represented a historic acknowledgment of the existence of racial discrimination in British society, a feat that contradicted much of the national mythology about race and racism in Britain. The regulation of race relations reflected a growing public awareness that the "colour bar" and the attendant racial prejudices and ideologies of White supremacy that accompanied it did not merely live in the minds of the disillusioned White "hooligans" castigated in the aftermath of the 1958 race riots and the death of Kelso Cochrane one year later. Instead, as policy makers crafted a race relations policy agenda, they began to publicly concede to some extent that the racial mores, colonializing mentalities, and culture of disenfranchisement that had long defined the everyday lives of Black Britons were widespread, pervasive, and deeply embedded in the structure of British society.

Unpacking the history of CARD, including the ideological battles over the organization's central mission and strategies of gaining a public profile, reveals much about the evolution of a national regulatory regime for policing race relations in Britain and the fault lines embedded in the articulation and representation of Black British political interests. Although the push for anti-discrimination policy had long figured into the political agendas of Black activists and organizations making claims for citizenship and belonging within British society throughout the twentieth century, in the mid-1960s, when the possibilities for achieving such legislation became viable, CARD emerged as the leading voice within the inner circles of a newly elected Labour Government lobbying on behalf of Black Britons and migrant communities of color. Whereas organizations such as the League of Coloured People and the Inter-Racial Friendship Coordinating Council had previously included anti-discrimination legislation as part of a broader state-sponsored program to address the pernicious "colour bar" in British society, by the spring of 1965, when CARD members began to formulate proposals for such a policy, they did so in a climate in which the question at hand for the political establishment was not *if* Government should address racial discrimination, but rather *how* Government should tackle this issue. Unlike their predecessors, by the mid-1960s CARD activists were debating with Government officials about the substance and reach of anti-discrimination policy rather than the merits of the proposition.

To be sure, both British officials and the CARD activists who pushed for the passage of anti-discrimination policy were well aware that racism and the management of a credible public image of domestic race relations carried a type of global cachet. In a world where news of a police massacre of people protesting Pass Laws in Sharpeville and images of innocent children facing police dogs and becoming bombing victims in Birmingham brought attention to the human-rights crisis that White supremacist violence posed globally, the move to regulate race relations in the form of anti-discrimination policy has to be understood through the prism of a growing international collective consciousness about the problem of racism. This crisis was a concern of the emerging Afro-Asian UN bloc that initiated the adoption of the Declaration on the Elimination of Racial Discrimination by the General Assembly just two days before US President John Kennedy was assassinated. Likewise, as Lyndon B. Johnson assumed office in the wake of Kennedy's death, the push to confront the inequities of access and opportunity caused by racism in American society became a core feature of his agenda as he pressed for the passage of historic civil rights legislation that sought to ban racial discrimination in US public life and create an infrastructure for the federal Government to monitor employment discrimination and participate in civil proceedings against institutions on behalf of victims of discrimination. Thus the rise and fall of CARD must be considered against the backdrop of critical developments both domestically and internationally that tremendously affected the scale and scope of the first Race Relations Act in 1965 and the passage of a second act in 1968, which expanded the regulatory purview of the National Race Relations Board and the range of public arenas where claims of discrimination could be investigated.[18]

But how did the Black British communities who would, in theory, benefit from such legislation weigh in on this policy matter? More specifically, how did Black Britons localize a global policy conversation about racial discrimination and the effects of racism to articulate the political interests of those disenfranchised by racial discrimination? Although the 1965 Race Relations Act represented a critical turning point in placing Black Britons' everyday experiences of exclusion and disenfranchisement on the agenda of policy makers, CARD members were at the forefront in outlining the shortcomings of the historic legislation, particularly its failure to address discrimination in the arenas of housing, employment, the issuance of credit, policing, and education. As noted in previous chapters, housing and employment in particular were two of the sectors of society most vital to migrant settlement and incorporation. Moreover, access to fair credit, educational resources, and equal treatment within the criminal justice system also shaped the quality of citizenship and manner in which people experienced disenfranchisement. Not only does this chapter explore how CARD influenced the debate about the structure of anti-discrimination policy, but it also examines how CARD members challenged the substantive limits of the first Race Relations bill and details their efforts to test the provisions of public policy and construct an empirical case for reform. Ultimately, however, before many of the amendments to the first Race Relations bill that CARD members lobbied for would take effect, the organization's internal struggles over strategies for engaging in official politics led to its eventual demise. To be sure, while CARD would not necessarily survive organizationally as the revised Race Relations bill of 1968 passed as the law of the land, the vision of the campaign's members and its mission to influence the development of public policy that would tackle the problem of racial discrimination in Britain would make an indelible imprint on legislation's role in articulating the politics of race, nation and citizenship in postwar Britain.

The Transnational Dimensions of Regulating Race Relations

Nine days prior to making his final public appearance at Manhattan's Audubon Ballroom before three armed assassins took his life, on 12 February 1965 Malcolm X spent an afternoon in the West Midlands town of Smethwick. This was Malcolm X's second trip to Britain in the months before his death, the first being his historic trip to debate at the Oxford Union in December 1964.[19] Flanked by a BBC reporting team that captured iconic footage of Malcolm X peering through the windows of vacant properties and staring at "For Sale" signs as he walked up Smethwick's Marshall Street, Malcolm X clearly intended his visit to, at the very least, visually disrupt the anti-Black British landscape that Smethwick—and Marshall Street in particular—had come to signify in the popular imagination following the general election of 1964.[20] Shortly after the election of Peter Griffiths as Smethwick's Parliamentary representative, the borough's Tory-led local council adopted a plan to use municipal funds to purchase homes on Marshall Street that went on the market and reserve sale for White occupants selected from the council-housing registry in an effort to halt the growth of a "ghetto."[21] Misappropriating Martin Luther King, Jr.'s critique of Black urban ghettos formed from socioeconomic conditions rooted in the "twin evils of discrimination and economic deprivation," proponents of the so-called Marshall Plan framed their efforts to publicly fund "White only" housing as part of an attempt to avoid the ghettoization of Marshall Street and promote "racial harmony" through the assimilation of "immigrants."[22] From their view, ghettos were racialized spaces synonymous with majority non-White residential areas that, by virtue of their inhabitants alone, were degenerate, undesirable, and disreputable.

While the West London neighborhoods in and surrounding Notting Hill and the activities of Teddy boys had become flashpoints for public debate about the "colour problem" during the late 1950s, by 1964, Smethwick began to eclipse Notting Hill as synecdoche for articulating White working-class backlash to Commonwealth migrants. In the first edition of the newly launched Black political organ *Magnet News,* a paper that hoped to continue the legacy of the *West Indian Gazette* in the wake of Claudia Jones's death, a story about Smethwick's troubling racial politics compared the town to Verwoerd's South Africa and contended that the "Marshall Street affair" was emblematic of a growing "crisis of civil rights."[23] Malcolm X likened the treatment of the town's Black and Asian residents to that of German Jews under the Third Reich.[24] And to be sure, as Labour leaders prepared to govern even before the Party's slim electoral victory in 1964, they too were well aware that Smethwick had become a placeholder for the mutually constitutive political issues of race and immigration or, more precisely, the contest between Britain's liberal image as a racially tolerant (White) society and growing anti-Black racism.

Defining themselves as the party of a "New Britain," in their 1964 election manifesto, alongside plans for modernizing industrial production and investing in social services that included education and health care, Labour Party leaders reaffirmed their commitment to pursuing legislation outlawing racial discrimination and incitement in public places and providing assistance to local authorities with significant "immigrant" settlement. On the more hotly contested issue of immigration policy, the Party prefaced its position by acknowledging its commitment to the Commonwealth, which it viewed as a key player in "grappling with the terrible inequalities that separate[d] the developed and under developed nations and the white and coloured races." Despite their initial opposition to the Commonwealth Immigration Act of 1962, however, Party leaders expressed intentions to maintain controls, pending future negotiations with Commonwealth Governments.[25] Thus the "New Britain" that Labour leaders promised contained a striking racial paradox. At the same time that Labour's "New Britain" welcomed a legislative agenda that sought to deter acts of racial discrimination by criminally penalizing those who engaged in such practices, it would also leave an "Old Britain" intact by upholding the very policy that codified the "immigrant" status marking Black Britons as patently un-British and subjecting them to surveillance, suspicion, criminalization, and deportation.

The pursuit of anti-discrimination legislation had been part of the Labour Party's platform for several years before their return to power in 1964. Just weeks after the violence in Notting Hill had begun to recede from national headlines, in late September 1958, under the leadership of Hugh Gaitskill, the National Executive Committee issued an official statement expressing the Party's intention to introduce legislation banning discrimination in public places in part "to meet the challenge of racialism in Britain and to develop a genuine sense of racial equality."[26] In the wake of the passage of the Commonwealth Immigration Act of 1962, a bill that Labour leaders including Gaitskill stridently opposed on grounds of racial discrimination, the Party reaffirmed its commitment to pursuing anti-discrimination legislation with a Labor majority as part of a comprehensive legislative agenda addressing immigration reform.[27]

Aside from declarations of intent, Parliamentary proposals of individual members throughout the 1950s and early 1960s also tied the Party to anti-discrimination policy. In 1950, Labour MP Reginald Sorenson introduced a Colour Bar Bill criminalizing racial discrimination in public places, but the bill received little Parliamentary support. Expanding on Sorenson's emphasis on prohibiting discrimination in public places, beginning in 1955, as non-White Commonwealth migration steadily increased, anti-colonial activist and Labour MP Fenner Brockway introduced a private members' bill outlawing racial discrimination and incitement in nine consecutive Parliamentary sessions. Evolving throughout the late 1950s and early 1960s to outlaw racial discrimination in public places such as hotels, restaurants, and pubs, as well as in housing covenants and establishments employing over fifty persons, the Brockway bills sought to impose statutory penalties, including fines and the revocation of licenses for those found guilty of racial discrimination or incitement.[28] Although the Brockway bills never received a second reading, they did gain a coalition of support over time, largely among Labour and Liberal backbenchers. However, it was not until the Labour Party stood poised to regain control of Government from a Tory Party besieged by the infamous Profumo Affair, a scandal involving the Secretary of War that ultimately discredited the Conservative Government, followed by the resignation of Prime Minister Harold Macmillan in late 1963, that the pursuit of anti-discrimination legislation became a viable political possibility.

When Fenner Brockway introduced his ninth consecutive bill to outlaw racial discrimination and incitement in January 1964, he had the support of a key ally, Opposition leader Harold Wilson. Wilson assumed leadership of the Labour Party upon the death of Hugh Gaitskill in the previous year. Although Gaitskill had been adamantly opposed to the discriminatory provisions of the Commonwealth Immigration Act of 1962, when the bill came up for renewal in November 1963 with widespread public support, Wilson, unlike his predecessor, attempted to scuttle a line that would identify Labour as an anti-control Party. Wilson hoped to do so by staking a position that acknowledged the need for restricted Commonwealth immigration but with a caveat that departed from Conservatives' closed-door approach to immigration reform by establishing measures for control in consultation with Commonwealth governments. Anticipating much of what became the Labour Party's campaign platform in the 1964 general election, Wilson pledged that a Labour Government would continue to find ways to negotiate immigration reform in partnership with Commonwealth governments, many of which included newly independent nations in Africa and the Caribbean. Moreover, he was careful to further distinguish the Labour Party's position by suggesting that comprehensive immigration reform would address not only the regulation of routes of entry, but also the conditions of settlement faced by a largely non-White Commonwealth migrant population. And to that point, in November 1963 Wilson shared plans to make good on a pledge that he had first made publicly at an anti-apartheid rally in Trafalgar Square shortly after Gaitskill's death—to pair legislation addressing controls with measures similar to those set forth in Fenner Brockway's earlier private member's bills that would impose a ban on racial discrimination in public places and make incitement to racial hatred illegal.[29]

Pair together

The Labour Party's support for the renewal of the Commonwealth Immigration Act of 1962 represented a decisive shift in electoral politics. Moving forward, as the new electoral cycle approached, the two major political parties fundamentally agreed on the legitimacy of a policy that essentially transformed British Commonwealth citizens into aliens who could obtain an immigrant (deportable) status through a labor voucher system that, by design, disproportionally excluded non-White migrants. Therefore, it is important to note that the Labour Party's emphasis on the pursuit of anti-discrimination legislation was arguably rooted in a desire to shore up a particular perception about the Party's liberal credentials in regard to race in the face of its support for a policy that Party leaders, including Hugh Gaitskill and Patrick Gordon Walker, found objectionable on the grounds that it was "based on race and colour discrimination."[30] From the view of Labour leaders, including Harold Wilson, an anti-discrimination policy agenda that effectively domesticated the problem of anti-Black racism proved to be a viable strategy for keeping the Party aligned with popular anti-immigrant sentiment among a majority White working-class electorate. Affirming the citizenship rights of Black Britons would then be by a possible byproduct rather than an intended purpose for Labour's anti-discrimination agenda going into the general election of 1964. But to even broach the issue and attempt to deracialize "immigration," Labour had to win in a climate in which Peter Griffiths's campaign for Smethwick's Parliamentary seat brought national attention to the so-called problem of the "coloured immigrant."

Griffiths's campaign and the local discourse about race and "immigration"
that it produced had significant implications for national electoral politics in
the weeks leading up to the general election. Not only did it resurrect the
trope of the "coloured immigrant" as a social problem and economic para-
site, devoid of citizenship rights in ways that echoed the racialized discourse
about Black Commonwealth migrants that arose in the aftermath of the
Nottingham and London "race riots" in 1958, but it also broadened the canvas
of anti-immigrationist–speak to more clearly include the denigration of populations of African and Asian descent. In the pages of Smethwick's leading
newspaper, editorials negatively associated immigrants with interracial sex,
prostitution, disease, filth, and squalor while headlines declared, "The Face of
the Midlands Is Fast Being Known as the Black Hole of Calcutta" because of
growing South Asian settlement.[31] Likewise, as Griffiths gained notoriety by
drawing sharp distinctions between his positions and those of his opponent,
Patrick Gordon Walker, he offered a platform that called for a five-year ban
on "unskilled immigration," as well as for assisted return passage for unemployed migrants, deportation of migrants found guilty of crimes, and special
consideration for non-English-speaking children, offering the caveat "integration insults the ancient culture of the Sikhs, Smethwick's largest immigrant
group."[32] Hoping to capitalize on a smear campaign against his opponent that
dubbed Walker a "nigger lover" and generated a whisper campaign on the eve
of the election to suggest that his daughter had "married a Negro," Griffiths
aimed to create a political dynamic that transformed Labour into the Party
that could be publicly perceived as an ally to "coloured immigrants," to the
detriment of the White working-class masses.[33]

Even though Harold Wilson expressed concern over Conservatives'
attempts at "whipping up colour feeling on the immigration issues" to under-
cut Labour's support, on the campaign trail in the week before the election,
Wilson confronted the stakes of this strategy as he stood before a crowd of
over 10,000 who had gathered at Bull Ring in Birmingham. There he encountered hecklers who interrupted his speech several times and demanded to
hear how he planned to address what one woman in the crowd reportedly
described as the "essential" issue of "the immigrants."[34] Eventually departing
from his scripted remarks as he responded to hecklers on the question of immigration, Wilson touted a Party line that he hoped would not only neutralize the
White working-class anti-immigrant sentiment being hurled at him but that
would also nullify race more generally as a political issue. By reminding the
Birmingham crowd of the Labour Party's pledge to maintain controls on the
inflow of Commonwealth migrants, he clearly aimed to find common ground
with his critics and position Labour as a friend of those who had joined the
growing popular chorus of anti-immigrant opinion among the White working

classes. However, as Wilson explained Labour's intentions to outlaw racial discrimination and incitement in an effort to achieve equality and address "the *problem of immigrants* who are already in this country," he challenged his White working-class constituents to view this issue as one that would allow the Labour Party to advance the common values of a purportedly tolerant and anti-racist British nation.[35]

Although Wilson assumed office with a slim Labour majority, the defeat of Patrick Gordon Walker had proven that the perception of pro-immigrant (or anti-control) could become a political liability—even if it was within the context of defending what were considered time-honored national virtues of tolerance, multiracialism, and equality before the law. As the Labour Party prepared to govern after thirteen years in the Opposition, in the aftermath of the Smethwick election the pursuit of official race policy became a priority that remained beholden to the task of appeasing two ideologically disparate factions—those, including Black Britons, who viewed the nation's moral duty to foster inclusion and keep the pernicious "colour bar" at bay, and those who viewed Britain as an island nation under siege in need of protection from the invasion of Commonwealth "immigrants."

With the specter of Smethwick still looming large, in Wilson's remarks at a political event held shortly after his election as Prime Minister, he declared that dismantling "divisions between first-class and second-class citizens, differentiated by the colour of their skin" was the "great moral imperative" facing every nation around the world. He further charged,

> We cannot condone in others or assert colour prejudice or the practice of racialism. And if we are going to speak with authority abroad, we have a duty at home to show our deep loathing and to condemn by our words, and outlaw by our deeds, racial intolerance, colour prejudice, anti-Semitism, whether they be found in the activities of squalid relics of prewar fascism, in the behavior of politicians of any party—or in the attitudes of so called Labour Clubs."[36]

Wilson's framing of the politics of race and perceptions of race relations as pressing domestic concerns with international ramifications took note of a crucial factor influencing the Labour Party's interest in pursuing anti-discrimination policy—the nation's image abroad. Just as Conservative leaders years before were well aware that headlines declaring "race war" in the streets of London had the potential to besmirch the nation's moral standing and political legitimacy in international affairs as the postwar world continued to embrace the "winds of change" that accompanied demands to end systems of racialized colonial rule, apartheid, and Jim Crow, the newly elected Labour Government was also keenly aware of the transnational political stage that their actions on race relations policy would be received.

Nearly a year before Wilson's speech on the "great moral imperative" of abolishing racism, on 20 November 1963, the General Assembly of the United Nations unanimously adopted the Declaration on the Elimination of All Forms of Racial Discrimination. Reaffirming the international body's commitment to upholding anti-discriminatory and anti-racist principles in accordance with the tenets of the United Nations Charter and the Universal Declaration of Human Rights, the declaration on racial discrimination resolved "to adopt all necessary measures for speedily eliminating racial discrimination in all its forms and manifestations, and to prevent and combat racist doctrines and practices in order to promote understanding between races." Whereas the Universal Declaration of Human Rights stopped short of including any explicit reference to race or racism, the goal of this statement directly stated a mission of engendering "an international community free from all forms of racial segregation and racial discrimination."[37] The declaration defined "racial discrimination" as "any distinction, exclusion, restriction, or preference based on race, colour, descent, or national or ethnic origin which has the purpose or effect of nullifying or impairing the recognition, enjoyment or exercise, on an equal footing, of human rights and fundamental freedoms in the political, economic, social, cultural or any other field of public life." [38]

The adoption of the Declaration represented the culmination of decades of struggle, protest, and petitioning by Black and disenfranchised communities of color throughout the world. Moreover, the statement demonstrated the growing international influence of an expanding contingent of newly independent Afro-Asian states that had steadfastly kept the overlapping global issues of colonialism and racism firmly planted in international politics.[39] Between 1964 and 1965, the UN General Assembly tasked the Commission on Human Rights with drafting the International Convention on the Elimination of All Forms of Racial Discrimination (ICERD), a legally binding document that implored signatories to actively seek measures to eradicate racial discrimination from public life and implement policy to address racial discrimination and incitement.[40] Although ICERD did not receive formal approval by the UN General Assembly until December 1965, the spirit of the UN Declaration began to manifest itself in historic civil rights legislation in the United States and the reversal of immigration policies designed to limit the influx of non-Whites in such places as Canada and Australia, beginning in 1964.[41] Although scholars have been careful to note the importance of the shifting domestic landscape that prompted the newly elected Labour Government to prioritize anti-discrimination policy during the early months of its return to power, including the fallout from the Smethwick election and the need to compensate for acquiescing to immigration controls that the Party had earlier vehemently condemned for their racist intent, it is important to remain cognizant of the broader international politics at play.[42] For Labour Party leaders, the introduction of a Race Relations bill was inextricably bound with the international political community's preoccupation with issues of race and the problem of racial discrimination.

As Labour prepared the way forward to regulate race relations, an official at the Foreign Office noted in a confidential memo to the Home Office that it was important to time the introduction of anti-discrimination legislation so that Parliamentary debate on the bill would coincide with UN General Assembly debates on ICERD. Well aware of the international political currency that the proposition of anti-discrimination policy might cultivate for the nation's image as a global power, the official explained,

> Although we can expect to gain some credit in the U.N. for the decision to legislate against racial discrimination, much of the credit may be lost if, when the domestic legislation is introduced into Parliament it is seen that little or no account has been taken of the draft U.N. Convention. Many delegations—especially the Afro-Asians—are likely to take the line that a good opportunity was being lost.[43]

The mere fact that considerations of domestic race-relations policy would be of concern to the Foreign Office speaks to the ways in which race and, more precisely, the perception of the nation's commitment to the international cause of eliminating racial discrimination to ensure basic human rights, civic freedoms, and equal justice points to the importance of understanding the links between the local and the global. Moreover, not only does a transnational field of vision shed light on the rationale behind British policy makers' consideration of anti-discrimination policy, but it is also crucial in tracing the substantive development of Britain's first national policy explicitly identifying and seeking to address the social problem of racism.

Defining a Legislative Agenda

On 7 April 1965 Home Secretary Frank Soskice introduced a Race Relations bill that extended the provisions of the Public Order Act of 1936. Under the bill, incitement to race hatred in any form carried fines up to £1,000 and the possibility of up to two years in prison; acts of discrimination in public places, including those maintained by public authority, carried criminal penalties with fines up to £100.[44] Despite the fact that much of the framework for Sockice's proposed Race Relations bill built upon the work of a Shadow Cabinet subcommittee that he had chaired during the previous year to develop recommendations for anti-discrimination legislation for the Labour Party's National Executive Committee, the bill drew immediate criticism from all sides.[45] Conservatives called for Sockice to withdraw the bill, describing it as "inept and ineffective" because of its limited scope and its adoption of criminal penalties that would be virtually unenforceable. Likewise, Conservatives charged that the extension of the provision of the Public Order Act of 1936 to include penalties for rhetoric promoting racial hatred constituted an infringement upon the right to free speech.[46]

Labour, Liberal, and leftist voices also remained skeptical of the efficacy of the bill's provisions in terms of its regulatory purview and machinery. Among these factions, there was a general consensus that the bill's focus on acts of discrimination occurring in public places without attention to the critical areas of housing and employment significantly undermined its potential impact in the public domains where racial minorities were most likely to encounter discrimination. While the London District Committee of the Communist Party acknowledged that the bill was the result of "public pressure from many progressive organisations," the committee concluded that a stronger draft was necessary for the policy to be effective.[47] The Movement for Colonial Freedom, the anti-colonial lobby chaired by Fenner Brockway, agreed, noting that the bill ignored religious discrimination in addition to neglecting to address discrimination in specific public arenas.[48] Editorials appearing in *The Observer* described the bill as a "botched job" that did little more than criminally stigmatize race prejudice, while an editorialist for *The Guardian* concluded that given its limited scope and emphasis on criminal prosecutions as a mechanism for adjudicating discrimination cases, the bill merely gave "statutory expression to the strong moral disapproval of racial prejudice."[49] Labour MP Lena Jeger touted the international significance of the bill. Jeger noted that the bill reflected UN recommendations made by the subcommittee on the Prevention of Discrimination and the Protection of Minority Rights, but stopped woefully short of being effective in outlawing common everyday practices of overt discrimination, including the posting of advertisements for jobs or sublets stating, "No coloured need apply."[50] Commenting in *The Times*, Peter Calvocoressi, a British member of the UN sub-commission that Jeger referenced, agreed with Jeger's overall assessment. Applauding the overarching intentions of a bill addressing racial discrimination, Calvocoressi also found the bill "inadequate" in terms of its scope and its ability to provide recourse to victims of discrimination, including the right to civil suit.[51] Instead, Calvocoressi joined a growing chorus of critics, including the Society of Labour Lawyers and the newly formed CARD, who proposed amending the bill along the lines of anti-discrimination and equity policies adopted in the United States and Canada to substitute conciliation for criminal prosecution as the central instrument for adjudicating individual cases of racial discrimination.[52]

add Conciliation

It was no coincidence that the Society of Labour Lawyers and members of the newly organized CARD were aligned in their support for amending Sockice's Race Relations bill to include conciliation as the central mechanism for compliance and enforcement. In the previous year Anthony Lester, a Harvard-trained barrister and one of the few White members involved in CARD from its inception, played a prominent role in formulating the Society of Labour Lawyers' anti-discrimination legislation proposals to the Labour Party's National Executive Committee that were considered alongside those offered by the Shadow Cabinet committee. As CARD worked to formalize its organizational mission and structure during the first few months of 1965, Lester became chair of CARD's legal committee, one of the most critical arms of the organization responsible for generating policy statements.[53] The Society of Labour Lawyers had served as an early incubus for debate surrounding the legal architecture of anti-discrimination legislative proposals that incorporated extrajudicial measures, including conciliation, as opposed to criminal prosecution as a means of confronting racism and protecting minority rights. However, as policy makers and political brokers grappled with the process of cultivating support for an actual bill in proffer, CARD emerged in the public sphere as the most prominent political lobby connected with the push to pass a Race Relations bill. And more specifically, CARD became the leading advocate of a statutory conciliation commission.

Although CARD was formed just months before the introduction of the Race Relations bill, by the time that the bill was formally introduced the organization had already begun to distinguish itself as an anti-racist advocate and political voice for Black and Asian communities. But at the time of the bill's proposal, CARD functioned with only a temporary executive committee. The committee was chaired by David Pitt, the well-known West Indian physician who had lobbied with the Inter-Racial Friendship Coordinating Council for anti-discrimination policy in the aftermath of Kelso Cochrane's death. Pitt had also launched an unsuccessful bid for Hampstead's Parliamentary seat as a Labour candidate in 1959. Besides Pitt, the early organizers who formed the core of the working executive committee also included Marion Glean, the Trinidadian peace activist who had initially convened the meeting with Martin Luther King, Jr. that spawned CARD, along with South Asian anti-colonial activist Ranjana Ash; C. L. R James' wife, Selma James; and Richard Small, a law student and James's aide, who had previously served in the West Indian Student Students' Union. Others who had ties to leftist groups and other organizations representing the interests of various Black and Asian constituencies that worked with CARD in the early months of its existence included Autar Dhesi, a member of the Southall Indian Workers Association; Gurmukh Singh of the anti-war Committee of 100; Hamza Alavi, a businessman associated with the National Federation of Pakistani Associations; Frances Ezzrecco, co-founder of the Coloured People's Progressive Association, who also served as vice-chair of the Standing Conference of West Indian Organizations; as well as Amoo-Gottfried, who had previously presided over the Council of African Organizations. In addition to representatives from the various migrant communities whom the organization aimed to represent, the working executive committee also included White allies such as Anthony Lester and Nicholas Deakin, who had recently begun work with the Institute of Race Relation on a long-term study of British race relations that was to culminate in the seminal report *Colour and Citizenship,* published in 1969. [54] Although none of the members of the working executive committee had formal roles in the political establishment, in part because the organization's early media profile cast it as Britain's version of a fledging "civil rights movement," born from the "gentlest of nudges" from one of the most publicly recognizable social justice advocates in the world, Martin Luther King, Jr., CARD leaders successfully leveraged the attention that the organization gained to fulfill its aim "to enter the discussion" on the course of anti-discrimination policy. [55]

In some of the earliest statements issued by CARD in reaction to the proposed Race Relations bill put forth by Home Secretary Frank Soskice, CARD representatives characterized the bill as a "token" gesture of a Labour Government's interest in achieving racial equality in Britain because it merely broached the oftentimes allusive yet pervasive issues of racial discrimination, racially incendiary speech, and racially motivated violence.[56] CARD members contended that the venues in which the legislation applied—"places of public resort"—were unspecific and ill-suited to regulate the arenas where a largely Black and Asian migrant population were likely to encounter overt discrimination or the types of exclusions that would serve as a social or economic detriment to the extent that one might experience in the job or housing market or in the issuing of credit and insurance. Noting the bill's failure to address religious discrimination, which certainly contributed to the ways in people of color, including Hindus, Sikhs, and Muslims from South Asia, Africa, and the Caribbean, were racialized as "immigrants," CARD leaders took issue with policy makers' narrow conception of the dynamics of the racial and ethnic identifications structuring how people of color experienced discrimination. Moreover, they also challenged the strength of the bill's mechanisms of compliance and enforcement.[57]

Much of CARD's critique of the bill reflected the distinction between the Home Secretary's proposal and a legislative package that the organization had devised in the two preceding months. In a public meeting held by CARD in February 1965, a body of approximately 600 voted on a resolution to accept a legislative proposal drawn up by CARD's legal committee and approved by the temporary executive committee. During the period between CARD's first public meeting and the second reading of the Race Relations bill in May 1965, CARD members organized a highly effective lobby of Cabinet and Parliament members across the political spectrum to push for amendments that would focus on replacing criminal penalties for acts of discrimination with the creation of a conciliatory commission. This lobbying effort involved circulating draft legislative proposals among Labour, Liberal, and Tory MPs; corresponding with Cabinet members; engaging the media; and holding meetings with high-ranking officials, including Frank Soskice and Shadow Home Secretary Peter Thorneycroft.[58] Members of the organization's legal subcommittee, headed by Anthony Lester, had compiled much of the research that informed CARD's legislative proposals. These proposals drew from extensive reviews of anti-discrimination law and statutory procedures at both the state and national level in North America. In particular, Jeffrey Jowell's research on New York State's Commission on Human Rights, which offered empirical data demonstrating the effectiveness of parajudicial conciliatory bodies with powers to receive complaints, investigate, and mediate discrimination cases, became central to the rationale that CARD members employed to persuade both Tory and Labour MPs not only to see the virtues in amending the Home Secretary's original bill but, in the case of conservatives, also to embrace the pertinence and utility of anti-discrimination policy more generally.[59]

In making their case for the establishment of a conciliation commission along the lines of those operating in the United States and Canada, CARD members noted that anti-discrimination policy should focus on "regulating conduct and codifying national disapproval of racialism."[60] On those issues, they found common ground with the Labour Party's efforts. But the CARD proposal went further. CARD members wanted an anti-discrimination policy that offered redress in a manner that affirmed the rights of those citizens most vulnerable to discrimination. The proposal explained, "There is at present no remedy in the courts, no tribunal to which any appeal for help can be made, and no declaration in any statute of the equality of her Majesty's Subjects regardless of their race, color, religion or national origin."[61] Thus, much like the federal Commission on Civil Rights and the newly established Equal Employment Opportunities Commission implemented under the 1964 Civil Rights Act in the United States, CARD members viewed a conciliatory commission as a means whereby victims of racial discrimination could have their rights due as British citizens acknowledged under a legal system that merely granted citizenship, irrespective of race, without explicit guarantee. With that

in mind, in regard to the portions of the bill dealing with racial discrimination, CARD offered three amendments. First, well aware that the racialization
of non-Whites involved more than phenotype and national origin, members
determined that religion should be added as a protected class alongside race,
color, and national origin. As one Labour MP had earlier noted, without the
inclusion of religion as a protected category, "they'll only say they'll be dis-
criminating against a man, not because he's black, but because he's Muslim."[62]
Additionally, CARD contended that laws should specifically apply to the
arenas of employment and housing—which were described as the "worst
problems"—as well as public facilities, including private establishments serving the public, advertising, education, insurance, credit, and Government
departments. Finally, CARD requested that an amended bill include provisions for a statutory commission staffed by an array of stakeholders, including
Government officials, race relations professionals, and representatives from
workers' and employers' unions, minority communities, and social welfare
organizations.[63]

The proposal went on to outline the specific legal function of the commission in the process of evaluating discrimination cases. Upon receiving a
complaint, the commission had a responsibility to investigate the complaint
and attempt to settle or gain voluntary compliance through private mediation. If mediation failed, the commission could hold a formal public hearing
with powers to subpoena witnesses under oath. Following a public inquiry,
the commission could order injunctive relief or offer compensation to a com-
plainant that would be legally binding and registered in the local county court.
In the event that there was no compliance with the orders of the commission,
the commission could turn to the county court for enforcement. Any appeals
would then move directly from the county court. Therefore, while voluntary
compliance was the ultimate goal, under these steps the work of the commission would serve as a clear precursor to any legal proceeding in a manner that
CARD members noted was very similar to how industrial relations tribunals
functioned to mediate workplace disputes.[64]

CARD circulated its legislative proposals to several high-ranking officials in the Labour Government, including the Home Secretary, the Lord
Chancellor, and Maurice Foley, the Under Secretary for Economic Affairs,
who had recently been appointed to serve as an official liaison between
Government agencies on race and immigration. Although interdepartmental correspondence reveals that Labour leaders seemed amenable to
CARD's proposal to replace criminal sanctions with conciliation as a means
of enforcing anti-discrimination legislation, it is clear that they did not necessarily agree on the legal authority that a conciliatory commission might
possess. In particular, an exchange between officials at the Lord Chancellor's

Office and the Home Office suggested that CARD's proposal for a statutory commission was completely "unacceptable," particularly because the work of the commission would concern issues that were "not matters of legal rights." Accordingly, the Lord Chancellor reasoned that "a Conciliation Commission with powers to make and enforce orders would be ineffective unless coloured persons were given civil rights in the field of employment, housing, etc. which are at present unknown to our law."[65] Whereas CARD members fully realized that the logic of effective anti-discrimination policy should doubly aim to root out racism and affirm citizenship, Labour leaders seemed less committed to the idea of safeguarding the rights of opportunity and access for Black Britons. CARD made a case for a policy whose enforcement mechanisms would subsequently establish the civil right not to be discriminated against on the basis of race in such areas as housing and employment without legal consequence; however, Labour leaders saw the role of anti-discrimination legislation as more of a deterrent from racist behaviors. For CARD members, the problem at hand was a social structure that did not affirm rights irrespective of race, yet Labour leaders saw only a need to address a problem limited to racist individuals.

Besides making direct entreaties to British officials, CARD also appealed to the national press and to grassroots news venues serving migrant communities. In a letter that members circulated to various news outlets, the organization explained that litigating discrimination cases in the criminal courts had previously proven "unworkable" in New York and Ontario to such an extent that it required amendments establishing extra-judicial commissions to investigate and adjudicate claims. CARD members explained that statutory commissions aimed at fostering conciliation rather than taking punitive action had provided an effective model for demonstrating the value of public policy in deterring discrimination and easing racial tensions. In addition to touting what CARD members believed to be the virtues of conciliation, the organization also emphasized that even with the bill's limited and arguably vague regulatory purview, any package that did not at the very least remove the investigation and litigation of discrimination cases from the criminal courts to a statutory commission should be patently rejected. The letter explained,

> There is disappointment that housing and employment are not only not in the Bill, but cannot be accepted as amendments. However, in the event of Parliament's rejecting an amendment to appoint a statutory commission to deal with discriminatory practices, there must be no doubt in the minds of persons who are seeking to improve the racial situation; their duty is then to oppose the Bill.[66]

For CARD members who clearly embraced the newly elected Labour Government's attempt to pursue anti-discrimination policy but determined that the Home Secretary's proposed bill failed on many accounts, conciliation was the line in the sand. Without it, they saw no path of support for the bill moving forward, and they wanted other proponents of anti-discrimination policy to take a similar stand.

The letters that CARD members circulated in the press to defend their position on the proposed Race Relations bill made their rounds just before the bill was scheduled for a second reading. And while one cannot unequivocally attribute the work of CARD members in shifting the framework of the Home Secretary's proposal, in introducing the bill for a second time in the House of Commons, the Home Secretary announced his willingness to consider an amendment that provided for the establishment of a conciliation commission with powers to mediate and settle matters of discrimination in the public places delineated in the original bill as an alternative route to criminal prosecution for those found in violation of the law. Only cases that the commission failed to adjudicate would then be referred to the Director of Public Prosecutions for review. With this change, ostensibly, the centerpiece of CARD's legislative agenda—conciliation—had prevailed. In reporting on the Home Secretary's shifting position, *The Guardian* characterized the change as a "victory" for CARD.[67] And despite the fact that the proposed changes gaining traction among both Labour and Tory MPs solely related to the instruments of compliance and enforcement for an arguably weak and narrowly conceived bill, in many ways this was still a solid feat for CARD members who hoped to establish the organization's political legitimacy as a pressure group lobby. In the time between the bill's initial publication and its second reading in the House of Commons, key groups, including the British Caribbean Association, a bipartisan voluntary organization of elected officials and citizens established in the wake of the 1958 violence to foster relations between Britain and the Caribbean; the Society of Labour Lawyers; the Fabian Society; and national press outlets endorsed CARD's research, rationale, and suggested interventions.[68] Moreover, as Parliamentary debate of the bill unfolded, points offered by the Opposition and those raised in support of conciliation by Labour MPs that included David Ennals, who read directly from CARD's draft proposals in expressing his support for a conciliation commission, cemented CARD's pivotal role in shaping the terms of public policy debate on the merits of anti-discrimination legislation in Britain.[69]

In terms of how CARD members may have measured the success of their lobbying efforts, the move toward the creation of a conciliation commission undoubtedly represented a critical pathway through which the organization's legislative strategists aimed to eventually strengthen the purview of the bill. At the very least, a conciliation commission provided a necessary platform to publicize individual cases of discrimination to highlight patterns and demonstrate the systemic nature of racism in British society. Moreover, conciliation, as opposed to criminal prosecution, created a means for Black Britons and other racially disenfranchised communities to exercise a type of citizenship right to initiate claims for redress and retribution when they experienced racial discrimination. Although these gains signaled progress, for CARD, the revised Bill did not equate to the type of "victory" for the organization that the national media reported.

In response to this particular depiction of the results of CARD's lobbying efforts, David Pitt, the organization's acting chairman, wrote the editor of *The Observer*, explaining that the characterization of the amended bill as a CARD "victory" had been "deeply wounding" to a movement that desired anti-discrimination policy that was more than mere "window dressing," in its scope of regulation and enforcement. Even though it is likely that members of CARD's legal committee welcomed the fact that Parliament members drew upon their research and the rationale presented in their legislative proposals to push for amendments to the Home Secretary's original bill, Pitt aimed to draw a sharp distinction between the work of CARD and what he described as the "absurd bill" introduced by the Labour Government, which remained vague in terms of where the bill would apply and failed to outline specific statutory powers for a conciliation commission.[70] Ultimately, CARD's goal remained seeking policy that addressed discrimination in the critical social and economic arenas that left Black Britons and other communities of color most vulnerable to the quotidian material effects of racial discrimination, including housing and employment. Undoubtedly, CARD organizers recognized that the proposed Race Relations bill represented a monumental initial step toward securing the citizenship rights of Black Britons and fulfilling some of the anti-racist demands characterizing a longer history of Black British political organizing, including those demands made by activists and organizers in the wake of the 1958 violence in Notting Hill, the murder of Kelso Cochrane, and the passage of migration restrictions targeting a largely Black Commonwealth migrant population. Yet Pitt wanted to make clear that CARD's agenda was much broader than the plans set forth in what was still largely considered to be a weak bill that merely gestured toward elements of CARD's legislative proposals. The battle had not been won, and under no uncertain terms did Pitt want to equate a political "victory" for CARD with an inadequate Labour bill that lacked substantive measures designed to rectify some of the socioeconomic effects of racism as experienced by people of color.

A Divided Movement

David Pitt's letter to the editor criticizing the Home Secretary's revised proposal for a Race Relations bill never reached the pages of *The Observer*. However, a month later in his opening speech at CARD's inaugural founding convention, held in July 1965, he took the opportunity to publicly declare opposition to the bill before a crowd that included over 200 individual members, representatives from 28 affiliated groups, and members of the national press.[71] Reiterating some of the points raised in his unpublished letter to *The Observer*, Pitt admonished the bill's failure to delineate statutory powers that would allow for investigations and the presentation of witness testimony under oath for the proposed Race Relations Board. Most disturbing, and what Pitt described as "indicative of the lack of bona fides on the part of Government" as it related to the bill, was the Home Secretary's rejection of a broader definition of "places of public resort" that did not exclude private establishments serving the public, including grocery stores, hotels, pubs, restaurants, and employment agencies. Pitt suggested that only one plausible rationale existed: "the Bill is merely intended as a sop and not as a serious measure." Anticipating the release of a new White Paper on Commonwealth Immigration, Pitt contended that the proposed Race Relations bill was merely a ploy "to cover up the reactionary measures which are being introduced for enforcing stricter immigration control." Pitt saw the newly elected Labour Party's embrace of the seemingly progressive agenda of regulating race relations not as representing Government's vested interest in passing effective anti-discrimination policy, but as a subterfuge to preserve its liberal anti-racist image while seeking a political advantage in the "competition for the support of prejudiced voters." With memories of the 1964 general election in mind, the political calculation was simple. Whereas Conservatives embraced "opposition to coloured people"—in the form of Commonwealth migration controls—as a "potential election winner," according to Pitt, among a majority White working-class electorate, Labour imagined "opposition to racialism as an election loser."[72]

It is likely that CARD delegates were overwhelmingly in agreement with Pitt's criticisms of the Government's proposed Race Relations bill. And undoubtedly, many in the room concurred with his assessment of the Party politics at play. But all was not well within the ranks, and as Pitt ended his opening remarks, he made a special plea for "tolerance and understanding and the maximum amount of goodwill" as delegates turned their attention toward conducting the business of formalizing CARD's constitution, its mission, and its leadership structure. Speaking directly to some of the internal schisms that had loomed over the early work of the temporary executive committee in the months leading up to the founding convention, in a somewhat patronizing tone, Pitt urged fellow delegates to give their "opponent[s] credit for being as passionately devoted to the welfare of the organisation" and for being "honest and well intentioned even though misguided," so that the meeting could produce "hard-hitting debates without rupturing relations."[73]

The final words with which David Pitt opened CARD's inaugural convention suggested that there were in fact competing visions about how the campaign would actually move toward embodying the type of movement that articulated and empowered the collective voices and experiences of people of color in Britain, as founder Marion Glean had initially imagined.[74] In the spring of 1965, just as national media outlets highlighted the organization's growing influence among those in positions to formulate and approve public policy, behind the scenes, members of the temporary executive remained deeply conflicted over CARD's immediate objectives. Interestingly, what began to harden dissent within the ranks was the timing of Parliamentary consideration of the Race Relations bill, a development that ran parallel to the formative months of CARD and served as a double-edged sword in shaping how members of the organization began to envision the mission and prioritize the work of the campaign. On one hand, the publication of the bill and the ensuing public debate that followed as it moved through Parliamentary channels provided an immediate cause for mobilization, which afforded CARD members a critical window of opportunity to gain an audience among British political elites for their ideas about the form that anti-discrimination legislation should take. On the other hand, perhaps to the detriment of the fledging organization, formulating its political voice and posture in the context of an extant public policy debate detracted from the business of defining precisely how the organization would go about building a grassroots movement that legitimately spoke for the collective interests of Black Britons and other marginalized and disenfranchised communities racialized as "immigrants" in Britain.

When CARD founders initially established the organization, they decided to delay holding an official founding convention so that they could use the early months of the campaign's existence to build a base of support. However, by the time David Pitt called the convention to order in Conway Hall in London on 24 July 1965, Marion Glean, the woman who helped set the wheels in motion to establish the campaign, had withdrawn her support. Explaining her decision to part ways with CARD, Glean contended that the push toward making a name for the campaign within the political apparatus of the new Labour Government had distracted from the organization's founding mission of building a grassroots movement that was intimately connected to and rooted within Britain's Black and Asian migrant communities. Glean charged, "CARD had failed to make the recruitment of immigrants its No. 1 priority." She claimed

that instead of attracting mass support from Black and Asian migrant communities, CARD's early activities "had alienated potential immigrant members."
From her view, the problem stemmed from the limited political vision of the
leadership and those within the executive committee who viewed "the recruitment of working class immigrants in any appreciable numbers" as a dynamic
that "would break the 'respectability' of the group and its promotional role."[75]

Glean's critique of CARD's early trajectory made an explicit indictment
of the types of intra-racial dynamics that had historically frustrated the mass
mobilization of collective movements for racial progress. At the heart of this
critique was the inherent tension between a leadership base comprised of
intellectuals, professionals, self-identified activists, and middle-class elites
who aimed to represent the collective will of a working-class coalition of
Caribbean, South Asian, and African masses whose immediate social, economic, political, and individual interests and perspectives did not necessarily
align with their own. Of course, these were not impossible obstacles to overcome. However, in Marion Glean's view they required attention to cultivating
relationships at the grassroots level that would allow CARD to best represent
Britain's Black and Asian citizens by working "through and with" rather than
simply "for" the "coloured community."[76] For Glean, the forms of participatory
democracy advocated by Ella Baker and the organizational models employed
in the Black freedom struggle in the United States provided case studies in
effective practices for building a grassroots movement and object lessons in
the pitfalls of taking a top-down approach to mass mobilization. In a report
issued to CARD's executive committee before her departure, Glean suggested
that organizations like the Student Non-Violence Coordinating Committee
(SNCC) and the Congress of Racial Equality (CORE), which focused on
mobilizing local communities and empowering students, everyday citizens,
and those who were oftentimes most alienated from formal political spheres,
arose out of a need to address the shortcomings of more exclusive civil rights
agendas aimed at seeking policy reform by dismantling the legal apparatus
buttressing Jim Crow through litigation and lobbying. Glean imagined the
birth of a racial justice movement in Britain in a world that had witnessed over
a decade of massive resistance to desegregation, where Medgar Evers's mur-
derer walked free from a Mississippi courthouse, and where the deaths of civil
rights workers James Chaney, Andrew Goodman, and Michael Schwerner
made news just weeks before President Lyndon B. Johnson signed the Civil
Rights Act of 1964. And like many Black Americans, she reckoned that policy reform was but one facet of a broader campaign for full citizenship. In the
spring of 1965, as images circulated around the world of local police assaulting
peaceful protestors with nightsticks and tear gas as they attempted to cross the
Edmund Pettis Bridge in Selma, Alabama in support of voting rights on a day

that the media dubbed "Bloody Sunday," and as racial tensions in cities across the United States mounted in anticipation of the eruption of violence in places like Los Angles, Cleveland, Newark, and Detroit, as Marion Glean and many others saw it, the tenor of the American civil rights movement was shifting, and different political grammars, agendas, and models of organizing were necessary. So with an eye toward what was happening in the United States in her assessment of the future of work of CARD, Glean concluded that the efforts of grassroots-oriented groups like SNCC and CORE were in fact "revolts against the old coloured, legalistic bourgeoisie of the NAACP," which CARD should seek to emulate. She warned, "It would be a pity if CARD became the NAACP equivalent in Britain." [77]

Glean's characterization of the NAACP as the presumably more conservative "legalistic bourgeoisie" wing of civil rights and anti-racist activism in the United States both appropriated and anticipated the rhetorical militancy and urgency that became characteristic of a burgeoning global Black Power movement in the United States that would eventually gain currency in Britain, beginning in the late 1960s. However, contrary to Marion Glean's warning that CARD should somehow avoid becoming a version of the NAACP and instead embrace the grassroots organizing models adapted by SNCC and CORE, recent scholarship on this critical phase in postwar US history has persuasively argued that the Black Power movement that gained traction during the late 1960s was not merely a backlash to earlier, more conventional civil rights activism of the early postwar years. Rather, the defiance, urgency, and militancy associated with Black Power leaders and organizations such as SNCC mutually coexisted with and were products of such activism that helped to usher in new modes of articulating racial pride, empowerment, and solidarity.[78] So while Glean's cautionary remarks for CARD members may have missed the mark in terms of acknowledging the ways in which SNCC and CORE drew from a methodological reservoir of civil rights activism that the NAACP and more reformist-oriented organizations had built during the first half of the twentieth century, her comments did reflect a keen awareness of the ways in which intra-racial and inter-ethnic class dynamics might prevent a group largely consisting of Black and Asian professionals and intellectuals from reaching and or identifying with the masses of working-class Black and Asian communities. In prioritizing the work of building relationships within Black and Asian communities, not only did Glean and her supporters' bottom-up approach to securing a national profile for CARD show an understanding of the need to attract and enlist the support of the masses, but it also indirectly acknowledged the exceptionality of their social positions in relation to the communities that they hoped CARD would serve. Glean knew that the majority of CARD leaders operated with limited first-hand knowledge about the social and economic lives of the average West Indian, African, or Asian worker in Britain and with that in mind she insisted that the campaign actively seek ties in local communities to bridge the gap.

Well aware of the importance of seizing the moment presented by the introduction of the Race Relations bill to harness political capital and press for effective anti-discrimination policy, Glean and a small but vocal faction in the temporary executive committee that included Ranjana Ash, Richard Small, and Selma James felt that making inroads among Government officials and Party powerbrokers should not divert from CARD's primarily goal of making itself a partner in arms with Black and Asian communities. Whereas David Pitt's opening speech at CARD's founding convention outlined an agenda for the organization that prioritized voter registration drives and rallying "liberal elements in the host community"—or presumably anti-racist White allies—as a means of shoring up CARD's status as a type of pressure group lobby within the confines of the political establishment, Glean and others strongly disagreed.[79] In a proposal addressing the future work of CARD that directly challenged Pitt's vision of CARD's premiere role as a political lobby, Selma James highlighted the importance of establishing "lines of communication" within local communities and between existing organizations serving people of color. To that end, James suggested that CARD generate promotional materials that could be easily translated for non-English-speaking migrants, partner with local organizations to hold neighborhood meetings and conferences to gain a sense of the specific needs and concerns of Black and Asian communities, and establish a newsletter that could function both as a type of public fact book and collate stories of interests relevant to various migrant populations. Asserting an alternative definition of pressure group that involved applying "joint pressure with the coloured community," as opposed to merely on behalf of that community, James insisted that placing emphasis in this direction was paramount to the success of CARD. She warned, "CARD can fail. It can fail to win the confidence and support and membership of ordinary working class coloured people, who are the majority of coloured people in Britain, and thus be unable to effectively fight racial discrimination."[80]

Those like David Pitt and CARD's chief legal strategist Anthony Lester who favored transforming CARD into *the* premiere political lobby advocating against racial discrimination certainly did not disagree with the position statements issued by James. However, they surmised that the burgeoning campaign's ability to develop relevance and produce tangible results toward addressing racial discrimination lay in the pursuit of a legislative agenda. As Pitt's opening speech at the convention suggested, Black and Asian Britons needed to create a space for their voices to be heard in an electorate in which the major political parties vied for White voters who opposed their growing presence. In principle, CARD's overarching aim of eradicating racial discrimination and becoming a conduit for representing the voices and interests of Black and Asian minorities in Britain should have allowed for the two dominant factions within the temporary executive to easily coexist and build bridges between ostensibly mutually reinforcing agendas. In this regard, the constitution adopted at CARD's founding convention incorporated ideas about the scope of the organization's structure drawn from both of the main camps that had emerged from debate about what strategies the campaign would employ for building an effective movement against racial discrimination in Britain. For those who wanted CARD to concentrate its efforts on mobilizing the support of a wide cross section of West Indian, African, and Asian constituencies, the fact that the central working body of the organization would largely be comprised of members of individual organizations already working among these populations was met with a degree of satisfaction. Moreover, because ensuring that CARD's leadership apparatus remained in the hands of those from within the Black and Asian communities whose collective interests the organization hoped to represent was of vital importance to both camps, both factions embraced this move as a means of preventing White liberal supporters from dominating the organization. For many of CARD's early supporters, avoiding this scenario became especially germane to maintaining its legitimacy, particularly since Anthony Lester as head of the legal committee had emerged in the press—to the dismay of some—as one of the faces of CARD during the early debates over the Race Relations bill.[81]

Beyond adopting a constitution, delegates at the founding convention also passed a series of resolutions, including a call for Black and Asian supporters and White sympathizers to join their cause. Directly implicating the state in contributing to the "deterioration of the racial situation" in Britain, delegates cited statements of British officials castigating "coloured people" as a source of socioeconomic problems and a Ministry of Education circular, issued in the previous month, calling for school quotas for "immigrant" and or "non-English-speaking" students as points of contention. Coupled with messages that "immigrants" rather than racialized structures of discrimination and disenfranchisement in such places as the labor market and education system were issues of concern, the convention also denounced the failure of the Home Office to address racial violence amidst an increase in police harassment and a "growing lack of confidence in the law enforcement machinery among coloured people living in Britain."[82] In regard to Government policy, delegates reaffirmed their opposition to what they regarded as an "ineffectual" Race Relations bill and renewed a call for the repeal of the Commonwealth Immigration Act of 1962 "on the grounds that it was racialist in concept and application" and created a "second-class citizenship for coloured people."

The lone action item among the series of resolutions passed by CARD delegates included a pledge to establish an official "census of the coloured population" to organize efforts for voter registration.[83]

On the whole, the resolutions passed at the founding convention spoke directly to a desire to harness the power of the state in affirming the rights and securing the citizenship status of Black Britons. And even though a resolution submitted by the West Indian Students' Union called for attention toward establishing a "membership drive as a matter of urgency," the founding convention oriented CARD's agenda toward building an audience for the organization's voice "at the centre of politics" or within the confines of the political establishment.[84] Under this formula, the push for grassroots organizing and the empowerment of ordinary citizens within the communities that CARD hoped to represent remained peripheral to the seemingly more pressing need to shore up a base of support that included a decidedly Black and Asian migrant voting bloc, an entity and form of political capital that would garner attention from those vested in protecting and expanding their own positions of power within the state, including brokers in the newly elected Labour Government. Nothing made this point more clearly than the election of David Pitt as Chairman. Even though Ranjana Ash offered competition for the position with support from those who wanted to see the campaign take a more grassroots approach, in many ways Pitt's biography made him a compelling choice.[85]

Born in Grenada in 1913, David Pitt first came to England in 1933 on scholarship to study medicine at the University of Edinburgh. After completing his studies he established a medical practice in Trinidad, where he became involved in nationalist politics and helped to organize the West Indian National Party in the early 1940s to advocate for self-government for the Caribbean colonies. Following World War II, Pitt moved his practice to London, where he followed in a tradition of Black medical workers, including Crimean War nurse Mary Seacole and League of Coloured Peoples founder Dr. Harold Moody, by melding his professional work with activism, in many instances offering his medical offices as a meeting space for community work. During the late 1950s and early 1960s, Pitt kept close ties with Claudia Jones and was active in the leadership of the London-based Afro-Asian Caribbean Conference in its work to expose the discriminatory character of the Commonwealth Immigration Act of 1962. After nearly two decades of activism with West Indian political circles in the Caribbean and in England in 1959, Pitt ran an unsuccessful campaign as the Labour candidate for a Parliamentary seat for the Hampstead district in a contentious election plagued with racial slurs. Two years later, he became the first Black person elected to the London County Council, where he represented Hackney and served for over a decade.[86] Pitt's social network and professional status set him apart from the masses of Black Britons who struggled to obtain decent housing and navigated a split labor market that oftentimes challenged their credentials, excluded them from workers' unions, and discriminated against them in hiring and promotion. But as CARD sought to champion the concerns of a broad multiethnic coalition of Black and Asian Britons, with an eye toward what was possible within the realm of state power, Pitt's exceptional West Indian biography and his standing as a known quantity within Party politics who had also established himself as an advocate for the plight of the Black Britons provided a palatable public figure who was readily acceptable to the political establishment, given that he clearly had aspirations to become a part of it.[87]

The inherent tensions between David Pitt's ability to identify and register as a West Indian, a Black British professional, a politician, and an agent of local authority all while serving as Chairman of CARD surfaced in dramatic fashion in the months following the founding convention with the release of a new White Paper on "Immigration from the Commonwealth." Issued in early August 1965, the position paper outlined a two-pronged legislative package that addressed migration from the Commonwealth and the place of Commonwealth migrants in British society. Under the provisions of the Commonwealth Immigration Act of 1962, only migrants who had made prior employment arrangements (Category A) or workers with skills deemed most valuable to the British economy (Category B), as well as spouses and dependent family members, were exempt from restrictions. All others (Category C) were selectively admitted on a first-come/first-served basis by applying for a predetermined annual allotment of vouchers distributed by the Ministry of Labour. Signaling Labour's full embrace of the principle of restricting a largely non-White Commonwealth migration by further tightening controls, the White Paper of 1965 announced the Government's intentions of prescribing an annual quota of 8,500 for workers in Categories A and B and proposed the abolition of Category C vouchers. In addition to instituting annual quotas for those hoping to enter the British labor market, citing figures of family reunification migrations estimated at approximately 30,000 annually, the White Paper included plans to curb the entry of dependents to exclude extended family members and children over the age of sixteen. In terms of regulating Commonwealth migrants who did gain entry or were already resident in Britain, the position paper outlined steps for broadening the discretionary powers of the Home Secretary, allowing him to bypass the need for a court recommendation before issuing repatriation orders for any Commonwealth citizen residing in Britain for under five years if the Home Secretary deemed that it was in the public interest. Furthermore, the paper called for a type of arbitrary police registration upon entry, at the discretion of the immigration officer.[88]

Beyond introducing the new provisions associated with Commonwealth migration, the policy proposal also addressed the Government's intentions to move forward with "positive" anti-discrimination measures, including the passage of a Race Relations bill, that would create a national Race Relations Board and local conciliation committees to mediate cases of discrimination under the terms that had been agreed upon following the bill's second reading. The White Paper also announced plans, aside from instituting the proposed national Race Relations Board, to reorganize the work of a National Committee on Commonwealth Immigration (NCCI) that would be comprised of race-relations professionals, social service workers, community liaisons, and individual Black and Asian migrants who would be "able to bring special knowledge and experience to bear on the problems arising from Commonwealth immigration." Although the committee would ostensibly be nonpartisan, it would function as the chief interlocutor between the Government and local organizations, educational institutions, and voluntary associations working in and with migrant communities.[89]

Upon the White Paper's release, CARD and other organizations representing Black and Asian interests swiftly condemned the policy agenda set forth in the paper. Much of the criticism focused on the move to place further restrictions on Commonwealth migrants, which CARD promptly labeled as nothing more than "a spur to racialism" that aimed to disenfranchise people of color, divide families, and subject Commonwealth migrants to arbitrary policing and surveillance.[90] Speaking on behalf of CARD in his role as Chairman, David Pitt reiterated some of the talking points in the speech that he had given before CARD delegates weeks earlier and characterized the new controls as "unnecessary" retrograde steps that reflected Government officials' attempts at "pandering to what they believed are the prejudiced views of the electorate."[91] A. S. Jouhl of the Birmingham Indian Workers Association, a group that touted a membership of over 1,000, agreed with Pitt's assessment. Jouhl insisted that the Labour Government's about-face on Commonwealth migration reform would do nothing more than provide a source of "encouragement to racialist organisations." Further, he expressed skepticism about the possibility that the work of the NCCI would produce the types of substantive reform necessary to improve conditions facing Britain's Black and Asian migrant communities.[92]

Less than a week after the White Paper was made public, CARD organized a public protest meeting at which participants passed a resolution calling upon members of Parliament and local officials to reject the proposal. Highlighting the detrimental effects that pursuing a racially discriminatory policy might have on Commonwealth relations, the resolution charged that the White Paper outlined an agenda that would prove "harmful to the good name of the country and to race relations."[93] The resolution's emphasis on the connections between migration controls and Commonwealth relations aligned with sentiments expressed by West Indian officials, including Trinidadian Prime Minster Eric Williams, who insisted that proposals to restrict Commonwealth migration were "racialist" and favored aliens over Commonwealth citizens.[94] Similarly, in an op-ed published days before the release of the White Paper, Jamaican High Commissioner H. L. Lindo made a point of countering anti-immigrationist arguments suggesting that Afro-Caribbean migrants could not successfully assimilate and "fit into British society." Lindo stressed that Jamaicans were particularly suited for integration, given that they spoke English and hailed from a place that shared Britain's "strong Christian and democratic tradition[s]." Anticipating some of the language of the CARD resolution, Lindo's editorial warned that if more effort was not given to "prevent immigrants from becoming second class citizens," the continued "discrimination against coloured immigrants will injure the image and weaken the influence of Britain not only in the Commonwealth but in the world."[95]

To be sure, West Indian officials and CARD supporters knew that it was unlikely that the Labour Government would completely reverse course on Commonwealth migration policy, particularly given that the Party had not resisted the renewal of the Commonwealth Immigration Act of 1962 and had ascended to power in 1964 on a platform acknowledging intentions to maintain controls. But what CARD organizers hoped was that the Party's abandonment of efforts to repeal an act that members agreed was rife with "pure discrimination" might be counteracted by more substantive efforts toward securing the rights of Black Britons and other non-White Commonwealth migrants.[96] And on this point, Labour's proposed "positive" measures toward "integration" sorely missed the mark, as they neglected to address the specific social and economic arenas where racial discrimination proved most detrimental.[97]

Undoubtedly, the publication of the White Paper on Commonwealth Immigration prompted CARD leaders such as David Pitt to reconsider how they could serve their desired purpose of creating a platform within the political establishment and cultivating ties within a Labour Government poised to enact policies that were hostile to the collective interests of what was still in 1965 a majority Black Commonwealth migrant population. How could CARD expect to work for anti-racist causes and ingratiate the work of the campaign into a system whose players were in fact perpetuating the "colour problem" by embracing and erecting polices designed to facilitate racialized exclusion and disenfranchisement? In an act of protest against the White Paper, David Pitt resigned his seat on the executive committee of the London Labour Party. Additionally, Pitt and Hamza Alavi, a Karachi-born Marxist scholar who served as vice-chair of CARD, withdrew from the British Overseas Socialist Fellowship, an organ of the Labour Party that aimed at cultivating ties with foreign socialists.[98] Pitt and Alavi's withdrawal from prominent Labour Party circles rendered a clear indictment of the Party's role in sanctioning policies rooted in a racialized conception of Britishness and citizenship. And in response, the executive committee of the London Labour Party immediately raised a motion urging the Government to reconsider the proposals in the White Paper—not explicitly on racial grounds—but because they would place Commonwealth migrants "at a disadvantage compared with other aliens."[99]

Pitt and Alavi's decisions to protest the White Paper by distancing themselves from Labour Party outlets sent a clear message that aligned with CARD and its affiliates' condemnation of the Labour Government's policies. But in a move that would ultimately cement some of the emerging intra-racial and inter-ethnic fault lines defining the struggle to articulate and adequately represent a collective political voice for Black Britons, the two ranking members of CARD's executive ultimately accepted invitations to join the newly reconstituted Government-sponsored NCCI. This decision drew the immediate ire of key CARD affiliates, including the National Federation of Pakistani Associations (NFPA) and the West Indian Standing Conference (WISC).[100] The NCCI represented a state-sanctioned body whose mandate had been established in the same White Paper that underscored the Labour Government's animosity at worst, and indifference at best, toward affirming the rights of Commonwealth citizens. As such, the work of the Committee would ostensibly function as a derivation of a broader policy agenda that directly conflicted with the central aims of CARD. Was it reasonable to think that Pitt and Alavi could reconcile their roles as chief advocates for a campaign designed to combat racism while serving as members of a public-policy-making apparatus committed to disproportionately restricting the rights of a largely Black and Asian Commonwealth migrant population?[101] In the eyes of the leadership of the NFPA and the WISC, this was an impractical scenario. Not only did it violate CARD's objective of opposing discriminatory legislation, but many felt that it also inherently compromised the interests of the communities that the campaign purported to represent.

Both Pitt and Alavi defended their decisions to join the NCCI by insisting that they would be functioning in their "personal capacities" as individual citizens and not as representatives of any specific organization.[102] However, ranking members of the NFPA and the WISC demanded that the two men make a choice and either reject the invitation to serve on the NCCI or resign their positions in CARD.[103] Writing in his capacity as General Secretary of the NFPA, Nurl Islam suggested that it was disingenuous for Pitt and Alavi to justify their involvement on the NCCI by claiming that their status on the committee would be viewed separately from their highly public positions as CARD leaders.[104] WISC Secretary Jeff Crawford concurred. And in a separate letter written specifically to David Pitt, Crawford explained that members of the WISC were "at a loss" to understand "how CARD is on record as being militantly opposed to that nauseating document called 'The White Paper on Immigration from the Commonwealth,'" while having "members serve on a committee which has been set up to implement the so-called Integration proposals laid down in the White Paper."[105] Crawford's letter suggested that Pitt, as CARD chairman, could not reject the White Paper on piecemeal terms. Moreover, it also highlighted the hypocrisies embedded in a policy agenda that professed a type of anti-racist integrationism while at the same time providing measures to stiffen racially coded migration controls grounded in the presumption that people of color—non-White British Commonwealth citizens, no doubt—embodied a socioeconomic problem for British society.

Because the legitimacy of the newly reconstituted NCCI—and, for that matter, CARD—depended on the support of prominent voices and established organizations within Black and Asian communities, as an expression of their unity against the Labour Government's call for further restrictions on Commonwealth migration and expanded powers of deportation, the Indian Workers Association (IWA) joined with the NFPA and the WISC to announce plans to boycott the NCCI. The leadership of these organizations—three of the largest serving Black and Asian constituencies in Britain—calculated that their refusal to support the work of the NCCI might offer some ground to leverage the Government's interest in promoting the appearance of meaningful efforts toward integration in the service of lobbying for a reconsideration of increased limitations on Commonwealth migration. In essence, the organizations hoped to employ the Government's strategy of linking a legislative agenda that included racially discriminatory migration controls with the ostensibly anti-racist goal of seeking integration to their political advantage.[106] However, with Pitt and Alavi's involvement in the NCCI—even in their "personal capacities"—in many ways this stance placed some of the leading Black and Asian organizations in direct contention with CARD. Moreover, this development exacerbated growing tensions between those in the leadership ranks of CARD and those in groups representing specific Black and Asian constituencies.

The IWA, the NFPA, and the WISC had already begun to mount a challenge to CARD's ability to claim a position as the leading collective voice for Black and Asian communities in Britain, even before the announcement of a joint boycott of the NCCI. In addition to holding a series of meetings in the weeks after the release of the White Paper to begin coordinating responses, delegates from each of these groups met in London with the purpose of establishing a separate national organization to ostensibly carry out CARD's professed mission of advocating for the interests of Black and Asian migrants and fighting against racial discrimination.[107] Although the IWA never formally affiliated with CARD, this move on the part of the leadership of the NFPA and the WISC—organizations that held formal representation on CARD's National Executive—spoke to a declining sense of confidence in both the motives and methods of CARD's leadership by key constituencies whose support was pivotal.

Among the three organizations, executive members of the Standing Conference were most critical of CARD and, more specifically, David Pitt's vision of CARD's role as a pressure group in the wake of the publication of the White Paper. Despite the early gains that CARD made in shaping Government opinion about the components of the Race Relations bill, the White Paper indicated that CARD's influence in Whitehall was virtually ineffectual. And if CARD planned to focus its efforts on lobbying for policy reform and building a Black and Asian voting bloc in a system in which both major political parties embraced racialized anti-immigrant policies, how would the particular everyday concerns of people of color fit into their agenda? CARD had yet to make these connections clear, and the presence of its top executives on the NCCI did not necessarily inspire confidence in the campaign's intent to foreground the specific concerns of the communities it professed to represent. In admonishing Pitt and Alavi's decision to join the NCCI, WISC Secretary Jeff Crawford suggested that their failure to resign their CARD positions would compel the Standing Conference to withdraw as a CARD affiliate.[108] But it is clear that in many ways Pitt and Alavi's decision to join the NCCI was the pretext for WISC leaders to make a clean break from an organization that they had already begun to work apart from even at the national level.

Less than a month after CARD's founding convention—which in theory was the official launch of a national coalition of organizations that included the WISC—members of the London and Birmingham branches of the Standing Conference held a joint meeting that unanimously voted to form a national organization to foster "self-protection" among West Indians.[109] While CARD's fledgling membership stood at about 400, between the two branches alone the WISC claimed a membership of approximately 11,000 through its affiliate groups and remained one of the largest and most influential organizations, particularly among London's West Indian communities.[110] Originally established as an arm of the Migrant Services Division of the West Indies High Commission in 1959, following the Notting Hill violence, the Conference's primary aims initially included mobilizing resources to provide assistance to largely first-generation West Indian migrant communities in their efforts to seek housing, employment, and successful incorporation into British society. As a central liaison between the short-lived West Indies Federal Government and local voluntary associations working among migrants from various islands, the Standing Conference played a key role in fostering a sense of West Indianness among the different colonial nationalities of Caribbean migrants forged through the shared experience of migration and the racial politics of settlement.[111]

After the disintegration of the West Indies Federation in the wake of Jamaica's withdrawal and subsequent independence in 1962, the internal dynamics of the organization began to shift. Backlit by the passage of the Commonwealth Immigration Act, as its diplomatic mission became less formal, the shifting political landscape in the Caribbean and Britain generated a heightened awareness of the precarious status of West Indians as citizens in British society. In particular, many WISC leaders began to embrace and articulate nascent "Black Power" ideologies rooted in a strident critique of the relationship between racism, disenfranchisement, and the power of the state that would crystallize in more tangible forms during the late 1960s. As the newly elected Labour Government began to pursue a national policy addressing racial discrimination in the early months of 1965, officials took note of the change in the political tenor of the Standing Conference. And before Home Official officials agreed in March 1965 to receive a deputation of WISC leaders expressing their support for comprehensive anti-discrimination legislation that would extend to employment and housing and address policing and the treatment of people of color in the court system—areas that CARD proposals neglected to tackle—Metropolitan Police began surveillance of the organization.[112]

Shortly after the publication of the White Paper on Commonwealth Immigration, WISC leaders announced plans to hold a series of town hall meetings to mobilize Black and Asian communities in self-defense after a home-grown branch of the Ku Klux Klan issued a series of threats, including plans to hold cross burnings targeting West Indians in September 1965.[113] Throughout the summer of 1965 news of Klan-initiated cross burnings, as well as increasing vandalism and threats of violence aimed at Black and Asian residents across the Midlands, made national headlines. Although prominent Government officials dismissed the violence as the work of "a small lunatic fringe" in places like Smethwick in an attempt to dislodge news-making expressions of anti-Black violence from the same forms of White racism that warranted the consideration of anti-discrimination policy, WISC leaders made a direct correlation between the two.[114] In fact, in announcing plans to combat threats by what appeared to be an organized Ku Klux Klan upstart that circulated letters stating it would never allow Britain "to become a dumping ground of Afro-Asian filth," members of the WISC linked their efforts toward achieving a sense of security within the confines of their homes and their neighborhoods with their objections to discriminatory immigration

policies and a broader diasporic Black freedom movement for socioeconomic justice. As WISC leaders made the case for the creation of a national
organization in defense of West Indian interests, they cited the threats of the
KKK- or, to be more precise, White supremacist violence-along with a White
Paper that they insisted contained provisions that "reek[ed] of South Africa,"
as well as the infamous Watts riots in Los Angeles that had captured headlines around the world and exposed the limits of a civil rights agenda that
did not foreground the relationship between racism, cycles of poverty, and
unequal access to social resources such as housing, jobs, education, and judi-
cious policing. In a resolution denouncing a recent decision to authorize the
Birmingham Corporation to regulate multi-occupied homes in such a manner
designed to "keep coloured people contained in substandard areas" or "forcibly disperse them," WISC delegates charged that the Labour Government
also appeared to be moving in a similar direction in failing to address discriminatory housing practices that had a negative disparate impact on people
of color. Thus, like the insurgent communities in Watts, Black communities in
Britain demanded more of their citizenship.[115]

Rallying WISC delegates to action, L. C. Dyke, Chairman of the North
London West Indian Association, suggested that building a strong and
active grassroots movement among West Indians was imperative, given the
Government's lack of interest in the particular concerns facing Black British
citizens. Dyke explained,

> If we have to mobilise forces to fight, it is because we find our backs
> to the wall. At this time we have no use for a Martin Luther King in
> Britain. The majority of West Indians are here to stay. The sooner we
> realize that the better. We must realise our right to be in this country.
> We are not going to fight as strangers, we are going to fight as citizens.
> If we cannot get protection and security from any of the Governments
> in this country, then we are going to let them know we need such pro-
> tection and we must get it. [116]

Invoking some of the more confrontational language that would later come to
define the rhetoric of a more cohesive articulation of Black Power in Britain,
Dyke implored,

> We must fight. I am not telling you what to fight with.... If the
> Government of this country is prepared to sit back and do nothing to
> stop this kind of hooliganism then we have to do something about it.
> A West Indian likes to protect his family. God help those caught put-
> ting up a burning cross.[117]

Dyke's strong words to Standing Conference delegates spoke to a long history of Black Britons' struggles to secure the right to belong as citizens entitled to protection from the state in the face of violence and racism. Moreover, his words suggested that in coalition, West Indians would be in an optimal position to make demands of the state and exercise their rights as citizens to defend themselves in the absence of adequate protection from state authority.

Aside from addressing the importance of joint action, Dyke's suggestion that the movement that he imagined had "no use for a Martin Luther King in Britain" also raised a critical issue related to the nature of the leadership required to carry forth the requisite "fight" for the right to belong. In the preceding decade, King had crafted and employed the currency of his media image as the leading spokesperson for a national movement for social justice that advocated civil disobedience and direct-action nonviolent protests.[118] Lyndon Johnson's signing of the 1964 Civil Rights Act followed by historic voting rights legislation just days after the release of the White Paper represented, in clear measurable terms, some of the legal gains that a coalition of activists and organizations who had embraced nonviolence as a protest strategy had made in the service of securing full citizenship for Black Americans. But even King himself acknowledged that the uprisings taking place in 1965 in cities such as Los Angeles and later Cleveland and Detroit expressed the frustrations of those who had not experienced a change in their material realities despite the passage of new anti-discrimination laws. To be sure, even within the variegated movement for Black freedom, King's commitment to nonviolence and his willingness to seek and placate White allies, including state authorities, placed him at odds with a growing segment of radical voices that included Stokely Carmichael and James Foreman, who famously proclaimed, "If we can't sit at the table, let's knock the fucking legs off" in response to the need for federal intervention in the wake of police attacks on demonstrators during Selma's "Bloody Sunday" voting rights protest.[119] Arguably, it was this type of non-conciliatory collective voice among West Indians that unabash- edly challenged and critiqued the configuration of state power, as opposed to merely finding a place for itself within the political establishment, that WISC leaders hoped to cultivate in making plans for a new national organization.

As WISC leaders began to coordinate their responses to the White Paper in conjunction with the Indian Workers Association and the National Federation of Pakistani workers in the fall of 1965, they continued to protest and lobby Government officials on behalf of West Indians and other populations racialized as "coloured immigrants" against the Ministry of Education's proposed quotas for migrant children in public schools, "vicious and unprovoked" racial violence, and malfeasant policing practices.[120] On the issues of racial violence and policing in particular, a delegation received by the Home Office and led by WISC General Secretary Jeff Crawford stressed what they believed to be the mutually constitutive relationship between the two. In urging the Home Office to investigate the rising number of assaults, similar to the critique offered by members of the IRFCC in the wake of the death of Kelso Cochrane, the delegation insisted that individual attacks were directly related to the inadequacies of police protection for Black Britons and other populations of color. Furthermore, in making a case for Government intervention that directly implicated the power of the state in compromising the citizenship rights of Black Britons, the delegation also highlighted allegations of violence occurring at the hands of police and proposals for discretionary police registration for Commonwealth migrants that would no doubt disproportionately subject Black and Asian migrants to police surveillance, regulation, and criminalization.[121] For WISC leaders, effectively confronting anti-Black racism required a willingness to both identify how the power of the state could be mobilized and vigorously articulate the ways in which the state, including officials in a purportedly liberal Labour Government, remained actively complicit in fomenting the structures and tacitly validating the social and cultural practices, including seemingly isolated incidents of racial violence, that contributed to Black Britons' experience of disenfranchisement. Taking this view required denouncing the terms devised to restrict non-White migrants' ability to exercise their right to enter Britain and scrutinizing the Labour Government commitment to a type of "integration" that allowed Black Britons to fully belong as citizens whose lives, bodies, property, and equal access to social resources warranted protection from the state. Therefore, as CARD leaders, including David Pitt, joined the ranks of a state-sanctioned body chartered to enact "integration" on the Government's terms, in the eyes of WISC officials, CARD's ability to provide the type of leadership for a movement that spoke for Black Britons was severely compromised.

Aside from the WISC's moves to challenge the legitimacy of CARD by establishing its own national organization and threatening to withdraw in the wake of David Pitt and Hamza Alavi's acceptance of membership on the NCCI, the publication of a manifesto by WISC Welfare Officer Neville Maxell in the summer of 1965 suggests that the issue of what constituted sufficient Black leadership had been a subject of debate and consideration among WISC leaders well before the release of the White Paper. Titled *The Power of Negro Action*, Maxwell's treatise made a case for the integration of people of African descent in British society in such a way that acknowledged their right to belong and their equality as citizens, as well as the diversity that they brought to the nation. Although he was careful to note that the pamphlet did not represent the official opinions of the Standing Conference, the ideas that he espoused originated from a paper that he had given at a conference held by the WISC a few months prior. In discussing what he dubbed "Operation Bootstraps," Maxwell outlined plans for organizing West Indian and other communities of African descent in Britain. Crucial to this endeavor was the development of "effective Negro leadership." Citing Paul Robeson's celebrated polemic *Here I Stand*, Maxwell insisted that, above all, Black leaders should possess independence in thought and action from "white do-gooders" and identify with the rank and file members of the constituencies that they hoped to speak for. In clarifying this particular point, Maxwell adopted a more personal and accusatory tone in describing the pitfalls of Black leaders who did not meet these standards. He noted that Black people should "watch with an eagle's eye for that kind of leadership which believes that white power must be relied upon rather than Negro power," and warned that "the best way to alienate rank and file support is to be openly seen to be relying on outside [white] advice and support, financial or otherwise." He further admonished,

> Useless is the leader who sees his position as a stepping stone to greater personal achievement or fame, or who is used by white liberals as the index, the living symbol of the progress of his race . . . Useless, too, is the leader who has come to be regarded by all except the majority of black people as "responsible" but who, at the same time is completely out of touch with the day to day problems and headaches of the people in the street. These "Uncle Toms" must be regarded as museum pieces.[122]

Although Maxwell did not identify any particular Black leader as the principal subject of his scathing critique, his commentary sheds light on some of the ways in which tensions between WISC and CARD officials were driven in part by competing visions of Black leadership. Among officers of the Standing Conference, including General Secretary Jeff Crawford, who declined an invitation to serve on CARD's Executive Committee because he was suspicious that CARD would become overrun by its White supporters, CARD Chairman David Pitt embodied the problem of Black leaders' collusion with White liberals and a Labour Government that had sanctioned, through policy and benign neglect, all of the insidious manifestations of the "colour bar" that they were working to dismantle.[123] From their view, the type of leadership that David Pitt—and ultimately CARD—represented was one that compromised the collective will of those whom they sought to speak for by exercising moderation rather than militancy to remain palatable and relevant in the eyes of a White political establishment.

In announcing a formal split between the WISC and CARD in the months following the establishment of the NCCI, Crawford insisted that CARD had "gradually become irrelevant" among the approximately 800,000 Black and Asian citizens that British officials suggested CARD represented. He explained, "We wanted a strong body that would speak for us, but it [CARD] has become soft and middle-class, working behind the scenes."[124] Crawford's critique of CARD spoke to the manner in which the organization operated, its leadership, and the composition of its membership base. Moreover, it dovetailed with many of the concerns that WISC Welfare Officer Neville Maxwell raised in regard to the pitfalls of a disjuncture between a type of bourgeois "Negro leadership" and the specific everyday concerns and grievances of the Black masses. Arguably, CARD Chairman David Pitt embodied many of these tensions. Pitt's middle-class upbringing, his educational credentials coupled with his professional status as a medical doctor, his ties to mainstream party politics, and his political ambitions clearly distinguished him from the average Black wage worker in Britain. And in many ways in the minds of Standing Conference leaders who maintained that their views were "quite contrary" and subsequently "ignored" under Pitt's leadership, CARD remained unable to adequately articulate the collective will of the rank and file members of the Black constituencies that it hoped to attract.[125]

Although WISC leaders took a firm stand against the inherent contradictions of Pitt and Alavi's membership on the NCCI, the fact that members of the Standing Conference later joined the ranks of the committee in an advisory capacity shortly after it began meeting suggests that their critique of CARD was more concerned with the manner in which an organization representing the interests of Black Britons engaged the power of the state than whether or not CARD should align with Government-sponsored entities promoting integration. However, aside from Pitt and Alavi's controversial acceptance of appointments to the NCCI, what is most critical to understanding the intra-racial politics that led to the split between CARD and the Standing Conference is recognizing how these organizational battle lines were part and parcel of a broader ongoing struggle to actualize a vision of citizenship for Black Britons, one that extended well beyond campaigning against racial discrimination. Top-down integration by way of tepid anti-discrimination policy did not equate to the affirmation of full citizenship and belonging for Black Britons. The fact remained that even with the passage of a Race Relations bill that finally acknowledged the existence of racial discrimination in British society, shops could still refuse to serve Black patrons, proprietors could continue to post advertisements refusing to rent to Black tenants, unions could deny membership to Black workers and Black families seeking credit, insurance, and a host of other economic resources were likely to pay more and receive less in the consumer marketplace than their White counterparts. Moreover, as Black men, women, and children walked the streets, acquired property, and established homes, they still did so in certain spaces in cities like London under the looming threat of violence enacted to remind them that they did not belong and were not entitled to protection. And while CARD continued to position itself as an advocate for Black Britons by lobbying to strengthen anti-discrimination policy, its inability to reckon with the germinating seeds of a more strident and unabashedly Black political consciousness that made demands of the state just as it implicated the Government in perpetuating anti-Black racism and White supremacy—in those terms—ultimately led to the eventual demise of the organization precisely when it seemed that some its early lobbying efforts were beginning to bear more fruit.

Britain's "Freedom Summer": Making a Case for Policy Reform

Parliament passed the nation's first Race Relations bill in November 1965, outlawing racial discrimination in "places of public resort," including hotels, restaurants, pubs, theaters, dance halls, or any facility maintained by public authority. Additionally, the Act established penalties of up to £1,000 in fines and two years in prison for those convicted of inciting racial hatred. While inciting racial hatred carried specific criminal penalties, the enforcement apparatus of the anti-discrimination provisions of the bill took shape in the form of the creation of a three-member national Race Relations Board charged with overseeing the establishment of local conciliation committees that would initiate the process of mediation.[126] Whereas the original CARD legislative proposals supporting conciliation as a mechanism for enforcement called for a commission with statutory powers to investigate and subpoena witnesses, the final Bill granted the Race Relations Board only the power to receive complaints, mediate within the realm of the law's narrow purview, and refer cases to the Attorney General for consideration in civil court if mediation failed. As other scholars have duly noted, although the act proved weak, due in part to its limited and somewhat ambiguous jurisdiction, in retrospect, the bill signaled a major paradigm shift in British public policy. Previously, the very idea of race relations—commonly framed by language typically associated with individual behaviors such as prejudice, intolerance, and bias—was a concept popularly relegated to the interpersonal realm. But as a matter of law and public policy, the Race Relations Act of 1965 made a declarative, albeit far from definitive, statement about the ways in which race structured systematic socioeconomic disadvantages for people of color that required some form of redress.[127]

If there was consensus within the Labour Government that the Race Relations Act of 1965 was a necessary "final step"—as outgoing Home

Secretary Frank Soskice had argued during closing debate—in a broader
agenda designed to depoliticize race by shifting the focus from discriminatory Commonwealth migration policies to anti-discriminatory integrationist measures, the fact that the first Chair of the Race Relations Board,
former Liberal MP Mark Bonham-Carter, accepted the appointment under
the condition that he could lobby for extending the provisions of the Board's
powers suggests that there were certainly some who viewed the bill as an
opening rather than a fait accompli. [128] Alongside those working directly for
Government-sanctioned entities, including members of the NCCI and the
three-member Race Relations Board, comprised of Bonham-Carter; Bernard
Langston, the former Lord Mayor of Manchester; and the former Trinidadian
High Commissioner, Learie Constantine, a well-known cricketer who previously served in the League of Coloured People, CARD played a decisive
role in helping a sympathetic new Home Secretary build a compelling case
for amending the first bill to widen its purview and expand the power of the
administrative bodies designated to enforce the law. As noted earlier, CARD's
push to include conciliation as the enforcement mechanism of Britain's
anti-discrimination policies grew from the legal committee's research on the
effectiveness of statutory commissions in North America, but also from a
desire to introduce an administrative mechanism that could be leveraged to
"put flesh on the enemy" by documenting, on a case-by-case basis, both the
existence and the specific nature of racial discrimination in British society.[129]
In doing so, not only did CARD leaders hope to reframe the "colour problem"
as one rooted in White racism as opposed to "coloured immigrants," but they
also aimed to empirically demonstrate the glaring shortcomings of the current
race-relations policy infrastructure and categorically shatter the myths that
underpinned the mystique of British anti-racism. And to that end, taking a cue
from students, activists, and grassroots organizers pressing for full citizenship
on behalf of Black Americans, CARD set out to test and showcase the limits of
the new policy, particularly in regard to the arenas of employment and housing, by launching a "Summer Project" in local communities that was modeled
after the "Freedom Summer" campaigns in the United States to draw public
attention to the quotidian realities of British racism as experienced by Black
Britons and other communities of color.[130]

   Bonham-Carter's appointment as Chair of the Race Relations Board suggested that from the outset the Board would seek to become a national clearinghouse of information about the manifestations of racial discrimination
occurring in the areas where the Board already had jurisdiction and in those
where it hoped to eventually extend its purview. But even before the Race
Relation Board joined forces with the NCCI to commission a study to examine
the magnitude of discrimination in areas not covered by the Race Relations

Act, CARD led the way in pursuing a fact-finding mission to expose and create greater public awareness about the day-to-day struggles of opportunity
and access that Black Britons and other groups racialized as "coloured immigrants" encountered—struggles that the 1965 Race Relations Act neglected to
address. Under the leadership of executive committee member Julia Gaitskill,
the daughter of former Labour Party leader Hugh Gaitskell, during the spring
of 1966 CARD established a subcommittee tasked with ultimately transforming the organization into a kind of informal satellite for filtering discrimination
cases to the media and to the Race Relations Board for review. In addition to
encouraging members and affiliate organizations to begin collecting individual
complaints of discrimination through personal contacts and by collectively
canvassing and hosting public meetings in neighborhoods and local communities, under the direction of South Asian scholar Dipak Nandy, an affiliate of
the Institute of Race Relations and chair of the Leister Campaign for Racial
Equality who had recently joined CARD's executive committee, the ad hoc
Complaints Committee helped coordinate efforts to strategically catalog discriminatory practices in the hiring process, the consumer marketplace, and the
leasing of accommodations during the summer of 1966. Inspired by the work of
SNCC activists and organizers during Freedom Summer in the United States,
CARD's Summer Project sent three teams of field workers to Manchester,
Southall, and Leeds for one month to test individual businesses and agencies,
conduct interviews, and observe conditions pertaining to race relations.[131]

Gathering evidence of discrimination through test cases emerged as
CARD's signature strategy during the Summer Project. Most of the volunteers recruited included young White, Black, and Asian school leavers and
college-age students whom CARD organizers trained on topics that included
job interviewing, employment qualifications, and home buying to adequately
prepare them to take on convincing roles in the testing process. Some of
the most popular forms of testing initially implemented by the Complaints
Committee involved having White volunteers apply for employment or seek
housing, credit, or insurance either in tandem with a Black or Asian applicant
or immediately after a person of color, typically with slightly better credentials, had been denied, duped, or subjected to arbitrary guidelines. In some
instances, this experiment involved a simple telephone inquiry about vacancies or sending pairs of letters of application with "one person making it clear
that he or she is coloured." At other times volunteers applied in person, no
doubt heeding the Complaints Committee's warning that in addition to paper
qualifications, particular expectations about "experience, voice and appearance" had to reasonably correspond with the advertised position.[132]

In addition to collecting evidence of racial discrimination that could be
presented to members of the Race Relations Board, a central goal of the

operation, much like that of Freedom Summer, entailed attracting media attention to educate and shape the consciousness of a majority White British public about the problem of racism as experienced by Black Britons and other Commonwealth citizens of color. In chronicling some of the findings of the Summer Project, one national newspapers declared that CARD had shown "It's No Fun Being a Brown Briton," as reports of test cases, including an experiment in which two young British-born West Indian women whose "speech and attitudes [were] entirely English" were consistently "met with lies, evasion or outright rejection" when applying for jobs that their less qualified White counterparts were routinely offered.[133] In other press coverage, the Summer Project also highlighted the fact that in communities like Southall, upwards of 85 percent of South Asian migrants who entered on priority work vouchers because of their education and professional experience were oftentimes relegated to semi-skilled or unskilled jobs because they were unable to secure employment in their field of training, in part because of perceptions about their level of competence and stereotypes about their ability to speak English.[134]

Just as much as the Summer Project was about building an arsenal of specific cases of discrimination, CARD volunteers were also expected to become the organization's eyes and ears on the ground in the local communities where they were sent to work. In addition to serving as testers, CARD organizers encouraged volunteers to document every aspect of the cases that they took part in and keep records or diaries of their encounters with ordinary people in the local community in regard to race relations in general.[135] In reflecting on some of her encounters with Black Britons in Moss Side, CARD volunteer Patricia Quick attempted to capture both the sense of frustration that Black Britons faced when confronting racial discrimination and the complexities associated with seeking to identify the myriad of ways in which anti-Black racism worked to simultaneously disenfranchise, offend, deny, violate, and exclude in everyday life. In one of her diary entries Quick explained,

> Apart from the question of discrimination we have managed to get some idea of what it is like to be a coloured person in Moss Side. The majority when asked say that they are treated well, or more commonly that "They keep to themselves." But my impression is that when we do manage to get through to people we discover that this is a front. Sometimes they say something like "It is a bit difficult but you get use to it," and it seems that after a time people do become almost immune to snubs. But occasionally we hear things like, "You have no idea how bad it is to be black in this country" and we hear about people cutting them dead in the streets, serving white people before them in shops,

refusing to sit next to them on the bus, and hundreds of petty little incidents that build up to make life unpleasant for people.[136]

Quick's entry highlights one of the central tensions between CARD's strategy of mounting a campaign focused squarely on seeking a public policy solution to address the more structural problem of racial discrimination and of effectively organizing a movement that represented and confronted how Black Britons and other populations of color in Britain experienced the insidious cultural nature of White racism. Challenging forms of racial discrimination were no doubt part of that struggle but, as Quick's observations suggested, what made life "unpleasant" for Black Britons—perhaps to put it mildly—was a constellation of experiences designed to remind them that their citizenship and rights of belonging were marginal, contested, and in many ways made fundamentally illegitimate.

In the spring of 1967 CARD submitted a summary report to the Race Relations Board, based on approximately 150 complaints compiled between April 1966 and March 1967. This report included both "spontaneous" cases filed with CARD by individual complainants and over 50 test cases initiated through the 1966 Summer Project. Of the 43 cases highlighted in the report, the overwhelming majority focused on discrimination occurring in the employment sector and in the housing market. Of the cases pertaining to employment discrimination, some documented instances in which an employer or hiring agency promised a Black or an Asian applicant a job interview over the phone, only to claim no vacancies existed when the applicant arrived in person. According to one Nigerian tester, after arriving early for a morning interview at the North of England British Rail Station, the manager seemed "very shocked" that the applicant was Black and embarrassingly explained to him that the position had already been filled earlier that morning even though he had arrived early enough to know that no one was waiting before him to be interviewed.[137] Other cases demonstrated how White applicants were offered opportunities for positions that Black applicants were refused and given preferential treatment in the hiring process. In one complaint a British-born woman of Jamaican parentage reported that a White woman had been asked to interview for a job at a local shop in Manchester shortly after the first woman had been told that the advertised position had been filled.[138] In another complaint filed against a bank in Manchester, a twenty-eight year old CARD tester who had migrated from Sierra Leone reported that after inquiring about positions he received a letter stating that the bank had "no vacancies for men in [his] age group with [his] particular qualifications," while a lesser-qualified White Englishmen of the same age was accepted for employment. To underscore the discriminatory treatment, the CARD tester later wrote to the bank under the

guise of a twenty-eight year old Australian man listing the exact same credentials as described in his previous inquiry. The bank responded by promptly
sending his alter ego an application for employment.[139]

Stories of preferential treatment toward oftentimes less qualified White
applicants abounded in the CARD report. Not only did Black and Asian
complainants report being passed over for interviews or positions that were
later offered to White applicants, they also cited encountering ambiguous and
irregular application procedures. In one case, when a Jamaican applicant edu-
cated in Britain with higher marks than his English counterpart asked why
he needed to complete additional forms to have his application considered by
a "prominent" London insurance company, the secretary promptly informed
him, "The fact that one applicant is offered an interview immediately and
another is not has nothing to do with nationality but with our interview programme." In a separate case involving another insurance company, a Jamaican
applicant was told that while it was the company's policy not to discriminate,
"the prejudice of the general public made it impossible for them to recruit
colored people as field staff unless they had exceptional qualities."[140]

To be sure, the CARD report also showed that instances of employment
discrimination were not limited to the private sector, nor were they confined to the hiring process. When applying to train as a radio and television
repairman at a London Government Employment Exchange, a Jamaican man
reported that he was told that he should select another trade "because the colour of [his] skin made employers prejudiced as well as English workers." After
being dismissed from a West London Government Training Center, an Indian
worker from Southall submitted a complaint indicating that he had been told
that he was "not a fit person to be trained for milling" because "Indians and
Pakistanis are not so good that they can learn handling English machines."
When he complained to the chief instructor, the manager responded, "Do not
waste our Government money . . . Your people are worthless and waste our
time for nothing."[141] In addition to racial bias, other cases highlighted unfair or
hostile working conditions for those Black and Asian workers who had secured
employment, including higher work expectations, salary and bonus deferen-
tials, exclusion from workplace facilities, social ostracism, and bullying.[142]

In the housing arena, CARD testers employed similar strategies used in the
labor market to uncover discrimination practiced by estate agents and private
landlords. They found oftentimes that rather than simply turn Black or Asian
tenants away, agents routinely steered them into or away from certain areas
and quoted higher rental rates. According to a British-born Indian resident
in Manchester who called to inquire about luxury flats advertised in the local
paper, "speaking with an obviously Indian accent," estate agents told him that
flats were available in Chorlton only for a rate of £4 per week. Thirty minutes

later a White friend called the same agency to inquire about the same advertisement and was told about cheaper flats in a different area. In cases involving complaints against private landlords, the report confirmed a long history of socially sanctioned apartheid practices involving advertised "whites only" leasing policies as well as the more respectable custom of telling potential Black tenants that advertised listings were no longer available.[143]

In addition to employment and housing, CARD also presented evidence of discrimination in the insurance market, where people of color were quoted higher premiums for car insurance even when they had no infractions on their driving record. In some cases, quoted rates for non-White customers were nearly double the rates offered to White customers. And although none of the previous CARD legislative proposals referenced policing practices as an arena of racial discrimination, the report presented to the Race Relations Board also included a few very detailed cases of alleged police bias, misconduct, and brutality submitted to CARD by individual complainants. In one complaint a woman described as "British by nationality, Grenadian by origin" charged that she was unfairly prosecuted for "police assault" after a violent encounter with a local White man who attacked her after she had apparently chided his eleven year old son for bullying "three small coloured children." The woman reported that after a bystander called police, the man continued to hurl verbal and physical assaults as the police restrained her. When she attempted to break free from police as her attacker "rained blows on her face and stomach," she fell to the ground and was later charged with assault on police and taken into custody after one of the officers claimed that she bit him. Even though two eyewitnesses to the attack on the woman and her encounter with police offered statements in support of her version of events indicating that she had not bitten the officer, her attacker was not charged and was instead brought in as a police witness against her. While her attacker remained uncharged, despite uncontroverted testimony that he had assaulted her and "used, foul, abusive and racist" language toward her, magistrates fined the woman £16 for the crime of assaulting police.[144]

In other accounts submitted about police misconduct, complainants reported sustaining injuries after violent encounters with police in the streets and at precinct stations.[145] And in one case, a man who identified as "British by nationality, Jamaican by origin" described his arrest on trumped-up charges after he apparently failed to cooperate during a raid in which a police detective allegedly threatened to plant drugs on him. Invoking popular stereotypes associating Black men with drug crimes, the detective warned that it would be difficult to beat the drug charges because "the magistrate knows that all coloured men are suppose to have drugs."[146] While it is unclear if CARD had a long-term strategy of pressing for reforms in the arena of policing and criminal justice—an issue that had long been a part of Black activists' demands for citizenship and equal justice—at the very least, the inclusion of complaints regarding policing no doubt helped to reinforce the connections that Black people knew all too well between stereotypes about Black bodies and the pathways to criminalization, police brutality, incarceration, and legal disenfranchisement.

In summarizing the results of the discrimination cases that CARD had compiled to argue for the urgency of new legislation, CARD Chairman David Pitt emphasized that the evidence pointed to three key issues: the variety of mechanisms facilitating discrimination, the systematic nature of discrimination, and the "pervasive helplessness" experienced by victims in part because of the "absence of any possibility of redress."[147] When the Race Relations Board issued its first annual report shortly after CARD released its finding, Board members echoed many of the talking points issued by CARD to build its case for amending the Race Relations Act and prioritizing race relations as a public policy concern. Although the Race Relations Board functioned as the official liaison between Government and an incestuous configuration of race-relations organizations, experts, professionals, and advocates, including local conciliation boards, the NCCI, the Society of Labour Lawyers, the Institute of Race Relations, and men and women of CARD's Executive Committee, in its function as a de facto legislative lobby the Board very much depended on the work of auxiliary organizations. It had no power to initiate complaints, so the work of the Board, as well as its ability to showcase its limitations, rested squarely on either individual volunteerism or the external efforts of advocacy groups, think tanks, and academic researchers. In their first report, the Board was careful to acknowledge the shortcomings of the voluntary complaints process as they emphasized, "that to suffer discrimination is to be humiliated." Therefore, the Board's work could be conducted only as a result of exceptional acts of individual determination that no doubt reflected experiences that were more widespread, given that it required "considerable courage to complain about humiliation."[148]

The annual report made a compelling case about the Board's impotence in regard to the arenas where Black Britons most commonly felt the social and economic sting of racial discrimination. Of the 327 complaints received by the Board between February 1966 and April 1967, 238, or nearly three-quarters of cases, were outside the scope of the Board's purview. Of those cases, nearly half related to employment. However, other arenas of complaint outside of the Board's reach included housing, financial facilities, shops, and policing.[149] Coupled with the findings of the CARD report and the release of the highly anticipated results of the Political and Economic Planning (PEP) committee's extensive survey of racial discrimination, a study jointly commissioned by the

Race Relations Board and the NCCI, by the summer of 1967, Home Secretary Roy Jenkins had a powerful arsenal of empirical evidence and national press support to lobby Parliament for new legislation and shatter the myth that racism was not a integral feature of everyday life in British society.

Much of the media traction and public attention given to the necessity of amending the Race Relations Act of 1965 came in reaction to Government-sponsored, purportedly nonpartisan efforts to investigate the scope of racial discrimination in Britain. Alongside the comprehensive PEP report, which ultimately became a benchmark in public and Parliamentary debate about race-relations policy, a separate study conducted by a University of Manchester law professor, Harry Street, on anti-discrimination law in other countries also bolstered arguments for reform.[150] Whereas the PEP report aimed to document discrimination by using a combination of nearly 1,500 interviews and 400 "situation tests" conducted in 6 different areas, the Street report provided a comparative international review of anti-discrimination policies.[151] But in terms of implementing a systematic study of the problem of racial discrimination as experienced by people of color in Britain, the early work of CARD organizers cannot be ignored. Inspired by the work of activists involved in the US Black freedom movement, CARD laid a foundation and established a model for exposing racial discrimination, testing the limits of anti-discrimination policy, and garnering publicity about the problem of White racism that the Race Relations Board endorsed and other entities emulated.

While the work of CARD's Complaints Committee and its Summer Project did not solely shift the terms of debate about the necessity of strengthening the 1965 Act, their efforts undoubtedly represented the first stage in a series of sociological evidence gathering, reporting, and analysis that made a majority White public more aware and the Labour Government more amenable to confronting some of the ways that race worked to exclude, disadvantage, and disenfranchise. But even as it appeared that CARD stood poised to see Government enact many of the core aspects of the vision of anti-discrimination policy that it had been campaigning for since its inception, by the fall of 1967, CARD reached a major impasse that jeopardized the future of the organization. While a number of factors certainly contributed to the decline of CARD at a moment when Government seemed most receptive to reforming anti-discrimination policy, it is clear that part of CARD's eventual demise derived from the inability of CARD leaders who had chosen the path of creating a voice for the organization within the political establishment to reckon with unyielding calls for a grassroots movement that spoke directly to the everyday grievances of Black Britons, as a cultural and political constituency, and against forms of state power that remained complicit in sanctioning and fomenting anti-Black racism.

The Rise of Black Power and the Fall of CARD

Armed with a wellspring of evidence documenting the "facts" of racial discrimination that Black Britons routinely lived, on 26 July 1967 Roy Jenkins announced plans to amend the Race Relations bill to include employment, housing, and the issuance of credit and insurance.[152] On that same day Jenkins also banned Stokely Carmichael from reentering Britain. During the previous two weeks, Carmichael had begun to boost his international profile by launching a speaking tour in London that included appearances at the Marxist-oriented International Congress on the Dialectics of Liberation Conference and meetings throughout London, where he stirred West Indian audiences by sharing stories of his formative years in Trinidad.[153] In the year before his arrival the British press paid close attention to Carmichael's rise to national prominence in the United States as head of SNCC, following a speech in Greenwood, Mississippi in which he made a vociferous call for "Black Power" to rally the disenfranchised Black masses to seek social justice. In particular, British newspapers cast Carmichael as an "extremist" in comparison to civil rights figures like Martin Luther King, Jr., suggesting that he embodied a violent brand of "Black Power" that one columnist suggested, "conjures up a biblical nightmare of Negro revenge with fire and sword" among White Americans.[154] Defining Black Power as an ideology that advocated Black unity, liberation, cultural awareness, institutional control, economic empowerment, and self-determination, Carmichael gave a new generation a language to voice a long history of Black nationalist thought. To be sure, this voice would be one that invoked a more strident tone emphasizing Black self-help and a more militant response to the violence inflicted by White supremacy.[155]

With news of the outbreak of racial violence in several US cities, including Newark as well as Detroit, a city where forty-three people died during the summer of 1967, Roy Jenkins did not want to imagine what the calls for "Black Power" as espoused by Stokely Carmichael might mean for British race relations. In the months leading up to his London tour, media reports attempted to link Carmichael to uprisings in such places as Nashville and Atlanta, while Congressional maneuvers to initiate federal legislation against inciting riots aimed at movement leaders like Carmichael only hardened popular perceptions of Black Power advocates as violent, dangerous, and criminal.[156] Part of the argument that Jenkins and many anti-discrimination policy supporters employed to make the case for extending the Race Relations Act rested on the premise that their plans were just as much preemptive strikes as they were a step toward enacting policies of redress for dealing with the problem of racial discrimination. In this respect, the extant realities of US race relations loomed large as supporters oftentimes invoked American racial geographies, including cities in turmoil and urban "ghettos," as cautionary tales about the dangers of failing to adequately address race relations.[157] And by the summer of 1967, imaginaries of Black Power and, more specifically, media-driven discourses focused on brash young militant leaders who called for anti-White-supremacist violence became one of the most powerful symbols of a purportedly American problem that British officials did not want to see cross the pond.

Despite Jenkins's half-hearted intentions of thwarting the impact of Black Power in Britain, the rising currents of a burgeoning grassroots Black Power movement were steadily taking shape well before Stokely Carmichael offered it a publicly legible namesake in 1966. In 1965 Michael de Freitas, who later changed his name to Michael X, founded the Racial Adjustment Action Society (RAAS), an organization that he described as "a child of the 1958 race riots." Taking its inspiration from the ideas of Black self-determination espoused by Malcolm X, RAAS began to gain media attention during the summer of 1965 as a "black men only" organization aiming to mobilize and unify Black workers by employing rhetoric that spoke directly to a Black struggle against White racism.[158] Alongside RAAS, the WISC also took on a media profile that positioned itself as a type of explicitly pro-Black organization with a confrontational posture that was most clearly articulated in its suspicion of the political establishment and White liberal patronage, particularly in contrast to CARD.[159] To be sure, with the publication of provocative treatises by prominent members, including Neville Maxwell's *The Power of Negro Action* (1965) and Joseph Hunte's *Nigger Hunting in England?* (1966), which highlighted the contentious relationship between Black Londoners and police, the Standing Conference certainly had begun to cast itself ideologically as a type foil to the more moderate, multiracial middle-class-led CARD operation even before the Standing Conference's short-lived affiliation with CARD came to an end in February 1966.

Although Michael X and members of the WISC had openly embraced Stokely Carmichael and the emerging Black Power politics that he championed during his tour of London, it was not until August 1967 that Nigerian writer Obi Egbuna established Britain's first organization explicitly advocating Black Power in Britain, the Universal Coloured People's Association (UCPA).[160] In the wake of the energy that Carmichael's visit generated within London's West Indian communities, as well as the backlash that it prompted from Government officials, in many ways the founding of the UCPA captured the growing appetite for what C. L. R. James famously described as the "banner" of Black Power being articulated in the late 1960s by staking a claim of representing a collective voice rooted in the political, cultural, and economic empowerment of Black people.[161] And as CARD attempted to remake itself and reconnect to grassroots movement building as the Labour Government moved to adopt many of its suggested policy reforms, some of its leading members recognized that the political climate in Britain was shifting. In a press interview, one CARD member explained, "Black Power just as relevant here as in the U.S."[162] So if CARD hoped to remain viable, it had to adjust.

By the time CARD convened its third annual national convention in November 1967, CARD remained in a holding pattern as its base of membership fractured in the wake of inactivity and loss of momentum. Moreover, as its leadership struggled to triangulate and redefine its role in relation to the state, the Black and Asian communities that it hoped to represent, and a fledgling grassroots Black Power movement skeptical of party politics and alliances with White liberals, the organization struggled to develop a coherent agenda for political action. In preparation for the national convention, a long-time associate of David Pitt, Johnny James, who served as CARD's Assistant General Secretary for membership, took the helm in making plans for the conference and recruiting new affiliates. Among his new recruits, James sought to develop ties with the newly formed Marxist group, the Caribbean Workers' Movement; the London Workers' Committee; the Indian Social Club; and Obi Egbuna's UCPA. In addition to swelling the number of voting delegates, James also made plans to introduce resolutions that called for constitutional amendments intended to reorient the mission and leadership base of CARD.[163]

When CARD's third annual convention opened on 4 November 1967 at Conway Hall in London, delegates immediately witnessed Johnny James's vision of CARD's political voice in the expanding milieu of a diasporically oriented British Black Power politics. Delegates gathered before posters of radical organizer Robert Williams, who advocated armed Black self-defense, and Pan-Africanist organizer and Kenyan independence leader Jomo Kenyatta. They stood before signs that reflected some of mantras of CARD's early history, declaring, "Outlaw racial discrimination. Provide effective laws," but also ones that imagined new futures for the organization, including one that stated, "Black Power means liberation, not integration as third-class citizens."[164] The juxtaposition of the signs underscored long-held debates about CARD's mission, its approach, and its relationship to state-sanctioned integration efforts. And many of these internal contestations, which had plagued CARD nearly from its inception, began to collide in dramatic fashion as two resolutions orchestrated in large part by Johnny James were set forth to call for constitutional amendments. Reflecting a more internationalist approach to anti-racism and the struggle against White supremacy, the first of the resolutions called for CARD members to declare their intentions to combat all forms of imperialism, while the more controversial of the two called for a new

Executive Committee comprised solely of "immigrant people or indigenous people of coloured origin." In this configuration, White members could only "support their coloured brothers and sisters in their struggle and not tell them how they are to fight."[165]

Subject to a general vote in a room comprised of newly minted delegates from organizations that Johnny James had handpicked to affiliate with CARD in the final weeks before the national conference, both resolutions received a majority vote, to the dismay of prominent White members of CARD's Executive Committee, including Anthony Lester, one of the chief architects of CARD's legislative proposals and former chair of the Complaints Committee, and General Secretary Julia Gaitskill. Other disaffected members included delegates from the Southall Indian Workers Association and Dipak Nandy, the South Asian scholar who had spearheaded CARD's Summer Project one year earlier.[166] When David Pitt refused to support an independent query to potentially disqualify votes that Nandy and other longer-standing active members of the organization felt had been illegally stacked, this refusal effectively provided a death blow to CARD.

In the weeks that followed, the divisions between CARD's old guard and a largely West Indian coalition of Black delegates and affiliate members who supported a change in mission and leadership intensified. In a press interview held a few days after the last day of the annual convention, Johnny James sought to clarify the position of those seeking to take the Campaign in a new direction. In outlining some of the grievances that prompted a reconsideration of CARD's structure and purpose, James prefaced his comments by explaining that he deplored "speaking to the white imperialist press reporters" in part because of the manner in which the media oftentimes distorted the work and assassinated the character of those fighting for human rights and Afro-Asian liberation by using labels such as "terrorists, rebels, extremists and other derogatory names" to describe their activities. He went on to offer a litany of grievances that stood at the root of what was now a growing "anger" about the status of Black and Asian people in Britain. Among the list of grievances James included the continuation of discriminatory immigration policies, "increasing cases of police brutality and terror against us," including "constant attacks against our women-folk," as well as use of the Race Relations Act's anti-incitement clause to prosecute and silence radical voices and political dissidents.[167] James's critique of the uses of the anti-incitement clause highlighted that some of the earliest prosecutions included RAAS leader Michael X, followed by four UCPA members charged in October 1967 for violating Section 6 of the Act during speeches given in Hyde Park in August of that year.[168]

In addition to highlighting some of the dynamics confronting Black Britons that pushed him and his fellow supporters in CARD to the "stage of red-hot explosion," James also expressed discontent with CARD's inability to embrace the connections between the domestic, imperial, and global dimensions of Black liberation. While CARD's early agenda had focused on a domestically oriented platform against racial discrimination, James insisted that the "coloured majority of CARD members and supporters" viewed their plight as part of a wider freedom struggle that included disenfranchised and oppressed

people in Africa, the Middle East, Asia, the Caribbean, and the United States. Frustrated by what he described as "white liberals and a few Uncle Toms" who did not support internationalizing CARD's mission and openly confronting "white imperialist oppression," James insisted, "THE BLOODY LIMIT HAS BEEN REACHED AND PASSED!" James concluded his interview by citing words of Asian radical Mao Tse Tung spoken in support of the 1963 March on Washington as he charged, "The evil system of colonialism and imperialism arose and thrived with the enslavement of negroes and the trade in negroes, and it will surely come to its end with the complete emancipation of the black people."[169]

After members convened a new annual delegates' conference in December 1967, following a series of emergency meetings of a lame-duck national executive, what media outlets described as the "takeover" of CARD was complete with the election of a new, predominately West Indian national

council.[170] Although Chairman David Pitt, who maintained his office, offered Dipak Nandy an opportunity to restate arguments in favor of conducting an independent investigation of the credentials of delegates, in many ways Pitt had already signaled his shifting allegiances when he unilaterally overruled a vote by the outgoing Executive in support of his action at the November convention. Before the close of the new convention, Nandy and six other veteran CARD organizers, including Anthony Lester, had walked out and the stage was set for a new era in the life of the Campaign that ideally would focus on gaining grassroots support and empowering Black Britons and other Commonwealth citizens of color to embrace self-determination. CARD's era as a national legislative lobby was effectively over.[171]

David Pitt claimed the title of CARD National Chairman into the early 1970s. But after the internal shift in power during the 1967 annual delegates' conference, the historical record is virtually silent about any specific platforms that the national Campaign adopted to attract more grassroots support among Black Britons or to secure further policy reform. Although several local CARD chapters refused to acknowledge the final delegates' conference of 1967, even in the midst of inertia at the national level, there is evidence that local chapters continued to function well into the late 1960s.[172] But ultimately, as the national umbrella organization of organizations and voice of Black and Asian Britons that founders imagined, CARD had disintegrated less than two years after it had begun. In many ways CARD's demise is emblematic of some of the intra-racial tensions that defined the shifting contours of Black politics in Britain during the late 1960s. These tensions occurred in the context of national debates about race-relations policies geared toward rectifying individual complaints and diasporically oriented calls for social justice that confronted the structural and institutional spaces—including the state itself—that systematically empowered anti-Black racism.

Epilogue

Black Britain, the State, and the Politics of Race

Forensic evidence indicated that twenty-nine year old Mark Duggan did not have a gun on his person before an officer with the Metropolitan Police fired a fatal gunshot to his chest on 4 August 2011. However, the results of an official inquest into the shooting issued over two years later ruled his death a "lawful killing."[1] But well before legal debate about whether or not officers had a reasonable belief that Mark Duggan posed an imminent threat as he exited a minicab blockaded by police, his family and those within the North London neighborhood where he resided took to the streets in protest, demanding justice and expressing long-simmering tensions between police and Britain's largely working-class Black communities. For over a week after images of Mark Duggan's slain body began to circulate alongside conflicting news stories—some of which suggested that Duggan appeared to surrender before he was shot—residents in Tottenham demonstrated outside the local police station and participated in a grassroots insurgency that resulted in damage to public property, looting, violent clashes with police, and the destruction of homes and local businesses.[2]

As the unrest continued, in an interview with a BBC reporter that quickly went viral, long-time activist and journalist Darcus Howe challenged media depictions of the uprisings as "riots." He insisted that the violence was not shocking, given that police "had been stopping and searching young Blacks for no reason at all." From his view, the violence was symptomatic of their frustrations and further proof of his own sense that "something was going seriously wrong in this country." Observing the events occurring in Tottenham with a lens sharpened by the experience of living as a Black man in London for over fifty years, unlike the news commentator, who accused him of not being "a stranger to riots," Howe understood that what was happening in the streets of London, and later Liverpool and Birmingham, was the product of "so many moods and moments." It was a reference point in a longer history—one that the death of Mark Duggan brought to life.[3]

During the course of his exchange with the newscaster, one of the "moments" that Darcus Howe urged the reporter and, ostensibly, his wider television audience to recall was the mass insurrection in Brixton that occurred thirty years before, resulting in eerily familiar scenes of burned buildings, violence, heavy policing, and street protests. In the months before the eruption of mass violence in Brixton during the spring of 1981, in response to a targeted deployment of the infamous stop-and-search (Sus) laws, Howe had been at the fore of local organizing in South London to highlight anti-Black violence, discriminatory policing practices, and an overall lack of confidence in law enforcement by Black Britons. On 2 March 1981, following the tragic deaths of thirteen Black youths in a house fire in New Cross that many believed was racially motivated, Howe led a "Black People's Day of Action" that attracted thousands of demonstrators, who took part in a seventeen-mile trek to Hyde Park.[4] At the heart of the demonstration of solidarity lay a simple plea for recognition and justice. As one participant reflected, "It was important for us to bring London to a standstill—to say we're here. Look at us. We're here. We're hurting and you're not doing anything about it. You're pretending it hasn't happened."[5]

Darcus Howe's work as an activist and radical anti-racist organizer grew in large measure from his early years as a member of the British Black Panther movement. During the late 1960s and early 1970s the Black Panthers emerged as one of the most visible symbols of Britain's appropriation of a global Black Power movement that found its wings in the transnational circulation of the iconography of Black freedom struggles in the United States.[6] Part of the political cachet that iterations of Black Power in Britain held concerned how this particular brand, ideologically, stylistically, and rhetorically, directly implicated the power of the state—along with its agents and its institutions—in a critique of the modalities through which Black people experienced the violence, insecurity, exclusion, invisibility, and indignity associated with racism and second-class citizenship. And in many ways, the rise of Black Power as a political vernacular in Britain can be seen as part of a resistance to a type of anti-racist politics that deemphasized the centrality of the state as a provocateur and conduit of racism and disenfranchisement. The types of anti-discrimination policies initially supported by CARD that began to find their way into the Race Relations bills enacted throughout the late 1960s and 1970s focused primarily on regulating opportunities to access public space, collective resources, and the consumer marketplace on equitable terms. Ultimately, what this integrationist style of anti-racist politics geared toward mending race relations did was transform the state into an arbiter of discriminatory complaints without accounting for the ways in which the state remained complicit in fomenting the very "colour bar" practices of anti-Black racism that it purportedly sought to regulate.[7]

To be sure, in characterizing the 2011 Tottenham uprisings as an "insurrection of the masses" against the power of the state wielded by law enforcement officers, Darcus Howe raised the specter of his own storied history of harassment and violence at the hands of police—a narrative that culminated in his prosecution in 1970 as part of the Mangrove Nine, where he demanded justice in the form of an all-Black jury trial.[8] Coupled with his reference to Brixton in 1981, his BBC interview also implicitly recalled confrontations between Black Britons and the police that spurred violence in Handsworth and Broadwater Farm in 1985, and those that had resulted in the deaths of David Oluwale, Cynthia Jarrett, and Dorothy "Cherry" Groce.[9] Essentially, Howe used the platform of the BBC to argue that the 2011 violence in Tottenham precipitated by Mark Duggan's death was intimately connected to a history marked by the state's inability to safeguard the rights of its Black citizens.

Only with the publication of the MacPherson report following the 1993 murder of Stephen Lawrence did the nation as a whole experience a moment when the state, in the form of the Metropolitan Police, was publicly indicted for "institutional racism." According to that report—which directly cited the definition of institutional racism offered by Stokely Carmichael and Charles V. Hamilton in their 1967 treatise *Black Power: The Politics of Liberation in America*—the Metropolitan Police as an organization had collectively failed "to provide an appropriate and professional service to people because of their colour, culture or ethnic origin" in such a manner that could be "detected in processes, attitudes and behaviour which amount to discrimination through unwitting prejudice, ignorance, thoughtlessness and racist stereotyping which disadvantage minority ethnic people."[10] As a result, state agencies, including the police, prisons, and health services, became subject to extensions of the Race Relations Act.[11] But just as the British Nationality Act of 1948 reflected sentiments that Black people in the British Empire had long expressed regarding their understanding of their relationship to the imperial nation-state, the findings of the MacPherson report only reiterated a long-standing refrain emanating from Black Britons in the Empire and the postcolonial metropolis about the chasm between their expectations of racial justice, full citizenship and belonging, and the realities of a British state unwilling to and or uninterested in guaranteeing their rights.

Following a historical thread rooted in formerly enslaved people's everyday struggles to make meaning of freedom in the post-emancipation Caribbean and tracking its connection to the invocation of citizenship as a tool of claim making and a language of belonging among those rendered marginalized, excluded, exploited, and unprotected by colonial society and the imperial

state, this study has attempted to provide an important backstory to more contemporary debates about the politics of race and Black Britons' status in British
society. It is a story that locates the histories of postcolonial Black Britain at
the crossroads of Empire, transnational race politics and diasporic movement,
settlement, and transformation. It is by far not the only story; however, it is one
that is integral to understanding why the authority of the British state—both
materially and rhetorically—remains a focal point for Black Britons' articulations of their sense of how the politics of race bears on their everyday lives as
citizens with rights. Narratives about the so-called Windrush generation must
begin to account for Black newcomers' claims "London is the place for me" as
more than a tagline capturing a naive belief in a welcoming Mother Country
and consider them instead as part of a historical continuum of citizenship
practices and imaginaries of belonging that shaped the evolution of race politics and the formation of postcolonial Black Britain. Black Britons were not
merely objects of a race politics governed by the actions and agendas of British
officials or a postwar welfare state. Rather, their lives, their aspirations, their
claims, and their experiences provide a rich source for understanding the politicization of race in Britain in the midst of moving people and movements for
Black freedom, citizenship, and social justice throughout the African Diaspora
in the second half of the twentieth century.

NOTES

Introduction

1. Mike Phillips and Trevor Phillips, *Windrush: The Irresistible Rise of Multi-Racial Britain* (London: Harper Collins, 1998), 66; "Lord Kitchener Steps off the Empire Windrush," *The Guardian*, 15 June 2011.

2. Matthew Mead, "Empire Windrush: The Cultural Memory of an Imaginary Arrival," *Journal of Postcolonial Writing* 45, no. 2 (2009): 140–144; Sandra Courtman, "Women Writers and the Windrush Generation: A Contextual Reading of Beryl Gilroy's *In Praise of Love and Children* and Andrea Levy's *Small Island,*" *EnterText* 9 (2012): 87; see also Incoming Passenger List for *Empire Windrush*, 22 June 1948, BT 26/1237/9395, The National Archives (TNA).

3. British Pathé Footage of Empire Windrush, Gaumont British Newsreel, Reuters, 22 June 1948; reprinted courtesy *London Is The Place For Me: Trinidadian Calypso in London, 1950–1956* (London: Honest Jon's Records, 2002), compact disc recording).

4. Phillips and Phillips, *Windrush*, 66.

5. Gordon Roehler, *Calypso and Society in Pre-Independence Trinidad* (Port of Spain, Trinidad: Gordon Roehler, 1990), 346. Roehler notes that during the 1940s, calypsonians oftentimes chose names for themselves and their tents "that reflected the idea of war." In her study of the cultural politics of carnival in Trinidad, Jocelyne Guilbault also notes that Aldwyn Roberts's Lord Kitchener "evokes imperial circuits" traveled by British war hero Horatio Kitchener. Jocelyn Guilbault, *Governing Sound: The Cultural Politics of Trinidad's Carnival Music* (Chicago: University of Chicago Press, 2007), 9.

6. On the subject of the cultural baggage that West Indians brought to Britain, see Bill Schwarz, ed., *West Indian Intellectuals in Britain* (Manchester, UK: Manchester University Press, 2003), 3.

7. British Pathé Footage of Empire Windrush, Gaumont British Newsreel, Reuters, 22 June 1948; Schwarz, *West Indian Intellectuals in Britain*, 1.

8. British Pathé Footage of Empire Windrush, Gaumont British Newsreel, Reuters, 22 June 1948.

9. Ibid.

10. Ashley Dawson, *Mongrel Nation: Diasporic Culture and the Making of Postcolonial Britain* (Ann Arbor: University of Michigan Press, 2007), 1–2.

11. Roehler, *Calypso and Society in Pre-Independence Trinidad*, 457–459; Harvey Neptune, *Caliban and the Yankees: Trinidad and the United States Occupation* (Chapel Hill: University of North Carolina Press, 2007), chap. 5.

12. Lara Putnam, "Citizenship from the Margins: Vernacular Theories of Rights and the State from the Interwar Caribbean," *Journal of British Studies* 53, no. 1 (2014): 162–191.

13. Frederick Cooper and Roger Brubaker, "Beyond 'Identity,'" in *Colonialism in Question: Theory, Knowledge, History,* ed. Frederick Cooper (Berkeley: University of California Press, 2005), 62–63, 71–73; Frederick Cooper, *Citizenship between Empire and Nation: Remaking France and French Africa, 1945–1960* (Princeton, NJ: Princeton University Press, 2014), 1–25; Putnam, "Citizenship from the Margins," 162–170; Keith McClelland and Sonya Rose, "Citizenship and Empire, 1867–1928," in *At Home with the Empire: Metropolitan Culture and the Imperial World,* ed. Catherine Hall and Sonya Rose (Cambridge, UK: Cambridge University Press, 2007), 277.

14. Paul Gilroy, *Ain't No Black in the Union Jack: The Cultural Politics of Race and Nation* (Chicago: University of Chicago Press, 1991), 11; other foundational works that also pay attention to Black people in Britain as political actors engaging state power include Trevor Carter, *Shattering Illusions: West Indians in British Politics* (London: Lawrence and Wishart, 1986); John Solomos, *Race and Racism in Britain* (New York: St. Martin's Press, 1993, 2nd ed.); Harry Goulbourne, *Black Politics in Britain* (Aldershot, UK: Avebury, 1990); Ambalavaner Sivanandan, *A Different Hunger: Writings on Black Resistance* (London: Pluto Press, 1991); and Kalbir Shukra, *The Changing Pattern of Black Politics in Britain* (London: Pluto Press, 1998).

15. Barnor Hesse notes that popular term "colour bar" was an "unofficial institution of British colonialism" that systematically excluded people of color both in the metropole and the colonies. Barnor Hesse, "Diasporicity," in *Un/Settled Multiculturalisms,* ed. Barnor Hesse (London: Zed Books, 2000), 106. Examples of state-centered scholarship on race, migration, and citizenship privileging the voices of policy-makers include Kathleen Paul, *Whitewashing Britain: Race and Citizenship in the Postwar Era* (Ithaca, NY: Cornell University Press, 1997); Ian Spencer, *British Immigration Policy since 1939: The Making of Multi-Racial Britain* (London: Routledge, 1997); Richard Weight and Abigail Beach, *The Right to Belong: Citizenship and National Identity in Britain, 1930–1960* (London: I. B. Tauris, 1998); Randall Hansen, *Citizenship and Immigration in Postwar Britain: The Institutional Origins of a Multicultural Nation* (Oxford: Oxford University Press, 2000); James Hampshire, *Citizenship and Belonging: Immigration and the Politics of Demographic Governance* (London: Palgrave Macmillan, 2005).

16. Cooper and Brubaker, "Beyond 'Identity,'" 72.

17. The historical construction of Blackness in Britain has been a highly contested debate; however, this study adapts a concept of Black Britishness that aims to historicize how this category has been both claimed by and associated with populations of African descent in Britain with colonial roots in Africa and or the Caribbean particularly in their engagement with state power and through the course of their racialization in public policy debates during the 1950s and 1960s. Tariq Modood, "Political Blackness and British Asians," *Sociology* 28, no. 4 (November 1994): 859–876; Avtar Brah, *Cartographies of Diaspora: Contesting Identities* (New York: Routledge, 1996), 96–101; Stuart Hall, "Ethnicity: Identity and Difference," in *Becoming National: A Reader,* ed. Geoff Eley and Ronald Suny (Oxford: Oxford University Press, 1996), 339–351; Stuart Hall, "New Ethnicities," in *Black British Cultural Studies: A Reader,* ed. Houston A. Baker, Jr., Manthia Diawara, and Ruth H. Lindborg (Chicago: University of Chicago Press, 1996); Claire E. Alexander, *The Art of Being Black: The Creation of Black British Youth Identities* (Oxford: Oxford University Press, 1996); Winston James, "The Making of Black Identities," in *The Oxford Reader in Ethnicity,* ed. John Hutchinson and Anthony Smith (Oxford: Oxford University Press, 1996), 155–161. Gilroy, *Ain't No Black in the Union Jack,* 39; Michelle M. Wright, *Becoming Black: Creating Identity in the African Diaspora* (Durham: Duke University Press, 2004), 197–199.

18. "Coloured People 'Have Lost Confidence' in Police: Open Letter to the Prime Minister," *Manchester Guardian,* 19 May 1959.

19. Zig Layton-Henry, *The Politics of Immigration: Immigration, 'Race' and 'Race Relations' in Postwar Britain* (Oxford: Blackwell Publishing, 1992), 13. The statistics that Layton-Henry cites that form the basis of this estimate are based on records maintained by the House of Commons. See also Colin Holmes, *John Bull's Island: Immigration and British Society, 1871–1971* (London: Macmillan Education, 1988), 218–228.

20. Emile C. Bartels, "Too Many Blackamoors: Deportation, Discrimination and Elizabeth I," *Studies in English Literature* 46, no. 2 (2006): 305–322; Kim Hall, *Things of Darkness: Economies of Race and Gender in Early Modern England* (Ithaca, NY: Cornell University Press, 1995), 11–24.

21. Peter Fryer's work remains the most comprehensive history of Black Britain from the early modern period through the twentieth century. Fryer, *Staying Power: The History of Black People in Britain* (London: Pluto Press, 1984); see also Edward Scobie, *Black Britannia: A History of Blacks in Britain* (Chicago: Johnson Publishing Co., 1972); James Walvin, *Black and White: The Negro in English Society, 1555–1945* (London: Penguin Press, 1973); Folarin Shyllon, *Black People in Britain, 1555–1833* (London: Oxford University Press, 1977); Ron Ramdin, *The Making of the Black Working Class in Britain* (London: Ashgate, 1987); Rainer Lotz and Ian Pegg, eds. *Under the Imperial Carpet: Essays in Black History, 1780–1950* (Crawley, England: Rabbit Press, 1986); Norma Myers, *Reconstructing the Black Past: Black in Britain, 1780–1830* (London: Frank Cass, 1996); Jeffrey Green, *Black Edwardians: Black People in Britain, 1901–1914* (London: Routledge, 1998); Gretchen Gerzina, *Black London: Life before Emancipation* (New Brunswick, NJ: Rutgers University Press, 1995); Kathleen Chater, *Untold Histories: Black People in England and Wales during the Period of the British Slave Trade, 1660–1807* (Manchester, UK: Manchester University Press, 2011).

22. Ruth Glass, *Newcomers: The West Indians in Britain* (London: George Allen and Unwin, 1960), 1; Ceri Peach, *West Indian Migrations to Britain* (Oxford: Oxford University Press, 1968), xv, 1.

23. On the history of imperial belonging see Daniel Gorman, *Imperial Citizenship: Empire and the Question of Belonging* (Manchester, UK: Manchester University Press, 2010); Sukanya Banerjee, *Becoming Imperial Citizens: Indians in the Late Victorian Empire* (Durham, NC: Duke University Press, 2010); Jinny Prais, "Imperial Travelers: The Formation of West African Urban Culture, Identity and Citizenship in London and Accra, 1925–1935," PhD Dissertation, University of Michigan, 2008.

24. Andrew Nichol and Ann Dummett, *Subjects, Citizens, Aliens and Others: Nationality and Immigration Law* (London: George Weidenfield and Nicholson, 1990).

25. Demetrius Eudell, *The Political Languages of Emancipation in the British Caribbean and the U.S. South* (Chapel Hill: University of North Carolina Press, 2002); Thomas Holt, *The Problem of Freedom: Race, Labor and Politics in Jamaica and Britain, 1832–1938* (Baltimore: Johns Hopkins University Press, 1991); Frederick Cooper, Thomas Holt, and Rebecca Scott, eds. *Beyond Slavery: Explorations of Race, Labor, and Citizenship in Post-Emancipation Societies* (Chapel Hill: University of North Carolina Press, 2000); Brian L. Moore and Michele A. Johnson, *Neither Led nor Driven: Contesting British Cultural Imperialism in Jamaica, 1865–1920* (Kingston, Jamaica: University of the West Indies Press, 2004); Anne Rush, *Bonds of Empire: West Indians and Britishness from Victoria to Decolonization* (Oxford: Oxford University Press, 2011); Brian L. Moore and Michele A. Johnson, *They Do as They Please: The Jamaican Struggle for Cultural Freedom after Morant Bay* (Kingston, Jamaica: University of the West Indies Press, 2011).

26. David Rooney, *Kwame Nkrumah: Vision and Tragedy* (Accra, Ghana: Sub-Saharan Publishers, 2007), 52–91; Deborah Posel, *The Making of Apartheid, 1948–1961: Conflict and Compromise* (Oxford: Clarendon Press, 1991), 23–60; Thomas Borstelmann, "Jim Crow's Coming Out: Race Relations and American Foreign Policy in the Truman Years," *Presidential Studies Quarterly* 29, no. 3 (2004): 549–569.

27. Paul Gorden Lauren, *Power and Prejudice: The Politics and Diplomacy of Racial Discrimination* (Boulder, CO: Westview, 1988); Johannes Morsink, *The Universal Declaration of Human Rights: Origins, Drafting, Intent* (Philadelphia: University of Pennsylvania Press, 2000).

28. Carole Boyce Davies, *Left of Karl Marx: The Political Life of Black Communist Claudia Jones* (Durham, NC: Duke University Press, 2007), xxiv.

29. For more on the life and work of Claudia Jones, see Buzz Johnson, *"I Think of My Mother": Notes on the Life and Times of Claudia Jones* (London: Karia Press, 1985); Marika Sherwood, *Claudia Jones: A Life in Exile* (London: Lawrence and Wishart, 2000); Bill Schwarz, "Claudia Jones and the *West Indian Gazette*: Reflections of the Emergence of

Post-Colonial Britain," *Twentieth Century British History* 14, no. 3 (2003): 264–285; Erik S. McDuffie, *Sojourning Freedom: Black Women, American Communism and the Making of Black Left Feminism* (Durham, NC: Duke University Press, 2011); Carole Boyce Davies, ed., *Beyond Containment: Autobiographical Reflections, Essays and Poems* (Boulder, CO: Lynne Reiner Publishers, 2011).

30. The literature here is vast and growing. See Brenda Gayle Plummer, *Rising Wind: Black Americans and U.S. Foreign Affairs, 1935–1960* (Chapel Hill: University of North Carolina Press, 1996); Brenda Gayle Plummer, *In Search of Power: African Americans in the Era of Decolonization, 1956–1974* (Cambridge, UK: Cambridge University Press, 2012); Penny Von Eschen, *Race against Empire: Black Americans and Anti-Colonialism* (Ithaca, NY: Cornell University Press, 1997); Mary Dudziak, *Cold War Civil Rights: Race and the Image of American Democracy* (Princeton, NJ: Princeton University Press, 2000); Thomas Borstelmann, *The Cold War and the Color Line: American Race Relations in the Global Arena* (Cambridge, MA: Harvard University Press, 2001); Carol Anderson, *Bourgeoisie Radicals: The NAACP and the Struggle for Colonial Liberation, 1941–1960* (Cambridge, UK: Cambridge University Press, 2014); Carol Anderson, *Eyes off the Prize: The United Nations and the African American Struggle for Human Rights, 1944–1955* (Cambridge, UK: Cambridge University Press, 2003); James H. Meriwether, *Proudly We Can Be Africans: Black Americans and Africa, 1935–1961* (Chapel Hill: University of North Carolina Press, 2001); Nico Slate, *Colored Cosmopolitanism: The Shared Struggle for Freedom in the United States and India* (Cambridge, MA: Harvard University Press, 2012); Gerald Horne, *Mau Mau in Harlem: The U.S. and the Liberation of Kenya* (New York: Palgrave, 2012); Robin D. G. Kelley, *Africa Speaks, America Answers: Modern Jazz in Revolutionary Times* (Cambridge, MA: Harvard University Press, 2012); Peniel Joseph, *Waiting 'Til the Midnight Hour: A Narrative History of Black Power in America* (New York: Henry Holt, 2006).

31. Susan Pennybacker, *From Scottsboro to Munich: Race and Political Culture in 1930 Britain* (Princeton, NJ: Princeton University Press, 2009); Minkah Makalani, *In the Cause of Freedom: Radical Black Internationalism from Harlem to London, 1917–1939* (Chapel Hill: University of North Carolina Press, 2011); Hakim Adi, *Pan-Africanism and Communism: The Communist International, Africa and the Diaspora, 1919–1939* (Trenton, NJ: Africa New World Press, 2013); Marc Matera, *Black London: The Imperial Metropolis and Decolonization in the Twentieth Century* (Berkeley: University of California Press, 2015).

32. Robin D. G. Kelley and Tiffany Patterson, "Unfinished Migrations: Reflections on the African Diaspora and the Modern World," *African Studies Review* 43, no. 1 (2000): 11–45; Brent Edwards, "Black Globality: The International Shape of Black Intellectual Culture," PhD Dissertation, Columbia University, 1997; see also Brent Edwards, *The Practice of Diaspora: Literature, Translation and the Rise of Black Internationalism* (Cambridge, MA: Harvard University Press, 2003).

33. Matera, *Black London*, 2.

34. Marika Sherwood, *Origins of Pan-Africanism: Henry Sylvester Williams, Africa and the Modern African Diaspora* (London: Routledge, 2010); Pennybacker, *From Scottsboro to Munich*, chap. 2; Christian Hosbjerg, *C. L. R. James in Imperial Britain* (Durham, NC: Duke University Press, 2014); Barbara Ransby, *Eslanda: The Large and Unconventional Life of Mrs. Paul Robeson* (New Haven, CT: Yale University Press, 2013); Tony Martin, *Amy Ashwood Garvey: Pan-Africanist, Feminist and Mrs. Marcus Garvey No. 1; or, a Tale of Two Amies* (Dover, MA: Majority Press, 2007); Leslie James, *George Padmore and Decolonization from Below: Pan-Africanism, the Cold War and the End of Empire* (London: Palgrave, 2014).

35. Uday Metha, *Liberalism and Empire: A Study in Nineteenth Century British Liberal Thought* (Chicago: University of Chicago Press, 1999); Barbara Bush, *Imperialism, Race and Resistance: Africa and Britain, 1919–1945* (London: Routledge, 1999).

36. Laura Tabili, *We Ask for British Justice: Workers and Racial Difference in Late Imperial Britain* (Ithaca, NY: Cornell University Press, 1994); Jacqueline Jenkinson, *Black 1919: Riots, Racism and Resistance in Imperial Britain* (Liverpool, UK: Liverpool University Press, 2009).

37. Winston James, "The Black Experience in Twentieth Century Britain," in *Blacks and the British Empire*, ed. Philip Morgan and Sean Hawkins (Oxford: Oxford University Press, 2006), 347–386; Simon Gikandi, *Maps of Englishness: Writing Identity in the Culture of Colonialism* (New York: Columbia University Press, 1996); Ian Baucom, *Out of Place, Englishness, Empire and Locations of Identity* (Princeton, NJ: Princeton University Press, 1999).

38. Hesse, "Diasporicity," 109; on the socio-cultural politics of decolonization in the metropole, see Stuart Ward, ed., *British Culture and the End of Empire* (Manchester, UK: Manchester University Press, 2001); Paul Gilroy, *Postcolonial Melancholia* (New York: Columbia University Press, 2006); Wendy Webster, *Englishness and Empire* (Oxford: Oxford University Press, 2007); Bill Schwarz, *The White Man's World* (Oxford: Oxford University Press, 2011); Jordanna Bailkin, *The Afterlife of Empire* (Berkeley: University of California Press, 2012).

39. Center for Contemporary Cultural Studies, *Empire Strikes Back: Race and Racism in 70s Britain* (London: Routledge, 1992); Paul Gilroy, *Ain't No Black in the Union Jack*; Sonya Rose, "Who Are We Now? Writing the Postwar 'Nation', 1948–2001," in *Race, Nation and Empire: Making Histories, 1750 to the Present*, ed. Catherine Hall and Keith McClelland (Manchester, UK: Manchester University Press, 2010), 154–174.

40. Schwarz, *The White Man's World*, 26–28; Bailkin, *The Afterlife of Empire*, 1–6, 11–15; Mark Mazower, *Dark Continent: Europe's Twentieth Century* (New York: Vintage, 2000), ix–xv, 286–326.

41. Barnor Hesse, "Introduction," in *Un/Settled Multiculturalisms: Diasporas, Entanglements, Transruptions*, ed. Barnor Hesse (London: Zed Books, 2000), 5–13, 15–16; Gilroy, *Postcolonial Melancholia*; Wendy Webster, *Englishness and Empire* (Oxford: Oxford University Press, 2007); Bill Schwarz, *The White Man's World*; Rush, *Bonds of Empire*; Bailkin, *The Afterlife of Empire*.

42. On the concept of the "imperial nation-state," see Gary Wilder, *The French Imperial Nation-State: Negritude and Colonial Humanism between the Two World Wars* (Chicago: University of Chicago Press, 2005), 3–23.

43. Paul, *Whitewashing Britain*. Other studies that reinforce this argument include Zig Layton-Henry, *The Politics of Immigration: Immigration, 'Race' and 'Race' Relations in Post-War Britain* (Oxford: Blackwell Publishers, 1992); Robert Miles, *Racism after Race Relations* (London: Routledge, 1993); Bob Carter, Clive Harris, and Shirley Joshi, "The 1951–1955 Conservative Government and the Racialization of Black Immigration," in *Inside Babylon: The Caribbean Diaspora in Britain*, ed. Winston James and Clive Harris (London: Verso Press, 1993), 55–72; Ian Spencer, *British Immigration Policy since 1939* (London: Routledge, 1997); Randall Hansen, *Citizenship and Immigration in Postwar Britain: The Institutional Origins of a Multicultural Nation* (Oxford: Oxford University Press, 2000); James Hampshire, *Citizenship and Belonging: Immigration and the Politics of Demographic Governance in Postwar Britain* (New York: Palgrave Macmillan, 2005).

44. Phillips and Phillips, *Windrush*. One might note that Phillips and Phillips are speaking of the rise of a more visible multiracial Britain in the British Isles, as the notion of a multiracial Britain in the form of an imperial nation-state existed well before the post–World War II era.

45. Ibid. This quotation describing the BBC television series and the companion history appears on the back of the written volume produced by Mike Phillips and Trevor Phillips.

46. "From Jamaica to the Imperial War Museum," *The Guardian*, 13 June 2008; Stuart Hall, "From Scarman to Stephen Lawrence," *History Workshop Journal* 48 (Autumn 1999): 187–197; Jo Stanley, "'Mapping Our Migrations': Afro-Caribbean History in Manchester," *History Workshop Journal* 47 (Spring 1999): 324–324.

47. Much of the earliest scholarly work examining Afro-Caribbean migration to Britain during the postwar period drew upon the sociological models of race relations scholarship that analyzed the experiences and conditions faced by Black people in urban settling largely by exploring the attitudes and behaviors of White Britons towards Black populations in urban area. See Kenneth Little, *Negroes in Britain: A Study of Racial Relations in English Society* (London: Routledge & Kegan Paul, 1972; original, 1948); James Wickenden, *Colour in Britain* (London: Oxford University Press, 1958); Michael Banton, *White and Coloured: The Behavior of British People Towards Coloured Immigrants*

(New Jersey: Rutgers University Press, 1960); Ruth Glass, *Newcomers: The West Indians in London* (London: George Allen & Unwin Ltd., 1960); Sheila Patterson, *Dark Strangers: A Sociological Study of the Absorption of a Recent West Indian Group in Brixton, South London* (Bloomington: Indiana University Press, 1963).

48. Paul Rich, *Race and Empire in British Politics* (New York: Cambridge University Press, 1986); Anne McClintock, *Imperial Leather: Race, Gender and Sexuality in the Colonial Contest* (London: Routledge, 1995); Ann Stoler, *Carnal Knowledge and Imperial Power: Race and the Intimate in Colonial Rule* (Berkeley: University of California Press, 2002).

49. Learie Constantine, *Colour Bar* (London: Kegan Paul, 1954).

50. Fryer, *Staying Power*, 299–309, 367–371.

51. Fryer, *Staying Power*; Philip Morgan and Sean Hawkins, eds., *Blacks and the British Empire* (Oxford: Oxford University Press, 2006).

52. Stuart Hall, "Racism and Reaction," in Commission for Racial Equality, *Five Views on Multi-Racial Britain* (London: Commission for Racial Equality, 1978); Hesse, "Diasporicity," 111.

53. Barnor Hesse, "Diasporicity," 97–99; Stuart Hall, "Preface," in Paul Gilroy, *Black Britain: A Photographic History* (London: Saqi Books, 2007), 7; Kennetta Hammond Perry, "Black Britain and Race Politics in the Twentieth Century," *History Compass* 12, no. 8 (2014): 651–652.

54. Hesse, "Diasporicity," 98.

55. British Pathé Footage of Empire Windrush, Gaumont British Newsreel, Reuters, 22 June 1948.

56. Catherine Hall, *Civilising Subjects: Metropole and Colony in the English Imagination, 1830–1867* (Chicago: University of Chicago Press, 2002); Demetrius Eudell, *The Political Languages of Emancipation*, 14; Diana Paton, *No Bond but the Law: Punishment, Race and Gender in Jamaican State Formation, 1780–1870* (Durham, NC: Duke University Press, 2004), 4.

57. Hesse, "Diasporicity," 99; Jacqueline Nassy Brown's work on Black Liverpool speaks directly to local and regional articulations of Black Britishness outside the London-oriented perspective represented in this work. See Jacqueline Nassy Brown, *Dropping Anchor, Setting Sail: Geographies of Race in Black Liverpool* (Princeton, NJ: Princeton University Press, 2005), 1–33.

58. Bob Carter, Clive Harris, and Shirley Joshi "The 1951–1955 Conservative Government and the Racialization of Black Immigration," 55–72; Paul, *Whitewashing Britain*, 111–130; Peach, *West Indian Migration to Britain*.

59. Hall, *Civilising Subjects*; Antoinette Burton, "Who Needs the Nation? Interrogating British History" in *Cultures of Empire: Colonizers in Britain and the Empire in the Nineteenth and Twentieth Centuries*, ed. Catherine Hall (New York: Routledge, 2002), 137–157; Rush, *Bonds of Empire*.

60. Lord Kitchener, "Sweet Jamaica," reprinted courtesy *London is the Place for Me: Trinidadian Calypso in London, 1950–1956* (London: Honest Jon's Records, 2002), compact disc recording.

61. Putnam, "Citizenship from the Margins," 188–189.

62. Randall Hansen, "The Politics of Citizenship in 1940s Britain: The British Nationality Act," *Twentieth Century British History* 10, no. 1 (1999): 67–95.

63. Stephen Castles and Mark Miller, *Age of Migration: International Population Movements in the Modern World* (New York: Guilford Press, 1993), 19–29, 45–46.

64. Donald Hinds, *Journey to an Illusion: West Indian Migrants in Britain* (London: Heinemann, 1966), 35.

65. Winston James, "Black Experience in Twentieth Century Britain," in *Black Experience and the Empire*, ed. Philip D. Morgan and Sean Hawkins (Oxford: Oxford University Press, 2006), 349.

Chapter 1

1. Quoted in Christopher L. Brown, "From Slaves to Subjects: Envisioning an Empire without Slavery, 1772–1834," in *Black Experience and the Empire*, ed. Philip D. Morgan and Sean Hawkins (Oxford: Oxford University Press, 2004), 114–118.

2. Fryer, *Staying Power*, 125. For more on the Somerset case, see Steven M. Wise, *Though the Heavens May Fall: The Landmark Trial That Led to the End of Human Slavery* (Cambridge, MA: Da Capo Press, 2005).

3. David Brion Davis, *The Problem of Slavery in the Age of Revolution, 1770–1823* (New York: Oxford University, 1999), 375–378; See also Robin Blackburn, *The Overthrow of Colonial Slavery, 1776–1848* (London: Verso Press, 1988), 99–100.

4. Brown, "From Slaves to Subjects," 139; See also Christopher L. Brown, "Empire without Slaves: British Concepts of Emancipation in the Age of the American Revolution," *William and Mary Quarterly* LVI (April 1999), 273–306; Roger Anstey, "The Pattern of British Abolitionism in the Eighteenth and Nineteenth Centuries," in *Anti-Slavery, Religion, and Reform: Essays in Memory of Roger Anstey*, ed. Christine Bolt and Seymour Drescher (Kent, England: William Dawson & Sons, 1980), 24; Eudell, *The Political Languages of Emancipation in the British Caribbean and the U.S. South*, 49.

5. Thomas Clarkson, "Thoughts on the Necessity of Improving the Condition of the Slaves in the British Colonies, with a View to Their Ultimate Emancipation" in *Slavery Abolition and Emancipation: Writings in the British Romantic Period*, Vol. 3, ed. Debbie Lee (London: Pickering and Chatto, 1999; original 1823), 99. Italics included as they appear in reprinted version.

6. Extract of Letter from Major General Murray to Earl Bathurst dated 24 August 1823 in Correspondence with Governors of Colonies in West Indies Respecting Insurrections of Slaves, 1822–1824, House of Commons Papers, Session 1824, Paper No. (333), Vol/Page XXIII. 465; Also quoted in Michael Craton, *Empire, Enslavement and Freedom in the Caribbean* (Kingston, Jamaica: Ian Randle Publishers, 1997), 314; Edwin Angel Wallbridge, *The Demerara Martyr: Memoirs of Rev. John Smith, Missionary to Demerara* (New York: Negro Universities Press, 1969; original, 1848), 89.

7. The testimony of Reverend John Smith notes that the term "'Buckra' is the term in the negro dialect for a *whit* person." Wallbridge, *The Demerara Martyr*, 91.

8. Brown, "From Slaves to Subjects," 139.

9. Putnam "Citizenship from the Margins," 162–191; Mimi Sheller, *Citizenship from Below: Erotic Agency and Caribbean Freedom* (Durham, NC: Duke University Press, 2012), 21, 27.

10. Building upon Anne Spry Rush's recent study, this chapter examines Britishness in the Caribbean among a cross section of post-emancipation Jamaican society. See Anne Spry Rush, *Bonds of Empire*.

11. Frederick Cooper and Ann Stoler, eds., *Tensions of Empire: Colonial Cultures in a Bourgeois World* (Berkeley: University of California Press, 1997), 4; Morgan and Hawkins, eds., *Black Experience and the Empire*, 2.

12. Gorman, *Imperial Citizenship*, 25–28; Cooper, Holt, and Scott, eds., *Beyond Slavery*, 5–26; Putnam, "Citizenship from the Margins," 164, 188–189.

13. Holt, *The Problem of Freedom*; Holt, Cooper, and Scott, *Beyond Slavery*, 1–60.

14. Quoted from Jeffrey Kerr Richie, *The Rites of August First: Emancipation Day in the Black Atlantic World* (Baton Rouge: Louisiana State University Press, 2007), 31–32.

15. Quoted from Mimi Sheller, *Democracy after Slavery: Black Publics and Peasant Radicalism in Haiti and Jamaica* (Gainesville: University of Florida Press, 2000), 178–179.

16. Ibid., 178–179.

17. Thomas Holt, *The Problem of Freedom: Race, Labor and Politics in Jamaica and Britain, 1832–1938* (Baltimore: Johns Hopkins University Press, 1992), 13–53.

18. William A. Green, *British Slave Emancipation: The Sugar Colonies and the Great Experiment, 1830–1865* (Oxford: Clarendon Press, 1976), 300.

19. Don Robotham, "'The Notorious Riot': The Socio-Economic and Political Basis of Paul Bogle's Revolt," Working Paper (Kingston: University of the West Indies Press for the Institute of Social and Economic Research, 1981), 41–42; Holt, *The Problem of Freedom*, 216–217.

20. Robotham, "'The Notorious Riot,'" 31–36; Holt, *The Problem of Freedom*, 73–74.

21. Holt, *The Problem of Freedom*, 269.

22. Holt, *The Problem of Freedom*, 297–300; Arvel B. Erikson, "Empire of Anarchy: The Jamaica Rebellion of 1865," *Journal of Negro History* 44 (April 1959), 101–102; Robotham, " 'The Notorious Riot," 50–64; Henry Bleby, *The Reign of Terror: A Narrative of Facts Concerning Ex-Governor Eyre, George William Gordon and the Jamaica Atrocities* (London: William Nichols, 1866), 37–38.

23. House of Commons. "Report of the Jamaica Royal Commission, 1866, Part I." Parliamentary Papers 1866 Cmd. [3683], vol. 30, p. 14; Bleby, *The Reign of Terror*, 38; Holt, *The Problem of Freedom*, 297, 459; Gad Heuman, *The Killing Time: The Morant Bay Rebellion in Jamaica* (Knoxville: University of Tennessee Press, 1994), 6.

24. Heuman, *The Killing Time*, 3–30; Holt, *The Problem of Freedom*, 297–302.

25. Quoted from Sheller, *Democracy after Slavery*, 150.

26. Ibid., 182–185. Swithin Wilmont's work on grassroots electoral politics in St. James parish between 1838 and 1865 makes a similar case regarding Baptist involvement in political mobilization among the black masses. See Swithin Wilmont, "Politics at the 'Grassroots' in Free Jamaica: St. James, 1838–1865," in *Working Slavery, Pricing Freedom: Perspectives from the Caribbean, Africa and the African Diaspora*, ed. Verene A. Shepherd (New York: Palgrave, 2002), 451–452.

27. Sheller, *Democracy after Slavery*, 185–186.

28. Ibid., 186–187.

29. C. A. Wilson, *Men of Vision: A Series of Biographical Sketches of Men Who Have Made Their Mark upon Time* (Kingston, Jamaica: Gleaner, 1929); Patrick Bryan, *The Jamaican People, 1880–1902* (Barbados: UWI Press, 2000), 242.

30. Quoted in Deborah Thomas, "Modern Blackness: What We Are and What We Hope to Be," *Small Axe* 12 (September 2002), 27. Original in italics as quoted by Thomas.

31. Douglas Lorimer, *Colour, Class and the Victorians: English Attitudes to the Negro in the Mid-Nineteenth Century* (New York: Holmes and Meier, 1978), 11–20.

32. Thomas, "Modern Blackness," 29.

33. Ibid., 29.

34. Ibid., 34.

35. Simon Gikandi, "Englishness, Travel and Theory: Writing the West Indies in the Nineteenth Century," *Nineteenth Century Contexts* 18, no. 1 (1994): 49–50.

36. James Anthony Froude, *The English in the West Indies: Or the Bow of Ulysses* (London: Longmans Green, 1888), 252.

37. Thomas Carlyle, "Occasional Discourse on the Negro Question," *Fraser's Magazine for Town and Country* (London: 1849), 528–538.

38. J. J. Thomas, *Froudacity: West Indian Fables by James Anthony Froude Explained by J. J. Thomas* (Philadelphia: Gebbie and Company), 127.

39. Ibid., 17.

40. Ibid., 125, 130–134.

41. Ibid., 15, 129.

42. Ibid., 117–118.

43. Catherine Hall, *Civilising Subjects: Metropole and Colony in the English Imagination* (Chicago: University of Chicago Press, 2002), 21–22.

44. Faith Smith, *Creole Recitations: John Jacob Thomas and Colonial Formation in the Late Nineteenth Century Caribbean* (Charlottesville: University of Virginia Press, 2002), 83–84.

45. Quoted in Jonathan Schneer, *London 1900: The Imperial Metropolis* (New Haven: Yale University Press, 1999), 215; for more on Williams and the origins of the Pan-African Conference, see Marika Sherwood, *Origins of Pan-Africanism: Henry Sylvester Williams, Africa and the African Diaspora* (New York: Routledge, 2011).

46. Rupert Lewis, "Garvey's Forerunners: Love and Bedward, *Race and Class*, 28, no. 3 (1987): 33.

47. Theophilus E. Samuel Scholes, *Glimpses of the Ages, Or the "Superior" and "Inferior" Races, So-Called, Discussed in the Light of Science and History* (London: John Long, 1908), 481.

48. Ibid., 91.

49. "Negroes and the Queen," *Daily Gleaner*, 25 February 1901.

50. Brian L. Moore and Michele Johnson, *Neither Led Nor Driven: Contesting British Cultural Imperialism in Jamaica, 1865–1920* (Kingston, Jamaica: University of the West Indies Press, 2004), 271–310.

51. "Memorial Services in Jamaica: The Country," *Daily Gleaner*, 4 February 1901; "The Queen's Funeral: The Country," *Daily Gleaner*, 2 February 1901.

52. "The Queen's Funeral: The Country," *Daily Gleaner*, 2 February 1901.

53. "The Passing of the Queen," *Daily Gleaner*, 4 February 1901.

54. Moore and Johnson, *Neither Led Nor Driven*, 273; Rush, *Bonds of Empire*, 51.

55. Moore and Johnson, *Neither Led Nor Driven*, 272. See also David Cannadine, "The Context, Performance and Meaning of Ritual: The British Monarchy and the 'Invention of Tradition,' 1820–1977," in *The Invention of Tradition*, ed. Eric Hobsbawm and Terence Ranger (Cambridge, UK: Cambridge University Press, 1983), 101–164.

56. "Celebration of Empire Day," *Daily Gleaner*, 23 May 1907.

57. "Empire Day: Programme For St. Andrew," *Daily Gleaner*, 22 May 1907.

58. Jervis Anderson, "England in Jamaica: Memories from a Colonial Boyhood," *The American Scholar* 69, no. 2 (Spring 2000): 25.

59. Hazel Carby, "Lost (and Found?) in Translation," *Small Axe* 13, no. 1 (March 2009): 28.

60. For more on the British education system in the Empire, see Rush, *Bonds of Empire*, 35–40.

61. On the idea of "inherited allegiance," see Anderson, "England in Jamaica," 25; Rush, *Bonds of Empire*, 60–61.

62. For more on the early history of the West India Regiments, see Norman Buckley, *Slaves in Redcoats: The British West India Regiments, 1795–1815* (New Haven, CT: Yale University Press, 1979).

63. Richard Smith, "'Heaven Grant You Strength to Fight the Battle for Your Race': Nationalism, Pan-Africanism and the First World War in Jamaican Memory," in *Race, Empire and First World War Writing*, ed. Santanu Das (Cambridge, UK: Cambridge University Press, 2011), 265.

64. Quoted in Moore and Anderson, *Neither Led nor Driven*, 304.

65. Marcus Garvey Circular Letter to Governors Inviting Declarations of Native Subjects to Celebration of Centenary Emancipation of West Indian Negroes 26 February 1934, CO 323/1282/10, TNA.

66. For more on UNIA activity globally, see Adam Ewing, *The Age of Garvey: How a Jamaica Activist Created a Mass Movement and Changed Global Black Politics* (Princeton, NJ: Princeton University Press, 2014).

67. Marcus Garvey, "The Principles of the Universal Negro Improvement Association," in *The Marcus Garvey and Universal Negro Improvement Association Papers*, Vol. V, ed. Robert Hill (Berkeley: University of California Press, 1986), 143–149.

68. Lara Putnam, "Citizenship From the Margins"; Lara Putnam, *Radical Moves: Caribbean Migrants and the Politics of Race in the Jazz Age* (Chapel Hill, NC: University of North Carolina Press, 2013), 21–48; Glenn Chambers, *Race, Nation and West Indian Immigration to Honduras, 1890–1940* (Baton Rouge: Louisiana State University Press, 2010), 97–114; David Killingray "'A Good West Indian, A Good African and in Short a Good Britisher': Black and British in a Colour Conscious Empire, 1760–1950," *Journal of Imperial and Commonwealth History* 36, no. 3 (2008): 368–369, 371–375; Laura Tabili, *'We Ask For British Justice'.*

69. Clayton Lloyd Alexander Jeffers to King George V, 20 January 1933, CO 318/40/3 TNA, as transcribed by Lara Putnam.

70. Smith, "Heaven Grant You Strength to Fight," 270–278. See also Reena Nicole Goldthree, "Shifting Loyalties: World War I and the Conflicted Politics of Patriotism in the British Caribbean," PhD Dissertation, Duke University, 2011.

71. "How the Country Towns and Districts of the Island Celebrated Signing of Peace Treaty by the Germans," *Daily Gleaner*, 23 July 1919; "Celebration At Buff Bay," *Daily Gleaner*, 23 July 1919.

72. "Grand Events at Falmouth in Celebrating Peace Day," *Daily Gleaner*, 23 July 1919.

73. Adriane Lentz-Smith, *Freedom Struggles: African Americans and World War I* (Cambridge, MA: Harvard University Press, 2009), 206–237.

74. Richard Smith, *Jamaican Volunteers in the First World War: Race, Masculinity and the Development of National Consciousness* (Manchester, UK: Manchester University Press, 2004), 163–164.
75. O. Nigel Bolland, *The Politics of Labour in the British Caribbean: The Social Origins of the Authoritarianism and Democracy in the Labour Movement* (Kingston. Jamaica: Ian Randle Publishers, 2001), 196–197; this is also the central argument of Smith, *Jamaican Volunteers in the First World War.*
76. Bolland, *The Politics of Labour in the British Caribbean*, 314.
77. Quoted in Bolland, *The Politics of Labour in the British Caribbean*, 316.
78. Nigel Bolland, *On the March: Labour Rebellions in the British Caribbean, 1934–1939* (Kingston: Ian Randle, 1995), 383; Howard Johnson, "The Black Experience in the British Caribbean in the Twentieth Century," in *Black Experience and the Empire*, ed. Philip Morgan and Sean Hawkins, 334–335.
79. Rush, *Bonds of Empire*, 128–130.
80. Reginald George Mason Interview, 2007, #30133, Imperial War Museum Sound Archives.
81. Ben Bousquet and Colin Douglas, *West Indian Women at War: British Racism in World War 2* (London: Lawrence and Wishart, 1991), 108.
82. Rush, *Bonds of Empire*, 132.

Chapter 2

1. "Isolyn Robinson," *Forty Winters On: Memories of Britain's Postwar Caribbean Immigrants* (London: South London Press and The Voice, 1998), 27.
2. Phillips and Phillips, *Windrush*, 74; Paul, *Whitewashing Britain*, 10–24; Hansen, *Citizenship and Immigration in Postwar Britain*, 35–49; Spencer, *British Immigration Policy since 1939*, 53–55.
3. Hampshire, *Citizenship and Belonging*, 16.
4. James, "Black Experience in Twentieth Century Britain, 377–379."
5. Stephen Castles and Mark Miller, *Age of Migration: International Population Movements in the Modern World* (New York: Guilford Press, 1993), 19–29, 45–46.
6. Hinds, *Journey to an Illusion*, 35.
7. Hakim Adi, "Amy Ashwood Garvey and the Nigerian Progress Union," in *Gendering the African Diaspora: Women, Culture and Historical Change in the Caribbean and Nigerian Hinterland*, ed. Judith Byfield, LaRay Denzer, and Anthea Morrison (Bloomington: Indiana University Press, 2010), 199–218; Tony Martin, *Amy Ashwood Garvey: Pan-Africanist, Feminist, and Mrs. Marcus Garvey, Wife No 1; or, a Tale of Two Amies* (Dover, MA: Majority Press, 2007). See also Lionel M. Yard, *Biography of Amy Ashwood Garvey: Co-Founder of the UNIA* (New York: Associated Publishers, 1990) and K. Natanya Duncan, "The 'Efficient Womanhood' of the Universal Negro Improvement Association: 1919–1930," PhD Dissertation, University of Florida, 2009, 43–69.
8. George Padmore, ed., *Colonial and Coloured Unity: A Programme of Action* (London: Hammersmith Bookshop, 1963), 6–8. Padmore published the original version of the conference proceedings under the same title in 1947.
9. Hesse, "Diasporicity," 109.
10. Padmore, ed., *Colonial and Coloured Unity*, 31.
11. Harold Moody to Colonial Secretary Copy of LCP, "News Notes," January, 1940, CO 323/1692/4, TNA; Anne Rush, "Imperial Identity in Colonial Minds," *Twentieth Century British History* 13, no. 4 (2002): 365–366; David Killingray, "'To Do Something for the Race': Harold Moody and the League of Coloured Peoples," in *West Indian Intellectuals in Britain*, ed. Bill Schwarz (Manchester, UK: Manchester University Press, 2004), 61–67.
12. Rush, "Imperial Identity in Colonial Minds," 365–381; Caroline Bressey, "It's Only Political Correctness—Race and Racism in British History," in *New Geographies of Race and Racism*, ed. Claire Dwyer and Caroline Bressey (Burlington, VT: Ashgate, 2008), 31–35.

13. LCP Memo to Colonial Secretary on Colour Bar in Military, Medical Schools and Hospitals, n.d., ca. 1939, CO 323/169/2/4, TNA.
14. Harold Moody to Colonial Secretary, 7 December 1939, CO 323/169/2/4, TNA.
15. Rush, "Imperial Identity in Colonial Minds," 367–369.
16. Quoted in Killingray, "'To Do Something for the Race'," 63.
17. Daniel Gorman, "Wider and Wider Still: Racial Politics, Intra-Imperial Immigration and the Absence of an Imperial Citizenship in the British Empire," *Journal of Colonialism and Colonial History* 3, no. 3 (2002): 1–24; Hansen, "The Politics of Citizenship in 1940s Britain," 69, 71–77; Hansen, *Citizenship and Immigration in Postwar Britain*, 37–45; Paul, *Whitewashing Britain*, 10–11.
18. Paul, *Whitewashing Britain*, 14; Hansen, "The Politics of Citizenship in 1940s Britain," 73; Kathleen Paul, "'British Subjects' and 'British Stock': Labour's Postwar Imperialism," *Journal of British Studies* 34, no. 2 (April 1999): 240–241.
19. "Break down" was the term used by Home Secretary, Chuter Ede, to characterize the impact of the Canadian Nationality Act of 1946 on the common code system derived from the 1914 nationality policy. Parliamentary Debates, House of Commons, 7 July 1948, Vol. 453, col. 387.
20. Hansen, "The Politics of Citizenship in 1940s Britain," 77.
21. Parliamentary Debates, House of Commons, 7 July 1948, col. 386.
22. Paul, *Whitewashing Britain*, 2; L. J. Butler, *Britain and Empire: Adjusting to a Post-Imperial World* (London: I. B. Tauris, 2002), 5; D. George Boyce, *Decolonisation and the British Empire, 1775–1997* (London: Macmillan Press, 1999), 78, 98, 142.
23. Parliamentary Debates, House of Commons, 7 July 1948, cols. 393, 398.
24. Parliamentary Debates, House of Commons, 7 July 1948, col. 393.
25. Robert Miles, "Nationality, Citizenship, and Migration to Britain, 1945–1951," *Journal of Law and Society* 16 (Winter 1989): 426–442; Paul, "'British Subjects' and 'British Stock,'" 237–240.
26. Butler, *Britain and Empire*, 189.
27. Chris Waters, "'Dark Strangers' in Our Midst: Discourses of Race and Nation in Britain, 1947–1963," *Journal of British Studies* 36, no. 2 (April 1997): 208, 214–215; Frank Heinlein, *British Government Policy and Decolonisation, 1945–1963: Scrutinizing the Official Mind* (London: Frank Cass, 2002), 88–89; Butler, *Britain and Empire*, 29–62; D. Boyce, *Decolonisation and the British Empire, 1775–1997*, 116–117.
28. Suke Wolton, *Lord Hailey, the Colonial Office and the Politics of Race and Empire in the Second World War: The Loss of White Prestige* (New York: St. Martins, 2000), 122; Rose, *Which People's War?* 277–284; Paul Rich, *Race and Empire in British Politics*, 206; for more on the history of the concept of imperial citizenship, see Gorman, *Imperial Citizenship*.
29. This is a reference used by MP Osbert Peake of Leeds, North to describe the purpose of the provisions of the British Nationality Act of 1948. Parliamentary Debates, House of Commons, 7 July 1948, col. 488. See also Hansen, *Citizenship and Immigration in Postwar Britain*, 17–18, 35–61, 66–67. In an alternative reading of the significance of the British Nationality Act of 1948, Bob Carter, Clive Harris, and Shirley Joshi maintain that the Act's relevance to imperial interests also entailed a desire to thwart the rising tide of colonial nationalism. See Bob Carter, Clive Harris, and Shirley Joshi, "The 1951–55 Conservative Government and the Racialisation of Black Immigration," in *Inside Babylon: The Caribbean Diaspora in Britain,* ed. Winston James and Clive Harris (London: Verso Press, 1993), 57.
30. Hansen, "The Politics of Citizenship in 1940s Britain," 93–95. See also Hansen, *Citizenship and Immigration to Postwar Britain,* esp. chap. 2; Spencer, *British Immigration Policy since 1939,* 53–55.
31. Telegram to the Acting Governor of Jamaica from the Colonial Secretary, 16 June 1948, CO 876/88, TNA. The *Windrush* sailed from Jamaica, but transported Caribbean migrants from various islands.
32. Parliamentary Debates, House of Commons, 16 June 1948, col. 421–422.
33. Kathleen Paul notes that unlike seamen and military personnel who traveled to Britain from the Caribbean during the first half of the twentieth century, postwar migrants came

to Britain as "independent British subjects" who "were thus beyond the public control of the Colonial Office." Paul, *Whitewashing Britain*, 114.

34. Phillips and Phillips, *Windrush*, 5.

35. "Connie Mark: Community Activist and Caribbean Champion," *The Guardian*, 16 June 2007; see also "Connie Goodridge-Mark," Imperial War Museum, Sound Archives, Ref.: 20577.

36. Phillips and Phillips, *Windrush*, 12.

37. On the concept of the "structure of feeling," see Raymond Williams, *The Long Revolution* (New York: Penguin Books, 1971), 64–88; for its application to understanding histories of Empire, see Catherine Hall, ed., *Cultures of Empire, A Reader: Colonizers in Britain and the Empire in the 19th and 20th Centuries* (Manchester, UK: Manchester University Press, 2000), 15.

38. Mary Chamberlain, *Narratives of Exile and Return* (London: Palgrave, 1997), 70–72; Hinds, *Journey to an Illusion*, 6–47; Brian L. Moore and Michele A. Johnson, *Neither Led nor Driven*, 271–325.

39. Moore and Johnson, *Neither Led nor Driven*, 271–325.

40. "Walter Lothen," *Forty Winters On*, 23.

41. Evelyn Brooks Higginbotham, "African-American Women's History and the Metalanguage of Race," *Signs* 17, no. 2 (Winter 1992): 251–274.

42. Mike Phillips, *London Crossings: A Biography of Black Britain* (London: Continuum, 2001), 11–12.

43. Holt, *The Problem of Freedom*, 160.

44. Clarence Senior and Douglas Manley, *A Report on Jamaican Migration to Great Britain*, 4; G. W. Roberts and D. O. Mills, *Study of External Migration Affecting Jamaica: 195–1955* (Kingston, Jamaica: Institute of Social and Economic Research, 1958), 1; Margaret Byron, ed., *Post-War Caribbean Migration to Britain: The Unfinished Cycle* (Aldershot, UK: Avebury, 1994), 32–37; Peter Fraser, "Nineteenth-Century West Indian Migration to Britain," in *In Search of a Better Life*, ed. Ransford Palmer (New York: Praeger Publishers, 1990), 19–37; Dilip Hiro, *Black British, White British: A History of Race Relations in Britain* (London: Grafton Books, 1991), 14; see also Lara Putnam, *The Company They Kept: Migrants and the Politics of Gender in Caribbean Costa Rica, 1870–1960* (Chapel Hill: University of North Carolina Press, 2001); and Glenn Chambers, *Race, Nation and West Indian Immigration to Honduras, 1890–1940*.

45. Winston James, *Holding Aloft the Banner of Ethiopia: Caribbean Radicalism in Early Twentieth Century America* (London: Verso Press, 1998), 26.

46. Senior and Manley, *A Report on Jamaican Migration to Great Britain*, 4; Roberts and Mills, *Study of External Migration Affecting Jamaica; 1953–55*, 1–2; Nancy Foner, *Jamaica Farewell: Jamaican Migrants in London* (Berkeley: University of California Press, 1978), 9.

47. Mae M. Ngai, "The Architecture of Race in American Immigration Law: A Reexamination of the Immigration Act of 1924," *Journal of American History* 86, no. 1 (June, 1999): 67, 69–70. For a more detailed discussion of the broader context of the nativist undertones represented in US immigration policy after World War I, see John Higham, *Strangers in the Land: Patterns of American Nativism, 1860–1925* (New Brunswick, NJ: Rutgers University Press, 1988); and Mae Ngai, *Impossible Subjects: Illegal Aliens and the Making of Modern America* (Cambridge, MA: Harvard University Press, 2004).

48. S. K. Ruck, ed., *The West Indian Comes to England: A Report Prepared for the Trustees of the London Parochial Charities by the Family Welfare Association* (London: Routledge and Kegan Paul, 1960), 7; Irma Watkins-Owens, *Blood Relations, Caribbean Immigrants and the Harlem Community, 1900–1930* (Bloomington: Indiana University Press, 1996), 53. See also Philip Kasinitz, *Caribbean New York: Black Immigrants and the Politics of Race* (Ithaca, NY: Cornell University Press, 1992), esp. chap. 1.

49. Letter from B. A. B. Burrows of the British Embassy in Washington, DC to the Under Secretary of State for the Colonies, 18 February 1952, CO 936/189, TNA.

50. "Claude Ramsey," *Forty Winters On*, 37.

51. Roberts and Mills, *Study of External Migration Affecting Jamaica, 1953–55*, 2–4. This report also alludes to unspecified "inherent weaknesses" in the census data used to mark

this figure. However, the authors are clear that "despite the known limitations of these census data," the figures "clearly emphasize the gravity of the unemployment situation." See also Peach, *West Indian Migration to Britain*, 24.

52. John Darragh, *Colour and Conscience: A Study of Race Relations and Colour Prejudice in Birmingham* (Leicester, UK: Leicester Printers, 1957), 13.
53. Paul, *Whitewashing Britain*, 4–5, 69; Paul, "'British Subjects' and 'British Stock,'" 254; Spencer, *British Immigration Policy since 1939*, 38.
54. Paul, *Whitewashing Britain*, 67.
55. Paul, *Whitewashing Britain*, 68; Miles, "Nationality, Citizenship, and Migration to Britain, 1945–1951," 430; Patterson, *Dark Strangers*, 64; Layton-Henry, *The Politics of Immigration*, 8; Colin Holmes, *John Bull's Island: Immigration and British Society, 1871–1971* (London: Macmillan Education, 1988), 211–213.
56. Paul, *Whitewashing Britain*, 71–75; Miles, "Nationality, Citizenship and Immigration to Britain," 431.
57. Draft Report of Working Party on the Employment in the United Kingdom of Surplus Colonial Labour, March 1949, LAB 8/1571, TNA.
58. Ibid.
59. Memo from D. J. Stewart to Mr. Goldberg and Mr. Hariman, 12 March 1949, LAB 8/1571, TNA.
60. Marcus Collins, "Pride and Prejudice: West Indian Men in Mid-Twentieth-Century Britain," *The Journal of British Studies* 40, no. 3 (July 2001): 391–418.
61. James Jackson and Leslie Moch, "Migration and the Social History of Modern Europe," *Historical Methods* (Winter 1989): 27–33; Monica Boyd, "Family and Personal Networks in International Migration: Recent Developments and New Agendas," *International Migration Review* 23, no. 3 (Autumn 1989): 638–670. See also Dirk Hoerder and Leslie Page Moch, eds., *European Migrants: Global and Local Perspectives* (Boston: Northeastern University Press, 1996); and Jan Lucassen and Leo Lucassen, eds., *Migration, Migration History, History* (Berlin: Peter Lang, 1997).
62. Memo, "Migrant Services Division of the Commission for the West Indies, British Guiana, and British Honduras," n.d., file dates 1957–1959, CO 1031/2945, TNA; Memo, "Migrant Services Division" by Commission for the West Indies, British Guiana and British Honduras, 22 September 1959, CO 1031/2545, TNA; Colonial Office Memo, "Commonwealth Immigrants' Advisory Council" undated, file dates 1960–1962, CO 1031/3942, TNA; Ruck, *The West Indian Comes to England*, 54; see also Report of the British Caribbean Welfare Association, 1 June 1956–31, December 1956, A. Sivanandan Collection, University of Warwick, Coventry, UK.
63. Pamphlet, *Before You Go to Britain*, n.d, file dates 1954–1956 CO 1028/34, TNA.
64. Ibid.
65. Even before significant numbers of Caribbean migrants moved to Britain during the 1950s, there were publications circulating that discouraged employment prospects in Britain. As early as 1948, in a telegram sent to the Colonial Secretary warning of the impending arrival of Jamaican migrants on the *Empire Windrush*, the Jamaican Governor noted, "Public announcements of the difficulty of obtaining work have not discouraged these bookings [referencing the booking of travel to Britain by Jamaicans aboard the *Empire Windrush*]." Telegram from Governor of Jamaica to Colonial Secretary, 11 May 1948, HO 213/714, TNA. See also Spencer, *British Immigration Policy Since 1939*, 32.
66. Peach, *West Indian Migration to Britain*, 31–36; See also Dennis Brooks, *Race and Labor in London Transport* (London: Oxford University Press, 1975).
67. Colonial Office Memo, "Commonwealth Immigrants Advisory Council," n.d., file dates, 1960–1962, CO 1031/3942, TNA. The bulk of these initiatives took place between 1952 and 1955.
68. Copy of Blank Bond Agreement for Barbadian Domestics Recruited for Service in Britain, 1952, CO 1028/20, TNA; see also Spencer, *British Immigration Policy since 1939*, 42.
69. Elyse Dodgson, *Motherland: West Indian Women to Britain in the 1950s* (London: Heinemann Educational Books, 1984), 10.

70. Roberts and Mills, *Study of External Migration Affecting Jamaica, 1953–1955*, 5–8; "Report of Bureau of Statistics on Jamaican Migration to U.K.," sent by Governor of Jamaica to Colonial Secretary, February 1955 CO, 1034/20, TNA.

71. Z. Nia Reynolds, ed., *When I Came to England: An Oral History of Life in 1950s and 1960s Britain* (London: Black Stock / Photo Press, 2001), 16.

72. "Report of Bureau of Statistics on Jamaican Migration to U.K.," sent by Governor of Jamaica to Colonial Secretary, February 1955, CO 1034/20, TNA.

73. "Thirty Thousand Colour Problems," *Picture Post*, 9 June 1956.

74. Stuart Hall, "Reconstruction Work: Images of Postwar Black Settlement," in *Writing Black Britain, 1948–1998: An Interdisciplinary Anthology*, ed. James Proctor (Manchester, UK: Manchester University Press, 2000), 82–94; Dick Hebdige, *Subcultures: The Meaning of Style* (London: Routledge, 2002), 102. See also Michael McMillan, "The West Indian Front Room: Reflections on a Diasporic Phenomenon," *Small Axe* 13, no. 1 (2009): 139–142.

75. Reynolds, *When I Came to England*, 84.

76. Hall, "Reconstruction Work," 84.

77. Barbara Krauthamer and Deborah Willis, eds., *Envisioning Emancipation* (Philadelphia: Temple University Press, 2013), 23; Laura Wexler, " 'A More Perfect Likeness': Frederick Douglass and the Image of the Nation," *Yale Review* 99, no. 4 (October 2011): 145–169.

78. Tina Campt, *Image Matters: Archive, Photography and the African Diaspora in Europe* (Durham, NC: Duke University Press, 2012), chap. 3; Kieran Connell, "Photographing Handsworth: Photography, Meaning and Identity in a British Inner City," *Patterns of Prejudice* 46, no. 2 (2012): 138.

79. Quoted from Kieran Connell, "Photographing Handsworth," 141.

80. Wendy Webster, *Imagining Home: Gender, 'Race' and National Identity, 1945–1964* (London: University College of London Press, 1998), 48; Elizabeth Buettner, " 'Would You Let Your Daughter Marry a Negro?': Race and Sex in 1950s Britain," in *Gender, Labour, War and Empire: Essays on Modern Britain* ed. Phillipa Levine and Susan R. Grayzel (London: Palgrave Macmillan, 2009), 219–237.

81. There are significant gaps in our knowledge of about the gender specific experiences of Black women in postwar Britain. See Hazel Carby, "White Woman Listen!: Black Feminism and the Boundaries of Sisterhood," in *The Empire Strikes Back: Race and Racism in 70s Britain*, ed. Center For Contemporary Cultural Studies (London: Hutchinson Ltd., 1982), 212–235; Beverley Bryan, Stella Dadzie, and Suzanne Scafe, *The Heart of the Race: Black Women's Lives in Britain* (London: Virago Press, 1985).

82. Collins, "Pride and Prejudice," 391–418; Webster, *Imagining Home*, xii, xv, 46, 50, 60, 122.

83. Jon Newman, "Harry Jacobs: The Studio Photographer and the Visual Archive," in *People and Their Pasts: Public History Today*, ed. Paul Ashton and Hilda Kean (London: Palgrave Macmillan, 2009), 260–270.

84. See Harry Jacobs Collection, Lambeth Archives, London, UK.

85. Stuart Hall, "Preface," in *Black Britain: A Photographic History* (London: Saqi, 2007), 5–10.

86. Patterson, *Dark Strangers*, 417; Glass, *Newcomers*, 5.

87. Roberts and Mills, *Study of External Migration Affecting Jamaica: 1953–1955*, 48–52.

88. Peach, *West Indian Migration to Britain*, 10–11.

89. Glass, *Newcomers*, 29–37.

90. Glass, *Newcomers*, 20–23, 29–37. According to Glass, non-manual occupations would include professionals, shopkeepers, salespersons, clerks, and typists, while manual workers would include craftsmen, mechanics, carpenters, and seamstresses.

91. Foner, *Jamaica Farewell*, 63, 67, 74–75, 87, 90. See also Margaret Byron, "Migration, Work and Gender: The Case of Post-War Labour Migration from the Caribbean to Britain," in *Caribbean Migration: Globalised Identities*, ed. Mary Chamberlain (London: Routledge, 1998), 226–241.

92. Lord Kitchener, "If You're Not White, You're Black," lyrics reprinted courtesy of *London Is the Place for Me: Trinidadian Calypso in London, 1950–1956* (London: Honest Jon's

Records, 2002), compact disc recording. In addition to treating darker-complexioned people of African descent as socially inferior, in subsequent verses of this song Kitchener as the narrator alludes to the ways in which those attempting to avoid identifying themselves with Blackness would also try to assume traits associated with Whiteness by transforming their physical appearance (skin bleaching, hair straightening), changing speech patterns, affiliating with people of European descent, and condemning "the name of Africa."

93. James, *Holding Aloft the Banner of Ethiopia*, 108–109; Winston James, "Migration, Racism and Identity Formation: The Caribbean Experience in Britain," in *Inside Babylon: The Caribbean Diaspora in Britain*, ed. Winston James and Clive Harris (London: Verso Press, 1993), 237–239; Ula Taylor, *The Veiled Garvey: The Life and Times of Amy Jacques Garvey* (Chapel Hill: University of North Carolina Press, 2002): 8–11.

94. Nancy Foner, "Race and Color: Jamaica Migrants in London and New York," *International Migration Review* 19, no. 4 (Winter 1985): 712–713.

95. James, "Migration, Racism and Identity Formation," 239.

96. Foner, *Jamaica Farewell*, 41.

97. Hinds, *Journey to an Illusion*, 50–51.

98. James, "Migration, Racism and Identity," 239–243; see also Carter, *Shattering Illusions*, 22–23.

99. See Barbara Fields, "Ideology and Race in American History," in *Region, Race, and Reconstruction: Essay in Honor of C. Vann Woodard*, ed. J. Morgan Kousser and James McPherson (New York: Oxford University Press, 1982), 143–177.

100. "May Cambridge," *Forty Winters On*, 32.

101. Glass, *Newcomers*, 58–59.

102. Noel B. W. Thompson, "Roots of Racial Prejudice," *Manchester Guardian Weekly*, 18 September 1958.

103. "Baron Baker," *Forty Winters On*, 19.

104. "So Sorry, No Coloured, No Children," *West Indian Gazette*, September 1960.

105. Reynolds, *When I Came to England*, 46.

106. M. J. Elsas, *Housing before the War and After* (London: Staples Press, 1946), 67.

107. Richard Sabatino, *Housing in Great Britain, 1945–1949* (Dallas: Southern Methodist University Press, 1956), 3; Edward Pilkington, *Beyond the Mother Country: West Indians and the Notting Hill White Riots* (London: I. B. Tauris, 1988), 53.

108. Patterson, *Dark Strangers*, 173.

109. John Davis, "Rents and Race in 1960s London: New Light on Rachmanism," *Twentieth Century British History* 12, no. 1 (2001): 69–92.

110. Layton-Henry, *The Politics of Immigration*, 37.

111. Susan J. Smith, *The Politics of "Race" and Residence* (Cambridge, UK: Polity Press, 1989), 51–52; Carter, *Shattering Illusions*, 30–32.

112. Layton-Henry, *The Politics of Immigration*, 37–38.

113. "Walter Lothen," *Forty Winters On*, 23.

114. "May Cambridge," *Forty Winters On*, 32, 34.

115. "Claude Ramsey," *Forty Winters On*, 37; Pamphlet, "Before You Go to Britain," CO 1028/34, TNA.

116. "So Sorry, No Coloured, No Children," *West Indian Gazette* September 1960; Note of Meeting between George Rogers, MP for North Kensington, Mrs. O. Wilson, Mr. Donald Chesworth, Mr. Richard Hauser and Mr. Renton of the Home Office, 20 January 1960, HO 325/161, TNA; Metropolitan Police Report, Metropolitan and City Police Fraud Department, 27 July 1959, HO 325/161, TNA.

117. Notting Dale Urban Studies Centre and Ethnic Communities Oral History Project, *Sorry, No Vacancies: Life Stories of Senior Citizens From the Caribbean* (London: Notting Dale Urban Studies Center & Ethnic Communities Oral History Project, 1992), 25.

118. Patterson, *Dark Strangers*, 84–130; 134–135.

119. Ibid., 131–142.

120. Ibid., 135–136.

121. Clive Harris, "Post-War Migration and the Industrial Reserve Army," in *Inside Babylon*, 18; Stephen Castles and Godula Kosack, *Immigrant Workers and Class Structure* (London: Oxford University Press, 1973), 57–115. See also Layton-Henry, *The Politics of Immigration*, 44–45.

122. Lydia Lindsey, "The Split-Labor Phenomenon: Its Impact on West Indian Workers as a Marginal Working Class in Birmingham, England, 1948–1962," *Journal of African American History* 87 (Winter 2002): 126.

Chapter 3

1. " 'Bombs' in Race Riot," *Daily Mail*, 2 September 1958.

2. Pilkington, *Beyond the Mother Country*, 121–122; "Baron Baker Interview," *Windrush*, DVD, David Upshal, Director, London: BBC, 1998.

3. " 'Lynch Him!' Heard in London," *Manchester Guardian Weekly*, 4 September 1958.

4. Ibid. In another report on this particular incident appearing in the *Daily Mirror*, Manning is described as Jamaican. This discrepancy is indicative of the ways in which categories of race, ethnicity, nationality, and, more precisely, Blackness were in part matters of perception. See "Riot Gangs Go by Car to Join the Mob," *Daily Mirror*, 2 September 1958.

5. " 'Lynch Him!' Heard in London," *Manchester Guardian Weekly*, 4 September 1958; "Riot Gangs Go by Car to Join the Mobs." *Daily Mirror*, 2 September 1958.

6. " 'Lynch Him!' Heard in London," *Manchester Guardian Weekly*, 4 September 1958.

7. "New Riot Terror," *Daily Herald*, 1 September 1958; "Racial Outburst in an English City," *Manchester Guardian Weekly*, 28 August 1958; "Race Violence Grows," *Daily Express*, 2 September 1958; "Thugs Hunt for Victims," *Daily Express*, 2 September 1958; "Midnight Riot in London," *Daily Mail*, 1 September 1958; see also Letter from Nottingham Chief Constable to Under Secretary of State, 2 September 1958, HO 325/8, TNA; and Home Office Memo, 4 September 1958, HO 325/8, TNA.

8. Statement of Geoffrey Golding, 1 September 1958, MEPO 2/9838, TNA; Statement of William Powell, 1 September 1958, MEPO 2/9838, TNA; Statement of Raymond Carter, 1 September 1958, MEPO 2/9838, TNA.

9. "Mosley's Man Opens Fire," *The Observer*, 7 September 1958; "Fight in Barricaded Houses," *Daily Mail*, 2 September 1958; Colin Eales, "Witness to Violence," *Kensington News and West London Times*, 5 September 1958.

10. Statement of John Meyrick, Notting Hill Police Station, 1 September 1958, MEPO 2/9838, TNA.

11. "Keep Britain White" was one of the unofficial mantras of Oswald Moseley's Union Movement during the late 1950s and was reported as a popular chant heard during the violence of 1958. "London Racial Outburst Due to Many Factors: Hooligan Invaders and Wild Charges," *The Times*, 3 September 1958; "Race Violence Grows," *Daily Express*, 2 September 1958.

12. " 'Bombs' in Race Riot," *Daily Mail*, 2 September 1958.

13. Memo to Assistant Chief Constable from Divisional Detective Superintendent, 5 September 1958, MEPO 2/9838, TNA. According to Metropolitan Police records, seventy-two of the perpetrators were white and twenty-six were "coloured." See also Telegram from Commonwealth Relations Office to Commonwealth Governments, 4 September 1958, DO 35/7992, TNA; and Pilkington, *Beyond the Mother Country*, 128.

14. Memo to Assistant Chief Constable from Divisional Detective Superintendent, 5 September 1958, MEPO 2/9838, TNA; "Notting Hill Men on 'Affray' Charge," *Evening Standard*, 4 September 1958. References to "race riots" are used in quotation marks to denote that this was a discursive formation or media construction of the violence, used to publicly discuss racial conflict between Black and White residents in Nottingham and London during the summer of 1958. On the concept of discursive formations, see Michel Foucault, *The Archaeology of Knowledge and the Discourse on Language* (New York: Tavistock Publications, 1972), 31–39.

15. "London Racial Outburst Due to Many Factors," *The Times*, 3 September 1958; "Riots: World Uproar," *Daily Herald*, 4 September 1958; See also Memo, "Ghana and the

Racial Riots," from A. Snelling to Sir H. Lintott, 4 September 1958, DO 35/7992, TNA. According to the memo, this characterization was also reproduced in Ghanaian papers.

16. This is one of the key threads of the only monograph on the riots: Pilkington, *Beyond the Mother Country*. See also Mike Phillips and Trevor Phillips, *Windrush*, 159–180.

17. Shirley Graham Dubois, "Howls from Lynch Mobs Shake Composure of British People," *Pittsburgh Courier*, 13 September 1958; "Nazis of Notting Hill," *Daily Gleaner*, 9 September 1958; "Nazis of Notting Hill," *The Statesman* (Calcutta), 7 September 1958 (according to the article this title was adopted from an article in *The Economist* with the same headline); "Race Riots Give Britain a Shock," *Sydney Morning Herald*, 4 September 1958.

18. Dudziak, *Cold War Civil Rights*, chap. 4; Kennetta Hammond Perry, "'Little Rock' in Britain: Jim Crow's Transatlantic Topographies," *Journal of British Studies* 51 (January 2012): 155–177.

19. Wilder, *The French Imperial Nation-State*, 3–23.

20. See Christopher Leslie Brown, *Moral Capital: Foundations of British Abolitionism* (Chapel Hill: University of North Carolina Press, 2006), epilogue; see also Derek Peterson, ed., *Abolition and Imperialism in Britain, Africa and the Atlantic World* (Athens: Ohio University Press, 2010), 4–5; J. R. Oldfield, *Chords of Freedom: Commemoration, Ritual and British Transatlantic Slavery* (Manchester, UK: Manchester University Press, 2007), 1–3, 88–90.

21. "Riots: World Uproar," *Daily Herald*, 4 September 1958.

22. "Alport—Race Riots Are UnBritish," *Daily Graphic*, 3 September 1958.

23. "Britain's Race Troubles," *Johannesburg Star*, 4 September 1958; "Race Riots Give Britain a Shock," *Sydney Morning Herald*, 4 September 1958.

24. Telegram from Paris, France to the Foreign Office, 6 September 1958, DO 35/7992, TNA.

25. Telegram from Wellington, New Zealand to Commonwealth Relations Office, 8 September 1958, DO 35/7992, TNA.

26. "Letters to the Editor: Britain's Race Riots," *Washington Post*, 2 September 1958; "Tolerance Remains High in Britain Despite Increase in Racial Collisions," *Washington Post*, 26 August 1958.

27. Telegram from Washington to Foreign Office, 4 September 1958, DO 35/7992, TNA.

28. "Manley Sees WI Leaders," *Trinidad Guardian*, 6 September 1958.

29. "Manley Tells West Indians 'Fear Nobody,'" *Trinidad Guardian*, 12 September 1958.

30. Letter from M. E. Allen to Mr. Chadwick, 1 September 1958, DO 35/7992, TNA; Confidential Letter from E. O. Asafu-Adjaye to Secretary of State for Commonwealth Relations, 3 September 1958, DO 35/7992, TNA; Telegram from E. Baring to Colonial Secretary, 31 October 1958, DO 35/7992, TNA; Telegram from Secretary of State for the Colonies to Federation of Nigeria, 5 September 1958, DO 35/7992, TNA.

31. Telegram from Karachi [Pakistan] to Commonwealth Relations Office, 4 September 1958, DO 35/7992, TNA.

32. Memo, "Racial Riots in the U.K.," 1 September 1958, DO 35/7992, TNA.

33. Memo from A. W. Snelling to Sir H. Lintott, "Ghana and the Racial Riots," 4 September 1958, DO 35/7992, TNA.

34. "Racial Attacks Cause Empire Crisis," *Sydney Morning Herald*, 7 September 1958.

35. Telegram from Karachi to Commonwealth Relations Office, 4 September 1958, DO 35/7992, TNA.

36. *Reuters* report, "British Entertainers Attack Race Violence," *Washington Post*, 11 September 1958.

37. "Manley Addresses London Meeting," *Daily Gleaner*, 8 September 1958.

38. "MacMillan Discusses Race Riots," *Trinidad Guardian*, 6 September 1958.

39. "Nigerian's Warning on Quotas," *Daily Worker*, 9 September 1958.

40. "Britain's Race Troubles," *The Star*, 4 September 1958; see also Letter from J. O. Wright, South African High Commissioner's Office to W. Preston, Commonwealth Relations Office, 18 September 1958, DO 35/7992, TNA. This article ran in the *Johannesburg Star* on 4 September 1958.

41. Telegram from South Africa to Commonwealth Relations Office, 1 September 1958, DO 35/7992, TNA.

42. Letter from J. O. Wright, South African High Commissioner's Office, to W. Preston, Commonwealth Relations Office, 18 September 1958 DO 35/7992, TNA.

43. Letter from J. O. Wright, South African High Commissioner's Office to W. Preston, Commonwealth Relations Office, 18 September 1958, DO 35/7992, TNA.

44. "Britain's Racial Problems: S. Africans Now Expect Greater Sympathy," *The Times*, 29 August 1958. Governor Faubus was the segregationist governor of Arkansas who dispatched the army reserves to stall the integration of Little Rock's Central High School in accordance with the mandate of Brown v. Board of Education. Charles Robberts Swart was the Minister of Justice in South Africa and came into power with the Nationalist Party that institutionalized apartheid in 1948. In 1959, he became the Union of South Africa's last Governor-General before the government left the British Commonwealth, and he became the first President of the Republic of South Africa, a position that he held until 1967.

45. "Britain's Racial Problems: S. Africans Now Expect Greater Sympathy," *The Times*, 29 August 1958.

46. Telegram from South Africa to Commonwealth Relations Office, 1 September 1958, DO 35/7992, TNA. For a discussion of British reactions to apartheid, see Ronald Hyam and Peter Henshaw, *The Lion and the Springbok: Britain and South Africa since the Boer War* (Cambridge, UK: Cambridge University Press, 2007), chap. 13.

47. Telegram from Bonn, Germany to the Foreign Office, 25 September 1958, DO 35/7992, TNA.

48. Telegram from Paris, France to the Foreign Office, 6 September 1958, DO 35/7992, TNA. For more on British reactions to French policy in Algeria and the Algerian War, see Martin Thomas, "The British Government and the End of French Algeria, 1958–1962," *Journal of Strategic Studies* 25, no. 2 (2002): 172–198; and Christopher Goldsmith, "The British Embassy in Paris and the Algerian War," *Journal of Strategic Studies* 25, no. 2 (2002): 159–171.

49. "Dear Governor Faubus . . ," *Daily Mail*, 6 September 1958. For a full discussion of how discourses about the Little Rock desegregation operated in domestic debate about racial violence in Nottingham and London, see Perry, "'Little Rock' in Britain," 155–117.

50. Here, I am drawing upon Antonio Gramsci's widely cited theories on the invisibility of cultural hegemony. See Antonio Gramsci, *Selections from Prison Notebooks*, ed. and trans. Quinton Hoare and Geoffrey Smith (London: Lawrence and Wishart, 1986). More recently, Georgie Wemyss has also appropriated Gramsci's concept of hegemony to describe the discursive "invisible empire" that marks Britishness as White, tolerant, and liberal. See Georgie Wemyss, *The Invisible Empire: White Discourse, Tolerance and Belonging* (Farnham, UK: Ashgate Publishing, 2009).

51. Brown, *Moral Capital*, epilogue; Richard Huzzey, *Freedom Burning: Anti-Slavery and Empire in Victorian Britain* (Ithaca, NY: Cornell University Press, 2012), chap. 3. See also Derek Peterson, ed., *Abolitionism and Imperialism*, introduction; J. R. Oldfield, *Chords of Freedom*, 1–3; Hall, *Civilizing Subjects*; Metha, *Liberalism and Empire*.

52. Teresa Zackdonik, "Ida B. Wells and 'American Atrocities in Britain," *Women's Studies International Forum* 28, no. 4 (2005): 259–273. See also Sarah Silkey, *Black Woman Reformer: Lynching and Transatlantic Activism* (Athens, GA: University of Georgia Press, 2015).

53. Paula M. Krebs, *Gender, Race and the Writing of Empire: Public Discourse and theBoer War* (Cambridge: Cambridge University Press, 1999).

54. Rich, *Race and Empire in British Politics*, 10, 26–27, 29; Sonya Rose, *Which People's War? National Identity and Citizenship in Wartime Britain, 1939–1945* (New York: Oxford University Press, 2004), 239; Suke Wolton, *Lord Hailey, the Colonial Office and the Politics of Race and Empire in the Second World War: The Loss of White Prestige* (New York: St. Martins, 2000), 19–34, 151–152.

55. Wendy Webster, *Englishness and Empire, 1939–1965* (Oxford: Oxford University Press, 2005), 28–29; see also Rose, *Which People's War?*; and Rose, "Race, Empire and British Wartime National Identity, 1939–45," *Historical Research* 74 (2001): 220–237.

56. Wolton, *Lord Hailey, The Colonial Office and the Politics of Race and Empire in the Second World War*, 152–154.

57. Rose, *Which People's War?*, 245.

58. Ibid., 258.

59. Quoted in Ian McLaine, *Ministry of Morale: Home Front Morale and the Ministry of Information in World War II* (London: Allen and Unwin, 1979), 271. See also Graham Smith, *When Jim Crow Met John Bull: Black American Soldiers in World War II Britain* (London: I. B. Tauris, 1987).

60. Wemyss, *The Invisible Empire*, 123–139; see also Wendy Brown, *Regulating Aversion: Tolerance in the Age of Identity and Empire* (Princeton, NJ: Princeton University Press, 2006).

61. Dudziak, *Cold War Civil Rights*, 1–6, 115–151.

62. "Renewed Call for Changes in Immigration Law," *The Times*, 28 August 1958; Perry, "'Little Rock' in Britain," 165–166.

63. Telegram from Foreign Office to HMG Representatives, 3 September 1958, DO 35/9506, TNA.

64. Telegram from Foreign Office to HMG Representatives, 3 September 1958, DO 35/9506, TNA.

65. Ibid.

66. Ibid.

67. Dudziak, *Cold War Civil Rights*, esp. chap. 1 and 2.

68. "Four-Year Terms for Nine 'Nigger-Hunting' Youths," *The Times*, 16 September 1958; "Race War in Britain," *Trinidad Guardian*, 25 August 1958; "'Keep Britain White' Call in Notting Hill Area," *The Times*, 10 September 1958.

69. "The Riots That Scar Britain," *Daily Express*, 25 August 1958.

70. "Why? What Fans the Hate? *Daily Express*, 2 September 1958; headline part of larger article entitled "Race Riots Meeting At Chequers," *London Observer*, 7 September 1958; "'Our Colour Problem,'" *London Observer*, 7 September 1958; Headline part of larger article entitled "Man's Inhumanity to Man ... In England," *London Observer*, 7 September 1958; "Why Racial Clash Occurred," *The Times*, 27 August 1958; "London Racial Outburst Due to Many Factors," *The Times*, 3 September 1958.

71. In her discussion of the "invisible empire," Georgie Wemyss also argues that White liberal discourses about Britishness pivot on the denial of an imperial past rooted in White violence. Wemyss, *Invisible Empire*, 3.

72. "Racial Outburst in an English City," *Manchester Guardian Weekly*, 28 August 1958.

73. Ibid.

74. "Letters to the Editor: Race Prejudice in Britain," *Manchester Guardian Weekly*, 4 September 1958. Home Office records indicate that Myrtle Shaw attended a public meeting held in Nottingham during the same week her editorial appeared in the press, sponsored by the Afro-West Indian Union, which focused on shifting attention from the "Teddy Boys or the Blacks" to the larger societal issues underlying the causes for the violence. See Report of Afro-West Indian Union to Assistant Chief Constable of the Nottingham Police, 7 September 1958, HO 325/8, TNA.

75. "Why Racial Clash Occurred," *The Times*, 27 August 1958.

76. Ibid.

77. "Riots That Scar Britain," *Daily Express*, 25 August 1958; "Prison Sentences for Five Nottingham 'Rowdies,'" *The Times*, 2 September 1958; "Nottingham Crowd 'Took Sides with Rowdies,'" *Manchester Guardian*, 2 September 1958; "The Colour Problem: Will It Solve Itself?" *Evening Standard*, 26 August 1958.

78. Dick Hebdige, *Subcultures: The Meaning of Style* (London: Routledge, 2002), 50–51, 81.

79. "Man's Inhumanity to Man ... in England," *London Sunday Observer*, 7 September 1958.

80. "The Hooligan Age," *The Times*, 3 September 1958. For a discussion of the longer cultural history of discourse of hooliganism in England during the twentieth century, see Bill Schwarz, "Night Battles: Hooligan and Citizen," in *Modern Times: Reflections on a Century of English Modernity*, ed. Mica Nava and Alan O'Shea (New York: Routledge, 1996).

81. "Clashes in the Streets: More Than Racial Issues Involved," *The Times*, 5 September 1958.

82. "Clashes in the Streets," *The Times*, 5 September 1958; Osbert Lancaster, "Pocket Cartoon," *Daily Express*, 2 September 1958.

83. "Menace behind the Brawl," *The Observer,* 31 August 1958.

84. "The Background of Notting Hill," *Manchester Guardian,* 2 September 1958.

85. "London Racial Outburst Due to Many Factors," *The Times,* 3 September 1958.

86. Webster, *Englishness and Empire,* 129–135.

87. "Language of Violence," *Manchester Guardian,* 11 September 1958.

88. "Roots of Racial Prejudice," *Manchester Guardian,* 18 September 1958.

89. "Race Riots Terrorise a City," *Daily Express,* 25 August 1958.

90. "Dozens Hurt in Racial Clash," *The Times,* 25 August 1958. Along with Mrs. Lowndes, *The Times* profiled the stories of Mrs. Ellen Byatt, Mrs. Charles Coyne, Mrs. F. Smith, and a Mrs. Slater, all of whom described either being attacked or witnessing attacks by "coloured men"; see also Majbritt Morrison, *Jungle West* 11 (London: Tandem Books, 1964).

91. "Why Racial Clash Occurred," *The Times,* 27 August 1958; "London Racial Outburst Due to Many Factors," *The Times,* 3 September 1958; "What Fans the Hate?" *Daily Express,* 2 September 1958; "Menace behind the Brawl," *The Observer,* 31 August 1958; "The Colour Problem," *Evening Standard,* 26 August 1958.

92. "'Brown Town' Speaks for Itself," *Manchester Guardian Weekly,* 11 September 1958.

93. Collins, "Pride and Prejudice," 391–418.

94. "Black and White," *Daily Mirror,* 6 September 1958.

95. Keith Waterhouse, "The Boys From Jamaica," *Daily Mirror,* 8 September 1958.

96. Keith Waterhouse, "The Men Who Come Here from West Africa to Learn," *Daily Mirror,* 9 September 1958.

97. Bailkin, *The Afterlife of Empire,* 5, 119–131. Bailkin is also careful to note that during this same period the state became quite concerned with distinguishing sojourning students and migrant laborers even among West African newcomers.

98. Keith Waterhouse, "The Boys from Jamaica," *Daily Mirror,* 8 September 1958.

99. Report of Proceedings at the 90th Annual Trades Union Congress, 1–5 September 1958, 378, 458–460, London Metropolitan University Trades Union Congress Library, London; "T.U.C. Statement," *The Times,* 5 September 1958.

100. This cartoon appeared on the front page of the *Daily Mirror,* headlined by an article describing violence in London. See "36 Arrests in New 'Colour Riots,'" *Daily Mirror,* 2 September 1958.

101. Report of Proceedings at the 90th Annual Trades Union Congress, 1–5 September 1958, 458–460, London Metropolitan University Trades Union Congress Library, London; "T.U.C. Statement," *The Times,* 5 September 1958.

102. "Entry Laws Are Being Revived," *Daily Mirror,* 4 September 1958.

103. Ibid.

104. "Government Warning on Race Riots," *The Times,* 4 September 1958.

105. "Race Riots Meeting at Chequers," *The Observer,* 7 September 1958.

106. "Four-Year Terms for Nine 'Nigger-Hunting' Youths," *The Times,* 16 September 1958.

107. "Four-Year Terms for Nine 'Nigger-Hunting' Youths," *The Times* 16 September 1958; "'You Started This Violence'—Judge Tells Gaoled Gang," *Daily Mirror,* 16 September 1958; "Great Britain: The Nigger Hunters," *Time,* 29 September 1958.

108. "9 London Youths Jailed for Colour Manhunt: Judge Says Attacks Were Vicious," *Trinidad Guardian,* 16 September 1958; "Trinidad Praise for British Justice," *The Times,* 17 September 1958.

109. James Nestor, "British Justice Has Justified Our Faith," *Trinidad Guardian,* 20 September 1958. Jimmy Wilson had been convicted of stealing less than $2.00 from a white woman in Alabama and received the death sentence for his crime. His case drew international headlines and served as a potent symbol of the virulence of American racism.

110. Telegram from Bonn, Germany to the Foreign Office, 25 September 1958, DO 35/7992, TNA.

111. Telegram from Paris to Foreign Office, 25 September 1958, DO 35/7992, TNA.

112. Telegram from Commonwealth Relations Office to Canada, New Zealand, South Africa, India, Pakistan, Ghana, and other Commonwealth countries, 26 August 1958, DO 35/7992, TNA.

113. "Nottingham M.P.s Urge Curb on Entry of Immigrants," *The Times*, 27 August 1958. A similar version of this article appeared in the Jamaican press on the following day. See "Nottingham MPs Seek Curb on Immigrants," *Daily Gleaner*, 28 August 1958.
114. "Renewed Call for Changes in Immigration Law," *The Times*, 28 August 1958.
115. Ibid.
116. "Government Warning on Race Riots," *The Times*, 4 September 1958; see also "Macmillan Warns Govt. Will Use 'All Strictness' to End Clashes," *Daily Gleaner*, 4 September 1958; and "Britain's PM Warns Race 'Troublemakers,'" *Trinidad Guardian*, 4 September 1958.
117. James and Harris, *Inside Babylon*, 59–68; Paul, *Whitewashing Britain*. Government consideration of migration controls in the early 1950s will be discussed in greater detail in Chapter 5.
118. "Easing Racial Tensions," *The Times*, 4 September 1958.
119. Fryer, *Staying Power*, 298–310, 367–371; see also Lorimer, *Colour, Class and the Victorians: English Attitudes towards the Negro in the Mid-Nineteenth Century* (Leicester, UK: Leicester University Press, 1978); Michael Rowe, "The Racialisation of Disorder: Sex, Race and Riot in Liverpool, 1919," *Immigrants and Minorities* (July 2000): 53–70; see also Kevin Searle, "Mixing of the Unmixables: The 1949 Causeway Green 'Riots' in Birmingham," *Race and Class* 54 (2013): 344–364.
120. "Nigeria Official Blames Influx of West Indians," *Trinidad Guardian*, 5 September 1958.
121. "Barbados Premier Arrives," *The Times*, 8 September 1958.

Chapter 4

1. "1,200 Mourn Cochrane: Scene at Graveside," *The Kensington News and West London Times*, 12 June 1959. For other news reports detailing the funeral of Kelso Cochrane, see "800 Mourners March to Graveside: Elaborate Precautions against Any Disorder," *Kensington Post*, 12 June 1959; "Big Crowd at West Indian's Burial," *The Times*, 8 June 1959; and "PM at Kelso's Burial," *Sunday Guardian*, 7 June 1959.
2. "Race Killer Hunted," *Daily Mail*, 18 May 1959.
3. Memo from Superintendent of Police, Antigua to Colonial Office, 9 June 1959, CO 1031/2541, TNA; Mark Olden, *Murder in Notting Hill* (Winchester, UK: Zero Books, 2011), 12–13. According to reports from the American Consulate General's Office, Cochrane's deportation may have also been triggered by an arrest for assault, a charge for which he never faced trial. See Memo from Philip C. Habib, American Consulate General Office, Port of Spain, Trinidad to Ian Turbott, Administrator, St. Johns, Antigua, 11 September 1959, CO 1031/2541, TNA.
4. "'Jim Crow' Taunts End in Death," *Daily Express*, 18 May 1959; "Race Killers Hunted: White Wife Sees Gang Murder at Window," *Daily Mail*, 18 May 1959; "Jamaican Is Stabbed to Death in Fight at Notting Hill," *News Chronicle and Daily Dispatch*, 18 May 1959; "Girl Who Saw a Murder," *Daily Mirror*, 18 May 1959; "'It Was *Not* a Racial Killing,'" *Daily Mirror*, 19 May 1959; see also Statement of George Isaacs, MEPO 2/9833, TNA; and Metropolitan Police Report, 25 August 1959, MEPO 2/9833, TNA.
5. "Race Tension Increased by Murder: Police Say Robbery Was a Likely Motive," *The Times*, 19 May 1959; "'It Was *Not* a Racial Killing,'" *Daily Mirror*, 19 May 1959.
6. Davies, *Left of Karl Marx*, 84.
7. Letter from Alao Bashorn to Harold Macmillan 18 May 1959, CO 1028/50, TNA.
8. "Coloured People 'Have Lost Confidence' in Police: Open Letter to the Prime Minister," *Manchester Guardian*, 19 May 1959; "2 Detained in Notting Hill Murder Probe," *Trinidad Guardian*, 20 May 1959; "Mass Funeral March Planned," *Daily Worker*, 20 May 1959.
9. Letter from Alao Bashorn to Harold Macmillan, 18 May 1959, CO 1028/50, TNA.
10. Ibid.
11. "The Human Race," *Daily Worker*, 8 September 1958.
12. Flyer, "Mass Demonstration of Inter-Racial Friendship," u.d., ca. 21 September 1958, Box 1, Folder 23, Claudia Jones Memorial Collection, Schomburg Center for Research, New York, NY.

13. "West Indian Chiefs Will Be at Rally," *Daily Worker,* 9 September 1958; "Will Too Many Do-Gooders Pave the Path to Notting Hell?" *Kensington News and West London Times,* 30 October 1959.

14. "Will Too Many Do-Gooders Pave the Path to Notting Hell?" *Kensington News and West London Times,* 30 October 1959.

15. "Fund to Defend Racist Victims," *Daily Worker,* 12 September 1958.

16. AACP Letterhead, undated, Box 1, Folder 25, Claudia Jones Memorial Collection, Schomburg; Fenner Brockway to Claudia Jones, 27 February 1959, Box 1, Folder 17, Claudia Jones Memorial Collection, Schomburg.

17. Claudia Jones, "An End to the Neglect of the Problems of Negro Women," *Claudia Jones: Beyond Containment,* ed. Carole Boyce Davies (Boulder, CO: Lynne Rienner Publishers, 2011), 83.

18. For more on Claudia Jones and the *West Indian Gazette,* see Johnson, *"I Think of My Mother;"* Sherwood, *Claudia Jones;* Davies, *Left of Karl Marx;* and Bill Schwarz, "Claudia Jones and the *West Indian Gazette,"* 264–285.

19. Sherwood, *Claudia Jones,* 93, 156.

20. Davies, *Claudia Jones,* 166–167.

21. Ibid., 166.

22. "Fund to Defend Racist Victims," *Daily Worker,* 12 September 1958; "Klan Joins Racist Attack on West Indians Here," *Daily Worker,* 28 August 1958; Sherwood, *Claudia Jones,* 129.

23. "'Jim Crow' Taunts End in Death," *Daily Express,* 18 May 1959.

24. Letter from Alao Bashorn to Harold Macmillan 18 May 1959, CO 1028/50, TNA.

25. Christabel Gurney, "'A Great Cause': The Origins of the Anti-Apartheid Movement, June 1959–March 1960," *Journal of Southern African Studies* 26 (March 2000): 123–144. See also Hakim Adi, *West Africans in Britain, 1900–1960: Nationalism, Pan-Africanism and Communism* (London: Lawrence and Wishart, 1998), 23–51.

26. Special Branch Report, New Scotland Yard, 28 May 1959, HO 325/9, TNA. This meeting is also documented in the minutes of the executive committee of the Movement for Colonial Freedom. See also Executive Committee Meeting Minutes, 21 May 1959, Movement for Colonial Freedom Papers, Box 1, School of Oriental and African Studies, London, UK.

27. "Notting Hill: 2 Quizzed 20 Hours," *Daily Mirror* 20 May 1959; "Man Who Helped Notting Hill Murder Probe Tells of MY 45 HOURS WITH POLICE," *Daily Mirror,* 21 May 1959; "Two Youths Leave Police Station," *The Times,* 21 May 1959. In a recent book, journalist Mark Olden asserts that circumstantial evidence proves that Patrick Digby was Kelso Cochrane's killer. See Mark Olden, *Murder in Notting Hill* (Alresford, UK: Zero Books, 2011), 115–126, 146–155.

28. "The Yard and the Notting Hill Murder," *Daily Mirror,* 19 May 1959; "Silent Streets Hide a Killer and Notting Hill Faces a New Danger," *Kensington News and West London Times,* 22 May 1959.

29. Memorandum of a Deputation Representing Interracial Friendship Co-Ordinating Council for Presentation to the Honourable R. A. Butler, Secretary of State for Home Affairs, Special Branch Report, New Scotland Yard, 28 May 1959, HO 325/9, TNA; "Coloured Plea to Mr. Butler," *The Times,* 28 May 1959.

30. Memorandum of a Deputation Representing Interracial Friendship Co-Ordinating Council for Presentation to the Honourable R. A. Butler, 28 May 1959, HO 325/9, TNA.

31. "Petition to the Right Honorable Mr. R. A. Butler, Home Secretary, Government of the United Kingdom," Claudia Jones Memorial Collection, Box 1, Folder 25, Schomburg.

32. "Home Office Deputation," *Kensington News and West London Times,* 5 June 1959; "A Petition to the Right Honorable Mr. R. A. Butler, Home Secretary, Government of the United Kingdom," Claudia Jones Memorial Collection, Box 1, Folder 25, Schomburg; Marika Sherwood, *Claudia Jones,* 95.

33. Memorandum of a Deputation Representing Interracial Friendship Co-Ordinating Council for Presentation to the Honourable R. A. Butler, Secretary of State for Home Affairs, Special Branch Report, New Scotland Yard, 28 May 1959, HO 325/9, TNA.

34. "Organisations Urge Govt to Make Public Appeal," *Daily Worker*, 28 May 1958; "Home Office Deputation," *Kensington News and West London Times*, 5 June 1959; "Coloured Plea to Mr. Butler," *The Times*, 28 May 1959; "Murder Search Goes On," *Kensington Post*, 29 May 1959. On Pearl and Edric Connor's work in Britain, see Amanda Bidnall, "West Indian Interventions at the Heart of the Cultural Establishment: Edric Connor, Pearl Connor and the BBC," *Twentieth Century British History* 24, no. 1 (2013): 58–83.

35. Special Branch Report, New Scotland Yard, 10 November, 1959, HO 325/9, TNA; Special Branch Report, New Scotland Yard, 21 July 1959, HO 325/9, TNA; Memo, "Inter-Racial Friendship Co-Ordinating Council: Central Executive Committee," undated, Claudia Jones Memorial Collection Box 1, Folder 27, Schomburg. The first Central Executive Committee for the organization was elected at a meeting held on 14 July 1959. See also Sherwood, *Claudia Jones*, 94–95.

36. "Many Voices on Notting Hill," *Kensington News and West London Times*, 29 May 1959.

37. For more on the All African People's Conference, see "All African People's Conference," *International Organization* 16, no. 2 (Spring, 1962): 429–431; see also Barbara Ransby, *Eslanda: The Large and Unconventional Life of Mrs. Paul Robeson* (New Haven, CT: Yale University Press, 2013).

38. "Deputy PM Blames Facists," *Trinidad Guardian*, 29 May 1959; Inter-Racial Friendship Co-Ordinating Council Report of Income and Expenditures through 30 June 1959, Claudia Jones Memorial Collection, Box 1, Folder 27, Schomburg; "Cochrane 'Killed because of Colour,'" *News Chronicle and Daily Dispatch*, 29 May 1959.

39. "West Indies Call for Ruthless Suppression of Race Hostility," *The Times*, 25 May 1958; "Many Voices on Notting Hill," *Kensington News and West London Times*, 29 May 1959.

40. "West Indies Call for Ruthless Suppression of Race Hostility," *The Times*, 25 May 1958; "Many Voices on Notting Hill," *Kensington News and West London Times*, 29 May 1959.

41. "WI Groom-to-Be Dies after Attack," *Trinidad Guardian*, 18 May 1959.

42. "Tensions Mount in Britain," *Trinidad Guardian*, 18 May 1959.

43. "WI Concerned over Migrants," *Trinidad Guardian*, 21 May 1959.

44. Lionel Hurst, General Secretary, Antigua Trades and Labour Union to the Administrator, St. John's, Antigua, 5 June 1959, CO 1031/2541, TNA.

45. Appendix A of Memorandum from the Administrator's Office, Antigua to Chief Secretary of the Leewards Islands, "Death of Kelso Cochrane," 5 June 1959, CO 1031/2541, TNA. According to the memo, this editorial appeared in the *Worker's Voice* on 21 May 1959.

46. "Confidence Lost," *The Daily Gleaner*, 19 May 1959; "Coloured Migrants Seek Protection," *The Daily Gleaner*; 28 May 1959; "W. I. Govt. Acts in Slaying of Antiguan," *The Daily Gleaner*, 21 May 1959; "PM Likely for UK on Stabbing," *Trinidad Guardian*, 20 May 1959.

47. Lord Perth to Governor-General of the West Indies, 21 May 1959, CO1031/2541, TNA; Governor General of the West Indies to Lord Perth, 23 May 1959, CO 1031/2541, TNA.

48. "Many Voices on Notting Hill," *Kensington News and West London Times*, 29 May 1959.

49. "Cochrane 'Killed because of Colour,'" *News Chronicle and Daily Dispatch*, 29 May 1959; "Coloured Plea to Mr. Butler," *The Times*, 28 May 1959.

50. "The Yard and the Notting Hill Murder," *Daily Mirror*, 19 May 1959.

51. Letter from Donald Ezzrecco, Coloured People's Progressive Association, to Labour Party, 23 October 1958, Labour History Archive and Study Center, Manchester, UK; Coloured People's Progressive Association Flyer, n.d., Claudia Jones Memorial Collection, Box 1, Folder 23, Schomburg; "Will Too Many Do-Gooders Pave the Path to Notting Hell?" *Kensington News and West London Times*, 30 October 1959.

52. "Many Voices on Notting Hill," *Kensington News and West London Times*, 29 May 1959.

53. "Home Office Deputation," *Kensington News and West London Times*, 5 June 1959; "In Action against the Colour Bar," *Daily Worker*, 2 June 1959.

54. Leigh Raeford, "Ida B. Wells and the Shadow Archive," in *Pictures and Progress: Early Photography and the Making of African American Identity*, ed. Maurice O. Wallace and Shawn Michelle Smith (Durham, NC: Duke University Press, 2012), 299–320; Mamie Till-Mobley and Christopher Benson, *Death of Innocence: The Story of the Hate Crime That Changed America* (New York: Random House, 2003), 139.

55. "'Jim Crow' Taunts End in Death." *Daily Express,* 18 May 1959; "Girl Who Saw a Murder," *Daily Mirror,* 18 May 1959; "Jamaican Is Stabbed to Death in Fight at Notting Hill," *News Chronicle and Daily Dispatch,* 18 May 1959.

56. Campt, *Image Matters,* 5–8, 150.

57. Bill Schwarz, "Our Unadmitted Sorrow: The Rhetorics of Civil Rights Photography," *History Workshop Journal* 72 (Autumn 2011): 143; see also Leigh Raiford, *Imprisoned in a Luminous Glare: Photography and the African American Freedom Struggle* (Chapel Hill: University of North Carolina Press, 2011), 1–28.

58. Claudia Jones, "Lament for Emmett Till," n.d., Claudia Jones Memorial Collection, Box 1, Folder 5, Schomburg.

59. Ibid.

60. Alrick Cambridge, "Black Body Politics," in *Where You Belong: Government and Black Culture,* ed. Alrick Cambridge and Stephan Feuchtwang (Aldershot, UK: Avebury, 1992), 108–110.

61. "Elaborate Precautions against Any Disorder," *Kensington Post,* 12 June 1959.

62. Inter-Racial Friendship Co-Ordinating Council Report of Income and Expenditures through June 30 1959, Claudia Jones Memorial Collection, Box 1, Folder 27, Schomburg.

63. "700 Mourn Murdered West Indian," *London Observer,* 7 June 1959; "1,200 Mourn Cochrane: Scene at Graveside," *Kensington News and West London Times,* 12 June 1959; Phillips and Phillips, *Windrush,* 186. Expense records show that the IRFCC purchased mourners' armlets for the services. See Inter-Racial Friendship Co-Ordinating Council Report of Income and Expenditures through 30 June 1959, Claudia Jones Memorial Collection, Box 1, Folder 27, Schomburg.

64. "Cochrane: Bishop for Funeral," *Daily Worker,* 4 June 1959; "800 Mourners March to Graveside: Elaborate Precautions against Any Disorder," *Kensington Post,* 12 June 1959.

65. Kelso Cochrane Funeral Program, 01/04/04/01/04/02/05, Black History Collection, Institute of Race Relations Archives, London, UK; "Cochrane's Funeral: Black and White At Graveside," *Daily Worker,* 8 June 1959; "800 Mourners March to Graveside," *Kensington Post,* 12 June 1959.

66. "Big Crowd at West Indian's Burial," *The Times,* 8 June 1959.

67. David L. Eng and David Kazanjian, eds., *Loss: The Politics of Mourning* (Berkeley: University of California Press, 2002), 2–5, 8–9.

68. Teju Cole, "Unmournable Bodies," *The New Yorker,* 9 January 2015; Judith Butler, "What's Wrong with 'All Lives Matter'?" *The New York Times,* 12 January 2015.

69. Fryer, *Staying Power*; Ramdin, *The Making of the Black Working Class in Britain*; Ron Ramdin, *Reimagining Britain: Five Hundred Years of Black and Asian History* (London: Pluto Press, 1999).

70. Phillips and Phillips, *Windrush,* 187.

71. "Statue for the Victim," *Daily Mirror,* 7 June 1959.

72. M. Z. Terry to George Rogers, 1 July 1959, CO 1031/2541, TNA; Memo from Under Secretary of State for the Colonies to Sir Austin Strutt of Home Office, 28 July 1959, CO 1031/2541, TNA.

73. "Kelso Cochrane Anniversary," *West Indian Gazette,* June 1960; "Gravestone Fund," *West Indian Gazette* June, 1960.

Chapter 5

1. "I Was Deported Because I Fought the Colour Bar," *Caribbean News,* June 1956, Claudia Jones Memorial Collection, Schomburg, New York.

2. Mae Ngai, *Impossible Subjects: Illegal Aliens and the Making of Modern America* (Cambridge, MA: Harvard University Press, 2004), 236.

3. "Text of Truman's Message to House on Veto of Immigration Bill," *New York Times,* 25 June 1952; "Anti-Colour-Bill-Lobby-Feb 13," *West Indian Gazette,* February 1962.

4. Memo, Claudia Jones on Behalf of the Afro-Asian-Caribbean Conference, 31 January 1962, Claudia Jones Research Collection, Schomburg, New York.

5. Paul, *Whitewashing Britain*, xii.
6. For examples of this interpretation see Carter, Harris, and Joshi, "The 1951–55 Conservative Government and the Racialization of Black Immigration," 55–72; Ian Spencer, *British Immigration Policy since 1939*; Kathleen Paul, *Whitewashing Britain*, especially chaps. 5 and 6.
7. Tabili, " 'We Ask for British Justice*, 117–121. Tabili notes that the non-White interwar maritime community was multiethnic and included Arab, Asian, Caribbean, and West African seamen. See also Spencer, *British Immigration Policy since 1939*, 10–11.
8. Tabili, *"We Ask for British Justice,"* 120–122; Spencer, *British Immigration Policy since 1939*, 10–12; see also Laura Tabili, "The Construction of Racial Difference in Twentieth Century Britain," *Journal of British Studies* 33, no. 1 (January 1994): 54–98; Paul, *Whitewashing Britain*, 113.
9. Tabili, "The Construction of Racial Difference in Twentieth Century Britain"; Tabili, *"We Ask For British Justice,"* chap. 6.
10. Spencer, *British Immigration Policy since 1939*, 23–24, 41.
11. Ibid., 31.
12. Spencer, *British Immigration Policy since 1939*, 22, 31–32, 44; Paul, *Whitewashing Britain*, 153; Hansen, *Citizenship and Immigration in Postwar Britain*, 66. Hansen notes that according to a Cabinet report in 1953, all of the African colonies were refusing passports to those who did not have stable employment or for those potential migrants who could not demonstrate a certain degree of financial solvency. This point is also referenced by D. Maxwell Fyfe, "Employment of Coloured People," Memo, 30 January 1954 CAB 129/65, TNA.
13. Spencer, *British Immigration Policy since 1939*, 51.
14. Layton-Henry, *The Politics of Immigration*, 13.
15. "Colonial Immigrants: Cabinet Conclusions on a Committee of Inquiry into Colonial Immigrants," Memo, 14 June 1955, CAB 128/29, TNA.
16. "Colonial Immigrants: Cabinet Conclusions on a Draft Bill to Restrict Colonial Immigration," Memo, 3 November 1955, CAB 128/29, TNA.
17. For a recent reconsideration of the legacies of the Bandung Conference, see Christopher J. Lee, ed. *Making A World after Empire: The Bandung Moment and Its Political Afterlives* (Athens: Ohio University Press, 2010).
18. Letter from Lord Swinton to Lord Salisbury, 15 March 1954, DO 35/5216, TNA.
19. The territories that comprised the West Indies Federation included Antigua, Barbuda, Barbados, Dominica, Grenada, Jamaica, Montserrat, St. Kitts and Nevis, Anguilla, St. Lucia, St. Vincent and Grenadines, and Trinidad and Tobago. For more on the West Indies Federation, see Cary Fraser, *Ambivalent Anti-Colonialism: The United States and the Genesis of West Indian Independence, 1940–1964* (Westport, CT: Greenwood Press); David Lowenthal, ed., *The West Indies Federation: Perspectives of a New Nation* (New York: Oxford University Press, 1961); Elisabeth Wallace, *The British Caribbean: From the Decline of Colonialism to the End of Federation* (Toronto: University of Toronto Press, 1977); Jason Parker, *Brother's Keeper: The United States, Race and Empire in the British Caribbean, 1937–1962* (New York: Oxford University Press, 2008); Eric Duke, *Building A Nation: Caribbean Federation in the Black Diaspora* (Gainesville: University of Florida Press, forthcoming, 2016).
20. Spencer, *British Immigration Policy since 1939*, 127.
21. Layton-Henry, *The Politics of Immigration*, 40.
22. Layton-Henry, *The Politics of Immigration*, 38–41; Spencer, *British Immigration Policy since 1939*, 98–102.
23. "Commonwealth Immigrants, Recommended Legislation: Cabinet Conclusions," 10 October 1961, CAB 128/35/2, TNA.
24. Working Party Report on the Social and Economic Problems Arising from the Growing Influx into the United Kingdom of Coloured Workers from Other Commonwealth Countries, 26 September 1961, LAB 8/2704, TNA.
25. "Early Law to Control Immigration: Jobs Must Be Waiting or Services in Demand," *The Times*, 12 October 1961.

26. Working Party Report on the Social and Economic Problems Arising from the Growing Influx into the United Kingdom," 26 September 1961, LAB 8/2704, TNA.

27. *Parliamentary Debates,* House of Commons, 1961–1962 (694), cols. 694–695.

28. Layton-Henry, *The Politics of Immigration,* 13; Working Party Report on the Social and Economic Problems Arising from the Growing Influx into the United Kingdom, 26 September 1961, LAB 8/2704, TNA. It is clear that the Working Party report issued in September 1961 followed the pattern of previous reports issued during the late 1950s by paying particular attention to the higher rates of West Indian migration in framing "the social and economic problems" of Commonwealth migration; however, it should be noted that the report did find "the substantial increase in the number of people from the Indian sub-continent ... particularly disturbing since many of these people do not speak English, and they are the more difficult group to assimilate." This is an important conclusion to highlight because although Black migration from the Caribbean might have been the initial targeted population of migration controls due to the higher rates of their migration to Britain during the 1950s and early 1960s, as Indian and Pakistani migration began to surpass West Indian migration in the mid-1960s, South Asian migrants became more prominently integrated into social narratives problematizing "immigration."

29. Wendy Webster, *Imagining Home,* 46, 60, 122.

30. Ibid., 123–127; Carby, "White Woman Listen!," 214–219.

31. "The Boys from Jamaica," *Daily Mirror,* 8 September 1958.

32. Webster, *Imagining Home,* 60.

33. *Parliamentary Debates,* House of Commons, 1961–1963 (694), col. 705.

34. Ibid., col. 710.

35. *Parliamentary Debates,* House of Commons, 1961–1962 (687), col. 710.

36. Ibid., col. 687.

37. Ibid., col. 710.

38. Ibid., col. 709.

39. *Parliamentary Debates,* House of Commons, 1961–1962 (649), col. 688.

40. Ibid., col. 708.

41. Ibid., col. 706.

42. Ibid., cols. 744, 747–748. Royle also noted that Irish migration to Britain at 353,000 between 1945 and 1959 exceeded total Commonwealth migration at 333,000 during the same years.

43. Ibid., cols. 778–779.

44. Ibid., col. 785.

45. Ibid., col. 802.

46. *Parliamentary Debates,* House of Commons, 1961–1962 (649), cols. 800,803. See also "Commons Storm over Immigration," *The Times,* 17 November 1961.

47. Telegram from Norman Manley to the Secretary of the Labour Party, 26 October 1961, Labour Party International Department Records, Box 1, File: Jamaica: Correspondence and Documents, 1955–1963, Manchester Labour History Archives, Manchester, UK.

48. Telegram from Norman Manley to the Secretary of the Labour Party, 26 October 1961, Labour Party International Department Records, Box 1, File: Jamaica: Correspondence and Documents, 1955–1963, Manchester Labour History Archives, Manchester. UK.

49. Telegram to the Colonial Secretary from K. Blackburne, 12 October 1961, PREM 11/3405, TNA.

50. "West Indies Government Oppose Colour-Bar Bill," *West Indian Gazette,* December 1961.

51. Ibid.

52. "W. Indies Appeal For Britain to Keep Door Open," *The Times,* 1 June 1961. See also "No Time to Curb Immigration," *West Indian Gazette,* June 1961.

53. Claude D. Ramsey, ed., "London Newsletter: Organ of the Standing Conference of Organisations Concerned with West Indians in Britain," February 1962, Edric and Pearl Connor Papers, Box 4, Folder 5, Schomburg Center for Research in Black Culture, New York, NY. This figure is an estimate of "postal remittances." In an article appearing in the *West Indian Gazette,* prominent West Indian political leader David Pitt noted that the annual figures for remittances were nearly as much as the total amount of colonial

development and welfare funding given to the West Indies by Britain during the 1950s. Considering this point, Pitt concluded that migrants "are therefore making a substantial contribution to bridging the gap between the poverty of the West Indies and the comparative wealth of Britain." See "David Pitt Says: W. I. Contribution Aids Britain," *West Indian Gazette,* October 1961.

54. Press Release, Office of the Commissioner for the West Indies, British Guiana and British Honduras, 17 November 1961, Movement for Colonial Freedom Papers, Box 73, School of Oriental and African Studies Special Collections, London, UK. See also "W. Indies Protest to Macmillan" *The Times.* 18 November 1961. Adams's reference to Lord Mansfield is a reference to the Somerset case, in which the English courts found that an enslaved person could not be forcibly sent out of England to be reenslaved in the colonies if he/she deserted his or her service in England. Although Mansfield's decision did not outlaw the practice of slavery in England, because it granted James Somerset freedom from enslavement and carved a new space to frame anti-slavery as antithetical to British law and tradition, it became a cause célèbre in the history of the abolition of slavery in the British Empire. See Douglas A. Lorimer, "Black Slaves and English Liberty: A Re-Examination of Racial Slavery in England," *Immigrants and Minorities* 3, no. 2 (1984): 121–150; William R. Cotter, "The Somerset Case and the Abolition of Slavery in England." *History* 79 (February 1994): 31–56.

55. "West Indies Government Oppose Colour-Bar Bill," *West Indian Gazette,* December 1961.

56. Ibid.

57. Spencer, *British Immigration Policy since 1939,* 127.

58. "West Indies Governments Oppose Colour-Bar Bill," *West Indian Gazette,* December 1961.

59. See Pennybacker, *From Scottsboro to Munich,* especially chap. 2; Makalani, *In the Cause of Freedom,* chaps. 6 and 7.

60. "Robeson at W.I.G. Anniversary Concert," *West Indian Gazette,* September, 1960; Flyer, "West Indian Gazette Features Talent in Town," 8 December 1960, Claudia Jones Papers, Donald Hinds Collection; Flyer, "*West Indian Gazette* Presents Paul Robeson," 28 September 1960, Claudia Jones Papers, Donald Hinds Private Collection.

61. Memo, Reception For Dr. Martin Luther King, 29 October 1961, Claudia Jones Papers, Donald Hinds Private Collection.

62. For more on Black globality, see Kelley and Patterson, "Unfinished Migrations," 11–45; Brent Edwards, "Black Globality: The International Shape of Black Intellectual Culture," PhD dissertation, Columbia University, 1997. Claudia Jones to Acting High Commissioner for Ghana, December, 1959, Claudia Jones Papers, Donald Hinds Collection. See also Claudia Jones, Memorandum for potential investors in *West Indian Gazette,* ca. 1962, Claudia Jones Papers, Donald Hinds Collection; Nico Slate, *Colored Cosmopolitanism: The Shared Struggle for Freedom in the United States and India* (Cambridge. MA: Harvard University Press, 2012).

63. Schwarz, "Claudia Jones and the *West Indian Gazette,* 264–285.

64. Flyer, "No Colour Bar on Immigration," November, 1961, 01/04/04/01/04/02/07, Black History Collection, Institute of Race Relations, London; "Protest Meeting," *The Guardian,* 2 November 1961.

65. Stephen Howe, *Anti-Colonialism in British Politics: The Left and the End of Empire, 1918–1964* (Oxford: Oxford University Press, 1993) ch. 6.

66. MCP Pamphlet, "No Colour Bar against Commonwealth Immigrants," n.d., 01/04/04/01/04/02/08, Black History Collection, Institute of Race Relations, London.

67. "Butler's Colour-Bar Bill Mocks Commonwealth," *West Indian Gazette,* November 1961.

68. "Dr. David Pitt Says: W.I. Contribution Aids Britain," *West Indian Gazette,* October 1961.

69. Ibid.

70. "The Commons Debate on Migration Restriction," *West Indian Gazette,* April 1960; "Memo to an M.P. on W.I. Migration," *West Indian Gazette,* September 1960; "No Time to Curb Immigration," *West Indian Gazette,* June 1961; "The New Arguments against Migration Restrictions," *West Indian Gazette,* September 1961.

71. "Butler's Colour-Bar Bill Mocks Commonwealth," *West Indian Gazette,* November 1961.

72. "The New Arguments against Migration Restriction," *West Indian Gazette,* September 1961.

73. "Butler's Colour-Bar Bill Mocks Commonwealth," *West Indian Gazette*, November 1961; Jordanna Bailkin, "Leaving Home: The Politics of Deportation in Postwar Britain," *Journal of British Studies* 47, no. 4 (2008): 853, 861–862.
74. Mae Ngai, *Impossible Subjects*, 2; Carole Boyce Davies, "Deportable Subjects: U.S. Immigration Laws and the Criminalizing of Communism," *South Atlantic Quarterly* 100, no. 1 (Fall 2001): 949–966.
75. Fenner Brockway, "The Immigration Bill," *Colonial Freedom News*, December 1961, Labour Party Archives Research Department Files on Race Relations and Immigration, Box 1, Manchester Labour History Archives and Study Center; "No Colour-Bar on Immigration March," *West Indian Gazette*, February 1962.
76. Claude D. Ramsey, ed., *London Newsletter*, Standing Conference of Organisations Concerned with West Indians in Britain, February 1962, Edric and Pearl Connor Papers, Schomburg Center for Research in Black Culture, New York, NY; "What Is the Afro-Asian-Caribbean Conference?" *West Indian Gazette*, February 1962.
77. "Anti-Colour-Bill-Lobby-Feb 13," *West Indian Gazette*, February 1962.
78. Flyer Announcing AACC Lobby, 13 February 1962, 01/04/04/01/04/02/09, Black History Collection, Institute of Race Relations, London .
79. "Labour Would Repeal Bill," *The Guardian*, 14 February 1962.
80. Memo, Commonwealth Immigration Bill, 13 February 1962, Claudia Jones Memorial Collection, Box 1, Folder 29, Schomburg Center for Research in Black Culture, New York, NY.
81. "British Law and Carmen Bryan," *The Observer*, 29 July 1962.
82. "Deportation Cancelled," *The Times*, 24 July 1962.
83. Ibid.
84. Confidential Telegram from Colonial Secretary to Sir K. Blackburne, Jamaica, 24 July 1962, DO 175/90, TNA; Jordanna Bailkin, "Leaving Home," *Journal of British Studies* 48, no. 4 (2008): 861–865.
85. "Anger over First Order for Deportation," *The Times*, 20 July 1962. See also Extract of Hansard Debate on Commonwealth Immigration, 7 February 1962, DO 175/90, TNA.
86. "Anger over First Order for Deportation" *The Times*, 20 July 1962.
87. Ibid.
88. Confidential Telegram from Colonial Secretary to Sir K. Blackburne, Jamaica, 24 July 1962, DO 175/90, TNA.
89. "Poor Start," *The Observer*, 22 July 1962; "Home Secretary in Storm over Deportation," *The Times*, 20 July 1962.
90. "Fair and Equal Treatment for All Subjects," *The Times*, 24 July 1962.
91. "British Law and Carmen Bryan," *The Observer*, 29 July 1962. During the first six months after the bill went into effect, of the 166 deportation orders issued by the Home Secretary, 108 were citizens of the Irish Republic. See Extract of Hansard Debate, 7 February 1963, DO 175/90, TNA; and Bailkin, "Leaving Home," 852–882.
92. List of March Slogans, n.d., Claudia Jones Memorial Collection, Box 1, Folder 29, Schomburg Center for Research in Black Culture. For more on the March on Washington held around the world, see Mary Dudziak, "The 1963 March on Washington: At Home and Abroad," *Review of French and American Studies* 107 (2006):, 61–76.
93. Committee of Afro-Asian Caribbean Organisations Press Release, 22 August 1963, Claudia Jones Memorial Collection, Box 1, Folder 29, Schomburg Center for Research in Black Culture, New York, NY. See also "March to U.S. Embassy: Solidarity Day," *Daily Worker*, 23 August 1963.
94. Committee of Afro-Asian Caribbean Organisations Press Release, 22 August 1963, Claudia Jones Memorial Collection, Box 1, Folder 29, Schomburg Center for Research in Black Culture, New York, NY.
95. "London Solidarity March," *West Indian Gazette*, 13 September 1963; List of March Slogans, n.d., Claudia Jones Memorial Collection, Box 1, Folder 29, Schomburg Center for Research in Black Culture.
96. Michael Stewart to Bernard Floud, 8 September 1965, FO 371/183147, TNA.
97. Miss M. Cooke to Bernard Floud, 21 August 1965, FO 371/183147, TNA.

98. Bernard Floud to Michael Stewart, 30 August 1965, FO 371/183147, TNA.
99. Secretary of State Memo, 23 September 1965, FO 371/183147, TNA.

Chapter 6

1. "Four Men Fight Pub Colour-Bar," *Daily Herald,* 14 September 1964.
2. "Colour Bar at London Pub: Four Stage Sit-In," *Peace News,* 18 September 1964.
3. "Intense Passions over Colour," *The Times,* 17 September 1964; see also "Elections and Racial Hypocrisy," *West Indian Gazette,* 19 October 1964.
4. In January1965 the Dartmouth Arms pub would again make news as the Brockley International Friendship Association led a picket outside of the club to protest its "colour bar" practices. See http://transpont.blogspot.com/2012/02/history-corner-colour-bar-pub-in-forest.html (accessed 30 December 2014).
5. "Matron Bans Coloured Nurses," *Daily Herald,* 7 September 1964; "Rent Problems of Coloured Students," *The Times,* 8 October 1964.
6. "Tories Disown Anti-Negro Posters," *The Guardian,* 8 October 1964; Alice Ritcherle, "Option out of Utopia," PhD Dissertation, University of Michigan, 2005, ch. 5.
7. "Candidate Seeks Apology," *The Guardian,* 11 March 1964; Paul Foot, *Immigration and Race in British Politics* (Hammondsworth, UK: Penguin Books, 1965), 63–79; Phillips and Phillips, *Windrush,* 199.
8. 1964 Labour Party Election Manifesto, *The New Britain,* ca. October 1964, Papers Related to the 1964 General Elections, Labour Party Records, Manchester Labour History Archives and Study Centre, Manchester, UK.
9. "A Sudden Storm over Smethwick," *The Times* 4 November 1964; " 'Leper' Jibe at M.P. Angers Opposition," *The Times,* 4 November 1964.
10. "Race: The Unmentionable Issue," *Peace News,* 25 September 1964.
11. "Race: The Unmentionable Issue," *Peace News,* 25 September 1964; "For Civil Right," *The Guardian,* 12 December 1964.
12. "Race: The Unmentionable Issue," *Peace News* 25 September 1964.
13. Benjamin Heinemann, *The Politics of the Powerless: A Study of the Campaign against Racial Discrimination* (London: Oxford University Press, 1972), 18; see also Howard Malchow, *Special Relations: The Americanization of Britain?* (Stanford, CA: Stanford University Press, 2011), 170–174
14. "Dr. Luther King's Warning," *West Indian Gazette,* December–January 1965; "Martin Luther King's Warning to Britain," *Peace News,* 11 December 1964. David Pitt also notes that Jones was involved in some of these early organizing efforts that would result in the formation of the Campaign Against Racial Discrimination. See "Dr. David Pitt's Pride and Sorrow," *West Indian Gazette,* February 1965.
15. "What Is CARD?" Brochure, ca. 1965, Uncatalogued CARD File, Black History Collection, Institute of Race Relations, London, UK.
16. Letter from Home Secretary, Frank Soskice, to Prime Minister, Harold Wilson, 4 January 1965, PREM 13/382, TNA; Letter from K. R. C. Pridham of the Foreign Office to Lord Caradon, British Representative to the United Nations, 1 January 1965, FO 371/178454, TNA; Parliamentary Sessional Papers, vol. xxviii, 1964–1965, Cmnd. 2739, London: HMSO, 1965.
17. Hansen, *Citizenship and Immigration in Postwar Britain,* 138–140, 144–146.
18. Jordanna Bailkin's recent work on decolonization in the imperial metropolis during the 1950s and 1960s also suggests that part of the international context for understanding British policy makers' ideas about the intent, scale and scope of race relations policy is tied to Cold War imperatives regarding the promotion of anti-communism in Africa. See Bailkin, *The Afterlives of Empire,* 117–118.
19. See Saladin Ambar, *Malcolm X at Oxford Union: Racial Politics in a Global Era* (New York: Oxford University Press, 2014); and Stephen Tuck, *The Night Malcolm X Spoke at the Oxford Union* (Berkeley: University of California Press, 2014).
20. Graeme Abernathy, " 'Not Just an American Problem': Malcolm X in Britain," *Atlantic Studies* 7 (September, 2010): 290–291; Joe Street, "Malcolm X, Smethwick and the

Influence of the African American Freedom Struggle on British Race Relations in the1960s," *Journal of Black Studies* 38 (July 2008): 932–950.

21. "Smethwick House Plan Opposed," *The Guardian,* 8 December 1964.

22. Alice Ritcherle, "Opting Out of Utopia: Race and Working Class Political Culture in Britain during the Age of Decolonization, 1948–1968," PhD Dissertation, University of Michigan, 2005, 218–220; Thomas F. Jackson, *From Civil Rights to Human Rights: Martin Luther King and the Struggle for Economic Justice* (Philadelphia: University of Pennsylvania Press, 2007), 177. In an address given at the University of Newcastle on the Tyne in 1967, King drew direct parallels between the ghettoization of Blacks and Asians in Britain and that of Black Americans. See Brian Ward, "A King in Newcastle: Martin Luther King, Jr. and British Race Relations, 1967–1968," *Georgia Historical Quarterly* 79, no. 3 (1995): 599–632.

23. "White Backlash in Leyton," *Magnet News,* 1 February 1965, Lambeth Archives, London, UK.

24. "Britain's Most Racist Election: The Story of Smethwick 50 Years On," *The Guardian,* 15 October 2014.

25. 1964 Labour Party Election Manifesto, *The New Britain,* ca. October 1964, Papers Related to the 1964 General Elections, Labour Party Records, Manchester Labour History Archives and Study Centre, Manchester, UK.

26. "Labour Plan to Outlaw Colour Bar," *The Observer,* 28 September 1958.

27. See Memo, National Executive Committee to M.P. Candidates and Party Workers, "The Labour Party and Commonwealth Immigration," 1962–1963; Flyer, "Immigration ... The Facts," Labour Party Archives Research Department Files on Race Relations and Immigration, File 1962–3, Box 1, Manchester Labour History Archives and Study Centre, Manchester, UK.

28. Keith Hindell, "The Genesis of the Race Relations Bill," *Political Quarterly* 36, no. 4 (October 1965): 390–391.

29. House of Commons Debate, 27 November 1963, Vol. 685, col. 367; Gavin Shaffer, "Legislating against Hatred: Meaning and Motive in Section Six of the Race Relations Act of 1965," *Twentieth Century British History* 25, no. 2 (2014): 253.

30. Memo from National Executive Cmte of Labour Party to M.P.s Candidates, and Party Workers Regarding Policy on Commonwealth Immigration, *The Labour Party and Commonwealth Immigration,* undated, but file date 1962–3, Manchester Labour History Archives, Manchester, UK.

31. Quoted from J. E. Richardson and B. Franklin, " 'Dear Editor': Race, Readers' Letters and the Local Press," *Political Quarterly* (2003): 184–185.

32. "10-Point 'Colour' Plan by Mr. Griffiths," *The Times,* 1 October 1964.

33. "Vile—It's All in Black and White," *The Times,* 13 October 1964; "Mr. Gordon Walker Tells of 'Lies,' " *The Guardian,* 15 October 1964.

34. "Mr. Wilson Rides Heckling on Immigration," *The Guardian,* 7 October 1964.

35. Ibid.

36. "No Compromise on Racial Challenge," *The Guardian,* 17 November 1964.

37. United Nations Declaration on the Elimination of All Forms of Racial Discrimination, LAB 13/1936, TNA.

38. Ibid.

39. Paul Gordon Lauren, *Power and Prejudice: The Politics and Diplomacy of Racial Discrimination* (Boulder, CO: Westview Press, 1996), 239–248.

40. Iyiola Solanke, *Making Anti-Racial Discrimination Law* (London: Routledge, 2009), 48–52.

41. Lauren, *Power and Prejudice,* 246.

42. For example, see Erik Bleich, *Race Politics in Britain and France: Ideas and Policymaking since the 1960s* (Cambridge, UK: Cambridge University Press, 2003), 44–47.

43. Letter from K. R. C. Pridham, Foreign Office to Home Office, 8 December 1964, FO 371/178454, TNA.

44. "£100 Fines for Colour Bar," *The Guardian,* 8 April 1965; Hindell, "The Genesis of the Race Relations Bill of 1965," 396.

45. Hindell, "The Genesis of the Race Relations Bill," 392–393; Heinemann, *The Politics of the Powerless,* 113–114.

46. "Race Bill 'Better Withdrawn,'" *The Guardian,* 13 April 1965.

47. Preface, *Against Racial Discrimination and Incitement: What Should Be in the Bill?* London District Committee of the Communist Party, 9 April 1965, CP/CON/RACE/1/5, Manchester Labour History Library and Study Centre, Manchester, UK.

48. Movement for Colonial Freedom Press Release, 8 April 1965, CP/LON/RACE/1/8, Manchester Labour History Archives, Manchester, UK.

49. "Government and Race Relations," *The Guardian,* 10 April 1965; "Race and the Law," *The Observer,* 11 April 1965.

50. Lena Jeger, "Double Talk," *The Guardian,* 9 April 1965.

51. "Race Relations Bill," *The Times,* 20 April 1965.

52. "Race Relations Bill," *The Times,* 20 April 1965; "Race Bill Welcomed By Labour Lawyers," *The Guardian* 10 April 1965.

53. Heinemann, *Politics of the Powerless,* 23.

54. Heinemann, *Politics of the Powerless,* 20, 23; E. J. B. Rose, *Colour and Citizenship: A Report of British Race Relation* (Oxford: Oxford University Press, 1969).

55. Colin McGlashan, "Integrating Britain's Anti-Racialists," *The Observer,* 24 January 1965.

56. "Race Bill 'Virtually Useless,'" *The Observer,* 11 April 1965.

57. Ibid.

58. "Teeth For Anti-Racial Law Urged," *The Guardian,* 15 March 1965; "Mr. Thorneycroft in Alliance with CARD?" *The Guardian,* 4 May 1965.

59. CARD Proposals for Legislation, April 1965, LAB 8/3070, TNA; Jeffrey Jowell, "The Administrative Enforcement of Laws against Discrimination," *Public Law* (Summer 1965): 119–186; "Anti-Racial Body Gains Support," *The Guardian,* 22 February 1965.

60. CARD Proposals for Legislation, April 1965, LAB 8/3070, TNA.

61. Ibid.

62. "New Laws to Combat Race Hate," *The Observer,* 7 March 1965.

63. CARD Proposals for Legislation, April 1965, LAB 8/3070, TNA.

64. Ibid.

65. Letter from Lord Chancellor's Office to Home Office, 13 April 1965, LAB 8/3070, TNA; see also Letter from Maurice Foley to Frank Sockice, 23 April 1965, LAB 3070, TNA; and Letter from Frank Sockice to Maurice Foley, 26 April 1965, LAB 8/3070, TNA.

66. Letter from CARD Organizing Secretary, 28 April 1965, CP/LON/RACE/1/8, Communist Party Records, Manchester Labour History Archives and Study Centre, Manchester, UK.

67. "Big Change in Race Relations Bill," *The Guardian,* 30 April 1965.

68. "Big Change in Race Relations Bill," *The Guardian,* 30 April 1965; "Government and Race Relations," *The Guardian,* 10 April 1965; "Race and the Law," *The Observer,* 11 April 1965.

69. "Mr. Thorneycroft on Tory Amendment," *The Guardian,* 4 May 1965; Heinemann, *The Politics of the Powerless,* 120.

70. Letter to the Editor of *The Observer* from David Pitt, 16 June 1965, CP/LON/RACE/1/9, Communist Party Records, Manchester Labour History Archives and Study Centre.

71. "Common Voice for the Coloured," *The Guardian,* 26 July 1965.

72. David Pitt, Opening Speech, National Founding Convention for the Campaign of Racial Discrimination, July 1965, CARD Papers, Institute of Commonwealth Studies, London.

73. Ibid.

74. "What Is Card?" Undated brochure, Uncatalogued CARD File, Black History Collection, Institute of Race Relations; Marion Glean, "Whatever Happened to CARD?" *Race Today,* 1972 or 1973, Uncatalogued CARD File, Black History Collection, Institute of Race Relations.

75. Marion Glean, "What Ever Happened to CARD?" *Race Today* 1972 or 1973, Uncatalogued CARD File, Black History Collection, Institute of Race Relations.

76. Heinemann, *Politics of the Powerless,* 27. For more on Ella Baker, see Barbara Ransby, *Ella Baker and the Black Freedom Movement: A Radical Democratic Vision* (Chapel Hill: University of North Carolina Press, 2005).

77. As quoted in Heinemann, *Politics of the Powerless*, 28.

78. Peniel E. Joseph, "The Black Power Movement: A State of the Field," *Journal of American History* (December 2000); 751–776; see also Peniel Joseph, *Waiting 'Til the Midnight Hour: A Narrative History of Black Power in America* (New York: Henry Holt, 2006).

79. David Pitt, Opening Speech, National Founding Convention for the Campaign of Racial Discrimination, July 1965, CARD Papers, Institute of Commonwealth Studies, London.

80. Selma James, "Memorandum on CARD's Future Work," undated, ca. spring 1965, Uncatalogued CARD File, Black History Collection, Institute of Race Relations.

81. CARD Constitution, adapted at National Founding Convention, July 1965, CARD Papers, Institute of Commonwealth Studies, London; Heinemann, *Politics of the Powerless*, 41–42, 47; see also "The Choice For Immigrants," *The Guardian*, 20 July 1965.

82. Resolutions, CARD National Founding Convention Papers, July 1965, Uncatalogued CARD Papers, Black History Collection, Institute of Race Relations.

83. Ibid.

84. Resolutions, CARD National Founding Convention Papers, July 1965, Uncatalogued CARD Papers, Black History Collection, Institute of Race Relation; CARD Secretary Annual Report for 1965, Uncatalogued CARD Papers, Black History Collection, Institute of Race Relations.

85. Heinemann, *Politics of the Powerless*, 50.

86. "David Pitt," in *The Oxford Companion to Black British History*, ed. David Dabydeen, John Gilmore, and Cecily Jones (Oxford: Oxford University Press, 2007), 366–368.

87. Lydia Lindsay, "Split Labor Phenomenon"; Heinemann, *Politics of the Powerless*, 87–90.

88. Parliamentary Sessional Papers, Vol. xxviii, 1964–1965 Cmnd. 2739 (London: HMSO, 1965); Spencer, *British Immigration Policy since 1939*, 134–136; Hansen, *Citizenship and Immigration in Postwar Britain*, 109–111, 129, 150–152; Layton-Henry, *The Politics of Immigration*, 75–78; Paul, *Whitewashing Britain*, 166, 174.

89. Parliamentary Sessional Papers, Vol. xxviii, 1964–1965, Cmnd. 2739 (London: HMSO, 1965); see also "National Group Will Co-ordinate Local Aid Programmes," *The Guardian*, 3 August 1965.

90. CARD Pamphlet, "The White Paper: A Spur to Racialism," undated, ca. August 1965, A. Sivanandan Collection, University of Warwick, Coventry, UK.

91. "'Unnecessary Step Back' on Immigration," *The Guardian*, 3 August 1965; "Immigration Policy Called 'Pandering,'" *The Observer*, 8 August 1965.

92. "'Unnecessary Step Back' on Immigration," *The Guardian*, 3 August 1965.

93. "London Party May Back Dr. Pitt," *The Guardian*, 8 August 1965.

94. Confidential Memo Port of Spain to Commonwealth Relations Office, 1 August 1965, PREM 13/384, TNA.

95. H. L. Lindo, "In Defence of the Emigres," *The Guardian*, 28 July 1965.

96. "'Unnecessary Step Back' on Immigration," *The Guardian*, 3 August 1965.

97. "'Unnecessary Step Back' on Immigration," *The Guardian*, 3 August 1965; "Immigration Policy Called 'Pandering,'" *The Observer*, 8 August 1965.

98. "CARD Men Resign from Party," *The Guardian*, 7 August 1965.

99. "London Party May Back Dr. Pitt," *The Guardian*, 9 August 1965.

100. "Immigrant Organisations Plan Boycott," *The Guardian*, 4 October 1965; see also "White Will Test for Colour-Bar," *The Observer*, 24 October 1965.

101. CARD Constitution, July 1965, CARD Papers, Institute of Commonwealth Studies, London.

102. Letter from David Pitt and Hamza Alavi to CARD membership, 21 October 1965, as quoted in Heinemann, *Politics of the Powerless*, 52; This description is also cited in Memo, Nurl Islam, General Secretary, National Federation of Pakistani Associations of Great Britain, undated, ca. October 1965, Uncatalogued CARD Papers, Black History Collection, Institute of Race Relations.

103. "Immigrant Organisations Plan Boycott," *The Guardian*, 4 October 1965.

104. Memo, Nurl Islam, General Secretary, National Federation of Pakistani Associations of Great Britain, undated, ca. October 1965, Uncatalogued CARD Papers, Black History Collection, Institute of Race Relations.

105. Jeff Crawford to David Pitt, 22 October 1965, Uncatalogued CARD File, Black History Collection, Institute of Race Relations; see also Rosalind Wild, "Black Was the Colour of Our Fight, Black Power in Britain, 1955–1976," PhD Dissertation, University of Sheffield, 2008, 61.
106. "Immigrant Organisations Plan Boycott," *The Guardian*, 4 October 1965.
107. "Immigrants to Unite against Racialism," *The Guardian*, 27 September 1965.
108. "Immigrant Organisations Plan Boycott," *The Guardian*, 4 October 1965.
109. "Protection Body for West Indians," *The Guardian*, 16 August 1965.
110. "Coloured Immigrants Set up Vigilantes," *The Observer*, 15 August 1965; "Protection Body for West Indians," *The Guardian*, 16 August 1965; Harry Goulbourne, "The Contribution of West Indian Groups to British Politics," in *Black Politics in Britain*, ed. Harry Goulbourne (Aldershot, UK: Avebury, 1990), 101–103.
111. Heinemann, *Politics of the Powerless*, 65–66; see also Winston James, "Migration, Racism, and Identify Formation" in *Inside Babylon: The Caribbean Diaspora in Britain*, ed. Winston James and Clive Harris (London: Verso Press, 1993), 240.
112. Memo, "Standing Conference of West Indian Organisations," 24 February 1965, HO 342/83, TNA; see also Special Branch Report, 17 February 1965, HO 342/83, TNA; Notes of Home Office Meeting with Standing Conference of West Indian Organisations, 15 March 1965, HO 325/83, TNA.
113. "Coloured Immigrants Set up Vigilantes," *The Observer*, 15 August 1965.
114. "Take Smethwick out of the Headlines: Lunatic Fringe at Work—Minister," *The Guardian*, 12 June 1965; "'Lunatics' Burn Klan Crosses," *The Guardian*, 14 June 1965; see also "Fiery Cross Put in Indian's Door," *The Guardian*, 8 June 1965, and "Report on Klan May Go to DPP," *The Guardian*, 1 July 1965.
115. "Protection Body for West Indians," *The Guardian*, 16 August 1965.
116. Ibid.
117. Ibid.
118. Mike Sewell, "British Responses to Martin Luther King Jr and the Civil Rights Movement, 1954–68," in *The Making of Martin Luther King and the Civil Rights Movement*, ed. Brian Ward and Tony Badger (New York: New York University Press, 1996), 194–212.
119. Quoted from *American Experience Eyes on the Prize* transcript, http://www.pbs.org/wgbh/amex/eyesontheprize/about/pt_106.html, accessed 1 February 2015.
120. "Court Threat on Choice of School," *The Guardian*, 6 October 1965; "Violence against Coloured Immigrants 'Increasing,'" *The Guardian*, 17 November 1965; "Immigrants See Minister about Assaults," *The Guardian*, 18 November 1965.
121. "Violence against Coloured Immigrants 'Increasing,'" *The Guardian*, 17 November 1965; "Immigrants See Minister about Assaults," *The Guardian*, 18 November 1965.
122. Neville Maxwell, *The Power of Negro Action* (London, 1965), 37–38, Duke University Rubenstein Library Pamphlet Collection.
123. Heinemann, *Politics of the Powerless*, 87.
124. "CARD 'Too Soft' Say Migrants," *The Observer*, 27 February 1966.
125. Ibid.
126. Erik Bleich, *Race Politics in Britain and France*, 58–59.
127. Ibid.
128. Bleich, *Race Politics in Britain and France*, 71–72; "Jenkins Going into the Attack against Racial Prejudice," *The Observer*, 20 February 1966.
129. CARD, "How to Expose Discrimination," 1966, Black History Collection, Institute of Race Relations, http://www.irr.org.uk/black_history_resource/Racial_Discrimination.pdf, accessed 1 February 2015.
130. Heinemann, *Politics of the Powerless*, 132.
131. "How To Expose Discrimination," Uncatalogued CARD Papers, Black History Collection, Institute of Race Relations, http://www.irr.org.uk/black_history_resource/Racial_Discrimination.pdf, accessed 5 July 2015; Heinemann, *Politics of the Powerless*, 132, n. 157; see also "Bus Work Ban on Turbans in 50 Racial Complaints," *Yorkshire Post* 25 August 1966 and "Welfare Delivering the Goods" *New Society*, 1 September 1966, Uncatalogued CARD Papers, Black History Collection, Institute of Race Relations.

132. CARD, "How To Expose Discrimination," 1966, Black History Collection, Institute of Race Relations, http://www.irr.org.uk/black_history_resource/Racial_Discrimination. pdf, accessed 5 July 2015.

133. "It's No Fun Being a Brown Briton," *Sunday Telegraph,* 11 September 1966.

134. "'Waste' of Indian Graduates," *The Observer,* 29 August 1966; see also "50 Complaints of Racial Discrimination," *Leicester Mercury,* 29 August 1966; and "Test of Racial Prejudice," *Manchester Guardian,* 30 August 1966, Uncatalogued CARD Papers, Black History Collection, Institute of Race Relations.

135. CARD, "How to Expose Discrimination," 1966, Black History Collection, Institute of Race Relations, http://www.irr.org.uk/black_history_resource/Racial_Discrimination. pdf, accessed 5 July 2015. For references to the diaries that the individual field workers maintained as part of the Summer Project, see Dipak Nandy, "Race and Community," 22 May 1968, CARD Papers, Black Cultural Archives.

136. Diary of Patricia Quick, quoted in Dipak Nandy, "Race and Community," Mayor's Lecture at University of Kent, 22 May 1968, CARD papers, Black Cultural Archives.

137. CARD Report on Racial Discrimination, Case 3, April 1967, CARD Papers, Black Cultural Archives.

138. CARD Report on Racial Discrimination, Case 10, April 1967, CARD Papers, Black Cultural Archives.

139. CARD Report on Racial Discrimination, Case 4, April 1967, CARD Papers, Black Cultural Archives.

140. CARD Report on Racial Discrimination, Cases 14 and 16, April 1967, CARD Papers, Black Cultural Archives.

141. CARD Report on Racial Discrimination, Cases 17 and 18, April 1967, CARD Papers, Black Cultural Archives.

142. CARD Report on Racial Discrimination, Cases 20–25, April 1967, CARD Papers, Black Cultural Archives.

143. CARD Report on Racial Discrimination, Cases 27–31, April 1967, CARD Papers, Black Cultural Archives; see Chapter 2.

144. CARD Report on Racial Discrimination, Case 38, April 1967, CARD Papers, Black Cultural Archives.

145. CARD Report on Racial Discrimination, Cases 36–38, April 1967, CARD Papers, Black Cultural Archives.

146. CARD Report on Racial Discrimination, Case 39, April 1967, CARD Papers, Black Cultural Archives.

147. CARD Report on Racial Discrimination, April 1967, CARD Papers, Black Cultural Archives.

148. Report of the Race Relations Board for 1966–1967 (London: Her Majesty's Stationary Office, 1967), 7, 26.

149. Report of the Race Relations Board for 1966–1967 (London: Her Majesty's Stationary Office, 1967), 7, 26. See also "'Bring Homes, Jobs under Race Act': Ghetto Warning by Board," *The Times,* 28 April 1967.

150. On press coverage of reaction to the PEP report, including editorials supporting the extension of the Race Relation Act, see "Settled Immigrants Find Increasing Discrimination," *The Guardian,* 18 April 1967; "New Laws Likely on Race Relations," *The Guardian,* 18 April 1967; "David Marquand, MP: Portrait of Prejudice," 19 April 1967; "Stronger Race Laws Needed," *The Guardian,* 28 April 1967; "Immigrants Face a 'Filter' When Seeking Jobs," *The Times,* 18 April 1967; "By Race and Colour," *The Times,* 18 April 1967; "The Lords: Challenge of Racial Discrimination: Clear Legislation Can Help," *The Times,* 7 June 1967. See also Heinemann, 136–139; James Hampshire, "Immigration and Race Relation," in *The Labour Governments, 1964–1970,* ed. Peter Dorey (London: Routledge, 2006), 324–325.

151. W. W. Daniel, *Racial Discrimination in England: Based on the PEP Report* (Hammondsworth, UK: Penguin Books, 1968); Harry Street, Geoffrey Howe, and Geoffrey Bindman, *Anti-Discrimination Legislation: The Street Report* (London: Political and Economic Planning, 1967).

152. "Tighter Race Laws for Britain," *The Times*, 26 July 1967.

153. "British Ban on Stokely Carmichael," *The Guardian*, 28 July 1967; "Mainspring of Black Power," *The Observer*, 23 July 1967; Peniel Joseph, *Stokely: A Life* (New York: Basic Books, 2014), 197–200.

154. "Marchers in KKK Country," *The Guardian*, 18 June 1966; "Civil Rights Movement Is Split," *The Observer*, 10 July 1966; "No Unity on Negro Strategy in the Struggle over Civil Rights," *The Guardian*, 23 August 1966; "Stokely Carmichael: A Profile," *The Guardian*, 11 April 1967.

155. Peniel, *Waiting 'Til The Midnight Hour*; Kalbir Shukra, *The Changing Patterns of Black Politics in Britain* (London: Pluto Press, 1999), 24–25.

156. "Third Night of Riots in Nashville," *The Guardian*, 12 April 1967; "Curb on 'Black Power' Chief?" *The Observer*, 25 June 1967.

157. Annual Report of the Race Relations Board, 1966–1967, 21; "Birmingham Is No Detroit but There Are Storm Signals," *The Times*, 27 July 1967; Bleich, *Race Politics in Britain and France*, 75–76.

158. "Race Problem in Great Britain," *Ebony*, November 1965; "White Paper Gives Fuel to the Militants," *The Observer*, 8 August 1965. See also "The Choice for Immigrants," *The Guardian*, 20 July 1965; and "Hit White Man Back, Says New Militant Group," *The Observer*, 4 July 1965; see also Michael Abdul Malik, *From Michael de Freitas to Michael X* (London: Andre Deutsch, 1968); and Jon Williams, *Michael X: A Life in Black and White* (London: Century, 2008).

159. "The Choice for Immigrants," *The Guardian*, 20 July 1965; "White Paper Gives Fuel to the Militants," *The Observer*, 8 August 1965.

160. R. E. R. Bunce and Paul Field, "Obi B. Egbuna, C. L. R. James and the Birth of Black Power in Britain: Black Radicalism, 1967–1972," *Twentieth Century British History* 22, no. 3 (2011): 393–414; Wild, "'Black Was the Colour of Our Fight'," 65–116.

161. C. L. R. James, "Black Power" speech delivered in London, 1967, https://www.marxists.org/archive/james-clr/works/1967/black-power.htm, accessed 1 February 2015.

162. "Black Power Leader Leaves Mark on Britain," *The Observer*, 6 August 1967.

163. Heinemann, *Politics of the Powerless*, 187–191.

164. Ibid., 190.

165. Heinemann, *Politics of the Powerless*, 191; "Battle for Power among Colour Bar Campaigners," *The Observer*, 12 November 1967; "Tempers Frayed as Extremists Fail to Oust CARD Leaders," *The Guardian*, 6 November 1967.

166. "Tempers Frayed as Extremist Fail to Oust CARD Leaders," *The Guardian*, 6 November 1967.

167. Johnny James, Press Interview Statement, 9 November 1967, Uncatalogued CARD Papers, Black History Collection, Institute of Race Relations.

168. Gavin Schaffer, "Legislating against Hatred: Meaning and Motive in Section Six of the Race Relations Act of 1965," *Twentieth Century British History* 25, no. 2 (2014): 271–273.

169. Johnny James, Press Interview Statement, 9 November 1967, Uncatalogued CARD Papers, Institute of Race Relations.

170. "CARD Walk-Out in Protest against Election 'Takeover,'" *The Guardian*, 4 December 1967.

171. Ibid.

172. "'Militants' Certain to Pack More Punch If CARD Splits," *The Guardian*, 2 December 1967; see Brent Area CARD Committee Flyer, March 1969, Uncatalogued CARD Papers, Black History Collection, Institute of Race Relations; Flyer of CARD Election Results, 19 January 1969, Uncatalogued CARD Papers, Black History Collection, Institute of Race Relations.

Epilogue

1. "Why So Many Find the Mark Duggan Verdict Hard to Accept," *The Guardian*, 19 January 2014; "Police 'Lawfully Killed' Unarmed Mark Duggan," *The Voice*, 1 August 2014.

2. Coverage of the case was extensive both nationally and internationally. See "Mark Duggan: Profile of Tottenham Police Shooting Victim," *The Guardian,* 8 August 2011; "Riots in Tottenham after Mark Duggan Shooting Protest," *BBC News,* 7 August 2011; "Rioting Widens in London on 3rd Night of Unrest," *New York Times,* 8 August 2011.

3. Darcus Howe BBC Interview on Riots, https://www.youtube.com/watch?v=mzDQCT0A Jcw, accessed 6 July 2015.

4. Robin Bunce and Paul Field, *Darcus Howe: A Political Biography* (London: Bloomsbury, 2014), 187–216.

5. Ros Howell Interview, *Windrush: A New Generation* (London: BBC2, 1998).

6. Bunce and Field, *Darcus Howe,* 27–136; Rosalind Wild, "Black Was the Colour of Our Fight!' Black Power in Britain, 1955–1976," PhD thesis, University of Sheffield, 2008; Anne-Marie Angelo, "The Black Panthers in London, 1967–1972," *Radical History Review* 103 (2009): 17–35.

7. One of the most influential text that tackles the relationship between state power and the structural and regulatory dimensions of anti-Black racism in Britain and beyond remains Stuart Hall, Chas Critcher, Tony Jefferson, John Clarke, and Brian Roberts, *Policing the Crisis* (Basingstoke: Palgrave Macmillan, 2013, 2nd ed.).

8. Bunce and Field, *Darcus Howe,* 93–152.

9. Kester Aspden, *The Hounding of David Oluwale* (London: Vintage Books, 2008); "What Caused the 1985 Tottenham Broadwater Farm Riot? *BBC News,* 3 March 2014 http://www.bbc.com/news/uk-england-london-26362633, accessed 1 February 2015; "Dorothy 'Cherry' Groce Inquest Finds Police Failures Contributed to Her Death," *The Guardian,* 10 July 2014.

10. Sir William MacPherson, *The Stephen Lawrence Inquiry,* Cmd 4262-1, February, 1999, chap. 6 https://www.gov.uk/government/uploads/system/uploads/attachment_data/file/277111/4262.pdf, accessed 17 February 2015; see also Doreen Lawrence, *And Still I Rise: A Mother's Search for Justice* (London: Faber and Faber, 2006), 180–205; "The Macpherson Report: Summary," *The Guardian,* 24 February 1999.

11. Iyiola Solanke, *Making Anti-Discrimination Law: A Comparative History of Social Action and Anti-Racial Discrimination Law* (Abington, UK: Routledge, 2009), 63–65.

BIBLIOGRAPHY

Audio/Visual Material

British Pathe Footage of *Empire Windrush*, 22 June 1948, Gaumont British Newsreel, *Reuters*.
London Is the Place for Me: Trinidadian Calypso in London, 1950–1956 (London: Honest Jon's Records, 2002).
Windrush, DVD, David Upshal, Director, London: BBC, 1998.

Black Cultural Archives, London, UK

Runnymede Collection
Periodical Collection

Donald Hinds Private Papers, London, UK

Private Collection of Claudia Jones Papers

Duke University Libraries, Durham, NC

British Parliamentary Papers
Pamphlet Collections

Imperial War Museum, London, UK

Sound Archives
From War to Windrush Exhibition

Institute of Commonwealth Studies, London, UK

CARD Files
C.L.R. James Papers

Institute of Race Relations, London, UK

Periodicals Collection
Black History Collection

Lambeth Archives, London, UK

Harry Jacobs Collection
Periodicals Collection

London Metropolitan Archives, London, UK

National Council of Social Services Records
West Indian Correspondences Files

Manchester Labour History Archive and Study Centre, Manchester, UK

Labour Party Archives Research Department Files on Race Relations and Immigration
Papers of the Manchester Negro Association
Communist Party Records
Labour Party Archives, International Department Records
Labour Party General Secretary's Papers
Labour Party Records, Papers Related to the 1964 General Elections

Metropolitan University Trades Union Congress Library

Trades Union Congress Annual Proceedings

The National Archives (Kew Gardens)

Records of the Colonial Office
Records of the Ministry of Labour
Records of the Home Office
Records of the Metropolitan Police Department
Records of the Dominion Office
Records of the Foreign Office

School of Oriental and African Studies, London, UK

Movement for Colonial Freedom Papers

Schomburg Center For Research in Black Culture, New York, NY

Claudia Jones Memorial Collection
Claudia Jones Research Collection
Edric and Pearl Connor Papers

University of Warwick, Warwick, UK

A. Sivanandan Collection

Newspapers

The Guardian
The Observer
Daily Gleaner
New Chronicle and Daily Dispatch
Picture Post

Manchester Guardian
West Indian Gazette
Daily Mail
Daily Mirror
Daily Herald
Daily Express
Daily Worker (London)
Kensington News and West London Times
The Times
New Statesman
Sydney Morning Herald
Daily Graphic (Ghana)
The Star (South Africa)
Washington Post
New York Times
Trinidad Guardian
Evening Standard
Magnet News
Flamingo
Peace News

Dissertations

Duncan, K. Natanya. "The 'Efficient Womanhood' of the Universal Negro Improvement Association: 1919-1930." PhD Dissertation, University of Florida, 2009.

Edwards, Brent. "Black Globality: The International Shape of Black Intellectual Culture." PhD Dissertation, Columbia University, 1997.

Goldthree, Reena Nicole. "Shifting Loyalties: World War I and the Conflicted Politics of Patriotism in the British Caribbean." PhD Dissertation, Duke University, 2011.

Prais, Jinny. "Imperial Travelers: The Formation of West African Urban Culture, Identity and Citizenship in London and Accra, 1925-1935." PhD Dissertation, University of Michigan, 2008.

Ritcherle, Alice. "Opting out of Utopia: Race and Working Class Political Culture in Britain during the Age of Decolonization, 1948-1968." PhD Dissertation, University of Michigan, 2005.

Wild, Rosalind. "'Black Was the Colour of Our Fight': Black Power in Britain, 1955-1976." PhD Dissertation, University of Sheffield, 2008.

Published Sources

Abernathy, Graeme. "'Not Just an American Problem': Malcolm X in Britain." *Atlantic Studies* 7 (September 2010): 285-307.

Adi, Hakim. "Amy Ashwood Garvey and the Nigerian Progress Union." In *Gendering the African Diaspora: Women, Culture and Historical Change in the Caribbean and Nigerian Hinterland.* Edited by Judith Byfield, LaRay Denzer, and Anthea Morrison. Bloomington, IN: Indiana University Press, 2010.

_____. "The Comintern and Black Workers in Britain and France, 1919-1937." *Immigrants and Minorities* 28 (2010): 224-245.

_____. *Pan-Africanism and Communism: The Communist International, Africa and the Diaspora, 1919-1939.* Trenton, NJ: Africa New World Press, 2013.

_____. *West Africans in Britain, 1900-1960: Nationalism, Pan-Africanism and Communism.* London: Lawrence and Wishart, 1998.

Alexander, Claire E. *The Art of Being Black: The Creation of Black British Youth Identities.* Oxford: Oxford University Press, 1996.

Ambar, Saladin. *Malcolm X at Oxford Union: Racial Politics in a Global Era.* New York: Oxford University Press, 2014.

Anderson, Carol. *Eyes off the Prize: The United Nations and the African American Struggle for Human Rights, 1944–1955.* Cambridge, UK: Cambridge University Press, 2003.

Anderson, Jervis. "England in Jamaica: Memories from a Colonial Boyhood." *The American Scholar* 69, no. 2 (Spring 2000): 15–30.

Angelo, Anne-Marie. "The Black Panthers in London, 1967–1972." *Radical History Review* 103 (2009): 17–35.

Anstey, Roger. "The Pattern of British Abolitionism in the Eighteenth and Nineteenth Centuries." In *Anti-Slavery, Religion, and Reform: Essays in Memory of Roger Anstey.* Edited by Christine Bolt and Seymour Drescher. Folkestone, UK: William Dawson and Sons, 1980.

Aspden, Kester. *The Hounding of David Oluwale.* London: Vintage Books, 2008.

Bailkin, Jordanna. *The Afterlife of Empire.* Berkeley: University of California Press, 2012.

_____. "Leaving Home: The Politics of Deportation in Postwar Britain." *Journal of British Studies* 47, no. 4 (2008): 852–882.

Banerjee, Sukanya. *Becoming Imperial Citizens: Indians in the Late Victorian Empire.* Durham, NC: Duke University Press, 2010.

Banton, Michael. *White and Coloured: The Behavior of British People Towards Coloured Immigrants.* New Jersey: Rutgers University Press, 1960.

Bartels, Emile C. "Too Many Blackamoors: Deportation, Discrimination and Elizabeth I." *Studies in English Literature* 46, no. 2 (2006): 305–322.

Baucom, Ian. *Out of Place, Englishness, Empire and Locations of Identity.* Princeton, NJ: Princeton University Press, 1999.

Blackburn, Robin. *The Overthrow of Colonial Slavery, 1776–1848.* London: Verso Press, 1988.

Bleby, Henry. *The Reign of Terror: A Narrative of Facts Concerning Ex-Governor Eyre, George William Gordon and the Jamaica Atrocities.* London: William Nichols, 1866.

Bleich, Erik. *Race Politics in Britain and France: Ideas and Policymaking since the 1960s.* Cambridge, UK: Cambridge University Press, 2003.

Bolland, O. Nigel. *On the March: Labour Rebellions in the British Caribbean, 1934–1939.* Kingston: Ian Randle, 1995.

_____. *The Politics of Labour in the British Caribbean: The Social Origins of the Authoritarianism and Democracy in the Labour Movement.* Kingston, Jamaica: Ian Randle, 2001.

Borstelmann, Thomas. *The Cold War and the Color Line: American Race Relations in the Global Arena.* Cambridge, MA: Harvard University Press, 2001.

_____. "Jim Crow's Coming Out: Race Relations and American Foreign Policy in the Truman Years." *Presidential Studies Quarterly* 29, no. 3 (2004): 549–569.

Bousquet, Ben, and Colin Douglas. *West Indian Women at War: British Racism in World War II.* London: Lawrence and Wishart, 1991.

Boyce, D. George. *Decolonisation and the British Empire, 1775–1997.* London: Macmillan Press, 1999.

Boyd, Monica. "Family and Personal Networks in International Migration: Recent Developments and New Agendas." *International Migration Review* 23, no. 3 (Autumn 1989): 638–670.

Brah, Avtar. *Cartographies of Diaspora: Contesting Identities.* New York: Routledge, 1996.

Bressey, Caroline. "It's Only Political Correctness—Race and Racism in British History." In *New Geographies of Race and Racism.* Edited by Claire Dwyer and Caroline Bressey. Burlington, VT: Ashgate, 2008.

Brooks, Dennis. *Race and Labor in London Transport.* London: Oxford University Press, 1975.

Brown, Christopher L. "Empire without Slaves: British Concepts of Emancipation in the Age of the American Revolution." *William and Mary Quarterly* LVI (April 1999): 273–306.

_____. *Moral Capital: Foundations of British Abolitionism.* Chapel Hill: University of North Carolina Press, 2006.

Brown, Jacqueline Nassy. *Dropping Anchor, Setting Sail: Geographies of Race in Black Liverpool.* Princeton, NJ: Princeton University Press, 2005.

Brown, Wendy. *Regulating Aversion: Tolerance in the Age of Identity and Empire*. Princeton, NJ: Princeton University Press, 2006.

Bryan, Beverley, Stella Dadzie, and Suzanne Scafe. *The Heart of the Race: Black Women's Lives in Britain*. London: Virago Press, 1985.

Bryan, Patrick. *The Jamaican People, 1880–1902*. Kingston, Jamaica: University of the West Indies Press, 2000.

Buckley, Norman. *Slaves in Redcoats: The British West India Regiments, 1795–1815*. New Haven, CT: Yale University Press, 1979.

Buettner, Elizabeth. " 'Would You Let Your Daughter Mayy a Negro?': Race and Sex in 1950s Britain." In *Gender, Labour, War and Empire: Essays on Modern Britain*. Edited by Phillipa Levine and Susan R. Grayzel. London: Palgrave Macmillan, 2009.

Bunce, R. E. R., and Paul Field. "Obi B. Egbuna, C. L. R. James and the Birth of Black Power in Britain: Black Radicalism, 1967–1972." *Twentieth Century British History* 22, no. 3 (2011): 393–414.

Bunce, Robin, and Paul Field. *Darcus Howe: A Political Biography*. London: Bloomsbury, 2014.

Bush, Barbara. *Imperialism, Race and Resistance: Africa and Britain, 1919–1945*. London: Routledge, 1999.

Butler, L. J. *Britain and Empire: Adjusting to a Post-Imperial World*. London: I. B. Tauris, 2002.

Burton, Antoinette. "Who Needs the Nation? Interrogating British History." In *Cultures of Empire: Colonizers in Britain and the Empire in the Nineteenth and Twentieth Centuries*. Edited by Catherine Hall. New York: Routledge, 2002.

Byron, Margaret, ed. "Migration, Work and Gender: The Case of Post-War Labour Migration from the Caribbean to Britain." In *Caribbean Migration: Globalised Identities*. Edited by Mary Chamberlain. London: Routledge, 1998.

_____. *Post-War Caribbean Migration to Britain: The Unfinished Cycle*. Aldershot, UK: Avebury, 1994.

Cambridge, Alrick. "Black Body Politics." In *Where You Belong: Government and Black Culture*. Edited by Alrick Cambridge and Stephan Feuchtwang. Aldershot, UK: Avebury, 1992.

Campt, Tina. *Image Matters: Archive, Photography and the African Diaspora*. Durham, NC: Duke University Press, 2012.

Cannadine, David. "The Context, Performance and Meaning of Ritual: The British Monarchy and the 'Invention of Tradition,' 1820–1977." In *The Invention of Tradition*. Edited by Eric Hobsbawn and Terence Ranger. Cambridge, UK: Cambridge University Press, 1983.

Carby, Hazel. "Lost (and Found?) in Translation." *Small Axe* 28 (March 2009): 27–40.

_____. "White Woman Listen!: Black Feminism and the Boundaries of Sisterhood." In *The Empire Strikes Back: Race and Racism in 70s Britain*. Edited by Center For Contemporary Cultural Studies, 212–235 (London: Hutchinson Ltd., 1982).

Carlyle, Thomas. "Occasional Discourse on the Negro Question." *Fraser's Magazine for Town and Country* (1849): 528–538.

Carter, Bob, Clive Harris, and Shirley Joshi, "The 1951–55 Conservative Government and the Racialization of Black Immigration." In *Inside Babylon: The Caribbean Diaspora in Britain*. Edited by Winston James and Clive Harris. London: Verson, 1993.

Carter, Trevor. *Shattering Illusions: West Indians in British Politics*. London: Lawrence and Wishart, 1986.

Castles, Stephen, and Mark Miller. *Age of Migration: International Population Movements in the Modern World*. New York: Guilford Press, 1993.

Cassar, George H. *Kitchener's War: British Strategy from 1914 to 1916*. Washington, DC: Brassey's, 2004.

Centre for Contemporary Cultural Studies. *The Empire Strikes Back: Race and Racism in 70s Britain*. London: Routledge, 1992.

Chamberlain, Mary. *Caribbean Migration: Globalised Identities*. London: Routledge, 1998.

_____, ed. *Narratives of Exile and Return*. London: Palgrave, 1997.

Chambers, Glenn. *Race, Nation and West Indian Immigration to Honduras, 1890–1940*. Baton Rouge: Louisiana State University Press, 2010.

Chater, Kathleen. *Untold Histories: Black People in England and Wales during the Period of the British Slave Trade, 1660–1807*. Manchester, UK: Manchester University Press, 2011.

Collins, Marcus. "Pride and Prejudice: West Indian Men in Mid-Twentieth-Century Britain." *The Journal of British Studies* 40, no. 3 (July 2001): 391–418.

Connell, Kieran. "Photographing Handsworth: Photography, Meaning and Identity in a British Inner City." *Patterns of Prejudice* 46, no. 2 (2012): 128–153.

Constantine, Learie. *Colour Bar*. London: Kegan Paul, 1954.

Cooper, Frederick. *Citizenship between Empire and Nation: Remaking France and French Africa, 1945–1960*. Princeton, NJ: Princeton University Press, 2014.

_____, ed. *Colonialism in Question: Theory, Knowledge, History*. Berkeley: University of California Press, 2005.

Cooper, Frederick, and Ann Stoler, eds. *Tensions of Empire: Colonial Cultures in a Bourgeois World*. Berkeley: University of California Press, 1997.

Cooper, Frederick, Thomas Holt, and Rebecca Scott, eds. *Beyond Slavery: Explorations of Race. Labor and Citizenship in Post-Emancipation Societies*. Chapel Hill: University of North Carolina Press, 2000.

Cotter, William R. "The Somerset Case and the Abolition of Slavery in England." *History* 79 (February 1994): 31–56.

Courtman, Sandra. "Women Writers and the Windrush Generation: A Contextual Reading of Beryl Gilroy's *In Praise of Love and Children* and Andrea Levy's *Small Island*." *EnterText* 9 (2012): 84–104.

Cowley, John. "London Is the Place: Caribbean Music in the Context of Empire, 1900–1960." In *Black Music in Britain: Essays on the Afro-Asian Contribution to Popular Music*. Edited by Paul Oliver. Philadelphia: Open University Press, 1990.

Craton, Michael. *Empire, Enslavement and Freedom in the Caribbean*. Kingston, Jamaica: Ian Randle Publishers, 1997.

Dabydeen, David, John Gilmore, and Cecily Jones, eds. *The Oxford Companion to Black British History*. Oxford: Oxford University Press, 2007.

Daniel, W. W. *Racial Discrimination in England*. Harmondsworth, UK: Penguin Books, 1968.

Darragh, John. *Colour and Conscience: A Study of Race Relations and Colour Prejudice in Birmingham*. Leicester, UK: Leicester Printers, 1957.

Das, Santanu, ed. *Race, Empire and First World War Writing*. Cambridge, UK: Cambridge University Press, 2011.

Dawson, Ashley. *Mongrel Nation: Diasporic Culture and the Making of Postcolonial Britain*. Ann Arbor: University of Michigan Press, 2007.

Davies, Carole Boyce, ed. *Beyond Containment: Autobiographical Reflections, Essays and Poems*. Boulder, CO: Lynne Reiner Publishers, 2011.

_____. *Black Women, Writing and Identity: Migrations of the Subject*. London: Routledge, 1994.

_____. ""Deportable Subjects: U.S. Immigration Laws and the Criminalizing of Communism." *South Atlantic Quarterly* 100, no. 1 (Fall 2001): 949–966.

_____. *Left of Karl Marx: The Political Life of Black Communist Claudia Jones*. Durham, NC: Duke University Press, 2007.

Davis, David Brion. *The Problem of Slavery in the Age of Revolution, 1770–1823*. New York: Oxford University, 1999.

Davis, John. "Rents and Race in 1960s London: New Light on Rachmanism." *Twentieth Century British History* 12, no. 1 (2001): 69–92.

Dodgson, Elyse. *Motherland: West Indian Women to Britain in the 1950s*. London: Heinemann Educational Books, 1984.

Duberman, Martin Bauml. *Paul Robeson: A Biography*. New York: Ballantine Books, 1989.

Dudziak, Mary. "The 1963 March on Washington: At Home and Abroad." *Review of French and American Studies* 107 (2006): 61–76.

_____. *Cold War Civil Rights: Race and the Image of American Democracy*. Princeton, NJ: Princeton University Press, 2000.

Duke, Eric. *Building a Nation: Caribbean Federation in the Black Diaspora*. Gainesville: University of Florida Press, forthcoming, 2016.

Edwards, Brent. *The Practice of Diaspora: Literature, Translation and the Rise of Black Internationalism*. Cambridge, MA: Harvard University Press, 2003.

Elsas, M. J. *Housing before the War and After*. London: Staples Press, 1946.

Eng, David L., and David Kazanjian, eds. *Loss: The Politics of Mourning*. Berkeley: University of California Press, 2002.

Erikson, Arvel B. "Empire of Anarchy: The Jamaica Rebellion of 1865." *Journal of Negro History* 44 (April 1959): 99–122.

Eudell, Demetrius. *The Political Languages of Emancipation in the British Caribbean and the U.S. South*. Chapel Hill: University of North Carolina Press, 2002.

Ewing, Adam. *The Age of Garvey: How a Jamaica Activist Created a Mass Movement and Changed Global Black Politics*. Princeton, NJ: Princeton University Press, 2014.

Fields, Barbara. "Ideology and Race in American History." In *Region, Race, and Reconstruction: Essay in Honor of C. Vann Woodard*. Edited by J. Morgan Kousser and James McPherson. New York: Oxford University Press, 1982.

Foner, Nancy. *Jamaica Farewell: Jamaican Migrants in London*. Berkeley: University of California Press, 1978.

———. "Race and Color: Jamaica Migrants in London and New York." *International Migration Review* 19, no. 4 (Winter 1985): 706–727.

Foot, Paul. *Immigration and Race in British Politics*. Hammondsworth, UK: Penguin Books, 1965.

Foucault, Michel. *The Archaeology of Knowledge and the Discourse on Language*. New York: Tavistock Publications, 1972.

Fraser, Cary. *Ambivalent Anti-Colonialism: The United States and the Genesis of West Indian Independence, 1940–1964*. Westport, CT: Greenwood Press.

Fraser, Peter. "Nineteenth-Century West Indian Migration to Britain." *In Search of a Better Life*. Edited by Ransford Palmer. New York: Praeger Publishers, 1990.

Froude, James Anthony. *The English in the West Indies: Or The Bow of Ulysses*. London: Longmans Green, 1888.

Fryer, Peter. *Staying Power: The History of Black People in Britain*. London: Pluto Press, 1984.

Gerzina, Gretchen. *Black London: Life before Emancipation*. New Brunswick, NJ: Rutgers University Press, 1995.

———, ed. *Black Victorians, Black Victoriana*. New Brunswick, NJ: Rutgers University Press, 2003.

Gikandi, Simon. "Englishness, Travel and Theory: Writing the West Indies in the Nineteenth Century." *Nineteenth Century Contexts* 18, no. 1 (1994): 49–70.

———. *Maps of Englishness: Writing Identity in the Culture of Colonialism*. New York: Columbia University Press, 1996.

Gilroy, Paul. *Black Britain: A Photographic History*. London: Saqi Books, 2007.

———. *Postcolonial Melancholia*. New York: Columbia University Press, 2006.

———. *'There Ain't No Black in the Union Jack': The Cultural Politics of Race and Nation*. Chicago: University of Chicago Press, 1987.

Ginzburg, Carlos. "'Your Country Needs You': A Case Study in Political Iconography." *History Workshop Journal* 52 (2001): 1–22.

Glass, Ruth. *Newcomers: The West Indians in Britain*. London: George Allen and Unwin, 1960.

Goldsmith, Christopher. "The British Embassy in Paris and the Algerian War." *Journal of Strategic Studies* 25, no. 2 (2002): 159–171.

Gorman, Daniel. *Imperial Citizenship: Empire and the Question of Belonging*. Manchester, UK: Manchester University Press, 2010.

———. "Wider and Wider Still: Racial Politics, Intra-Imperial Immigration and the Absence of an Imperial Citizenship in the British Empire." *Journal of Colonialism and Colonial History* 3, no. 3 (2002).

Goulbourne, Harry, ed. *Black Politics in Britain*. Aldershot, UK: Avebury, 1990.

Gramsci, Antonio. *Selections from Prison Notebooks*. Edited and translated by Quinton Hoare and Geoffrey Smith. London: Lawrence and Wishart, 1986.

Green, Jeffrey. *Black Edwardians: Black People in Britain, 1901–1914*. London: Routledge, 1998.

Green, William A. *British Slave Emancipation: The Sugar Colonies and the Great Experiment, 1830–1865*. Oxford: Clarendon Press, 1976.

Guilbault, Jocelyn. *Governing Sound: The Cultural Politics of Trinidad's Carnival Music*. Chicago: University of Chicago Press, 2007.

Gurney, Christabel. "'A Great Cause: The Origins of the Anti-Apartheid Movement, June 1959–March 1960." *Journal of Southern African Studies* 26 (March 2000): 123–144.

Hall, Catherine. *Civilizing Subjects: Colony and Metropole in the English Imagination.* Chicago: University of Chicago Press, 2002.

———, ed. *Cultures of Empire, A Reader: Colonizers in Britain and the Empire in the 19th and 20th Centuries.* Manchester, UK: Manchester University Press, 2000.

Hall, Catherine, and Sonya Rose, eds. *At Home with the Empire: Metropolitan Culture and the Imperial World.* Cambridge, UK: Cambridge University Press, 2007.

Hall, Kim. *Things of Darkness: Economies of Race and Gender in Early Modern England.* Ithaca, NY: Cornell University Press, 1995.

Hall, Stuart. "From Scarman to Stephen Lawrence." *History Workshop Journal* 48 (Autumn 1999): 187–197.

———. "Racism and Reaction." *Five Views of Multi-Racial Britain.* London: Commission for Racial Equality, 1978.

Hall, Stuart, Chas Critcher, Tony Jefferson, John Clarke, and Brian Roberts. "Ethnicity: Identity and Difference." In *Becoming National: A Reader.* Edited by Geoff Eley and Ronald Suny, 339–351. Oxford: Oxford University Press, 1996.

———. "New Ethnicities." In *Black British Cultural Studies: A Reader.* Edited by Houston A Baker, Manthia Diawara, and Ruth Lindborg, 163–172. Chicago: University of Chicago Press, 1996.

———. *Policing the Crisis*, 2nd ed. Basingstoke: Palgrave Macmillan, 2013.

———. "Reconstruction Work: Images of Postwar Black Settlement." In *Writing Black Britain, 1948–1998: An Interdisciplinary Anthology*, 82–94. Edited by James Proctor. Manchester, UK: Manchester University Press, 2000.

Hampshire, James. *Citizenship and Belonging: Immigration and the Politics of Demographic Governance in Postwar Britain.* New York: Palgrave Macmillan, 2005.

———. "Immigration and Race Relation." In *The Labour Governments, 1964–1970.* Edited by Peter Dorey. London: Routledge, 2006.

Hansen, Randall. *Citizenship and Immigration in Postwar Britain: The Institutional Origins of a Multicultural Nation.* Oxford: Oxford University Press, 2000.

———. "The Politics of Citizenship in 1940s Britain: The British Nationality Act." *Twentieth Century British History* 10, no. 1 (1999): 67–95.

Harris, Clive. "Post-War Migration and the Industrial Reserve Army." In *Inside Babylon: The Caribbean Diaspora in Britain.* Edited by Winston James and Clive Harris. London: Verso, 1993.

Hebdige, Dick. *Subculture: The Meaning of Style.* London: Routledge, 2002.

Heinemann, Benjamin. *The Politics of the Powerless: A Study of the Campaign against Racial Discrimination.* Oxford: Oxford University Press, 1972.

Heinlein, Frank. *British Government Policy and Decolonisation, 1945–1963: Scrutinizing the Official Mind.* London: Frank Cass, 2002.

Hesse, Barnor, ed. *Un/settled Multiculturalisms: Diasporas, Entanglements, Transruptions.* London: Zed Books, 2000.

Heuman, Gad. *The Killing Time: The Morant Bay Rebellion in Jamaica.* Knoxville: University of Tennessee Press, 1994.

Higham, John. *Strangers in the Land: Patterns of American Nativism, 1860–1925.* New Brunswick. NJ: Rutgers University Press, 1988.

Higginbotham, Evelyn Brooks. "African-American Women's History and the Metalanguage of Race." *Signs* 17, no. 2 (Winter 1992): 251–274.

Hill, Donald R. *Calypso Calaloo: Early Carnival Music in Trinidad.* Gainesville: University of Florida Press, 1993.

Hill, Robert, ed. *The Marcus Garvey and Universal Negro Improvement Association Papers.* Vol. V. Berkeley: University of California Press, 1986.

Hindell, Keith. "The Genesis of the Race Relations Bill." *Political Quarterly* 36, no. 4 (October 1965): 390–405.

Hinds, Donald. *Journey to an Illusion: West Indian Migrants in Britain.* London: Heinemann, 1966.

Hiro, Dilip. *Black British, White British: A History of Race Relations in Britain.* London: Grafton Books, 1991.

Hobsbawm, Eric, ed. *The Invention of Tradition.* Cambridge, UK: Cambridge University Press, 1983.

Hoerder, Dirk, and Leslie Page Moch, eds. *European Migrants: Global and Local Perspectives.* Boston: Northeastern University Press, 1996.

Holmes, Colin. *John Bull's Island: Immigration and British Society, 1871–1971.* London: Macmillan Education, 1988.

Holt, Thomas. *The Problem of Freedom: Race, Labor and Politics in Jamaica and Britain, 1838–1938.* Baltimore: Johns Hopkins University Press, 1992.

Horne, Gerald. *Mau Mau in Harlem: The U.S. and the Liberation of Kenya.* New York: Palgrave, 2012.

Hosbjerg, Christian. *C. L. R. James in Imperial Britain.* Durham, NC: Duke University Press, 2014.

Howe, Stephen. *Anti-Colonialism in British Politics: The Left and the End of Empire, 1918–1964.* Oxford: Oxford University Press, 1993.

Huzzey, Richard. *Freedom Burning: Anti-Slavery and Empire in Victorian Britain.* Ithaca, NY: Cornell University Press, 2012.

Hyam, Ronald, and Peter Henshaw. *The Lion and the Springbok: Britain and South Africa since the Boer War.* Cambridge, UK: Cambridge University Press, 2007.

Jackson, James, and Leslie Moch. "Migration and the Social History of Modern Europe." *Historical Methods* (Winter 1989): 27–36.

Jackson, Thomas F. *From Civil Rights to Human Rights: Martin Luther King and the Struggle for Economic Justice.* Philadelphia: University of Pennsylvania Press, 2007.

James, Leslie. *George Padmore and Decolonization from Below: Pan-Africanism, the Cold War and the End of Empire.* London: Palgrave, 2014.

James, Winston. *Holding Aloft the Banner of Ethiopia: Caribbean Radicalism in Early Twentieth Century America.* London: Verso Press, 1998.

_____. "The Making of Black Identities." *The Oxford Reader in Ethnicity.* Edited by John Hutchinson and Anthony Smith. Oxford: Oxford University Press, 1996.

James, Winston, and Clive Harris, eds. "The Black Experience in Twentieth Century Britain." In *Blacks and the British Empire.* Edited by Philip Morgan and Sean Hawkins. Oxford: Oxford University Press, 2006.

_____. *Inside Babylon: The Caribbean Diaspora in Britain.* London: Verso Press, 1993.

Jenkinson, Jacqueline. *Black 1919: Riots, Racism and Resistance in Imperial Britain.* Liverpool, UK: Liverpool University Press, 2009.

Johnson, Buzz. *'I Think of My Mother': Notes on the Life and Times of Claudia Jones.* London: Karia Press, 1985.

Johnson, Howard. "The Black Experience in the British Caribbean in the Twentieth Century." In *Black Experience and the Empire.* Edited by Philip Morgan and Sean Hawkins. Oxford: Oxford University Press, 2006.

Joseph, Peniel E. "The Black Power Movement: A State of the Field." *Journal of American History* (December 2009): 751–776.

_____. *Stokely: A Life.* New York: Basic Books, 2014.

_____. *Waiting 'Til The Midnight Hour: A Narrative History of Black Power in America.* New York: Henry Holt, 2006.

Jowell, Jeffrey. "The Administrative Enforcement of Laws against Discrimination." *Public Law* (Summer 1965): 119–186.

Kasinitz, Philip. *Caribbean New York: Black Immigrants and the Politics of Race.* Ithaca, NY: Cornell University Press, 1992.

Kelley, Robin D. G. *Africa Speaks, America Answers: Modern Jazz in Revolutionary Times.* Cambridge, MA: Harvard University Press, 2012.

Kelley, Robin D. G., and Tiffany Patterson. "Unfinished Migrations: Reflections on the African Diaspora and the Modern World." *African Studies Review* 43, no. 1 (2000): 11–45.

Killingray, David. "'A Good West Indian, A Good African and in Short a Good Britisher': Black and British in a Colour Conscious Empire, 1760–1950." *Journal of Imperial and Commonwealth History* 36, no. 3 (2008).

Killingray, David. " 'To Do Something for the Race': Harold Moody and the League of Coloured Peoples." In *West Indian Intellectuals in Britain*. Edited by Bill Schwarz. Manchester, UK: Manchester University Press, 2004.

Krauthamer, Barbara and Deborah Willis, eds., *Envisioning Emancipation* (Philadelphia: Temple University Press, 2013.

Krebs, Paula M. *Gender, Race and the Writing of Empire: Public Discourse and the Boer War*. Cambridge: Cambridge University Press, 1999.

Lambeth Council. *Forty Winters On: Memories of Britain's Postwar Caribbean Immigrants*. London: South London Press and The Voice, 1998.

Lauren, Paul Gordon. *Power and Prejudice: The Politics and Diplomacy of Racial Discrimination*. Boulder, CO: Westview Press, 1996.

Layton-Henry, Zig. *The Politics of Immigration: Immigration, 'Race' and 'Race Relations' in Postwar Britain*. Oxford: Blackwell Publishing, 1992.

Lee, Christopher J., ed. *Making a World after Empire: The Bandung Moment and Its Political Afterlives*. Athens: Ohio University Press, 2010.

Lee, Debbie, ed. *Slavery Abolition and Emancipation: Writings in the British Romantic Period*. Vol. 3. London: Pickering and Chatto, 1999.

Lentz-Smith, Adriane. *Freedom Struggles: African Americans and World War I*. Cambridge, MA: Harvard University Press, 2009.

Lewis, Rupert. "Garvey's Forerunners: Love and Bedward." *Race and Class* 28, no. 3 (1987): 29–40.

Lindsey, Lydia. "The Split-Labor Phenomenon: Its Impact on West Indian Workers as a Marginal Working Class in Birmingham, England, 1948–1962." *Journal of African American History* 87 (Winter 2002): 83–109.

Little, Kenneth. *Negroes in Britain: A Study of Race Relations in English Society* London: Routledge and Kegan Paul, 1972.

Lorimer, Douglas A. "Black Slaves and English Liberty: A Re-Examination of Racial Slavery in England." *Immigrants and Minorities* 3, no. 2 (1984): 121–150.

_____. *Colour, Class and the Victorians: English Attitudes towards the Negro in the Mid Nineteenth Century*. Leicester, UK: Leicester University Press, 1978.

Lotz, Ranier and Ian Pegg, eds. *Under the Imperial Carpet: Essays in Black History, 1780–1950*. Crawley, England: Rabbit Press, 1986.

Lowenthal, David, ed. *The West Indies Federation: Perspectives of a New Nation*. New York: Oxford University Press, 1961.

Lucassen, Jan, and Leo Lucassen, eds. *Migration, Migration History, History*. Berlin: Peter Lang, 1997.

Makalani, Minkah. *In the Cause of Freedom: Radical Black Internationalism from Harlem to London, 1917–1939*. Chapel Hill: University of North Carolina Press, 2011.

Malchow, Howard. *Special Relations: The Americanization of Britain?*. Stanford, CA: Stanford University Press, 2011.

Malik, Michael Abdul. *From Michael de Freitas to Michael X*. London: Andre Deutsch, 1968.

Martin, Tony. *Amy Ashwood Garvey: Pan-Africanist, Feminist, and Mrs. Marcus Garvey Wife No. 1; or, a Tale of Two Amies*. Dover, MA: Majority Press, 2007.

Matera, Marc. *Black London: The Imperial Metropolis and Decolonization in the Twentieth Century*. Berkeley: University of California Press, 2015.

Mazower, Mark. *Dark Continent: Europe's Twentieth Century*. New York: Vintage, 2000.

McClintock, Anne. *Imperial Leather: Race, Gender and Sexuality in the Colonial Contest*. London: Routledge, 1995.

McDuffie, Erik S. *Sojourning for Freedom: Black Women, American Communism and the Making of Black Left Feminism*. Durham, NC: Duke University Press, 2011.

McLaine, Ian. *Ministry of Morale: Home Front Morale and the Ministry of Information in World War II* (London: Allen and Unwin, 1979).

McMillan, Michael. "The West Indian Front Room: Reflections on a Diasporic Phenomenon." *Small Axe* 13, no. 1 (2009): 135–156.

Mead, Matthew. "Empire Windrush: The Cultural Memory of an Imaginary Arrival." *Journal of Postcolonial Writing* 45, no. 2 (2009): 137–149.

Meriwether, James H. *Proudly We Can Be Africans: Black Americans and Africa, 1935–1961.* Chapel Hill: University of North Carolina Press, 2001.

Metha, Uday. *Liberalism and Empire: A Study in Nineteenth Century British Liberal Thought.* Chicago: University of Chicago Press, 1999.

Miles, Robert. "Nationality, Citizenship, and Migration to Britain, 1945–1951." *Journal of Law and Society* 16 (Winter 1989): 426–442.

——. *Racism after Race Relations in Postwar Britain.* London: Routledge, 1993.

Modood, Tariq. "Political Blackness and British Asians." *Sociology* 28, no. 4 (November 1994): 859–876.

Moore, Brian L., and Michele Johnson. *Neither Led nor Driven: Contesting British Cultural Imperialism in Jamaica, 1865–1920.* Kingston, Jamaica: University of the West Indies Press, 2004.

——. *They Do as They Please: The Jamaican Struggle for Cultural Freedom after Morant Bay.* Kingston, Jamaica: University of the West Indies Press, 2011.

Morgan, Philip, and Sean Hawkins, eds., *Blacks and the British Empire.* Oxford: Oxford University Press, 2006.

Morrison, Majbritt. *Jungle West 11.* London: Tandem Books, 1964.

Morsink, Johannes. *The Universal Declaration of Human Rights: Origins, Drafting, Intent.* Philadelphia: University of Pennsylvania Press, 2000.

Myers, Norma. *Reconstructing the Black Past: Black in Britain, 1780–1830.* London: Frank Cass, 1996.

Neptune, Harvey. *Caliban and the Yankees: Trinidad and the United States Occupation.* Chapel Hill: University of North Carolina Press, 2007.

Newman, Jon. "Harry Jacobs: The Studio Photographer and the Visual Archive." In *People and Their Pasts: Public History Today.* Edited by Paul Ashton and Hilda Kean. London: Palgrave Macmillan, 2009.

Ngai, Mae M. "The Architecture of Race in American Immigration Law: A Reexamination of the Immigration Act of 1924." *Journal of American History* 86, no. 1 (June 1999): 67–92.

——. *Impossible Subjects: Illegal Aliens and the Making of Modern America.* Cambridge, MA: Harvard University Press, 2004.

Nichol, Andrew, and Ann Dummett. *Subjects, Citizens, Aliens and Others: Nationality and Immigration Law.* London: George Weidenfield and Nicholson, 1990.

Olden, Mark. *Murder in Notting Hill.* Winchester, UK: Zero Books, 2011.

Oldfield, J. R. *Chords of Freedom: Commemoration, Ritual and British Transatlantic Slavery.* Manchester, UK: Manchester University Press, 2007.

Padmore, George, ed. *Colonial and Coloured Unity.* London: Hammersmith Bookshop, 1963.

Parekh, Bhikhu C. *The Future of Multi-Ethnic Britain.* London: Profile Books, 2000.

Parker, Jason. *Brother's Keeper: The United States, Race and Empire in the British Caribbean, 1937–1962.* New York: Oxford University Press, 2008.

Paton, Diana. *No Bond But the Law: Punishment, Race and Gender in Jamaican State Formation, 1780–1870.* Durham, NC: Duke University Press, 2004.

Patterson, Sheila. *Dark Strangers: A Sociological Study of the Absorption of a Recent West Indian Migrant Group in Brixton, South London.* London: Tavistock Publications, 1963.

Paul, Kathleen. "'British Subjects' and 'British Stock': Labour's Postwar Imperialism." *Journal of British Studies* 34, no. 2 (April 1999): 233–276.

——. *Whitewashing Britain: Race and Citizenship in the Postwar Era.* Ithaca, NY: Cornell University Press, 1997.

Peach, Ceri. *West Indian Migration to Britain.* Oxford: Oxford University Press, 1968.

Pennybacker, Susan. *From Scottsboro to Munich: Race and Political Culture in 1930s Britain.* Princeton, NJ: Princeton University Press, 2009.

Perry, Kennetta Hammond. "'Little Rock' in Britain: Jim Crow's Transatlantic Topographies." *Journal of British Studies* 51 (January 2012): 155–177.

Peterson, Derek, ed. *Abolition and Imperialism in Britain, Africa and the Atlantic World.* Athens: Ohio University Press, 2010.

Phillips, Mike. *London Crossings: A Biography of Black Britain.* London: Continuum, 2001.

Phillips, Trevor, and Mike Phillips. *Windrush: The Irresistible Rise of Multi-Racial Britain.* London: Harper Collins, 1998.

Pilkington, Edward. *Beyond the Mother Country: West Indians and the Notting Hill White Riots.* London: I. B. Tauris, 1988.

Plummer, Brenda Gayle. *Rising Wind: Black Americans and U.S. Foreign Affairs, 1935–1960.* Chapel Hill: University of North Carolina Press, 1996.

_____.*In Search of Power: African Americans in the Era of Decolonization, 1956–1974.* Cambridge, UK: Cambridge University Press, 2012.

Posel, Deborah. *The Making of Apartheid, 1948–1961: Conflict and Compromise.* Oxford: Clarendon Press, 1991.

Proctor, James, ed. *Writing Black Britain, 1948–1998: An Interdisciplinary Anthology.* Manchester, UK: Manchester University Press, 2000.

Putnam, Lara. "Citizenship from the Margins: Vernacular Theories of Rights and the State from the Interwar Caribbean." *Journal of British Studies* 53, no. 1 (2014): 162–191.

_____. *The Company They Kept: Migrants and the Politics of Gender in Caribbean Costa Rica, 1870–1960.* Chapel Hill: University of North Carolina Press, 2001.

_____.*Radical Moves: Caribbean Migrants and the Politics of Race in the Jazz Age.* Chapel Hill, NC: University of North Carolina Press, 2013.

Quevedo, Raymond. *Atilla's Kaiso: A Short History of Trinidad Calypso.* St. Augustine, Trinidad and Tobago: University of the West Indies Press, 1983.

Raiford, Leigh. "Ida B. Wells and the Shadow Archive." In *Pictures and Progress: Early Photography and the Making of African American Identity.* Edited by Maurice O. Wallace and Shawn Michelle Smith. Durham, NC: Duke University Press, 2012.

_____.*Imprisoned in a Luminous Glare: Photography and the African American Freedom Struggle.* Chapel Hill: University of North Carolina Press, 2011.

Ramdin, Ron. *The Making of the Black Working Class in Britain.* Brookfield, VT: Gower Publishing, 1987.

_____. *Reimagining Britain: Five Hundred Years of Black and Asian History.* London: Pluto Press, 1999.

Ransby, Barbara. *Ella Baker and the Black Freedom Movement: A Radical Democratic Vision.* Chapel Hill: University of North Carolina Press, 2005.

_____. *Eslanda: The Large and Unconventional Life of Mrs. Paul Robeson.* New Haven, CT: Yale University Press, 2013.

Regis, Louis. *The Political Calypso: True Opposition in Trinidad and Tobago, 1962–1987.* Gainesville: University of Florida Press, 1999.

Reynolds, Z. Nia, ed. *When I Came to England: An Oral History of Life in 1950s and 1960s Britain.* London: Black Stock / Photo Press, 2001.

Rich, Paul. *Race and Empire in British Politics.* Cambridge, UK: Cambridge University Press, 1986.

Richie, Jeffrey Kerr. *The Rites of August First: Emancipation Day in the Black Atlantic World.* Baton Rouge: Louisiana State University Press, 2007.

Roberts, G. W., and D. O. Mills. *Study of External Migration Affecting Jamaica: 1953–1955.* Kingston, Jamaica: Institute of Social and Economic Research, 1958.

Robotham, Don. "'The Notorious Riot': The Socio-Economic and Political Basis of Paul Bogle's Revolt." Working Paper. Kingston, Jamaica: University of the West Indies Press for the Institute of Social and Economic Research, 1981.

Roehler, Gordon. *Calypso and Society in Pre-Independence Trinidad.* Port of Spain, Trinidad: Gordon Roehler, 1990.

Rooney, David. *Kwame Nkrumah: Vision and Tragedy.* Accra, Ghana: Sub-Saharan Publishers, 2007.

Rose, E. J. B. *Colour and Citizenship: A Report on British Race Relations.* London: Oxford University Press, 1969.

Rose, Sonya. "Race, Empire and British Wartime National Identity, 1939–45," *Historical Research* 74 (2001): 220–237.

_____. *Which People's War? National Identity and Citizenship in Wartime Britain, 1939–1945.* New York: Oxford University Press, 2004.

_____. "Who Are We Now? Writing the Postwar 'Nation', 1948–2001." In *Race, Nation and Empire: Making Histories, 1750 to the Present*. Edited by Catherine Hall and Keith McClelland. Manchester, UK: Manchester University Press, 2010.

Rowe, Michael. "The Racialisation of Disorder: Sex, Race and Riot in Liverpool, 1919." *Immigrants and Minorities* (July 2000): 53–70.

Ruck, S. K., ed. *The West Indian Comes to England: A Report Prepared for the Trustees of the London Parochial Charities by the Family Welfare Association*. London: Routledge and Kegan Paul, 1960.

Rush, Anne Spry. *Bonds of Empire: West Indians and Britishness from Victoria to Decolonization*. Oxford: Oxford University Press, 2011.

_____. "Imperial Identity in Colonial Minds." *Twentieth Century British History* 13, no. 4 (2002): 356–383.

Sabatino, Richard. *Housing in Great Britain, 1945–1949*. Dallas: Southern Methodist University Press, 1956.

Schaffer, Gavin. "Legislating against Hatred: Meaning and Motive in Section Six of the Race Relations Act of 1965." *Twentieth Century British History* (January 2013): 251–275.

Schneer, Johnathan. *London 1900: The Imperial Metropolis*. New Haven, CT: Yale University Press, 1999.

Scholes, Theophilus E. Samuel. *Glimpses of the Ages, Or the "Superior" and "Inferior" Races, So-Called, Discussed in the Light of Science and History*. London: John Long, 1908.

Schwarz, Bill. "Claudia Jones and the West Indian Gazette: Reflections on the Emergence of Post-Colonial Britain." *Twentieth Century British History* 14, no. 3 (2001): 264–285.

_____. "Our Unadmitted Sorrow: The Rhetorics of Civil Rights Photography." *History Workshop Journal* 72 (Autumn 2011): 138–155.

_____, ed. *West Indian Intellectuals in Britain*. Manchester, UK: Manchester University Press, 2003.

_____. *The White Man's World*. Oxford: Oxford University Press, 2012.

_____. "Night Battles: Hooligan and Citizen." In *Modern Times: Reflections on a Century of English Modernity*. Edited by Mica Nava and Alan O'Shea. New York: Routledge, 1996.

_____. "Our Unadmitted Sorrow: The Rhetorics of Civil Rights Photography." *History Workshop Journal* 72 (Autumn 2011): 138–155.

Scobie, Edward. *Black Britannia: A History of Blacks in Britain*. Chicago: Johnson Publishing, 1972.

Searle, Kevin. "Mixing of the Unmixables: The 1949 Causeway Green 'Riots' in Birmingham." *Race and Class* 54 (2013): 344–364.

Senior, Clarence, and Douglas Manley. *A Report on Jamaican Migration to Great Britain*. Kingston, Jamaica: Government Printers, 1955.

Sewell, Mike. "British Responses to Martin Luther King Jr and the Civil Rights Movement, 1954–68." In *The Making of Martin Luther King and the Civil Rights Movement*. Edited by Brian Ward and Tony Badger. New York: New York University Press, 1996).

Sheller, Mimi. *Citizenship from Below: Erotic Agency and Caribbean Freedom*. Durham, NC: Duke University Press, 2012.

_____. *Democracy after Slavery: Black Publics and Peasant Radicalism in Haiti and Jamaica*. Gainesville: University of Florida Press, 2000.

Shepherd, Verene A., ed. *Working Slavery, Pricing Freedom: Perspectives from the Caribbean, Africa and the African Diaspora*. New York: Palgrave, 2002.

Sherwood, Marika. *Claudia Jones: A Life in Exile*. London: Lawrence and Wishart, 2000.

_____. *Origins of Pan-Africanism: Henry Sylvester Williams, Africa and the African Diaspora*. New York: Routledge, 2011.

Shukra, Kalbir. *The Changing Patterns of Black Politics in Britain*. London: Pluto Press, 1998.

Shyllon, Folarin. *Black People in Britain, 1555–1833*. London: Oxford University Press, 1977.

Silkey, Sarah. *Black Woman Reformer: Lynching and Transatlantic Activism*. Athens, GA: University of Georgia Press, 2015.

Sivanandan, Ambalavaner. *From Resistance to Rebellion: Asian and Afro-Caribbean Struggles in Britain*. London: Institute of Race Relations, 1981.

_____. *A Different Hunger: Writings on Black Resistance*. London: Pluto Press, 1991.

Slate, Nico. *Colored Cosmopolitanism: The Shared Struggle for Freedom in the United States and India*. Cambridge, MA: Harvard University Press, 2012.

Smith, Faith. *Creole Recitations: John Jacob Thomas and Colonial Formation in the Late Nineteenth Century Caribbean*. Charlottesville: University of Virginia Press, 2002.

Smith, Graham. *When Jim Crow Met John Bull: Black American Soldiers in World War II Britain*. London: I. B. Tauris, 1987.

Smith, Richard. "'Heaven Grant You Strength to Fight the Battle for Your Race': Nationalism, Pan Africanism and the First World War in Jamaican Memory." In *Race, Empire and First World War Writing*. Edited by Santanu Das. Cambridge, UK: Cambridge University Press, 2011.

_____. *Jamaican Volunteers in the First World War: Race, Masculinity and the Development of National Consciousness*. Manchester, UK: Manchester University Press, 2004.

Smith, Susan J. *The Politics of "Race" and Residence*. Cambridge, UK: Polity Press, 1989.

Solanke, Iyiola. *Making Anti-Racial Discrimination Law*. London: Routledge, 2009.

Solomos, John. *Race and Racism in Britain*. 2nd ed. New York: St. Martin's Press, 1993.

Spencer, Ian. *British Immigration Policy since 1939: The Making of Multi-Racial Britain*. London: Routledge, 1997.

Stanley, Jo. "'Mapping Our Migrations': Afro-Caribbean History in Manchester." *History Workshop Journal* 47 (Spring, 1999): 324–324.

Stoler, Ann. *Carnal Knowledge and Imperial Power: Race and the Intimate in Colonial Rule*. Berkeley: University of California Press, 2002.

Street, Harry, Geoffrey Howe, and Geoffrey Bindman, *Anti-Discrimination Legislation: The Street Report*. London: Political and Economic Planning, 1967.

Street, Joe. "Malcolm X, Smethwick and the Influence of the African American Freedom Struggle on British Race Relations in the1960s." *Journal of Black Studies* 38 (July 2008): 932–950.

Surridge, Keith. "More Than a Great Poster: Lord Kitchener and the Image of the Military Hero." *Historical Research* 74 (2001): 298–313.

_____. "The Politics of War: Lord Kitchener and the Settlement of the South African War, 1901–1902." In *Writing a Wider War: Rethinking Gender, Race and Identity in the South African War, 1899–1902*, 213–232. Edited by Greg Cuthbertson, Albert Grundlingh, and Mary-Lynn Suttie. Athens: Ohio University Press, 2002.

Tabili, Laura. "The Construction of Racial Difference in Twentieth Century Britain." *Journal of British Studies* 33, no. 1 (January, 1994): 54–98.

_____. *'We Ask For British Justice': Workers and Racial Difference in Late Imperial Britain*. Ithaca, NY: Cornell University Press, 1994.

Taylor, Ula. *The Veiled Garvey: The Life and Times of Amy Jacques Garvey*. Chapel Hill: University of North Carolina Press, 2002.

Thomas, Deborah. "Modern Blackness: What We Are and What We Hope to Be." *Small Axe* 12 (September 2002): 25–48.

Thomas, John Jacob. *Froudacity: West Indian Fables by James Anthony Froude Explained By J. J. Thomas*. Philadelphia: Gebbie and Company, 1890.

Thomas, Martin. "The British Government and the End of French Algeria, 1958–1962." *Journal of Strategic Studies* 25, no. 2 (2002): 172–198.

Till-Mobley, Mamie, and Christopher Benson. *Death of Innocence: The Story of the Hate Crime That Changed America*. New York: Random House, 2003.

Tuck, Stephen. *The Night Malcolm X Spoke at the Oxford Union*. Berkeley: University of California Press, 2014.

Von Eschen, Penny. *Race against Empire: Black Americans and Anti-Colonialism*. Ithaca, NY: Cornell University Press, 1997.

Wallace, Elisabeth. *The British Caribbean: From the Decline of Colonialism to the End of Federation*. Toronto: University of Toronto Press, 1977.

Wallbridge, Edwin Angel. *The Demerara Martyr: Memoirs of Rev. John Smith, Missionary to Demerara*. New York: Negro Universities Press, 1969; original, 1848.

Walvin, James. *Black and White: The Negro in English Society, 1555–1945*. London: Penguin Press, 1973.

Bibliography 299

Ward, Brian. "A King in Newcastle: Martin Luther King, Jr. and British Race Relations, 1967–1968." *Georgia Historical Quarterly* 79, no. 3 (1995): 599–632.

Ward, Stuart, ed. *British Culture and the End of Empire*. Manchester, UK: Manchester University Press, 2001.

Waters, Chris. "'Dark Strangers' in Our Midst: Discourses of Race and Nation in Britain, 1947–1963." *Journal of British Studies* 36, no. 2 (April 1997): 207–238.

Watkins-Owens, Irma. *Blood Relations, Caribbean Immigrants and the Harlem Community, 1900–1930*. Bloomington: Indiana University Press, 1996.

Webster, Wendy. *Englishness and Empire, 1939–1965*. Oxford: Oxford University Press, 2005.

———. *Imagining Home: Gender, 'Race' and National Identity, 1945–1964*. London: University College of London Press, 1998.

Weight, Richard, and Abigail Beach. *The Right to Belong: Citizenship and National Identity in Britain, 1930–1960*. London: I. B. Tauris, 1998.

Wemyss, Georgie. *The Invisible Empire: White Discourse, Tolerance and Belonging*. Farnham, UK: Ashgate Publishing, 2009.

Wexler, Laura. "'A More Perfect Likeness': Frederick Douglass and the Image of the Nation." *Yale Review* 99, no. 4 (October 2011): 145–169.

Wickenden, James. *Colour in Britain*. London: Oxford University Press, 1958.

Wilder, Gary. *The French Imperial Nation-State: Negritude and Colonial Humanism between the Two World Wars*. Chicago: University of Chicago Press, 2005.

Williams, Jon. *Michael X: A Life in Black and White*. London: Century, 2008.

Williams, Raymond. *The Long Revolution*. New York: Penguin Books, 1971.

Wilmont, Swithin. "Politics at the 'Grassroots' in Free Jamaica: St. James, 1838–1865." In *Working Slavery, Pricing Freedom: Perspectives from the Caribbean, Africa and the African Diaspora*. Edited by Verene A. Shepherd. New York: Palgrave, 2002.

Wilson, C. A. *Men of Vision: A Series of Biographical Sketches of Men Who Have Made Their Mark upon Time*. Kingston, Jamaica: Gleaner, 1929.

Wise, Steven M. *Though the Heavens May Fall: The Landmark Trial That Led to the End of Human Slavery*. Cambridge, MA: Da Capo Press, 2005.

Wolton, Suke. *Lord Hailey, The Colonial Office and the Politics of Race and Empire in the Second World War: The Loss of White Prestige*. New York: St. Martins, 2000.

Wright, Michelle. *Becoming Black: Creating Identity in the African Diaspora*. Durham: Duke University Press, 2004.

Yard, Lionel. *Biography of Amy Ashwood Garvey: Co-Founder of the UNIA*. New York: Associated Publishers, 1990.

Zackdonik, Teresa. "Ida B. Wells and 'American Atrocities in Britain." *Women's Studies International Forum* 28, no. 4 (2005): 259–273.

INDEX

Figures are indicated by "f" following page numbers.

Pigmentocracy, 81
Pitt, David
  AACC, role in, 178
  background, 216–217
  CARD role of, 203, 214–215, 216, 236, 241,
    242, 277n14
  Cochrane memorial service, as speaker
    at, 139
  Cochrane murder, response to, 135
  Commonwealth Immigration Bill,
    opposition to, 174–175
  London Labour Party, resignation from,
    219–220
  NCCI work, criticisms of, 220–222, 228
  participation in IRFCC deputation, 138
  on postal remittances, 274–275n53
  as problematic Black leader, 227, 228
  Race Relations bill, opposition to, 209–210
  at St. Pancras Town Hall rally, 130
  White Paper, reaction to, 218
Places of public resort, 192, 204, 210, 229
A Plan for the Abolition of Slavery
  (Morgann), 24
Plantations, Jamaica
  plantation economy, 30–32
  plantation workers, protests by, 45–46
Plantocracy, White male elite, 29
Police bias, 136–137, 235–236
Policy reform, case for, 229–237
Polish Resettlement Act (1947), 66
Political and Economic Planning (PEP)
  committee, 236–237
Political candidates, qualifications for, under
  Franchise Act, 30
Political parties. *See* Labour Party; Tory Party
Politics of mourning, Black bodies and,
  146–152
Politics of race. *See* Race and racism
Portraiture, as cultural practice for
  Afro-Caribbean migrants, 73–75
Postwar Britain, state of racial violence in,
  135–146
Postwar Caribbean migrants. *See*
  Afro-Caribbean migrants
The Power of Negro Action (Maxwell),
  226–227, 239
Prevention of Discrimination and the
  Protection of Minority Rights (UN
  subcommittee), 202
Propaganda, racist, Cochrane murder and, 136
Public dialogue
  AACC's impact on, 180
  Commonwealth Immigration Act as
    instigation for, 155–156
  on race politics, 137
  racism as subject of, 6
  Shaw and, 109–110

Waterhouse and, 115
Public housing, residency requirements
  for, 84–85
Public Order Act (1936), 202, 203
Putnam, Lara, 26

Quick, Patricia, 232–233
Quotas, 64–65, 163, 217, 225

RAAS (Racial Adjustment Action
  Society), 239
"Race: The Unmentionable Issue" (magazine
  column), 189–190
Race and racism. *See also* "Colour bar";
  "Colour problem"; Mystique of British
  anti-racism; Official racial discourse,
  voices of dissent and; Stereotypes; *entries
  beginning "racial"*
  after Race Relations Act, 228
  American racism, virulence of, 268n109
  anti-communism policy in Africa
    and, 277n18
  belonging and, 48–88
  in Black Britain, 24–47, 244–247
  Black Power, rise of, and fall of CARD,
    238–243
  British anti-racism, "race riots" and mystique
    of, 89–125. *See also* Mystique of British
    anti-racism
  CARD, role of, 210–229, 233–237
  Cochrane murder, politics of, 126–152. *See
    also* Cochrane, Kelso
  colonial racism, 35
  of Commonwealth Immigration Act, 184
  Commonwealth migration policies and,
    160–161
  definition of racial discrimination, 200
  discrimination test cases, 231–232
  experiences of, in Caribbean vs. in
    Britain, 80–88
  immigration controls, racial politics of,
    153–186. *See also* (Im)migration
  impact of Afro-Caribbean migrants on, 16
  imperial citizenship and, 27
  inciting racial hatred, penalties for, 229
  as international issue, 106, 193
  legislative agenda, creation of, 201–209
  limits of campaigning against, 187–243
  narratives of, after "race riots," 100–104
  overview, 21, 187–194
  Pan African Congress consideration
    of, 51–52
  policy reform, case for, 229–237
  race relations scholarship, sociological
    models of, 253n48
  racial boundaries, under slavery, 27
  racial classifications, 57, 95–96, 157

Union Movement (fascist organization), 90,
    118, 136
United Committee of Coloured People's
    Association (Cardiff), 52
United Kingdom Coloured Citizens'
    Association, 151
United Nations
    Afro-Asian bloc at, 193
    Declaration on the Elimination of Racial
        Discrimination, adoption of, 193, 200
    ICERD, approval of, 200
    Pan African Congress's appeal to, 51
    Universal Declaration of Human Rights,
        adoption of, 9
United States
    Britain's "race riots," Southern reaction
        to, 99–100
    civil rights movement, changes in, 213
    immigration restrictions, 64
    Jamaican migrants in, 64
    Jim Crow laws, 8, 103–104, 122, 212
    McCarran-Walter Act, 64–65, 127, 153–154
    racial violence in, 238–239
    racism, virulence of, 268n109
    sugar plantations, Blacks on, 43
Universal Coloured People's Association
    (UCPA), 239, 240
Universal Declaration of Human Rights, 9, 200
Universal male subjecthood, 29
Universal Negro Improvement and
    Conservation Association and African
    Committees League (UNIA), 43

Valentine, Johanna, 126, 140
Vass, Ken, 187
Vernacular theories of rights, 26
Victoria, Queen, response to death of, 38–41
Violence. *See* British anti-racism; Racial
    violence
Visas, German requirements for, 185–186
Voices of dissent and official racial discourse.
    See Official racial discourse, voices of
    dissent and
Voting rights, 30, 33, 225. *See also*
    Disenfranchisement

Wade, Cecelia, 86
Walker, Patrick Gordon, 165–167, 168, 188,
    197, 198, 199
Washington Post, reaction to Britain's "race
    riots," 93–94
Waterhouse, Keith, 115–117
Waterloo station, Black family arrival at, 74*f*
Waters, Chris, 57
Watts riots, 224
Webster, Wendy, 78, 164–165
Weddings, photographs of, 75, 75–76*f*

Welfare and Reception department (Migrant
    Services Division), 68–69
Wellington Dominion, reaction to Britain's "race
    riots," 93
Wells, Ida B., 102, 144
"We Mourn Cochrane" memorial, 139,
    142–143, 150
Wemyss, Georgie, 266n50, 267n71
West African governments, compliance with
    Colonial Office, 158
West African Students Union, 52, 173
West Indian Federal Labour Party, 148
*West Indian Gazette and Afro-Asian Caribbean
    News (WIG,* periodical)
    AACC creation and, 177
    Cochrane murder and, 134, 151–152
    Commonwealth Immigration bill and,
        175–176
    establishment of, 9, 128
    importance, 172–173
    Claudia Jones and, 131–132
    London solidarity march, photograph
        of, 183*f*
    as rally organizer, 130
    title change, 178
West Indian governments. *See also* West Indies
    Federation
    non-compliance with Colonial Office,
        158–159
    officials in England, after
        "race riots," 94–95
West Indian migrants, 72*f*, 164. *See also*
    Afro-Caribbean migrants
West Indian National Party, 174, 216
West Indian Standing Conference (WISC)
    AACC creation and, 177
    CARD, split with, 220–222, 226, 227–228
    Home Office, delegation to, 225–226
    King and, 190
    Maxwell manifesto, 226–227
    media profile for, 239
    West Indian Federation and, 222–223
    White Paper on Commonwealth
        Immigration, response to, 223–225
West Indian Students' Union, 130, 133–134,
    177, 178, 216
West India Regiments, 42
West Indies, Commonwealth Immigration Bill,
    opposition to, 178
West Indies Federal Parliament, 141
West Indies Federation
    calls for reorganization of, 177
    Commonwealth Immigration bill and,
        170–172
    establishment of, 68, 160
    postal remittances to, 274–275n53
    support for, 177